Pulling Strings

SUNY Series in Israeli Studies
Russell Stone, Editor

A publication from the Center for Study and Documentation of Israeli Society, The Hebrew University of Jerusalem.

Pulling Strings

Biculturalism in Israeli Bureaucracy

Brenda Danet

State University
of New York Press

Published by
State University of New York Press, Albany

© 1989 State University of New York

For information, address State University of New York
Press, State University Plaza, Albany, N.Y. 12246

Library of Congress Cataloging in Publication Data

Danet, Brenda.
    Pulling strings : biculturalism in Israeli bureaucracy / Brenda
Danet.
        p.   cm.
    Bibliography: p. 335
    Includes index.
    ISBN 0-88706-788-3. ISBN 0-88706-790-5 (pbk.)
    1. Bureaucracy—Israel. 2. Patronage. Political—Israel.
3. Israel—Politics and government. I. Title.
JQ1825.P32D36   1988
306'.24—dc19   87-26776
                                                                            CIP

10 9 8 7 6 5 4 3 2 1

In Memory of

**Naomi E. Kies
(1941–1985)**

"I never heard of protektzia. Could you explain to me what it is, and how I could get some?"

> —Young woman, an American immigrant, three months in Israel, on a phone-in, English-language radio program, *Kol Yisrael* (The Voice of Israel), 1982.

"B'drom Tel Aviv merimim kisaot; b'tsfon Tel Aviv merimim telefon."

"In south Tel Aviv they lift/pick up chairs (i.e., threaten violence); in north Tel Aviv they pick up the telephone."

> —Shlomo Lahat, mayor of Tel Aviv, known as "Chich".

Contents

List of Tables and Figures

x

FIGURES

Preface

This book has been germinating for more than twenty years. In the spring of 1962, when I was taking courses in sociology at the Hebrew University, with an eye toward an eventual Ph.D., I was offered a job by Elihu Katz. The project was called "Petitions and Motivating Mechanisms," and was funded by the American National Science Foundation, with funds transferred to Jerusalem via the University of Chicago. Katz explained that the project was about bureaucracy and the public. "Bureaucracy?—what a dull, dry subject!" I thought. "My interests are in values and value conflict, in *mizug galuyot* (the ingathering of the exiles in Israel)." "No, thank you," I told him, "I'm off to the United States next year to do a Ph.D." Forty-eight hours later I was back, having realized that bureaucracy was merely the institutional setting in which we would be studying the very thing that interested me, and having recognized that here was a golden opportunity, not to be missed.

With Elihu Katz as our leader, a team of researchers, which also included Michael Gurevitch and Tsiyona Peled, conducted four studies in the 1960's. First, there was a pilot study of the persuasive appeals clients of Israeli organizations would use to persuade an official to do something. This was followed by a full-fledged study of persuasive appeals in letters to the Israel Customs Authorities. Eventually, this study was to be the topic of my Ph.D. dissertation for the University of Chicago, with Katz as my adviser. We also investigated patterns of interaction between doctors and patients in Sick Fund clinics in Jerusalem. Finally, there was a national survey of attitudes and experiences of Israelis with respect to government and public bureaucracy, which I directed. In this book I will refer to this latter study frequently; its data were collected only in 1968, having been postponed because of the Six Day War. In that same year, Tsiyona Peled and I conducted a graduate research seminar at the Communications Institute, in which we carried out what is probably the world's first empirical study of an ombudsman's office.

Between 1972, the year of publication of the last of the papers to emerge from these studies, and 1979, I rested from the study of bureaucracy and the public, although in the interim I did publish one paper, in which I explored some ideas on how to evaluate the functioning of ombudsmen. Then, after an extended stay in the United States, during which the growing attention to complaint-handling devices there rekindled my own earlier interests, I returned to Israel, and obtained the grants for the case study reported in this book.

Two foundations supported this research, the Israel National Council for Research and Development, Fund for Basic Research (then anchored in the Ministry of Energy and Infrastructure, now located in the Ministry of Science and Development), and the Israel Academy of Sciences. To both, I am most grateful for making the Israeli study possible and for displaying patience when my collaborators and I did not always meet deadlines. My collaborators were the late Naomi E. Kies and Hadassah Haas, both of whom participated in the design and execution of the case study. Hadassah Haas was also responsible for the early stages of data analysis. I would like to take this opportunity to thank her for her invaluable contribution to the research. Special thanks also to Zvi Richter, programmer for the department of sociology and social anthropology at the Hebrew University, for his help and patience as data analysis went through several stages.

Like most authors of academic books, I have been helped by many people. Four colleagues at the Hebrew University, Reuven Kahane, Ehud Sprinzak, Ehud Harari, and Eyal Ben Ari, read various parts of the manuscript and made valuable comments. The influence on the manuscript of Ehud Sprinzak's work on illegalism will be apparent to all who know his work. Alex Weingrod, of Ben Gurion University, Paul King, of the Jerusalem Foundation, and Martha Ramon also commented on portions of the manuscript. I have benefited greatly from their reactions, as well. Two colleagues in Jerusalem, Luis Roniger and Elihu Katz, generously read the entire manuscript. Drawing on his vast knowledge of patronage and brokerage around the world, and particularly the scene in Latin America,

Luis Roniger helped me to put the Israeli case into comparative perspective.

It was especially gratifying for me to have Elihu Katz serve as one of the readers of this manuscript for the State University of New York Press. It is only a slight exaggeration to say that he invented the topic of bureaucracy and the public in academic sociology, and was the first to recognize its centrality in the raw society that was the Israel of the late 1950's. Although much has changed in the years since our early bureaucracy project, the issues I wrestle with in this book are, ultimately, those I first learned to formulate as his student and assistant.

In the period of my training as a sociologist I learned most about the challenges, the joys and the frustrations of empirical social research, not from lectures or books, but from the daily struggles of our research team, which Katz led during those years. I hope that something of the example he set is detectable in this book. Because he has not been involved in empirical work on bureaucracy and the public in Israel since the late 1960's, in a way, this book (especially Chapter VIII, "Biculturalism versus " 'Modernity' ") is a kind of private report to him on what has happened in this area since then.

Continuing dialogue with various other collaborators over the years has also benefited me. In the 1960's Michael Gurevitch and Tsiyona Peled shared in the challenge of developing theory and method for our topic. Peled and I designed the questionnaire for the 1968 survey together. Then, in the early 1970's Harriet Hartman served as my research assistant and collaborator on the analysis and write-up of the results of this survey.

Turning to the more recent past, I owe a special debt to my former teaching and research assistant, Neta Ha-Ilan, and to the students in my 1984–85 seminar on "The Study of Organizational Culture," for many stimulating discussions which led to major improvements in the conceptualization of the problem tackled in this book. Chapter II has especially profited from their criticisms. Discussions with Ha-Ilan often helped me to clarify muddy thinking. Her M.A. thesis, an analysis of the networks invoked in about a hundred instances of the use of protektzia, complements this book in important ways.

Another person to whom I owe a special debt is Baruch Kimmerling. His invitation to prepare a paper for the June 1986 conference on "Rethinking Israeli Society," sponsored by the Center for the Study and Documentation of Israeli Society and the Department of Sociology and Social Anthropology of the Hebrew University, led to several important reformulations of issues discussed in this book.

I am also grateful to him for his continuing encouragement as the manuscript went through several drafts, and for his invaluable help and patience in the role of coordinator between Russell Stone, editor of the SUNY Israeli Studies Series, and myself.

I should also like to acknowledge with gratitude the influence of Irving Louis Horowitz on the manuscript. His encouraging reactions to Chapter VI in particular led to my focusing the book on the theme of protektzia.

With the ever-plentiful wisdom of hindsight, I now see all too clearly many of the weaknesses of the case study reported in the coming pages. But it is too late to change the conceptualization, or to ask our respondents questions I now know we should have asked. In particular, I hope that future researchers will investigate the role of familism and illegalism in promoting biculturalism more thoroughly than we have done. I very much regret the lack of case materials on actual use of protektzia—along the lines Neta Ha-Ilan began to explore in her M.A. thesis.

Another shortcoming of this book is that it is only about Jews in Israel. Considering that one in six Israeli citizens is an Arab, and that a million-and-a-half residents of the occupied territories are *de facto* clients of Israeli bureaucracies, a book which deals exclusively with Jews clearly tells only a part of the story. For too long, social science writing about "Israelis" has only been about Jews. A small corrective step, in the area of this book, has been taken by my student, Taher El-Makawi, whose M.A. thesis explores orientations toward *waasta*—the Arab equivalent of protektzia—among Israeli Arabs and residents of the administered territories.

With much sadness, I dedicate this book to the memory of Naomi E. Kies, who died tragically of leukemia in May, 1985. Hers was a life devoted in more ways than one to the cause of social justice.

Brenda Danet
Jerusalem, August, 1987

I

Introduction

In the last 10 to 20 years we have witnessed the rise of a host of devices for the processing of citizens' complaints about unfair treatment in organizational encounters. These include ombudsmen, small claims courts, newspaper Action Line columns, Better Business Bureaus, and media programs which investigate complaints. Arising initially in the West,[1] these devices have spread rapidly around the world, both in industrialized countries and in those on the road to industrialization. Their appearance is a response to the call for greater accountability of public institutions, and for at least partial redress of the tremendous imbalance of power between individual citizens and these huge institutions.

Recognition of the rights of citizens to complain about unjust treatment or bad service is an extension of the basic normative code which is supposed to govern bureaucratic organizations in both democratic and socialist societies. Although the avowed goals and actual functioning of complaint-handling devices may be quite different in the two types of regimes, in both, bureaucratic role relations are supposedly governed by the principles of universalism, specificity and affective neutrality: Officials are supposed to grant clients goods and services in accordance with entitlements alone. Neither their ethnicity, nor the color of their eyes, nor even the ability of clients to provide them with desired resources—whether financial or otherwise—should influence decision-making. Second, officials are required to relate only to those aspects of clients' identities which are relevant to the task at hand; neither their mutual preferences in films nor their tastes in food should be brought into the conversation. Finally, officials and clients are supposed to keep their emotions to themselves and to relate to one another impersonally.

1

In fact, all over the world, patterns of actual behavior frequently differ quite dramatically from this model. Think first of the various practices which involve money: bribery, graft, embezzlement, misappropriation of funds, and so on. Then there is a vast array of practices in which no money is necessarily involved at all, including nepotism, patronage, brokerage, and activation of old-boy networks. Most countries and languages have special terms for the use of personal connections to get something one wants. In the United States it is usually called "pull" or "pulling strings"; Russians call it *blat*. In Eastern Europe and in Israel it is known as *protektzia*. Peruvians call it *palanca*. Italians need *racommandazioni,* letters of recommendation, or at least access to persons who would write such letters for them.

Given the persistence of these various forms of particularistic behavior, the question arises: What elements of the universalistic complaints culture are actually being transferred outside the West, and what processes of modification do they undergo? Does a device like the ombudsman function in similar fashion, say, in Zambia, as in Sweden, the country where the idea first arose in 1809? From the vantage point of citizens, what are the social-psychological components of the culture of redress? What kinds of knowledge, attitudes and behavioral dispositions must they acquire if they are to be competent to demand and receive a fair share of what their society claims to offer them? Is the competent client necessarily the one who uses only universalistically-based strategies? Can the success of institutionalization of complaint channels be judged without imposing Western criteria of what is acceptable behavior?[2]

I. Research on the Response to Organizational Injustice

In the last decade social scientists have begun to study the response of citizens to injurious experiences in organizational encounters. Some investigate the files of particular complaint-handling devices, to see who complains about what and with what effect (e.g., Hill, 1976; Nader, 1980; Steele, 1975; Hannigan, 1977). Others have focused on which of a variety of channels people choose in connection with a particular problem (e.g., Ladinsky and Susmilch, 1982). Still others have begun to analyze how the act of complaining relates to general feelings of political efficacy, or how effective the public believes various channels to be (e.g., Friedmann, 1974).[3]

Despite the variety of goals, methods, and theoretical formulations characterizing this growing body of research, the various studies share a common limitation: They all tend to be concentrated only on formal channels for the processing of complaints. Yet as I have just pointed out, in most countries of the world, personal connections and bribery continue to be important and even legitimate ways of getting what one wants. Moreover, some individuals and groups are known to resort to violence and threats, even when there are strong sanctions against such behavior.

Even in the West, where routine transactions like applying for unemployment compensation or getting a telephone installed may be quite free of bribery or pull, scandals involving illegitimate transactions and influence attempts erupt periodically. Two examples which rocked the United States in the 1970's were the whitewashing of illegitimate political campaign funds by the Nixon administration in Mexico and Lockheed's payment of funds to Japanese officials to win contracts for the construction of aircraft.

In societies on the brink of modernization and in various stages of development, monetary payments or gifts to officials, whether before or after a service is rendered, as well as the mobilization of personal connections to intervene on the client's behalf, are often not only tolerated but even viewed as perfectly legitimate, routine ways of doing business. In Ghana, for instance, small payments to civil servants are a routine matter, not necessarily deserving the label bribery (Price, 1975). In Bantu bureaucracy, chiefs were expected to provide relatives with preferential treatment (Fallers, 1956). In southern Italy the mobilization of personal connections has long been a way of life (Galt, 1974; Smart, 1983).

II. THE INSTITUTIONAL TRANSFER OF COMPLAINT-HANDLING DEVICES: THE CASE OF THE OMBUDSMAN

A. Spread of the Ombudsman Around the World

Among the new devices for the handling of grievances, the best known is probably the ombudsman. The so-called classical ombudsman is an official appointed by a legislative body to serve as an address for citizens who believe they have been treated unjustly. Typically, ombudsmen have free access to files, are independent of the organizational hierarchy, but have few, if any, legal sanctions they may bring against offending officials; rather, they must use the powers of persuasion to influence them. The term *ombudsman,* like the institution to which it refers, comes from Sweden: The word means "representative" in Swedish (Lundvik, 1982). But about 100 years had to pass before the idea began to spread to other countries. In the last 20 years in particular many countries have instituted ombudsmen.

Among the other Scandinavian countries, Finland adopted the idea at the national level in 1920; Denmark followed suit in 1955, and Norway in 1963.[4] New Zealand was the first country outside of Scandinavia to adopt the idea, in 1962. By 1979 nine industrialized nations had national ombudsmen; 26 countries had state, regional or provincial ombudsmen; there were 15 municipal ombudsmen, and another 15 specializing in the areas of the military, languages, health, prisons, and privacy; 16 emerging nations had also created ombudsmen (Anderson, 1982). Ombudsmanship has become a profession in its own right, with its own international organization, the International Ombudsman Association, and its own journal; the association holds a congress every 4 years (the third took place in 1984).

National ombudsmen took office in the United Kingdom in 1967, in Israel in 1971, in France in 1973, in Portugal in 1976, and in Australia and Austria in 1977. Canada has opted primarily for ombudsmen at the provincial level. In the United States only four states have full-fledged legislative ombudsmen (Hawaii, Iowa, Nebraska, and Alaska), although another nine have ombudsmen appointed by the executive, and many cities and counties now have them.[5]

B. Goals of the Ombudsman

Hill listed five basic goals of the ombudsman: (1) to right individual wrongs; (2) to humanize administrative relationships and to lessen alienation; (3) to bring about administrative reform; (4) to serve as a watchdog against administrative abuse; (5) to bolster officials' morale by backing them up when they are right (Hill, 1976: 13).[6] Apart from these substantive goals, it is generally agreed that the ombudsman is to serve as a symbol of justice, a sympathetic person with whom citizens can identify, who cares about their fate at the hands of impersonal bureaucratic agencies.

C. The Ombudsman as a Problem in Institutional Transfer: New Zealand

Hill's (1976) study of the first 12½ years of the New Zealand ombudsman office developed theoretical and empirical criteria to assess whether the institution had been transferred successfully. Applying four criteria of institutionalization previously proposed by Huntington (1965; 1969),[7] he concluded that the transfer had indeed been successful, primarily because the host environment was already a highly universalistic one.

D. Transfer of the Ombudsman to Countries Outside the West

At the level of formal enactment of the ombudsman function, it is already evident that non-Western versions of the role often differ sharply from Western ones, both in jurisdictions and in basic operating features. Scott (1982; 1983) noted that the Zambian Commission of Investigations must report directly to the executive,[8] thereby opening up the office to political manipulation. And the Tanzanian Permanent Commission of Inquiry is almost as constrained; although the President cannot stop an investigation, he can direct the commission to conduct one. Similarly, complaint-handlers in socialist countries are responsible to the executive (International Ombudsman Institute, 1980).

Ombudsmen are sometimes seen as a means to combat bureaucratic corruption, sometimes as a kind of management consultant to the civil service, sometimes as a combatant of racial or ethnic discrimination. When citizens lack socialization to universalistic ways, ombudsmen frequently take on a teaching function. The mediating functions of ombudsmen may be even more important than the quasi-judicial ones. In Western contexts, ombudsmen hand down judgments as to whether complaints are justified. In contrast, Scott (1982) found that the Fijian ombudsman classed significant numbers of complaints as "explained," rather than justified or unjustified— in Scott's view this reflects the strong emphasis placed on mediation by the Fijian ombudsman.

Although in studies like Scott's some account is taken of the sociocultural setting to which the ombudsman idea has been transplanted, no account is taken of the ways in which use of the ombudsman interrelates with more traditional ways of obtaining things in countries like Fiji. Ombudsmen must not only teach citizens their rights and rouse them from apathy, but must compete with traditional modes of coping.

If behavior considered corrupt by local criteria is nevertheless extremely widespread, or if such behavior enjoys some kind of legitimacy, or again, if organizations are grossly inefficient and unfair, we may well ask just what a lone ombudsman, without formal sanctions, stands to accomplish. In such situations, ombudsmen might be little more than a means to "cool out" disgruntled clients, providing only the semblance of justice, or justice for rare individuals, all the while leaving the system fundamentally unchanged. If this danger exists in the West—evidence is already coming in that it does (see Nader, 1980)—is it not all the more likely outside the West, where citizens are far more passive, far less aware of their rights?

Consider the case of India: Two observers of the Indian scene have expressed quite pessimistic views of the prospects of the ombudsman idea for improving the quality of public life there. Dhavan (1977) has argued that India has adopted the idea, at the state level if not at the federal one, in order to be given credit for being against corruption and guaranteeing justice, all the while looking the other way at corruption and maladministration. Summing up the long parliamentary struggles to pass ombudsman legislation and the experience of four states with the institution, Jain (1983) issued a ringing condemnation:

> The Indian record is not impressive. Given the large population, ubiquitous governmental regulation of private activity, sprawling administration and general belief in widespread corruption and maladministration, the number of complaints has been very low. The reasons are obvious—illiteracy, lack of knowledge, inaccessibility, fear of offending authority, and a general feeling that nothing will come of an ombudsman's intervention. The executive has been and remains hostile. . . . Public agencies do not exhibit good will or cooperation. The ombudsman offices are starved of adequate resources, cannot conduct their own investigations and rely on the public agencies to investigate themselves. They cannot do anything in the face of hostility and apathy. In the absence of deep-seated democratic values in the polity and public administration, the ombudsman idea has resulted in merely a symbolic institution rather than a real protector of the people. (Jain, 1983)

III. THE THESIS OF THIS BOOK

The thesis of this book is that in hybrid organizational cultures, the universalistic culture of redress is very likely to be *under-institu-*

tionalized. In such settings, individuals with grievances will tend to relate to the official system in an instrumental manner. Even if an elaborate machinery for the processing of grievances in universalistic (U) fashion exists, the official code will not be sufficiently infused with value for citizens to prize the right to a principled decision. They will easily *opt out, abdicate from the system, waive the demand for universalistic justice* (see Chapters 3 and 7).

When particularistic (P) channels are at least as rewarding for citizens as U ones, and in hybrid organizational cultures this will often be the case, the latter will have to compete for customers not only among themselves (e.g., ombudsmen with media complaint handlers), but with P channels, too. As a result, U channels of redress will be even more hampered than their counterparts in the West in promoting administrative reform. Only a biased sampling of the problems actually encountered by clients will ever reach them. Perhaps even more important is the likelihood that administrative elites will not strive seriously for reform, because they themselves tend to benefit from the status quo. In such societies, the more fully people are integrated into the social structure, the more likely they are to be hybrid types, who display now U features, now P ones, both in their regular patterns of doing business in bureaucratic encounters, and in the pursuit of redress of grievances. People will switch to P channels not because they believe U channels to be ineffective, or not only because they know them to be less effective than P channels, but because they do not prize the right to use official channels.

This might have been called a study in organizational deviance. The term *deviance* implies something marginal, of dubious status, engaged in by only a minority of persons who have strayed from the right path. But in situations where forms of white, gray, and black corruption flourish,[9] it may be the purely U person who is viewed by others as deviant, or even as a naive fool who doesn't know the score.

To side-step this problem, the theoretical perspective developed in this book draws on an analogy to bilingualism. I shall argue that to be an organizational hybrid is to be a kind of *bilingual.* In formalistic societies in which behavior departs radically from official norms (cf. Riggs, 1964), citizens command two codes, the U and P codes. This book will demonstrate that in one society at least—that of Israel—U and P elements are simultaneously internalized by the public, who are in effect, bicultural; to be a competent client is to use personal influence at least some of the time; and the better integrated into the social structure, the more likely the individual is to be a hybrid in the pursuit of redress, mobilizing personal connections as well as using official complaint channels.

IV. INTELLECTUAL ROOTS OF THE
PRESENT STUDY

Five research traditions have enriched this study. Their topics are, respectively, (1) the civic culture, (2) bureaucracy and the public, (3) dispute-processing and the sociology of law, (4) patronage and brokerage, and (5) political and administrative corruption.

A. The Civic Culture

The agenda for the study of the civic culture was laid down by Almond and Verba (1965) in *The Civic Culture*. Pursued mainly by political scientists, and focused on comparative political culture, this type of work examines modes of political participation, the factors which socialize individuals to participate, and the consequences of participation for the emergent polity.[10] Both conventional and non-conventional forms of participation are studied (cf. Barnes, Kasse et al., 1979).

At least one passage in *The Civic Culture* may be read as a mandate for studies of redress behavior:

> we are concerned with the perceptions that individuals have about the amount of influence they can exercise over governmental decisions. Several questions may be asked about their attempts to influence the government.
>
> 1. Under what circumstances will an individual make some conscious effort to influence the government? Direct political influence attempts are rare. For the citizen the activities of government . . . may seem quite distant. At the time that a decision is being made the citizen is not aware that it is being made or of what its consequences for him are likely to be. It is probable, then, that only in situations of some *stress* (italics supplied), where a government activity is perceived to have a direct and serious impact upon the individual, will a direct influence attempt be stimulated.
> 2. What method will be used in the influence attempt? Some major dimensions . . . include: the kinds of channels . . . that are used, whether the individual attempts to influence the government alone or attempts to enlist the support of others.
> 3. What is the effect of the influence attempt? . . . We shall consider (the citizen's) view of the likelihood that an attempt made by him to influence the government will have any effect. (Almond and Verba, 1965: 140)

It is only necessary to focus on the reference to *stress* to see that this passage may be read as a call for the study of responses to personally injurious experiences. If citizens are not efficacious— attitudinally as well as behaviorally—when it is in their personal interest to pursue redress, can they be expected to be active in other modes of political participation? Any society that claims to be a participatory democracy and welfare state based on principles of social justice ought to pay attention to how mechanisms for the allocation of goods and services work in practice—what determines whether citizens get a fair deal, and, more generally, who gets what and how.

In the political participation literature rather limited attention has been given to contacts with officials having to do with the interests of citizens and their families (e.g., Almond and Verba, 1965; Verba and Nie, 1972; Barnes, Kaase, et al., 1979). Researchers have not focused specifically on complaints or grievances; moreover, no distinction is made between future-oriented petitions and past-oriented complaints.[11] One view sometimes expressed is that it is the alienated, the powerless, who turn to non-conventional means. In cross-national research, Barnes, Kaase and their colleagues (1979) found, on the contrary, that it is the relatively stronger groups who are high in use of both the conventional and the non-conventional means.

B. Bureaucracy and the Public

Another research tradition which has consolidated over the last 20 years investigates relations between bureaucracy and the public. Until about 1960, social scientists had mainly written about organizations as if clients did not exist. Eventually, researchers saw that client-official encounters deserved study. By the 1970's, the titles of publications began to mention clients explicitly.[12]

The study of bureaucracy and the public analyzes the ways that environmental, organizational, and situational factors constrain interaction between clients and officials. Environmental features include degree of structural differentiation and size of a society; organizational variables include goals of the organization and degree of elaboration of hierarchy; situational ones include the latent social identities of participants and the furniture arrangements (see Danet, 1981, Figure 1; Katz and Danet, 1973b, Introduction).[13]

In the last decade, the emphasis has shifted from a relatively dispassionate stance to a more problem-oriented one. Many researchers recognize that the benefits ostensibly available to citizens in fact often reach them only to the extent that they are skilled in extracting them from organizations. In earlier work on the sociology and social psychology of organizations perspectives from the top down, or from the outside looking in were stressed, whereas in work focused on the public the view from the outside looking in and from the bottom up was stressed (McKinlay, 1975; Danet, 1981). Researchers asked: To what extent do complaint-handling devices help to equalize the imbalance between citizens and organizations?

C. Dispute-Processing and the Sociology of Law

The third tradition which has influenced this research is the study of dispute-processing, as practiced by researchers in law and social science. The study of dispute-processing encompasses disputes between neighbors and kin, as well as those between individuals and organizations. Anthropologists have recently broadened the spectrum of topics studied to include not only the modes of disputing in traditional societies (e.g., Nader, 1969; Nader and Todd, 1978; Roberts, 1979), but access to justice in modern societies as well (Nader, 1980).

The sociology and anthropology of law shifted attention from courts to non-judicial means of dispute resolution, as it became evident that civil disputes reaching court are only the tip of the iceberg and that the courts alone are grossly incapable of providing access to justice (Cappelletti, 1981; Abel, 1982; Galanter, 1981; Nader, 1980). Another development is that attention has moved from the later stages of a dispute to earlier ones—the perception of an experience as injurious, the assignment of blame, making the grievance known, deciding to act, etc. (Felstiner, Abel and Sarat, 1980–81).[14]

Two main approaches have emerged, termed by Steele (1975) the institutional and individual approaches, respectively. In the institutional approach, the researcher typically analyzes the files and procedures of a dispute-processing device like a newspaper Action Line column (e.g., Hannigan, 1977; Mattice, 1980), a Consumer Protection Agency (Steele, 1975; Silbey, 1980–81), an ombudsman's office (Hill, 1976), or an elected official's services to constituents (Karikas, 1980). Researchers ask who complains, about what, and with what results.

In the second, individual approach, survey methods are used to assess the incidence of various types of problems and what people do about them (Curran, 1977; Best and Andreasen, 1977; Ladinsky and Susmilch, 1982; Fitzgerald, 1982; Miller and Sarat, 1980–81).

Each of these two approaches has major advantages and disadvantages. The institutional approach allows for extensive analysis of the workings of particular complaint-handling devices, but takes no account of the masses of grievances which either go unexpressed or have been taken elsewhere (cf. Danet, 1978). The individual approach allows for questioning about injurious experiences both among those who take action and among those who do not. Depth of detail about particular problems is often sacrificed, however, and little or nothing can be learned about the long-term impact of complaint-handling devices from attitudinal data.

D. Patronage and Brokerage

A fourth research tradition is that focussing on patronage and brokerage, a tradition practiced mainly by anthropologists (e.g., Wolf, 1966; Gellner and Waterbury, 1977; Boissevain, 1974), although political scientists interested in machine politics and party patronage have also made important contributions to this topic (e.g., Scott, 1972; Heidenheimer, 1970; Clapham, 1982). The use of personal influence in organizational settings is often a form of brokerage: Typically, a third party intervenes on the client's behalf, urging the official to grant what he or she has previously refused.

In the anthropological literature patronage is viewed as a type of asymmetric exchange relationship, prominent in underdeveloped peasant societies and in developing countries. In an oft-cited paper, Wolf (1966) focused his analysis on situations where "the formal framework of economic and political power exists alongside, and intermingled with various other kinds of informal structure which are interstitial, supplementary, parallel to it." The informal structure fills functional gaps and protects individuals against insecurity. A full patron-client relationship is one which is asymmetric—one person has more valued resources than the other; the dependent person offers deference and loyalty in return for favors; the relationship is personal and maintained in face-to-face interaction, and persists through time. Typically, the relationship is cultivated, consciously created. In one well-known variation, that of *compadrazgo,* common in Southern Europe and Central and South America, godparents may be chosen for a child with an eye to the resources the chosen couple can offer the family—status, potential help, and protection—in a hostile, unpredictable world (see, e.g., Mintz and Wolf, 1977; Nutini and Bell, 1980).

Boissevain (1977) has suggested that over the past hundred years, three forms of patronage have evolved. He calls them patronage, patron/brokerage, and organizational brokerage. Simple patronage is much like the definition given earlier—it involves long-term personal relationships in which the client offers loyalty in exchange for desired benefits. Patron/brokers are typically local "big men," such as a notary, a lawyer, parish priest or doctor. As Boissevain suggested, this type of patron/broker arises when big government begins to impinge on the lives of villagers. People need help to make use of newly available, bureaucratized services. The local patron can provide fewer and fewer of these services personally, but now "he can use his influence with people he knows well in the increasingly complex government, who, in turn, dispense these prizes" (Boissevain, 1977: 89). There is still a personal relationship with the client, but it is no longer exclusive. Finally, in a third stage, there is organizational brokerage. Here, organizations like political parties and unions serve as brokers to clients. The relationship is no longer necessarily personal at all. These brokers consciously cultivate the dependence of their clienteles, who activate them to get desired benefits.

There is quite another type of informal brokerage which occurs in many organizational settings and which has not received the sociological attention it deserves. This form is characterized not by assymetry, but by symmetric exchange of favors among comparative status equals. Suppose a well-known surgeon wishes to make sure his son is accepted at a prestigious university. He telephones the dean of admissions, who happens to be an old college friend. If the dean sees to it that the son is accepted, the surgeon will owe him one. The Russian aphorism, "You scratch my back, I'll scratch yours," is illustrative of the principle which underlies such exchanges. This study will focus on symmetric, as well as asymmetric forms of exchange outside the universalistic system.

E. Political and Administrative Corruption

In the 1960's, political scientists studying corruption saw it as a byproduct of modernization and development, whose effects were thought to be mainly positive. Corruption was claimed to stimulate the economy and to encourage integration of weak or alienated groups. It was thought to self-destruct. In the 1970's many writers came to reject these functionalist views. A post-functionalist approach crystallized, whose tenets are that (1) corruption is not confined to developing countries but is universal and flourishes in developed countries as well; (2) it does not disappear; on the contrary, it is self-perpetuating; (3) it is systemic in origin, rather than merely individual; (4) its negative consequences probably outweigh the positive ones (Werner, 1983a, 1983b; Caiden and Caiden, 1977; Ben Dor, 1974).[15]

Heidenheimer (1970) distinguished between black, gray and white corruption. Behavior which is viewed by both leaders and the public as requiring condemnation and the application of sanctions is deemed black. That which is condemned by the one but not the other is gray; and behavior to which both turn a blind eye is white. This distinction is useful because it helps the researcher to draw back from the value-laden connotation of corruption as bad or immoral. Empirical studies have examined to what extent leaders or the public view various acts as corrupt or undesirable. For example, Peters and Welch (1978) studied perceptions among American state legislators of 10 forms of deviation from U criteria, nearly all of which involved money. Sebba (1983) compared the perceptions of Russian and American immigrants to Israel with those of native Israelis regarding a set of deviant acts, including embezzlement, giving a bribe, taking a bribe, tax evasion, use of personal influence (protektzia), and consumer fraud.[16]

Ostensibly corrupt behavior is difficult to study, because so often it takes place under the table. Nevertheless, my collaborators, Naomi Kies and Hadassah Haas, and I found in the 1980 study reported in this book that in Israeli society enough people are willing to talk to a stranger about one particular type of non-U behavior—the use of personal connections—to make systematic empirical analysis based on structured interviews not only possible but fruitful and illuminating.

V. ISRAEL AS A SETTING FOR THIS STUDY

A number of features of Israeli society make it especially appropriate for research of the kind undertaken in this study.

A. General Features

Israel is a quite modern, industrialized, and urbanized society with high levels of literacy and health standards. In per capita income it resembles the less affluent of the Western European societies, such as the United Kingdom or Italy. As Ben-Dor has put it, somewhat paradoxically, it is a "highly developed developing society" (Ben-Dor, 1974). In many ways it resembles the societies of the West. Now 40, it is, or at least wishes to be known as, a pluralist democracy—with a political structure much like the consociational societies of Switzerland, the Netherlands or Austria.[17] Whether Israel can continue to call itself a pluralist democracy, given the continuing occupation of territories conquered in the Six Day War, is, however, a matter of some debate. Kimmerling (1988) has recently suggested that it should be thought of, instead, as a "control system." Israel's economy is a mixed socialist-capitalist one. As a welfare state, Israel is committed to providing many services to the public.

It has the largest public sector of any democracy in the world and holds a world record in the proportion of total economic resources expended by the public sector. In 1980 20.7% of the gross national product was expended on public services and as much as 28.1% of the labor force was employed in providing these services (Ofer, 1983). Planning and implementation of these services are highly centralized, even excessively so, in the eyes of some (cf. Marx, 1980). The private sector is not autonomous either, because investors are heavily dependent on government for subsidies and benefits.

B. Immigration, Cultural Heterogeneity

For anyone interested in the competition between U and P norms, Israel is an especially interesting case because it is an immigrant society. There was an initial period of nation-building between 1880 and 1948, when the British Mandate over Palestine ended and the State was declared. Israel is a very small country, with a population in 1988 of only a little over 4 million. Population increase has derived mainly from massive waves of immigration of Jews both in the pre-State period and following the establishment of the State. In 1948 there were only 700,000 persons residing in Palestine; in the short span of 35-or-so years the population increased by a factor of about six. Jews now constitute about 84% and Arabs the other 16% of the population.

Most Jewish immigrants came from Eastern Europe and from North Africa and the Middle East, though smaller numbers came from Western Europe and the English-speaking countries (the United States, the United Kingdom, South Africa, Australia), and even from such far-flung places as China and India. In much social science writing about Israel it is typical to speak of Western and of Middle Eastern or Oriental Jews, or of *Ashkenazim* and *Sephardim* (i.e.,

Jews whose ancestors hail from *Ashkenaz,* or Germany, and Jews from *Sepharad* or Spain). A great deal has been written about the so-called ethnic gap between these two large groups of immigrants and their descendants (e.g., Smooha, 1978; Shama and Idris, 1977; Inbar and Adler, 1977). This book will explore the significance of differentials in the distribution of access to protektzia for the ethnic gap in Israel. Although such differentials are discernible, they turn out to be of only secondary importance in the present study.

For the purposes of analysis of organizational culture, it is necessary to think in terms of three, rather than two, main cultural groupings. These are (1) persons of Western European origin, or who came from English-speaking countries; (2) immigrants from Eastern and Central Europe and their descendants; and (3) immigrants from North Africa and the Middle East. These three groups come from three quite different types of societies, which Eisenstadt (1981) has labelled pluralist democratic, monolithic, and neo-patrimonial, respectively. Persons from Western Europe or the United States bring with them experience of a relatively well-institutionalized pattern of universalistic allocation of goods and services in a more or less efficient public administration. Those coming from the socialist countries of Eastern and Central Europe—the USSR, Hungary, Czechoslovakia, Poland, Romania, Yugoslavia, and Bulgaria—bring experience of a monolithic bureaucracy permeating all areas of life, whose dysfunctional aspects give rise to a wealth of ways to circumvent it, whether through bribery or through informal exchange of favors. Finally, immigrants from North Africa and the Middle East (Morocco, Tunisia, Greece, Turkey, Iraq, etc.), especially those of poor education and from rural areas, have had little experience of bureaucracy, or are used to obtaining benefits through traditional networks of patronage and brokerage.

C. The Official Commitment to Universalism

On paper, Israel's is a universalistic organizational culture. In the public sector there is official commitment to bureaucratic norms, derived in large part from exposure to universalism and the other paraphernalia of bureaucracy during the British Mandate between 1917 and 1948. The large public sector consists of a vast array of bureaucratic agencies with all the Weberian characteristics of hierarchy, specialization, formal stipulation of goals, hiring based (in theory) on merit, written specification of rights and duties, universalistic allocation of goods and services, and so on. Although the economy retains some of the phenomena of the Middle and Far Eastern bazaar, by and large, the private sector is also dominated by bureaucratized structures—corporations, supermarkets, department stores, bank chains.

A major indication of the official commitment to universalism is the proliferation of ombudsmen in Israel. Both the speed and the extent of adoption of the idea have been remarkable. Not only was Israel a leader in being one of the first countries outside of Scandinavia to create a national ombudsman (in 1971), but it can boast of having the first municipal ombudsman anywhere: The city of Jerusalem opened the first municipal ombudsman office in the world in 1967. By 1977 Israel had two of the 15 existing municipal ombudsmen, the city of Haifa having also created an office by then.[18] Israel has also been quick to adopt specialty ombudsmen. It has one of the three existing military ombudsmen. There are not one but two in the police, one for the public, and one for the police themselves. The Hebrew University has an ombudsman for students only. In the light of all these developments, it is no exaggeration to say that Israel's public sector has rushed to offer citizens at least the semblance of universalistic justice.

In the private sector, there have been parallel developments. The consumer movement, imported from the West, has had an important impact in the last decade, although there is still a long way to go to catch up with North America or Western Europe. Besides four consumer organizations, Israel now has small claims courts. A highly popular television program used to process individual complaints. It still did so at the time of the 1980 survey which is reported in this book. More recently it has specialized in features which socialize citizens to consumer awareness. Another television program broadcasts live small claims cases. In addition, much consumer legislation has been passed in the last decade.

D. Protektzia: The Prevalence of Particularistic Behavior

Pitted against all these features of modernization, Westernization, and bureaucratization is the prevalence in Israel of protektzia, or the use of personal connections—what English-speakers call pulling strings, or using pull. One of the standard dictionaries of the Hebrew language, the Evan-Shoshan Dictionary (1983), defines protektzia as "patronage, a recommendation for preferential treatment; support by a person of influence of someone in order to obtain for him a right to a certain preferential advantage in obtaining work, and so forth." This dictionary traces the term to the Latin *protectio*, meaning the granting of patronage or protection. A dictionary of Hebrew slang (Ben-Amotz and Ben-Yehuda, 1972) defines protektzia as "the granting of preferential treatment in circumvention of official rules by an important person, because of kinship or social ties, and so forth."

To take an illustration, one of the most common situations in which citizens encounter problems in Israeli bureaucracy has to do with having a telephone installed. The demand for telephones has far exceeded the capacity of the telephone authority—formerly a government agency in the Ministry of Communications and now a public corporation—to supply them. To help cope with pressures from the public, telephone officials established a set of priorities, such that heart patients and high-ranking public officials have priority over ordinary citizens. Faced with the possibility of having to wait years for a telephone, many Israelis try instead to mobilize protektzia.

Although cases of bribery and other forms of corruption in high places are occasionally brought into public view, and may even be increasing (see chapter 4), in general, at the level of routine everyday transactions between citizens and low-level officials, bribery is probably rare. Protektzia, on the other hand, flourishes. Our own empirical study in the late 1960's (Danet and Hartman, 1972a, 1972b), as well as Avruch's mid-1970's research (Avruch, 1981) both demonstrated that this is the case. And contrary to the contention of Nachmias and Rosenbloom (1978), based on very fragmentary data, that the use of protektzia has been diminishing, the present study found it to be more entrenched than ever. In Heidenheimer's (1970) terms, Israelis view protektzia as a form of white corruption. Its use is widely recognized as a departure from the official rules but treated very permissively by both the establishment and the public (Sebba, 1983; Werner, 1983b).

E. The Research Question

What are people in this type of organizational culture likely to do when bureaucrats infringe on their rights, deny them unemployment compensation, overcharge them on income tax? Will they choose U channels, or will they opt for protektzia? This study is cast primarily at the social-psychological level: the attitudes and behavior of individuals are investigated. To assess the degree of institutionalization of the U code of redress, four sets of issues are addressed:

1. Knowledge. What do people know about the possibility of obtaining redress of grievances? Do they know of the existence of various channels? Who are the most knowledgeable persons, and who are the uninformed?

2. Attitudes. What beliefs and attitudes do people hold about the possibility of demanding redress through U channels? Do they feel they have a right to complain through them? Do they believe that it pays to use them? Or do they believe that particularistic ties must be mobilized in order to obtain entitlements? How do they rank the various channels available, U and P, as to the likelihood that using them can really help people? Do they believe it is all right to use P channels, or do they go on record, verbally, as condemning them?

3. Action. Do people, in fact, take action when they feel aggrieved or when the road to some desired resource is blocked? Do most people give up, or do they try again, whether through a P or a U channel? Which of the two basic types do they tend to choose? Do they mainly use U channels alone, P channels alone, or some combination of them? Is it important for them to obtain principled redress of grievances to get justice or do they opt out, abdicate, forego their right to have established who is right and who is wrong, and about what? Do they behave in a manner which is governed more by interest than by principle?[19]

4. Outcomes. Does it in fact pay to use U channels of redress? Which ones work best for citizens? Do they compete successfully with P channels not only in recruiting users, but in their ability to help people? Which channels are judged accurately by the general public? Which are the ones whose effectiveness they over-estimate and which are under-estimated? What is the empirical distribution of help? Are some more likely than others to obtain favorable outcomes? If there is a differential distribution of help, what accounts for sub-group differences—sociocultural characteristics of clients, or some other factors? What are the long-term consequences of outcomes not only for organizational culture but for social justice?

VI. DESIGN AND SAMPLE

A. Method and Sample

This study is based on a survey of the attitudes and experiences of the Jewish population of Israel in dealings with public and private organizations during the year 1979–1980. Approximately 1000 residents of Jerusalem, Haifa, and metropolitan Tel Aviv, the three main cities, were sampled. Further details of the construction of this sample are presented at the end of Chapter IV and in Appendix C.

Our original plan had been to combine the survey with case studies of four complaint-handling devices, thereby overcoming at least in part some of the limitations of either method used separately. Unfortunately, two obstacles prevented us from carrying out this plan and forced us to abandon the idea of carrying out case studies. First, it became evident that we could not obtain research funds sufficient to support both. Second, very early on, we realized that it was impossible to obtain the cooperation of the national ombudsman's office, despite the avowed commitment of the then-incumbent, Dr. I.E. Nebenzahl, to the importance of evaluation.

I had been interested in the ombudsman idea since the 1960's. In 1968 Tsiyona Peled and I had conducted a research seminar on the office of the new Jerusalem ombudsman. As the first national ombudsman, Dr. Nebenzahl had acquired an international reputation; in fact, his personal prestige had led to his being responsible for the planning and hosting of the Second World Congress of Ombudsmen in Jerusalem in November, 1980. Dr. Nebenzahl included in the program a panel discussion on "Evaluation of the Effectiveness and Efficiency of the Ombudsman." Despite this public commitment to evaluation, he avoided cooperating with us by arguing that he was required to preserve confidentiality of the files to protect the privacy of complainants and that it would be disloyal to expose bureaucrats to outsiders, especially because he was dependent on their cooperation.[20]

Although the issues are thorny and it is difficult to prove that Dr. Nebenzahl wished to protect his office from scrutiny, the experience of Nader and her team of researchers, summarized in Nader (1980) in studying the files and operations of a large variety of American complaint-handling devices suggested that this was, indeed, the case. The Nader group found that organizations blocked public disclosure of information not only to them personally, but to the public at large, to the media, and to other organizations with an interest in public accountability and social reform. As noted earlier, the overriding conclusion of their research was that American complaint-handlers may ultimately be little more than cooling-out devices which in the long run serve the interests of big organizations and not of the individual client.[21]

B. Reasons for Exclusion of the Arab Population from the Study

As mentioned in the Preface, regrettably, the Arab population of Israel has not been included in this study. Christian and Moslem Arabs constitute about 16% of the population of Israel, a sizable minority of persons residing within the pre-1967 borders. Unfortunately, a variety of considerations led us to exclude them, despite our recognition of several very good reasons for the importance of investigating their experiences in encounters with organizations.

The most obvious of the reasons arguing for their inclusion is the fact that minority groups are especially likely to be victims of injustice. Given the same type of problem or grievance, for example, are Arabs as likely as Jews to take action, either through channels like the ombudsman, or through the mobilization of personal connections? Still more critical is the question of outcomes: Is there any evidence of discrimination in the operations of complaint channels? Are Arabs less likely than Jews to be vindicated when a complaint is processed by the ombudsman? Another interesting question is whether their networks of personal influence are reported to be as effective as those available to Jews. Chances are, in some settings, at least, that they are not.

A second consideration arguing for their inclusion is that there is theoretical interest in investigating their experiences because they are less modernized and more rural. Only 50% of Israeli Arabs, as opposed to 90% of Jews, live in cities (Central Bureau of Statistics, 1981). The quality of the experiences of rural Arabs and the types of strategies they use in organizational encounters are likely to be quite different from those of urban Jews. A pioneering, exploratory study strongly suggested that Israeli Arabs are likely to make extensive use of more traditional forms of patronage and brokerage (El-Makawi, 1988).

In spite of these very persuasive considerations, there were others which led to the exclusion of Arabs from this study. First of all, a study of rural Arabs would require a very different research design from the one used in this study. It would have to be far less structured, with intensive ethnographic work in the villages, as well as observations of encounters between urban Arabs and bureaucrats.[22] Second, we felt at the time that it is difficult to study Arab Israelis' experiences of injustice and poor service without being drawn into larger issues of their problematic status in a Jewish state. Third, the research team for the 1980 study consisted of three Jewish women (Naomi Kies and Hadassah Haas, in addition to myself), only one of whom, Naomi Kies, knew even a little Arabic. To carry out such a study effectively would require the assistance of a male Arab able to move about freely. For all these reasons, then, this study was restricted to the Jewish population.[23]

C. Scope of the Study: Both Public and Private Sectors

This study differs radically from most of those surveyed, and also from my own past research, in that it extends the scope of analysis to include both the public and the private sectors. Usually, only one or the other is studied. Political participation studies naturally are focused only on government-citizen relationships. And, like most studies of consumer behavior by persons trained in marketing and business administration, the socio-legal studies of client-organization disputes emphasize consumer relationships in the private sector. Only Nader's (1980) group has looked at how the sector affects client-organization relationships, though even in their studies problems with private-sector purchases were emphasized.

As Nader (1980) has suggested, the condition of monopoly is one of the main constraints on the freedom of action of citizens in pursuing a fair deal, whether in the public or the private sectors. In the public sector, citizens are dependent on a sole source for services and many contacts are not initiated by them. In the private sector, on the other hand, in theory at least, the consumer has bargaining power, can go elsewhere if not satisfied, and tell others not to patronize the store involved. While the main theme of this book is the interrelations between U and P elements within the public sector, a secondary theme is the difference that the sector itself makes for use of channels.

VII. CLARIFICATION OF CONCEPTS

There are four concepts which are frequently used in this book and which deserve clarification. They are organizational culture, redress, personal influence, and biculturalism.

A. Organizational Culture

I define organizational culture as "patterns of orientations toward formally constituted organizations, including knowledge and beliefs about them, and feelings and evaluations about the performance of

participants in them, as well as patterns of behavior so regular as
to become discernible features of organizational life." This definition
includes the orientations of both the public and officials, though the
book will focus only on the public. I will speak of organizational
rather than bureaucratic culture (cf. Nachmias and Rosenbloom,
1978), to call to mind both public and private sectors and to avoid
a term which appears to assume that organizations function universalistically. The domain of organizational culture covers a wide
range of phenomena, including supervisor-subordinate relationships
and worker output norms.[24] Here the topic is limited to client
attitudes and behavior in the pursuit of benefits, and, particularly,
in the pursuit of redress.

B. Redress

Generally, the terms *culture of redress* and *complaints culture* will
be used interchangeably, to mean people's knowledge, beliefs, attitudes, and behavioral dispositions relating to perceived injurious
experiences in formal organizations. Three terms often crop up in
discussions of redress: petition, complaint, and appeal. I mentioned
earlier the difficulties in distinguishing complaints from petitions
(see footnote 10). Empirically, things are still more complicated,
because what appears to be redress behavior may not be that at all.
Suppose a client receives a negative reply to some request and then
goes to a higher official. This client may not necessarily be complaining about perceived injustice at all—he or she may just be
unhappy with a refusal, might even think the refusal was legitimate,
and may just be using the machinery of appeal to try again. Thus,
in some indeterminate percentage of the cases, citizens genuinely
feel aggrieved and seek U-grounded justice. Others may experience
no grievance but use grievance machinery as a strategem. Still others,
though aggrieved, may opt out of the U-grounded system, either
switching to P channels or simply lumping it, i.e., taking no action.
   Avoiding a positivistic view that rule-application necessarily results
in correct or incorrect decisions, I see much room for negotiation,
in both the private and the public sectors. Most generally, then, this
is a study not merely of redress, but of how clients get what they
want in organizations. Viewed most broadly, U rules and regulations
on the one hand, and the non-U normative bases upon which extra-
organizational ties may be mobilized, on the other, constitute two
kinds of games, each having many possible moves, which clients
can use to maximize their interests. This conceptualization of official-

client encounters places analytic emphasis on patterns of behavior, on strategy in encounters with officials, rather than on clients' experience of injustice per se.

The reservations about redress expressed earlier reflect what is known about the functioning of bureaucracy outside the West. Might it be, in fact, that they apply to all settings? In Mayhew's (1975) study of what people in the city of Detroit did about serious problems in five areas, including those with public organizations, only a minority claimed they sought justice or vindication of rights.

> The interests of individuals are often less broad, abstract and long term than the interests implied in conceptions of social justice. . . . The individual facing a problem tends to be more interested in the necessity of resolving a practical difficulty than in vindicating a right. . . . Even when given . . . an opportunity to choose directly between the law and expedience in explaining the grounds of their satisfaction or dissatisfaction with the outcomes of their problems, respondents chose practical rather than legal terms by ratios varying from 1.7 to 7.1 depending on the area involved. (Mayhew, 1975)

Only systematic comparative research can tell us whether interest predominates over principle to the same extent in the West as in countries outside the West. Until evidence to the contrary becomes available, my hypothesis is that, relatively speaking, the average American or British citizen of at least some high school education cares more about principle in encounters with organizations than does his or her counterpart in developing countries, and that this concern for principle is more predictive of behavior than it would be outside the West.

C. Personal Influence

To pull strings, to use personal influence in supposedly U dealings is to attempt to activate some particularistic normative obligation on the part of the official, or of some third party, to obtain a benefit which is otherwise blocked.

1. Two-party influence attempts: the impingement of latent identities. The simplest case is that where latent identities of official and client (Katz and Danet, 1973a) impinge on their relationship, and clients implicitly or explicitly exploit these identities to receive benefits. For instance, suppose that a person seeking unemployment compensation learns that among the officials working in that agency is a person who happens to be his or her neighbor. To choose deliberately to see the neighbor is to attempt to activate a normative obligation of neighbors to help one another. The fact of knowing each other as neighbors might of course affect the encounter even if the client does not consciously seek to exploit the relationship. The mere appearance of the client in the office might motivate the official to give him or her preferential treatment. In this book I shall be interested primarily in those instances where clients consciously seek to mobilize personal influence to undermine organizational regulations. Other aspects of interlocutors' social identities which clients might mobilize are common ethnic origin, schooling, or work experience, having served in the army together, kinship ties, and the varieties of friendship ties, from casual to intimate ones.

2. Personal connections: The activation of interpersonal networks. These same types of particularistic ties provide the basis for activation of interpersonal networks to intercede on the client's behalf. Suppose, for instance, that the person seeking unemployment compensation wants to receive an extra 3 months' benefits and the official has refused. The client approaches the official's boss, who happens to be his cousin, thereby activating (or at least trying to activate) the norm that relatives should help each other. The boss will then pressure the official to comply or order him or her do so, even if the order is illegitimate—and the official will find it difficult to refuse, being dependent on the positive opinion held by the supervisor of him or her.

In theory, there is no limit on the size of chains of influence that can be mobilized. If, for example, the client's cousin happens to be married to the official's boss, there would be a chain with four nodes in it. The size of these chains and the types of relationship mobilized at each link are topics which await systematic empirical research.[25] Granovetter (1973, 1974) has argued that it is weak ties, rather than strong ones, which are most often and most successfully mobilized in influence attempts. His thesis is that the location of individuals in the social structure is more important than their psychological motivation in determining their ability to provide help.

D. Biculturalism

As suggested earlier, individuals living in hybrid organizational cultures may usefully be viewed as biculturals. Like bilinguals, they command two distinct codes. And like bilinguals, they develop switching capabilities. Research on bilingualism is extremely suggestive for the study of organizational behavior. Ferguson (1964), one of the first to write about bilingualism from a macro-sociological viewpoint, noted that when high and low varieties of speech co-exist, usually one enjoys public prestige, but speakers often feel more comfortable using the other, which they feel is more homelike, more natural. I propose that when two organizational codes co-exist, a similar phenomenon occurs—people publicly claim to respect one code, but in fact they feel more comfortable using the unofficial one. The notion of biculturalism is further developed in Chapter III.

VIII. A PREVIEW OF THE COMING CHAPTERS

There are eight more chapters in this book. Two are devoted to elaboration of a theoretical framework, whose outlines have only been hinted at in this Introduction. Chapter 2 develops a way to classify patterns of organizational culture around the world, identifying two key sets of variables, namely, the presence of objective difficulties in obtaining resources, and cultural factors, usually the survival and continuing salience of pre-modern forms of social relations in modern or modernizing settings. Chapter 3 seeks to translate the macro-sociological discussion of chapter 2 into terms which facilitate predictions about the behavior of individuals. It sets out the basic hypotheses of the book.

Chapters 4 through 8 are devoted to presentation of the Israeli case study. Chapter 4 provides an introductory overview of Israel's organizational culture, as it had developed by the time of the present study. The basic parameters of this culture are described and the main factors which have shaped it are surveyed. It is suggested that there is *prima facie* evidence that hybrid patterns of behavior are a product both of genuine objective difficulties in obtaining benefits and of unique cultural and historical factors which have characterized the history of the Jewish people and the creation of the State of Israel.

In chapters 5 through 7 the main findings of the survey described above are reported. Chapter 5 shows how Israelis are socialized into a bicultural system, on the one hand acquiring many elements of a U-based code, yet at the same time learning that to get along in this society, to be a savvy client, protektzia must be used at least some of the time. Chapter 5 deals with the issues only at the level of attitudes, or of Israelis' cognitive map of the nature of organizational life. In contrast, in chapters 6 and 7 patterns of behavior and their consequences are examined. Chapter 6 demonstrates that protektzia is firmly rooted in Israeli society and, more important, that it filters down from the top—that the better integrated the individual is in the society, the more likely the person is to have access to protektzia and to use it. In chapter 7 the relation between protektzia and redress is analyzed. Among other things, the predictors of hybridization, or of biculturalism in the choice of channels of redress are examined. Of special interest is what the data show about the cultural transformation of immigrants hailing from Western European or English-speaking countries—those countries which are supposed bastions of universalism.

Chapter 8 discusses the results of the present study in the light of about 30 years of research on bureaucracy and the public in Israel. Its aim is to reconstruct how and why the researchers of the late 1950's and early 1960's erred in believing that Israel was on the road to becoming a Western-style society that was universalistic in practice, as well as in theory. The chapter traces the history of the so-called absorption-modernization paradigm (Eisenstadt, 1954) which characterized much social science thinking about the emerging society in those years, and concludes that biculturalism is a much more appropriate characterization of organizational culture in contemporary Israel than is modernity.

Finally, chapter 9 explores the more general, societal implications of the case study. It seeks to relate the findings to the theoretical formulation presented in chapters 2 and 3 and returns to two themes which are threaded throughout the book: (1) the double advantage of the stronger social groups, in hybrid organizational cultures, and (2) the difficulties in implementing social change in societies having such cultures.

Also in the last chapter the pro's and con's of the phenomena of organizational biculturalism are debated. I acknowledge that societies with widespread biculturalism do pay a price for it. Yet, there may be important benefits for individuals or societies, or both. For instance, the availability of choice in social situations is the essence of human freedom. Second, the use of personal connections not only humanizes bureaucracy but, at least under certain conditions, even promotes social integration. The explanatory power of the concept of biculturalism may be more limited in those cases where there are major social cleavages and where exploitation of underdog groups is ruthless and widespread. Nevertheless, the position of this book is that the concept of biculturalism is useful in pointing to differing cultural patterns, enabling researchers, as it does, to avoid the pitfalls of value-laden concepts like corruption.

II
Patterns of Organizational Culture

Suppose we were to observe encounters between social welfare officials and clients in Chicago or Zagreb or Jerusalem. Probably, we would immediately notice some very striking differences. Assuming that we had a basic command of the local language and culture— so that initial strangeness of the culture was not a barrier to perception of the situation—we might be struck by the bland but not uncomfortable impersonality and cool efficiency of the Chicago encounters, as contrasted with those in the other two cities, where officials often treat clients officiously. Met with a refusal to a request, most clients in all settings might simply lump it. But the Americans would probably trust in the legitimacy of the decision and some would appeal or complain through proper channels. The Zagreb or Jerusalem clients, on the other hand, might perceive the situation as one requiring manipulation behind the scenes, and Zagreb clients, if not Jerusalem ones, might also perceive the refusal to be unnecessarily arbitrary.

There might also be considerable differences in what is happening just outside the door—in Chicago the line would probably be quite orderly and those waiting would be neither surly nor especially subservient. In Zagreb or Jerusalem, on the other hand, people might be crowding around the door, arguing over whose turn is next, with one or more seeking to get ahead of their turn, and responding either impassively or in anger when some well-connected person is ushered through the door without having had to wait his or her turn.

In this chapter and the next, I attempt to develop a theoretical framework for the study of official-client encounters as a problem in organizational culture. This chapter will focus on encounters from a macro-sociological perspective; in the following one, I reframe the issues at the level of the individual.[1]

I. DEFINING THE PROBLEM

It is no easy task to establish the boundaries of the topic of this book. The general area of inquiry is extraordinarily complex and elusive. Moreover, there are large areas of overlap with the domains of political and administrative corruption and of white collar crime, as well as of what has become known as the parallel economy. The scheme shown in Figure II.1 helps to create some order among these various phenomena.

This scheme is what Guttman (1957; 1970) called a mapping sentence. It is used to order the variables in a given domain without necessarily implying causal relations among them. Reading through the sentence, it can be seen that a given act X counts as an instance of non-universalistic behavior if an actor (A) who is an official or employee of an organization, or a client or citizen, or a politician (B) gives or receives, or attempts to do one of the two, a resource which is either (C) material or non-material, and (D) either substantive, procedural or interpersonal, in exchange for another resource which is again either (E) material or non-material, and (F) substantive, procedural or interpersonal, and this act takes place in (G) the domain of politics, public-sector organizations, or private-sector organizations, and (H) does or does not require the cooperation of another person, in any of the roles listed in (I), and finally, the act constitutes a violation of a norm which is of a (J) legal, organizational, or general moral nature.[2] It will become evident shortly that of these ten facets, two are most critical.

Political scientists interested in machine politics and political corruption typically study illegal or immoral bureaucrat-politician and politician-citizen exchanges. Examples are a minister intervening in the hiring of a new employee to see that his close friend gets the job, and a party hack who offers material benefits to citizens in exchange for their votes. Criminologists specializing in white collar crime focus on illegal cooperation between employees of the same organization (for example, conspiring to misappropriate funds), between officials belonging to different organizations (for instance, a bribe by a cement factory owner to a builder to obtain a contract to supply cement for some housing), between officials and clients (say, a policeman receiving a bribe in exchange for waiving a traffic ticket) or solo offenses where cooperation of another person is not

Figure II.1.

A Mapping Sentence for Analysis of Types of Deviations from Universalistic Norms

An act X counts as an instance of non-universalistic behavior in a universalistic context if:

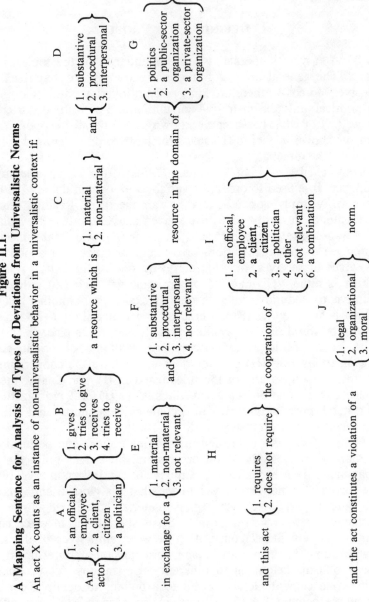

involved at all, as in embezzlement or tax evasion.[3] Much of the recent literature on parallel economies has been written by economists whose main interest is in estimating the total amount of national economic activity which is illegal. The sociological distinction between solo and cooperative forms of rule-violation is not particularly of interest to them and neither are they interested in offenses which are technically legal although they violate other types of norms. Thus, although this literature is pertinent to the topic in a general way, it is difficult to make use of it.

Figure II.1 helps us to focus on violations of universalistic rules which are generally neglected by these researchers: first of all, I focus specifically on client organization exchanges (facets A and I), particularly in those organizations which provide goods and services to individual clients. Here, Blau and Scott's (1962) *cui bono* typology is helpful. They distinguished between organizations whose prime beneficiary is the individual client (e.g., service organizations like a private employment agency); those whose prime beneficiary is the public-at-large (police, tax authorities; these are called commonweal organizations); business concerns whose prime beneficiary is, of course, their owners; and finally, mutual benefit organizations like unions. Empirically, many organizations are, of course, mixed types. Public-sector organizations have both commonweal and service components. Thus a government social welfare agency juggles service to clients with checks of eligibility. In theory, both public-sector and private-sector organizations may be included, though the main interest in this book is in the former (facet G).

Students of white collar crime deal with offenses against commonweal organizations or private-sector businesses. They are not interested in particularistic transactions in service organizations unless they are illegal. I propose to isolate for sociological analysis instances of rule-violation (1) in which it "takes two to tango,"[4] (2) which involve pairs of officials and clients, and which (3) violate formal or informal organizational norms, and may or may not be illegal. It is these which have hardly been studied, and for which the tools of sociological analysis are especially appropriate. It is now evident that the critical facets in Figure II.1 are facets H and J: I concentrate on violations of universalistic rules requiring the co-operation of at least one other person. Additionally, I narrow the topic to such exchanges between officials and the public.

Bureaucratization profoundly transforms the basic ways that people relate to one another. The differentiation between public and private spheres requires that persons relate to one another in public settings according to the norms of universalism, specificity, and affective neutrality (Parsons, 1951; Inkeles and Smith, 1974; Katz and Danet, 1973a). The commitment to universalism requires that goods and services be allocated in accordance with general rules which specify the rights of categories of persons, independent of characteristics with which they were born, such as caste, ethnicity, race or sex. The requirement of specificity means that individuals are supposed to avoid bringing into interaction aspects of their identity such as their family roles, ethnicity, or occupational status, unless these aspects happen to be relevant to the situation. Finally, affective neutrality means that people are supposed to keep their feelings out of organizational encounters, maintaining an impersonal orientation toward those with whom they come into contact.

Apparently, there are limits to the extent that people can be made to conform to these requirements, even in the most controlled environments. Many have argued that bureaucratization seriously conflicts with basic human needs. The work of Goffman on total institutions like prisons and mental hospitals (Goffman, 1961), the novels of Solzhenitsin on dissidents in the Soviet Union, and Mars' (1982) analysis of *fiddling*—petty bureaucratic crime in occupational settings—all suggested in different ways that the greater the effort to control behavior through bureaucratization, the more likely it is that people will find ways to break the rules. People exploit the cracks in institutional arrangements not only to maximize instrumental interests, but to keep a portion of the human spirit free from domination.

At the same time, people do not violate these norms simply on ideological grounds; behavior which departs from them is highly structured. The job in this chapter is to illuminate the factors which constrain behavior in client-official encounters. Such departures can occur in either of two directions. In the first instance, there is the granting of favors not due by law or bureaucratic regulation. I call this positive particularism. In the second instance, individuals are denied their due. This is negative particularism, commonly called discrimination. I restrict the domain of this book to the varieties of positive particularism and the social conditions that foster behavior which falls under this label. A fully elaborated theory would, of course, have to encompass both types of phenomena. Notice that in Figure II.1 only instances where resources are illegitimately transferred are covered, not those where they are illegitimately denied; hence, it does not apply to what I have just called negative particularism.

II. Patterns of Organizational Culture: A First Approximation

The literature on organizations in different cultural and structural settings invites speculation that there may be three main patterns in official-client encounters. In one pattern there is considerable correspondence between the official U code and actual behavior. In the other two, there is a marked gap between the official U code and actual behavior. Empirical research suggests that the three basic patterns correspond, more or less, to Eisenstadt's (1973, 1981) classification of (1) pluralistic democratic societies; (2) monolithic societies; and (3) neo-patrimonial societies. Figure II.2 contrasts the features of organizational culture in the public sector in the three types of society; in Figure II.3 the same contrasts are shown for the private sector.[5]

The quality of the evidence for patterns of official-client relations in each of these three types is extremely uneven. For the democracies there is relatively good information, including empirical research. For the socialist societies there are only the unsystematic though often insightful reports of Western journalists, and social science research based on secondary sources both by emigres from Eastern Europe and by Western social scientists. Finally, despite a huge literature on administration in developing countries, there is remarkably little suitable empirical research of the kind needed.[6]

A. The Public Sector

In Figure II.2 are listed ten features of either societies or organizations, or the relations between them, which together shape organizational culture. The first nine may all be viewed, loosely, as independent variables which combine to produce the degree of conformity or lack of conformity to U norms which is characteristic of each type and which appears as the tenth and final feature in Figure II.2.

1. The official commitment to bureaucratic norms. The most basic question to be asked in assessing organizational culture is the extent of normative bureaucratization. I would want to know to what extent goods and services are supposed to be distributed by universalistic bureaucratic structures. Both in the socialist societies where bureaucratization is total—the State is literally one huge bureaucracy—and in the West, where a private sector is demarcated, goods and services

Figure II.2

Organizational Culture in Pluralist Democracies, Monolithic Socialist Societies, and Neo-Patrimonial Societies: Public Sector

Feature	Pluralist Democracies	Monolithic Socialist Societies	Neo-Patrimonial Societies
Normative institutionalization of U code	strong	strong	weak
Availability of channels of redress	many	some	few
Civic orientation	civic	subject	subject/parochial
Dependence on government	moderate	high	low
Availability of material resources	plentiful	scarce	scarce
Politicization of the bureaucracy	low	high	high
Homogeneity of the population	relatively homogeneous	relatively homogeneous	very heterogeneous
Efficiency	high	low	low
Service ethic	strong	weak	weak
Conformity to U code	high	low	low

are overwhelmingly supplied by such structures. Official documents and pronouncements of organizations call for workers and clients to relate to one another according to the requirements of the U code. In developing countries the code is only weakly institutionalized on the official level.

Second, at least on paper, organizational cultures committed to universalism have generally invested in complaint-handling devices, or are investing in them at present. The heaviest investment in these devices is the pluralist democracies of the West, because of strong ideological commitment to the notion of accountability of institutions to the public. In the socialist countries mechanisms for redress of grievances, or at least for the airing of grievances do exist, including letters to the editor and criticism sessions, although, as will be shown later, citizens may not feel free to use them. These devices are rarer still in developing countries, though as I mentioned in chapter 1, a growing number of them are instituting ombudsmen.

The official commitment to universalism should go hand in hand, theoretically, with socialization of the public to the civic culture, in Almond and Verba's (1965) sense. To be competent in obtaining their entitlements, clients must not only be aware of influence from above, but must also perceive themselves to have influence on organizations. In the democracies, significant numbers of citizens are socialized to be full citizens. In socialist regimes, despite the official commitment to universalism, citizens would have mainly a subject orientation, reinforced by past domination by autocratic bureaucracies in the pre-socialist era. In third world countries, elites would probably have a mixed citizen and subject orientation, whereas the masses would be parochial, only dimly aware, if at all, of modern organizations and what they offer.

2. Objective ease of access to resources. Four factors affect access to resources: the presence of monopoly; the degree of effectiveness

Figure II.3
Organizational Culture in Pluralist Democracies, Monolithic Socialist Societies, and Neo-Patrimonial Societies: Private Sector*

Feature	Pluralist Democracies	Monolithic Socialist Societies	Neo-Patrimonial Societies
Institutionalization of bureaucratic norms	strong	strong	weak
Availability of channels of redress	many	some	few
Government regulation of standards	strong	strong	weak
Availability of goods	plentiful	scarce	scarce
Prices	market-determined	fixed	flexible
Negotiation	absent	absent	present
Conformity to bureaucratic norms	high	low	low

* Strictly speaking, for socialist societies, the term *private sector* does not apply; however, they are included here because certain factors are shown to be distinctly different in them which did not emerge from the analysis in Figure II.2.

and efficiency of the organization; scarcity of resources; and degree
of rigidity or flexibility in decision-making. Other things equal, monopoly is likely to create difficulties because the citizen is dependent
on a sole source for service. The higher the proportion of all benefits
provided by the state, the more dependent citizens will be. At the
same time, monopoly does not guarantee such difficulties; there are
public bureaucracies which are extensive and which nevertheless
work in relatively efficient, responsive fashion, e.g., those in Sweden.
And inefficiency and lack of responsiveness to legitimate needs and
requests may occur even when organizations do not control a monopoly. Wherever inefficiency and red tape flourish, people will try
to circumvent the official system. Both large size of organizations
and centralization often result in these dysfunctional consequences
for citizens.

One of the most important factors in shaping organizational culture
is whether resources are scarce or plentiful. In the West, resources
are generally plentiful and there is little competition for them. In
contrast, in socialist and developing countries there are chronic
shortages of goods and services and, consequently, intense competition for them (in the latter countries it may be only the urban
groups who know about these benefits who will try to compete for
them). The relation between scarcity and behavior is probably curvilinear: When resources are either extremely plentiful, or so scarce
that efforts to obtain them are guaranteed to fail, people will remain
within universalistic restrictions.[7] As for rigidity or flexibility of
bureaucrats, in societies with a strong service ethic (generally, those
in the West, although the rigidity of the French bureaucracy is famous
(cf. Crozier, 1964), officials are likely to be relatively flexible; where
a service ethic is lacking, officials are more likely to be sticklers for
the rules.

3. Social structure. Two features of social structure are pertinent.
First is the extent of structural differentiation between institutional
spheres, in particular, the degree of politicization of public administration. One hallmark of a fully differentiated civil service is that
it is immune to political influences. Generally, politicization is low
in the West, although this has not always been true and political
patronage has been known to influence the handing out of high-
level positions. At the level of daily transactions between low-ranking
officials and clients, however, politicization is unlikely, unless, for
example, a benefit is rare—say, the services of a particularly well-
regarded surgeon in a public hospital. In the socialist regimes, the

opposite trend is found: deliberate cultivation of overlap between the political and administrative spheres, for purposes of social control. In third world countries, politicization is also high, either because the process of differentiation is incomplete or unintentionally arrested or because it is intentionally blocked in one-party regimes.

Another aspect of social structure which casts its shadow on organizational culture is the composition of the population. Are there wide gaps between masses and elites in education, in socialization to the U code, or is the population relatively homogeneous? Although there *are* gaps between middle and lower classes in the West, they are relatively small, compared to the yawning gaps in the developing world; in the latter, educated elites may have quite thoroughly internalized the U code, while for illiterate masses personalistic styles of relating are still the normatively approved way. It may be assumed that citizens in socialist countries generally know the rules, because all-pervasive indoctrination has no doubt reached out to all groups.

B. The Private Sector

Next, I examine the constellation of features characterizing the private sector in these societies. Of course, in monolithic societies there is no separate private sector, or if there is one, it is small and insignificant; I include the socialist societies here because the features that surround obtaining consumer goods are not necessarily those that are relevant for analysis of services, where eligibility is often the critical variable.

1. Commitment to bureaucratic norms. In regimes which distinguish between public and private sectors, formally constituted written rules are not as central in the management of relationships between organizations and the public as they are in the public sector; what determines access to a resource is not the individual's formally stipulated right but the ability to pay.[8] Nevertheless, universalism is present at least in the fact that clerks are supposed to treat all customers in the same way and charge the same price. Second, the relationship is supposed to be specific; it should not be relevant that the customer is a high-status person or a friend of the salesperson. Finally, feelings are not expected to be salient. The same constellation of normative expectations would supposedly characterize consumer transactions in Moscow or Bucharest, even though these socialist regimes do not demarcate an official private sector (or allow only a small one). In developing societies there may be a mixed situation, in which the bureaucratic norms have been institutionalized in city shops which charge fixed prices and are patronized by elites, whereas in the villages and city outdoor markets particularistic, diffuse, emotionally-charged styles of relating dominate the bazaars.

We have seen that the West has invested in complaint-handling devices in the private as well as the public sectors. Socialist countries also offer citizens having problems with consumer goods help with these problems, though information on this is hard to come by. In developing countries, presumably, little attention is paid to the need for such channels, or if they are present, there are serious problems in their institutionalization.

2. Government regulation of standards. One factor which helps create consciousness of consumer rights is government regulation of standards for consumer goods. More exactly, consumer consciousness can hardly arise if there has not been an attempt to create standards. Both in the West and in socialist countries, government does take responsibility for standards. In the West in the last 20 years there has been much attention paid to consumer protection legislation. In developing countries little attention is paid to this issue because it is of lower priority than other matters of nation-building.

3. Availability of goods. In the West, consumer goods are plentiful; in socialist and developing countries they are not, at least not for groups without privileges. We shall see, later on, just how critical a variable scarcity is in shaping organizational cultures.

4. Prices and negotiation. In the Western pluralist democracies with their capitalist or mixed capitalist and socialist economies, prices are market-determined.[9] In the socialist countries prices are fixed by the state and are supposed to be the same everywhere. In practice, however, there is a flourishing black market, with unregulated higher prices for scarce items. Prices are flexible to an even greater extent in developing countries than in the West: Although in a Western city different stores may have different prices for the same item on the same day, in the markets of developing countries, prices may vary with the same seller on the same day. How much he or she likes the customer, the social status of the customer, and whether business is good may all influence the price. Wherever prices are fixed, there is, of course, no bargaining (except for those who know someone who can get it wholesale or in the occasional street market).[10] When prices are not fixed, as in the developing nations, negotiation is part of the game, expected, and normatively approved. The contrast between the impersonal, efficient Western supermarket and the leisurely, colorful third world market with genial haggling could not be greater.

III. A Typology of Patterns of Organizational Culture

The above grouping of countries into three general categories is useful as a first approximation of types of organizational culture. On closer inspection, however, it is not analytically very powerful. The countries are divided on the basis of either geographical location—the West, Eastern Europe, or Asia-Africa—or political system—democracy or one-party state. Neither of these inherently dictates the shape of organizational culture, except for the fact that monopoly is a direct consequence of totalitarian regimes. Thus, in a rough way these three categories point to three empirical types, but they cannot serve as theoretical types. By focussing on two critical features of societies, we can arrive at a more satisfactory mode of classification of patterns of organizational culture. These are: (1) the extent to which clients encounter objective difficulties in obtaining resources, and (2) the presence of competing cultural factors which legitimate particularistic behavior.

A. Objective Difficulties in Obtaining Resources

We have already seen that four types of factors lead to objective difficulties in obtaining resources: dependence of citizens on monopolistic organizations, inefficiency (whether or not monopoly obtains), scarcity of resources, and rigidity in application of rules.

B. Cultural Factors: The Persistence of Pre-Modern Types of Social Relations

Competing cultural factors providing legitimation for particularistic behavior are most typically found in the developing societies. Two types of structural features of these societies produce strong pressures toward particularistic decision-making. Where familism is strong and membership in corporate groups is a salient part of an individual's identity, there will be pressure toward egalitarian, or symmetrical particularism. Where hierarchical patron-client relationships continue to be salient, asymmetrical particularism will be found.

C. A Four-Fold Classification

Cross-classification of these two basic dimensions of societies should enable researchers to distinguish among four, rather than three, types of organizational cultures. Consider Figure II.4: Type I societies would be those which are quite universalistic in practice, as well as on paper. Neither are there objective difficulties in obtaining resources, nor do pre-modern types of social relations persist. Societies falling into this category are, of course, mainly the pluralistic democracies of the West. Type II societies are those in which citizens struggle to obtain resources but in which there is no particular trend toward the persistence of traditional ways of relating; clearly, the totalitarian societies belong here. Type III societies should report no scarcity of resources, nor dysfunctional effects of monopoly and bureaucratization, though corporate group membership or patron-client ties would influence decision-making in organizational encounters. Finally, in Type IV societies, both objective difficulties in obtaining resources and the persisting salience of pre-modern bases of social identity would be found.

D. Difficulties in Applying the Typology

There are a number of difficulties to be aware of in applying the typology. To begin with, even if criterion of economic well-being used by the World Bank or the United Nations were adopted to

Figure II.4
Four Types of Organizational Culture

Objective Difficulties in Obtaining Resources

Presence of Cultural Factors Legitimating Particularism	−	+
−	Type I	Type II
+	Type III	Type IV

distinguish the developing from the more developed countries, there would still be problems in trying to locate many countries in this classification. We lack the knowledge to identify the critical level of prosperity at which availability of resources is no longer important in shaping organizational behavior. Another problem is that regional variation within a given country may make it difficult, if not impossible, to place that country in a single one of the four types. There may be uncertainty as to whether the perpetuation of particularism is restricted to underdeveloped areas within a country, or whether it is a general characteristic of a society.

Italy is a good case in point, with its gaps between the more developed north and the less developed south. It is a relatively prosperous European country, not a Third World country, yet one whose bureaucracy is know for its inefficiency and rigidity, and in which patterns of patron-client relations persist to this day. There is an ongoing debate among students of Italian society as to whether these phenomena are limited to, or most present in the poor, relatively undeveloped south, or are characteristic of the country as a whole.[11]

One thing is clear: Persons socialized into environments where objective constraints mainly account for non-U behavior know that their behavior is "wrong," that it is a departure from the official rules. In contrast, persons raised in cultures where traditional ways of relating not only foster, but may even require P behavior, see it as fully legitimate and perhaps even as enjoying more legitimacy than the "foreign," imported U values of public administration. Thus, when Russians use blat, they know they are breaking the rules; when Thais or Indians engage in what appears to be the same behavior, they may not see themselves as breaking rules at all, or, at best, they may have only weakly internalized the U code. Riggs (1964) called this phenomenon "polynormativism."

IV. UNIVERSALISTIC ORGANIZATIONAL CULTURES: THE WESTERN DEMOCRACIES

Several kinds of solid empirical evidence document that the U code is well institutionalized in the West and that behavior in routine encounters conforms more with it than in the rest of the world. One type of evidence comes from survey data on citizens' expectations of treatment by government officials and their evaluations of experiences in contact with them.

A. Citizens' Evaluations of Service

1. Public sector. In Almond and Verba's (1965) study of the United States, Britain, Germany, Italy, and Mexico, the American and British respondents were most likely to say that they expected equal and considerate treatment by bureaucrats and police; the Germans were in the middle, and the Italians and especially the Mexicans were more negative in their views. Nelson (1981) reviewed American studies by Goodsell (1981), Katz et al. (1975), and Schmidt (1977), as well as her own work, in all of which was painted a quite favorable picture of client evaluations of government service programs. Bureaucrats were generally seen as courteous, considerate, and, in Schmidt's study, willing "to adapt rules and methods to meet (the client's) needs" (Schmidt, 1977: 412).

Are these rosy assessments of the fairness, responsiveness, and manner of public officials to be taken literally? I suspect that it is politicians who are mainly thought of as corrupt, whereas civil servants are trusted. If there is unfairness, it is probably (1) at the level of policy, (2) in the under-utilization of services by disadvantaged groups (cf. McKinlay, 1975; Nelson, 1980), and (3) in negative discrimination against minority groups, not in positive discrimination toward groups without rights.

2. Private sector. Research on private-sector encounters is mainly focused on a problem somewhat different from that which concerns us here. The central question asked is not, do officials make universalistic decisions, but do organizations give value for money? In the private sector fairness means, primarily, an equitable balance between rewards and costs, not fairness in the application of general rules. There is plenty of evidence that even in the West consumers do not always get value for money. Schrag (1972) was dismayed by the amount of landlord corruption, loan sharks, abuses relating to cars, medicine, food and appliances, and other types of exploitation in New York City. The Small Claims Study Group's report (1972) called *Little Injustices,* described a state of endemic lawlessness. In another American study, cited in Nader (1980), in every 100 urban households there were about 28 perceived consumer problems per year that led to complaining and to full dissatisfaction with the results of complaining. In Miller and Sarat's (1980–81) study, about a tenth of all households had at least one grievance against an organization in each of the public and private sectors, respectively.

Consumer problems are, of course, especially severe among disadvantaged consumers (cf., Caplovitz, 1963).

B. Complaints

A number of researchers and practitioners have suggested that data on complaints can be employed as a useful social indicator (e.g., Krendel, 1970; Danet, 1978; Hill, 1981). In an exploratory exercise, I worked with data on the numbers of complaints sent to ombudsmen in eight Western countries in 1972 (Danet, 1978).[12] I developed a standardized measure of rate of complaining, which neutralized the effects of absolute volume of complaints and absolute size of population (a volume of 5000 complaints per year means different things in societies with 5 million or with 50 million persons).

Of the eight countries, Canada had the highest rate of complaining; in the five provinces which had an ombudsman by 1972, the ombudsman received an average of 80 complaints per 100,000 citizens (Table II.1). In the Scandinavian countries, including Sweden, the home of the ombudsman idea, the rate ranged from 25 per 100,000 in Finland to 58 in Sweden; New Zealand was close to Sweden with 52 per 100,000 persons. Britain and France had exceedingly low rates: In the former there were only 1/3 complaints per 100,000 persons, and in the latter only 3.5.

These rates are difficult to interpret because of variation in such factors as the size and scope of jurisdiction, diffusion of knowledge about the ombudsman, ease of access (whether oral complaints are accepted), need to contact an MP rather than the ombudsman directly (as in the British case). Still, I believe that these rates indicate a relatively well-functioning public bureaucracy. The comparable rate for Israel for the same period was 250 complaints per 100,000 citizens, a far higher rate than in any of these eight European or Anglo-Saxon countries (see Danet, 1978).

The proportion of complaints found justified also varies from country to country, but, at the same time, again suggests that these countries have well-functioning bureaucracies. With the exception of Norway, the range was from 10% to 31%. The comparable figure for Israel for the same year was 47%.[13]

Solid information on what people complain about to ombudsmen in Western societies is not yet available, though some information can be gleaned from ombudsmen's annual reports or from their files.[14] It is quite likely that most people who take the trouble to complain object not to an official's failure to smile, but to more

Table II.1

Comparative Statistics on Complaints to the Ombudsman in Eight Western Countries*

Country	A Year	B Population in millions	C Total files handled	D Total closed with final decision	E Total pending	F Total justified complaints	G[a] Rate of petitioning/complaining	H[b] % fully investigated complaints found justified
Sweden	1971	7.6	4,381	1,973	1,271	618	57.6	31%
Finland	1971	4.6	1,182	558	237	54	25.7	10%
Denmark	1972	4.7	1,896	646	202	140	40.3	22%
Norway	1972	3.7	1,607	513	213	273	43.4	53%
New Zealand	1972/73	2.7	1,409	554	497	154	52.2	28%
Britain	1972	55.0	729	261	150	79	1.3	30%
Canada[c]	1972	9.9	7,949	2,831	1,530	786	80.3	28%
France	1973	50.0	1,773	469	740	70	3.5	15%

* Source: Danet (1978), Table 1.

a) $G = \dfrac{C}{B}$; figures are total petitions/complaints per 100,000 population.

b) $H = \dfrac{F}{D}$.

c) Figures are for the five Canadian provinces which had an ombudsman as of 1972.

serious matters—what they believe to be unfair deprivation or harassment or grossly unreasonable procedures.[15]

C. Old-Boy Networks and Political Patronage

Two forms of particularistic behavior which persist in generally universalistic settings are so-called old-boy networks and political patronage. Studies of elites in the United States (Hunter, 1959; Mills, 1956; Domhoff, 1970) report on chains of contact among members. Exclusive secondary schools, universities, clubs, and resorts are fertile meeting places for making contacts and gaining entrance into high-status positions. Similarly, in studies of the English elite system the importance of coming from an "Oxbridge" (Oxford or Cambridge) background to gain access to elite status (Guttsman, 1974) is emphasized. Not only in politics and big business but in academia, too, knowing the right people can play an important part in receiving academic appointments, obtaining grants, and so on.

Machine politics and party patronage are known to have flourished in many Western societies, and still do in some, to this day. In Etzioni-Halevy's comparative study of four countries it was revealed that, although important in all of them at one time, party patronage has declined in Britain and Australia, and persists to a relatively greater extent in the United States, but most strongly in Israel (Etzioni-Halevy, 1979).[16] To my knowledge, no empirical studies exist of the extent to which clients mobilize political or old-boy network connections to obtain things from organizations. But my impression is that in the English-speaking countries as well as in the non-Mediterranean countries of Western Europe, their use is extremely rare, when it comes to everyday, routine goods and services—because the system is generally responsive. However, when it comes to goods and services which are more difficult to come by—for example, wanting to have surgery performed by a particular physician in great demand, rather than by a staff physician in a bureaucratized health service, or getting a son or daughter into a prestigious university—personal or political connections may indeed continue to be important on occasion.

D. Direct Measurement of Universalistic and Particularistic Orientations

Few researchers have attempted to measure universalistic versus particularistic orientations in officials or clients. In two studies which

I shall discuss in detail later on, of civil servants in Egypt and Ghana, questionnaires were used.

In Goodsell's (1976) cross-cultural study of encounters between postal clerks and clients in Costa Rica and the United States cleverly designed observations were made. Observers played the role of client in two tasks, mailing a small package by surface transportation, and purchasing stamps for an airmail letter to a relatively unknown country. In each country there were two observers, one of high status and one of low status. Goodsell found that postal officials maintained a neutral manner more often in the United States than in Costa Rica (Table II.2). In both countries there was a slight tendency to depart from this more often with low-status clients, though it is even rarer in the United States than in Costa Rica, as one would expect. The Costa Rican officials were more likely to receive the customer in a negative manner, by either not responding to the client's greeting or responding in a discourteous manner, especially if the client was of low status.

The tendency to introduce nonessential talk during the encounter was also influenced by culture and social status. Although American postal clerks did this more often than the Costa Ricans, counter to what one would expect, on closer examination their remarks were almost exclusively task-oriented whereas the Costa Ricans volunteered pleasantries. In Costa Rica the pleasantries were offered mainly to the high-status client; in the United States, both high-status and low-status clients were more likely to have task-oriented than expressive talk directed to them.

When the client questioned the amount of postage requested, the Costa Rican official actually lowered the cost of the postage in 16% of the cases, and in 63% simply denied the client's claim without giving a reason. The American clerks, on the other hand, mainly explained why the customer was wrong (38%); in some instances they also rechecked the calculation (which the Costa Ricans never did), and were also more likely either to show the manual documenting the correct postage, or at least to quote it. In short, the Americans behaved more in accordance with the demands of rational-legal authority; they not only pointed to the rules but to the reasons for them. Thus, they acknowledged the right of the client to question the dictates of their authority. The Costa Ricans, on the other hand, either behaved in a more arbitrary manner, or actually bargained over the price of the service!

Social status of the client also influenced the response to disagreement in both countries. In Costa Rica, the low-status client

Table II.2

Universalism, Specificity, and Affective Neutrality in the Manner of Postal Clerks Toward Clients in Costa Rica and in the United States*

Country and Client	Universalism: Neutral greetings	Specificity: % having nonessential talk			Universalism: Responses to client disagreement about postage					N
		All Types	Volunteered pleasantries	Task-oriented talk	Rate adjusted	Simple denial	Error explained	Rate rechecked	Manual quoted as shown	
Costa Rica	17.1	15.6	15.6	—	15.6	62.5	12.5	—	9.4	100.0 (35)
United States	54.2	47.5	7.5	40.0	2.5	22.6	37.5	17.5	20.0	100.0 (40)
Costa Rica										
High-status	22.2	23.5	23.5	—	5.9	53.0	23.5	—	17.6	100.0 (18)
Low-status	11.8	6.7	6.7	—	26.7	73.3	—	—	—	100.0 (17)
United States										
High-status	56.4	57.1	4.8	52.3	5.0	—	45.0	15.0	35.0	100.0 (39)
Low-status	50.0	36.9	10.5	26.4	—	45.0	30.0	20.0	5.0	100.0 (20)

* Based on Goodsell (1981), Tables 1, 2 and 3.

mainly met with the arbitrary response of unjustified denial; some got a break in the price of postage, much as low-status clients of the Israel customs authorities did (Danet, 1973; see chapter 4). Although the high-status client also mainly met with straight denial, he also had his error explained or was referred to the manual in a fair number of cases. In the United States the low-status client was far more likely to meet with straight denial, whereas the high-status client was more likely to receive a response which showed the official's concern with objective substantive justice—whether by explaining the error, rechecking the rate, or referring to the manual.

E. The Parallel Economy

The parallel economy in Western democracies is acknowledged to be enormous, though its extent is exceedingly difficult to estimate. In testimony during American Congressional Hearings, Voss offered an estimate of between $100 billion and $200 billion a year (Voss, 1979, cited in Bawli, 1982: 115). Bawli (1982) claimed that subterranean economies are about as extensive in the Netherlands, Belgium, and France as in the United States. Analysts of data on parallel economies do not separate behavior which indicates non-compliance with organizational rules from that which extracts resources from organizations on a non-universalistic basis. Thus, there is no way of knowing how much parallel economy activity in the West falls into the latter category. My guess is, however, that as long as resources are plentiful, as they are in the West, there is little need to create subterranean arrangements to obtain them.

V. SOCIETIES COPING
WITH OBJECTIVE DIFFICULTIES

The second type of organizational culture identified in Figure II.4 was that in which the public must cope with objective difficulties in obtaining resources. In Type II societies, the other set of factors, having to do with the persisting salience of pre-modern types of social relationships, is not present. The societies which easily come to mind in this category are, of course, the socialist countries of Eastern Europe, the Soviet Union, and the People's Republic of China.

A. The Dysfunctions of Total Bureaucratization

The negative consequences of bureaucratization are found everywhere, but they are especially prominent in the socialist regimes.

Efforts at total bureaucratization almost dictate that this will be so. Hirszowicz, a Polish sociologist now living in England, listed six dysfunctions of bureaucratization under socialism: (1) excessive growth of rules and regulations; (2) inevitable rigidity of organizational structures; (3) over-centralization, causing severe delays; (4) excessive time and effort spent on coordinating activities; (5) displacement of goals because employees spend more energy on avoiding disapproval of superiors than on the tasks to be performed; and (6) defense mechanisms of functionaries against clients, customers, and outsiders (Hirszowicz, 1980: 135).

Several features of bureaucratization combine to produce these negative effects. Sheer size is one important factor; both the huge numbers of citizens to be provided for and the huge numbers of bureaucrats themselves pose enormous difficulties of coordination, planning, implementation. No less important is the extraordinary range of goods to be provided, since the State is responsible for the distribution of everything. Centralization is part of the problem too; as Hirszowicz suggested, it paralyzes low-level officials who cannot act without clearance. Finally, monopoly itself has important consequences; because citizens have no alternative, there is no pressure on the system to perform well.[17] All of these problems are further exacerbated by chronic shortages of all kinds of goods, from meat to Western jeans to electrical appliances.

B. The Parallel Economy

In response to all these difficulties, parallel economies have developed, over time, and continue to flourish, in the Soviet Union as well as in the other socialist states of Eastern Europe.[18] Russians call theirs the *na levo* economy; *na levo* means on the left, or, what in English is called under the table. The term includes bribery and unreported moonlighting (even during the hours a worker is supposedly on the main job), among others. A bribe might be anything from a bottle of vodka to a large sum of money. Analysts have estimated that black market activity constitutes anywhere from 20% to 50% of total economic activity in the Soviet Union (Kaiser, 1976; Seeger, 1982). Predictably, the People's Republic of China too has a flourishing black market, though its scope may be smaller (Fraser, 1980). There is not only illegal selling of goods, but quasi-legal trading of ration stamps for food and consumer goods. A person wanting to buy a pair of leather shoes may be willing, say, to exchange coupons with someone wanting a service for which he or she has no need (Fraser, 1982). And when scarce goods come on the market, scalpers buy them up and sell them at a higher price (Bonavia, 1982).

A common feature of socialist economies is the *tolkach,* a kind of pusher kept on the payroll of factories. With its heavy emphasis on five-year planning, the Soviet system sets output targets which it cannot meet. Enormous pressure is put on people to meet production requirements. It is the job of the tolkach to cultivate good contacts, to bypass bureaucratic snags and to mobilize the raw materials needed to meet production quotas.[19] Once again, the same phenomenon occurs in the People's Republic of China. There, pushers are euphemistically called purchasing agents, and, according to Bonavia, inevitably become corrupt. Favorite kickbacks are foodstuffs which are perishable and leave no trace (Bonavia, 1982: 218–219).

C. Protektzia; Blat

Personal connections are widely used in all the socialist countries. The use of such connections is called protektzia in all the Eastern European countries except the Soviet Union, where it is called blat. According to the historian Seton-Watson, *protekcija,* as he spells it, is a Serbian form of a word used with different terminations in all the languages and countries of Eastern Europe to denote special protection, connection, graft, or pull. It is indispensable for the making of a career (Seton-Watson, 1967: 167). The old (presocialist) Russian and Eastern European bureaucracies were marked by dictatorial arbitrariness, inefficiency, and great emphasis on status; Balkan officials regarded themselves as greatly superior to peasants. Balkan bureaucracies put great emphasis on obscure, complicated formalities and documents, the result of an accumulation of laws and taxes superimposed from earliest times. Seton-Watson commented that a contempt for the public, laziness and a love of formality and fear of responsibility have always characterized Eastern European bureaucrats more than those in the West.

> The Balkan official regards himself as immeasurably superior to the peasants among whom he lives and from whose ranks he has sprung. To be an official is the fondest dream of every able young son of a peasant. The Balkan official does not like to work. He considers himself so fine a fellow that the State and the public should be proud to support him for life, and should not ask him to make efforts that will tax his intellect or character. A visitor to a Balkan Ministry or Police headquarters in the middle of the morning will find the rooms filled with good-natured fellows comfortably enjoying a cup of Turkish coffee and a chat with their friends.

The papers lie on their desks. Outside stand, sit and squat patient queues of peasants awaiting their various permits and receipts. Foreigners and citizens with *protekcija* obtain swift and polite attention, but the people can afford to wait. They have waited many hundreds of years already for justice, and a few more hours will not make much difference. Time counts little in the Balkans. (Seton-Watson, 1967: 146–147)

It is probably no accident that *The Trial* was written by an Eastern European, the Czech Franz Kafka. While people continue to debate the meaning of *The Trial,* it is easily read as a devastating critique of arbitrary bureaucratic despotism. According to Connor (1979), Seton-Watson's observations about Eastern European countries between the two world wars, made in the 1960's, are still quite pertinent today, despite the change to Communist regimes and the years that have passed.

Smith, former bureau chief for the *New York Times* in Moscow, explained about blat in the Soviet Union:

The Soviet counter-economy has its own lore and lingo, its channels and conventions, understood by all and employed by practically everyone on an almost daily basis. Its mutations and permutations are innumerable. But the most common and innocent variety is what the Russians call *blat*—influence, connections, pulling strings. In an economy of chronic shortages and carefully parceled-out privileges, *blat* is an essential lubricant of life. The more rank and power one has, the more *blat* one normally has. But actually almost everyone can bestow the benefits of *blat* on someone else—a doorman, a railroad car porter, a cleaning lady in a food store, a sales clerk, an auto mechanic, or a professor—because each has access to things or services that are hard to get and that other people want or need. *Blat* begins to operate when someone asks someone else a favor with the understanding of eventually doing a favor in return. Technically, *blat* does not involve money. '*Blat* doesn't involve corruption,' an actress contended, 'it's just *ty mne i ya tebe*' (you for me and me for you). In other words, "I'll scratch your back and you scratch mine." (Smith, 1976: 115)

Various forms of nepotism, favoritism and cultivation of personal connections occur in the People's Republic too (Duncanson, 1982; Fraser, 1980; Bonavia, 1982). There, using personal connections is known as "using the back door" (Fraser, 1982: 409–410). As in the Soviet Union, there are institutionalized privileges for high-ranking persons, including special stores to buy goods at favorable prices with foreign currency certificates. Or, to return to the person wanting leather shoes, access to well-connected persons can relieve a person of the need for coupons.

D. Tolerance for Deviance

A great deal can be learned about organizational culture from how people feel about violations of the official rules. If situational constraints encourage violations, as in the case of the socialist societies, internalization of norms should be weakened, and we should find evidence of permissiveness and of a tolerant attitude toward violations. This is just what Sebba (1983) found, in a comparison of North American and Russian immigrants to Israel. He interviewed samples of both groups of immigrants as to their attitudes toward white-collar crime, including giving or taking a bribe, and giving protektzia—positive discrimination in favor of a friend or relative by an official.

Table II.3
Attitudes Toward Three Bureaucratically Deviant Acts Among North American and Russian New Immigrants to Israel*

		Russian (N=82)	North American (N=61)
A)	Percentage who would report to police		
	Protektzia	3.7	3.3
	Giving a bribe	18.3	45.9
	Taking a bribe	25.6	50.8
B)	Percentage who would report act to no one		
	Protektzia	59.8	37.7
	Giving a bribe	39.0	16.4
	Taking a bribe	22.0	3.3
C)	Mean seriousness score of offense**		
	Protekzia	83.0	134.0
	Giving a bribe	125.0	197.0
	Taking a bribe	170.0	216.0
D)	Percent believing officials should take a tough line		
	Protekzia	7.3	36.1
	Giving a bribe	17.1	42.6
	Taking a bribe	23.2	57.4

* Based on Sebba (1983), Tables 2, 3, 7, 8.
** Scores ranged from 0 to 300.

Highlights from Sebba's study are summarized in Table II.3. Note, first of all, that for both groups, the perceived relative seriousness of the three forms of deviance is the same; taking a bribe is viewed as most serious, giving a bribe as almost as serious, but granting protektzia is not viewed as serious by large numbers in either group. The more important result, however, is that on 3 out of 4 measures, the Americans take a tougher line. More Russians than North Americans would report an instance of granting protektzia to no one; Russians rated protektzia lower on a scale of seriousness of offense, and are far less likely to believe that officials should take a tougher line with persons engaging in this practice.[20]

E. Complaints

In a 1966 survey of complaint-handling devices in Scandinavia, New Zealand, Japan, Yugoslavia, Poland, and the Soviet Union, Gellhorn (1966a) found that there is usually a strong commitment to legislation to protect the individual from the evils of maladministration. Along with complaint-handling by persons in political positions, there are special administrative bodies to hear and process complaints. The media are also heavily involved. Newspapers often investigate complaints themselves, instead of merely referring them to appropriate agencies, as is common in the West. Letters to the editor complaining of bad service are extremely common (Hirszowicz, 1980; Inkeles and Geiger, 1952; Gellhorn, 1966a; Chu and Chu, 1981). In the Soviet Union of the 1960's, which Gellhorn observed, there was even a television program airing complaints. Of the three socialist countries studied, Gellhorn found Yugoslavia to be the most committed to justice for the individual, a finding that fits with the generally more democratic orientation of Yugoslavia, compared with other Eastern European States.

Just how effective complaint-handling devices are in socialist countries is extremely difficult to assess, not only because of lack of empirical research. The meaning of the act of complaining is quite different in the context of socialist ideology. On the one hand, citizens not only have a right to complain, but a duty to do so. "The close policing of administration is aimed at assuring the suitable discharge of the official's obligations to the state he serves, rather than at assuring fairness to individual interests" (Gellhorn, 1966a: 337).

In practice, however, citizens are more supplicants than contestants, and are often afraid to complain. Ostensibly a constructive act, a complaint is also by definition a criticism of the system, and thus an act which borders on intolerable full-fledged dissent (cf. Hurvitz, 1981; Chalidze, 1974). The restraining effects of the totalitarian regime are typically reinforced by pre-socialist traditions of despotic bureaucracy, as has been seen is true of the Balkans. Nevertheless, a recent content analysis of letters to the editor of the People's Daily in the People's Republic of China concluded that these letters serve as a safety valve—as an important channel for the expression of conflict (see Chu and Chu, 1981).[21]

VI. SOCIOCULTURAL PRESSURES
TOWARD PARTICULARISM

Many societies of the developing world, as well as some of the more developed ones (e.g., Italy or Spain), show evidence of pressures toward particularism deriving from traditional cultural sources. Symmetric, or asymmetric forms of particularism, or both, may be present.

A. Constraints toward Symmetric Particularism

1. Role conflict in officials. One of the first studies in which the conflicting loyalties of civil servants outside the West were empirically documented was Berger's (1957) research on the Egyptian civil service. When asked, for example, whether an official should make an acquaintance wait his turn like all the others, 85% of his sample said it was proper to keep the person waiting; yet, when asked what a civil servant would actually do in such a situation, the same figure of 85% said that the official would take the man out of turn.

In another hypothetical situation, a civil servant learns he is about to be transferred from Cairo to a new post in the provinces. Because he wishes to remain near his aged parents, he goes to the director general in his ministry and asks him to intervene, so that he may remain in Cairo. Three-quarters of the sample said that they could expect the director general to keep the man in Cairo, both when the director general was presented as a friend and when he was presented as a cousin of the official. In both cases, three-fifths believed the director general would actually do this. The large majority believed that the family of the official would expect this, too, and more than half said the family would perceive the director general as disloyal if he did not keep his cousin in Cairo.

Students of African societies agree as to the dominance of corporate kinship groups in these societies:

When, as in traditional Africa, society is organized on the basis of corporate groups, social and political rights, obligations and identities reside in the group, not, as in the contemporary West, in the individual. Society is perceived by its members as a collectivity of groups; individuals are viewed as extensions of their corporate groups—they have no autonomous existence and identity outside of their group membership. Thus, interaction can be conceived of as taking place not between individual social actors but rather between representatives of corporate groups. (Price, 1975: 26–27)

Thus, in Fallers' (1956) study of Bantu bureaucracy in Uganda he found that Soga chiefs employed as civil servants were torn between the universalistic requirements of their position in the civil service and pressures from kinship groups to benefit kinsmen. In Price's own (1975) study of the Ghanaian civil service, which drew on Berger's (1957) work, he presented a sample of civil servants with scenarios similar to those that Berger had used. Asked whether it would be proper to keep a relative waiting because others had come before him, three-quarters said it would be proper. At the same time, 93% said the relative would expect to be seen before the others. Three-quarters of the sample professed to the universalistic norm, yet predicted that the average official would see the relative out of turn.

In the second scenario, an official is again notified of an impending transfer, and goes to the head of his department, who happens to be his cousin, and asks to be kept where he is located. Four-fifths of the sample claimed that the relatives did not have a right to expect the department head to comply—again, giving the normative, universalistic answer, as Berger had found. At the same time, 85% said that the relatives would expect the department head to yield.[22]

Many Mediterranean societies are also characterized by the kinds of cultural pressures just described. In Southern Italy and in Greece, bureaucrats frequently resolve similar role conflicts by giving preferential treatment to kinsmen. Banfield (1964) described what he called "amoral familism" among the people of the town of Montenegro in southern Italy: people related with distrust and even hostility toward non-kinsmen.[23] Boissevain's (1966) observations on Sicily are complementary:

Civil servants generally favour their close relatives, and try to derive a personal advantage from their position. Since most are members of the *borghesia,* this means that the upper classes receive preferential treatment . . . it is illegal for a civil servant to let a public contract to a person who gives him a large commission or present. But, seen from the point of view of his relatives, this act is not immoral. On the contrary, by performing it he fulfils his primary obligation to aid his own family and his nearest kinsmen. In practice this means that the civil servant is only impartial to persons who are neither relatives nor friends. (Boissevain, 1966: 20–21)

2. Pressures for conspicuous consumption. Another aspect of Price's (1975) research on Ghana, as well as Mars and Altman's (1983) study of the parallel economy in Soviet Georgia, demonstrated yet another way in which traditional forms of social relations and the norms and values that accompany them encourage and even require peers to engage in deviant acts. Mars and Altman theorized that the values of this "honor-and-shame" culture require men (1) to prove their manhood by engaging in conspicuous display and by taking risks, and (2) to demonstrate their honor by participating in networks whose deviant acts require great mutual trust. "White" sources of income do not suffice to finance the competitive display involved in bouts of feasting and drinking, or dressing up, they claimed.

Similarly, Price (1975) argued that status pressures on Ghanaian civil servants constrain them to engage in conspicuous consumption at a cost beyond that which their official salaries can finance and to provide financial help to relatives which they could not otherwise afford. Both the civil servants interviewed and a sample of the public substantially agreed with the proposition that "If a rich man does not buy an expensive car and build a large house he will lose standing in the eyes of his relatives and friends." More important, members of his sample were presented with two descriptions of senior government officials: (1) one who has used his official position to "chop" (appropriate public funds for personal use) a great deal of money but has shown great generosity, coming to the aid of many people who are in need; (2) one who follows all rules and regulations and has not chopped money, but as a result, although he would like to show generosity, constantly refuses to help any of his people who are in need. Although the bureaucrats themselves thought the first official was the more admirable, 83% believed that most Ghanaians would prefer the second.[24]

3. Client strategies. Price's civil servants were asked which of three alternative strategies used by clients to obtain something would be most effective: going straight to an official (that is, using the U code), seeing a relative who is also a government official, or seeing a friend who knows the official. Two-thirds thought the client should go straight to the official, but only a quarter thought this would be the most effective approach. Fully 85% of them predicted that the client would actually choose one of the particularistic routes. These findings are confirmed by data on perceptions of the Ghanaian public. Price also asked a sample of Ghanaian students which of five strategies would be most and least effective.

Nearly half the students thought going the U route would be most effective, but many chose one of the P routes (Table II.4). About 38% chose one of the alternatives in which the client would seek out a go-between—28% said finding a friend of the official would be most effective. "Dashing" the official, or making a payment of a material benefit, is widely practiced in Ghana, as I noted in chapter 1—it is more like a tip than a bribe in Western terms.

B. Constraints toward Asymmetric Particularism

1. Bureaucratization and types of patronage. In an unpredictable and even hostile world, having kinsmen to whom one can turn is not enough. Local affairs in remote rural areas are increasingly impinged upon by the forces of modernization from above and afar. Peasants are ill at ease in dealing with bureaucratic agencies and lack the knowledge and skills to get what they need, or to conform with State requirements. They cannot simply ignore these agencies; they need things like permits to farm or to raise their sheep; they need official recognition of land transfers, and so on.

But the higher one needs to go in a bureaucratic hierarchy, the less likely one is to have a friend or relative to whom one can turn. Consider the dilemma of intimidated Greek shepherds:

> . . . the Sarakatsanos in facing the hierarchy of Government confront persons of higher social status who share with him no bond of kinship or community. As a rule only nationality and common humanity link them together. In Greek society this is not an adequate basis for the acceptance of social obligations other than the common duty to defend the nation against its external enemies. The indifference or hostility of junior officials may be bought off. . . . But the indifference of senior officials cannot be directly countered with bribes, nor is it easy because of the social distance which separates them for a shepherd to approach successfully a senior official. (Campbell, 1964: 246)

The response of Greek peasants to such a dilemma bears many similarities to patterns of behavior in many other Mediterranean, as well as Latin American and Asian countries: Individuals cultivate ties with more powerful patrons as protectors and benefactors, and,

Table II.4

Evaluations of Alternative Methods of Doing Business in Ghanaian Government Offices*

Method	Routine Business		Urgent Business	
	Most effective	Least effective	Most effective	Least effective
1. You go straight to the government office and state your business.	46.1	43.8	32.2	45.8
2. See a friend who knows the official with whom you must deal.	27.9	12.1	27.0	11.6
3. You find someone to fix things.	10.3	16.9	14.8	19.3
4. You visit the official in charge at his house prior to going to his office, and offer to do something.[a]	13.7	10.9	19.4	8.6
5. You go to the office and dash the official.[b]	2.1	16.3	6.6	14.6
	100.1	100.0	100.0	99.9
	(N=380)	(N=313)	(N=366)	(N=301)
Not answered	5	72	19	80

* Source: Price (1975), Table 20, p. 115.

a) 'Do something' is a euphemism for offering a material benefit in Ghana.

b) 'Dash' is roughly a bribe, but seen in the context of traditional Ghanaian culture is an appropriate act; see Price (1975), pp. 116–129.

most important, as brokers to goods and services they are not competent or not able to obtain in any other way. In traditional or feudal societies, classic patron-client relationships flourished: A peasant would have one patron with whom he would establish a particularistic, diffuse relationship characterized by unequal but relatively stable exchange—of loyalty and small services, say, in exchange for protection, financial aid in time of trouble, and so forth.

But with the rise of bureaucratization and the other concomitants of modernization, such as urbanization, the ability of single individuals to provide a person's needs becomes eroded, and a second type of patronage arises, in which—instead of providing resources themselves—well-connected individuals like lawyers, priests, and bureaucrats provide access to resources controlled by still more powerful persons. As mentioned in chapter 1, Boissevain (1977) calls these persons patron/brokers. There is still a personal relationship between client and patron/broker, but it is no longer exclusive; clients may now have several specialized patrons. Although Campbell's (1964) Greek shepherds chose men of many professions—doctors, engineers, merchants—as patrons, they most often chose lawyers, who not only gave legal advice and attended clients in court, but acted as fixers, or intermediaries between peasants or shepherds and the State authorities.

Eventually, a third type of relationship develops, which Boissevain (1977) calls "organizational brokerage," and which he found to be common on the island of Malta. In this third type,

> both organizational broker and client are members of the same group. They . . . share a certain group loyalty. Both expect support from each other as members of the same group. Their relationships have become formalized, in the sense that they may be expressed as rights and duties. The party or union secretary represents the interests of his client/constituent fellow member to civil service decision makers. He does this not so much as a personal friend but as a representative. If he does not succeed he can mobilize further pressure on the civil servants to the same extent as the patron/broker . . . the personal element in social relations may continue to remain strong. Organizational brokerage is becoming the most prominent type of relation with authorities. (Boissevain, 1977: 90)

2. The incidence of use of brokers. Although illiterate peasants are especially likely to need patrons and brokers, urbanites in certain settings are quite likely to find themselves needing them too. But just how often people use brokers instead of dealing directly with officials in any given society is extremely difficult to estimate. Many studies offer impressionistic evidence, enriched with vivid stories, that their use is extremely widespread. For example, in Italy, especially southern Italy, the impression is that clients can hardly move without raccomandazioni (recommendations from influentials; Galt, 1974; White, 1980; Boissevain, 1966; Littlewood, 1974). Kenny (1962) described a similar pattern for Spain; apparently, the only way to cope with bureaucratic inefficiency and lack of responsiveness is to have *enchufe* (literally, a plug), an *amigo,* a friend in the right place at the right time.[25]

In a few studies survey methods have been employed to estimate the incidence of use of personal connections, despite the obvious problem that the more their use is officially condemned, the more people may hesitate to admit using them.[26] In a 1965 study of Turkish bureaucrats (Roos and Roos, 1971) 40% of employees of six different agencies said that political pull or knowing the right person was important for citizens to get help with a problem. In a 1964 study in India, 70% of a rural sample and 54% of an urban sample believed that pull was important (Eldersveld et al., 1968).[27]

3. Compadrazgo. One of the best-known forms of patronage which exists to this day in both urban and rural areas of Mediterranean and Latin American countries is the compadrazgo, or godparent system (Mintz and Wolf, 1977; Nutini and Bell, 1980; Davis, 1977, chap. 5). Parents choose godparents at the time of baptism of their newborn children.[28] A particular couple may be chosen, among other things, because they can offer potential resources like cash loans or introductions to important people. For example, in the Mexican village of Tzintzuntzan studied by Foster (1961; 1963) people often sought out godparents among wealthy city relatives, local ranchers or storekeepers and curried favor with them by giving meals and presents. Among the types of help often provided by godparents is mediation in obtaining benefits from bureaucratic organizations.

4. The incidence of bribery. It is still more difficult, if not impossible, to attempt to estimate the incidence of bribery, or, more neutrally, material payments, in exchange for services than it is to estimate use of personal connections. Even when both tend to be under the table, people may be less secretive about the latter than the former, mainly because bribery is usually illegal. And although under certain conditions small payments are viewed as legitimate, as in Ghana, there may not necessarily be any covert prestige involved in making them, as I believe is often true in the case of activation of personal connections.

The major puzzle for the theorist is to sort out the conditions under which bribery thrives, as opposed to those under which activation of personal ties is most common, and those under which there is a high incidence of both within the same country. The present state of theory and research does not allow for very precise statements on this problem. It seems reasonable to argue that activation of personal ties presupposes conditions of trust and social integration, whereas bribery, being a contractual arrangement, closes off ties and disposes of interpersonal obligations, rather than creating or extending them. Yet, paradoxically, in situations of covert if not overt bribery, people also have to trust one another—not to reveal one another to the authorities.

Unsystematic as it is, the evidence has suggested that most Third World countries have widespread bribery, as well as activation of personalistic norms, whether of a symmetrical or an asymmetrical nature. But there is no way of comparing countries to see where bribery is most common. It is hard to imagine a more extreme case than that of Morocco. Waterbury (1973) has stated that citizens need to pay bribes for small services of every kind, from passports to birth certificates to documents attesting that a child has been sick. He did not investigate or comment on whether Moroccans view these payments as legitimate, but the general tone of his article suggested that they do not. It is unlikely that members of the elite have to make these payments—more likely, it is seen as a matter of *noblesse oblige* to provide them with these services without charge.

C. Complaints

I pointed out in chapter 1 that many developing countries have rushed to adopt ombudsmen, under conditions in which citizens lack the necessary skills to use their services—literacy, for one—and in which problems of inefficiency, corruption, and basic lack of services are so severe that ombudsmen are seriously handicapped in their ability to help individual citizens. More serious, under such conditions, I argued, even if policy-makers were interested in using information on complaints as a source of feedback to improve services, the obstacles to implementing reform are often so great as to boggle the mind. The most formidable obstacle to reform is probably the fact that it is in the interest of elites to maintain the *status quo,* because it is they who benefit from it most. This is probably one of the main reasons why campaigns to wipe out corruption invariably fail.

In the Introduction, I used the case of India as an example. Compare the pessimism of Jain (1982) and of Dhavan (1977) about India, cited there, with Waterbury's (1972) view of Morocco as a society where

> corruption serves only one "positive" function—that of the survival of the regime. Resources are absorbed in patronage and are drained away from rational productive investment. Morocco remains fixed in a system of scarcity in which the vulnerable seek protection and thus regenerate the links of dependency and patronage that perpetuate the system. The dilemma for the ruler in such a system is whether, in the short term, his survival can be made compatible with rational administration and economic development, or whether, in the long term, it can be made compatible with planned corruption. (Waterbury, 1972: 555)

Although Morocco may be an extreme case, the introduction of ombudsmen in countries having the general characteristics Waterbury described must surely be problematic. Empirical research on how ombudsmen function in these countries has, of course, hardly begun. But even after the evidence starts coming in, it seems a foregone conclusion that, having instituted ombudsmen, those in power can bask in the reflected glow of what appears to be a commitment to redress personal injustices and imbalances between social groups, all the while reaping the benefits of a system which perpetuates injustice.

D. Other Cultural Factors

This discussion of constraints toward particularism by no means exhausts the potential for cultural factors to influence what goes on in organizational cultures. Among other such factors I may mention the general political and legal culture of a society, especially attitudes toward rules and rule-breaking, and whether the society tends to be permissive or strict with respect to rules, for example. In chapter 4 I expand on this topic, in relation to Israel, and examine the notion of Israel as a "delinquent community" (cf. Pitts, 1963).[29]

VII. Some Speculations about Japan

It is impossible to conclude a chapter about patterns of organizational culture without paying attention to the special case of Japan. As is well-known, Japan has attracted world-wide attention for its extraordinary industrial success. The puzzle of this success, all the while preserving important elements of Japanese traditional culture, has preoccupied many persons in the West (e.g., Vogel, 1975; 1979; Pascale and Athos, 1982; Ouchi, 1981; Johnson, 1982). Because far less attention has been paid by non-Japanese to its public sector, this section is necessarily quite speculative.

The single most distinctive feature of Japan's organizational culture is the strong paternalistic tie between individuals and the organization. Instead of the transformation of traditionally diffuse relationships into narrowly specific ones in work settings, at least in the large corporations, Japanese workers tend to be hired for life; they both express a preference for, and actually enjoy highly involving personalistic relationships with their supervisors (Abegglen, 1975; Dore, 1973; Marsh and Mannari, 1976). Nakane (1973) sees the secret of Japan's success in the transfer of core identity from the traditional extended family to the modern corporation or factory. Because the traditional extended family was primarily an economic rather than a kinship unit, individuals were able to transfer their identification to organizations, as the newer types of production unit emerged with industrialization. Modern organizational familism apparently supersedes even kinship ties, and is often expressed through group rituals.[30]

As for client-official encounters in the public sector, researchers are in quite unknown territory. Given a rich, developed society with a Western-style democracy, Japanese client-official dealings might be quite universalistic in practice, as well as on paper. The relative plenitude of resources and a reasonably well-functioning bureaucracy[31] make it likely that organizations are responsive to legitimate needs and requests of the public. On the other hand, if employer-employee relationships are so radically different from those in the West, it is tempting to suppose that relationships between organizations and their clients must also be distinctively different. Moreover, patron-client relationships remain extremely important in many aspects of life in modern Japan, including politics, academic life, and advancement in corporations (Ike, 1972; Nakane, 1973; Ishino, 1953; Befu, 1974; Kahane, 1984a). Might the use of patron/brokers in client-organization transactions also be common?

Despite the lack of empirical research on bureaucratic encounters in Japan,[32] available evidence on other important aspects of Japanese culture suggests that there is little deviation from official rules, at least with respect to substance, if not procedure. First of all, there is no reason to assume that because employer-employee relationships are unusually diffuse, there is any necessary carry-over into official-client relationships. A basic component of Japanese culture is the strong distinction made between in-group and out-group relations (Nakane, 1973; Lebra, 1976, chapter 2). Thus, although solidarity is extremely strong among workers inside the organization, officials are likely to see clients as outsiders, especially in contacts which are fleeting and lack continuity over time, and perhaps even in those settings in which clients are repeat players. Moreover, the mere fact of, say, living in the same neighborhood as an official who is familiar by sight is unlikely to provide a basis on which a client can expect or demand special treatment.[33]

In addition, for both officials and clients, interaction in organizational encounters is typically interaction with a stranger. Because status considerations are extremely important in Japanese culture, a person is always somewhat ill at ease with a stranger (Lebra, 1976, chapter 5). Speakers must mark in their speech, posture, and demeanor their status relative to their interlocutors; to an extent unknown in Western languages they must use expressions of appropriate deference. This interactional burden must inevitably cause difficulties of communication in organizational encounters, in which people may have little or no information about each other, and hence simply do not know how to behave.

An especially important factor mitigating against particularism is the reticence of the Japanese when it comes to revealing information about their private lives to out-group persons (Barnlund, 1975). This would make it quite unlikely that clients would casually bring officially irrelevant aspects of their selves into interaction with officials as a way of manipulating them. Yet another reason to expect universalistic behavior is the reluctance of persons to become indebted to others. Although indebtedness may be experienced as onerous in any society, in Japan it is particularly so (Lebra, 1969; 1976, chapter 6). Thus, clients would not lightly ask for favors in organizational encounters.

Finally, there is the matter of Japanese attitudes toward authority. Traditional submissiveness to authority, inherited from pre-modern times, may condition many Japanese to find behind-the-scenes manipulation and circumvention of rules unthinkable. According to Reischauer (1981), the pre-war bureaucracy had treated the people with condescension. Besides Reischauer, at least two other Western observers have also cited the Japanese aphorism, *kanson mimpi,* which means "official exalted—people despised" (Ike, 1972; Vogel, 1979; Reischauer, 1981). A 1953 handbook, called *How to Come*

Into Contact with Others, advised readers that "the best way to come into contact with government officials is to apologize humbly" (cited in Minami, 1971: 5).[34]

Against the backdrop of these traditional attitudes to authority, Japanese public administration began to institute complaint-handling devices in the 1960's. At that time, interviews with knowledgeable professionals led Gellhorn, a student of administrative law and of the diffusion of complaint-handling devices around the world, to write:

> Still operative in Japan, although diminishing in intensity, is a tradition of deference to authority that forestalls complaints. Centuries of feudalism dictated uncritical obedience to overlords. In pre-war times, officials were distinctly masters of the public at large. Today, in democratized Japan, officials are public servants, no longer masters, In some quarters, nevertheless, the atmosphere of olden days lingers on. Some officials still think of themselves as superior beings, and some citizens share their thought. In a status conscious society . . . inferiors do not easily disagree with or complain against their superiors. . . . The prevalence of this attitude in present-day Japan is not precisely measurable, but many . . . believe it to be widespread, especially . . . in rural areas. (Gellhorn, 1966a: 376–377)

The views of Lebra, an anthropologist specializing in Japanese culture and of Japanese origin herself, on Japanese morality, are complementary to those of Gellhorn:

> Japanese morality . . . is characterized by an overwhelming sense of unpayable debt to countless benefactors, which makes one at once humble and obligation-bound. From the standpoint of the sociology of law, Kawashima characterized the Japanese as *gimu chusin* ("obligation-preoccupied"), in contrast to the Western *kenri chusin* ("right-preoccupied") orientation. (Lebra, 1976: 106)

Given such deference to authority, and such reluctance to become indebted to others, if people use brokers in organizational dealings, it is probably to help them to obtain what is their due according to the rules, and not illegitimate benefits or procedural favors.[35]

There is reason to believe that traditional attitudes to authority have undergone considerable change since the 1960's, when Western observers characterized Japan in the fashion just cited. At least in urban areas where people are better educated, official-client contacts have begun to have a different flavor. Thus, in a personal communication, Ben Ari reported hearing many complaints from city officials in the mid-1980's about lack of respect on the part of

citizens.[36] Despite these impressions of the growth of a more egalitarian style of relating, and of a greater demand on the part of
citizens today for their legitimate rights, rights-consciousness is probably less developed in Japan today than in, say, the United States,
Sweden or Britain. Consequently, there may be serious obstacles to
the development of a universalistic redress culture—perhaps not so
formidable as those in Third World countries, but formidable, none-
theless.

A small piece of empirical evidence, discovered after developing
the above speculations provides striking support for some of them.
Hayashi et al. (1965) presented subjects with a hypothetical stiuation
which resembles those used by Berger (1957) and Price (1975).
Respondents were asked to imagine themselves as the president of
a company who must choose between two candidates for employment, the one who ranks highest on an examination or the one who
is second highest but is the president's relative. Seventy-five percent
of the respondents chose the first candidate, and only 19% chose
the relative. When the second candidate was not a relative but the
benefactor or patron of the president, the proportion giving the
universalistic reply dropped to 48%, with 44% saying they would
choose the benefactor (Hayashi et al., 1965; cited in Lebra, 1969,
1974: 204–205).

The response to these situations confirms three points: (1) that
the dominant orientation on the attitudinal level is universalistic;
(2) that in those probably rare situations in which pre-existing *on*[37]
relations exist, and impinge on official-client encounters, indebtedness
to patrons will take priority over universalistic norms; e.g., officials
will feel obligated to give special treatment to a client to whom they
happen to be personally indebted; and finally, (3) that the social
bonds created by *on*-obligations are stronger than those of kinship.

In short, despite radical wider sociocultural differences from the
Western democracies, as well as in the intra-organizational aspects
of organizational culture, in its patterns of interaction between clients
and officials, Japan may resemble the Type I societies of the West.
Or, alternatively, it may be moving from a Type III society where
traditional cultural constraints affect encounters in the direction of
the Type I societies.

VIII. Summary and Discussion

In this chapter I have attempted to identify patterns of interaction
between clients and officials in ostensibly modern, bureaucratized

organizations around the world. We saw that the topic of organization-client encounters, and of gaps between official universalistic rules and behavior in practice overlaps with at least three other areas of inquiry: those of administrative and political corruption, white-collar crime, and the parallel economy. A mapping sentence was developed to help delineate the domain of the book (Figure II.1); the critical facets of the general area of investigation turned out to be whether or not the cooperation of one or more persons was involved in the violation of a universalistic rule, and what type of norm was violated—a legal one, or an organizational one (whether formal or informal), or a moral one. The topic chosen for intensive analysis in this book is rule-violations involving the cooperation of others, typically of a non-legal, organizational nature, and taking place between officials and citizens.

I began by discussing three empirical types, found generally in the Western democracies, the monolithic socialist societies and the developing countries, respectively. But mere identification of these empirical types did not tell us enough about the variables which produced them. A more promising approach was to single out two constellations of factors which predispose individuals to depart from universalistic rules. The first group was those which present objective difficulties for citizens intent on obtaining benefits from organizations. Four factors were examined: monopoly and its consequences; inefficiency, which may be present even when organizations are not monopolistic; scarcity of resources; and rigidity in the application of rules.

The other major constellation of factors promoting particularistic decision-making derives, typically, from normative traditions which existed in modernizing, and even in quite modern societies, before the rise of bureaucratization and the other processes of modernization. I distinguished between symmetric and asymmetric particularism. In the former, various bases of corporate group identity are experienced as exerting stronger normative pressure on individuals than the official rules in organizations. Asymmetric particularism is rooted in traditional forms of patronage. Even though modernization radically changes the forms of patronage, the predisposition of individuals to look to persons of higher status and superior control of resources for help in bureaucratic dealings persists in many countries.

Although isolation of these two sets of factors fostering rule-violation moved the analysis forward considerably, it too proved fraught with problems. It turned out to be extremely difficult to tease apart the ways in which cultural sources of particularism interrelate with the presence or absence of objective difficulties in obtaining benefits. Even in countries in which resources are generally plentiful, those resources which are scarce will be subject to the types of constraints I have discussed and will be vulnerable to unofficial manipulation.

But what kinds of ties will be mobilized? Ha-Ilan's (1986) study of the use of personal connections in three areas in Israel is suggestive. Horizontal ties were mobilized mainly in connection with services, whereas vertical ties were more often mobilized in pursuit of jobs or business deals. These results suggested that the scarcer the resource, the more likely that asymmetrical ties will be critical for success in obtaining benefits through unofficial channels.

Full elaboration of the ideas presented in this chapter would require a separate book. My agenda is not to work out these ideas, nor to solve all the problems identified in this chapter, but to outline a general theoretical framework for the study of client behavior in hybrid organizational cultures and to show how that framework accounts for the behavior of the public in one society—that of Israel. The next step in completing that agenda is to switch from macro-sociological analysis to a micro-sociological perspective, to formulate hypotheses to be tested with data on attitudes and behavior of Israelis. To take this next step, I turn now to chapter 3.

III
Becoming Bicultural

I propose that four sets of social-psychological variables account for how clients go about getting what they want from organizations. The first two are: (1) evaluations of the rewards and costs engendered by choosing either U or P strategies, and (2) perceptions of the legitimacy of particularistic strategies. The notion of perception of rewards and costs is a micro-level conceptualization of the macro-level notion of presence of objective difficulties, as discussed in chapter 2. Similarly, whereas there I talked of the persistence of traditional forms of particularism, here I speak of individuals' perceptions of the right to expect particularistic help, or of the legitimacy of monetary payments. To these two sets of variables I add two others, (3) the individual's perceived control of resources necessary for using P strategies, and (4) perceptions of the behavior of others.

I. INSTITUTIONALIZATION OF THE UNIVERSALISTIC AND PARTICULARISTIC CODES

To assess the extent and nature of organizational biculturalism in any setting, it is necessary first to know just how thoroughly the U code has been institutionalized. I follow Selznick (1957), Price (1975), and Hill (1976) in stressing that full institutionalization means that people have a more than merely instrumental orientation toward the U code. As Selznick aptly put it,

. . .organizations become institutions as they are *infused with value,* that is, prized not as tools alone but as sources of direct personal gratification and vehicles of group integrity. (Selznick, 1957: 40)

Thus, clients and bureaucrats should feel that the U code is not only efficient, but that using it is rewarding for its own sake.

As Price (1975) suggested, institutionalization links roles to transcendental individual and social goals; it provides both internalized motivation and social support for carrying out organizational roles according to official prescriptions. When institutionalization is deficient, individuals lack both personal motivation and social support for conforming to this code. There may be greater rewards and social support for violating the code than for conforming to it. As we saw in chapter 2, Price's own study of Ghanaian civil servants revealed this to be the case in Ghana.

In situations of successful institutionalization, there is a state of equilibrium in the relationship between the organization and the environment. Factors external to the organization's official mandate do not impinge inappropriately on its functioning. Neither does the organization acquire excessive power and come to dominate the environment. In Eisenstadt's terms, this is the state of balanced bureaucratization, rather than either de-bureaucratization or over-bureaucratization (Eisenstadt, 1959). Alternatives to U-governed procedures have not particularly flourished in the context of client-organization encounters, because structural and cultural conditions have not worked to undermine these procedures. Because organizations are generally responsive to legitimate needs, individuals do not perceive that going outside the system is more rewarding than staying within it. As I argued in chapter 2, the Western democracies generally fall into this category.

In contrast, where there is de-bureaucratization, organizations are poorly integrated with their environments. In Type III and Type IV societies, individuals exposed to the U code experience conflict between the normative obligations of their organizational roles, on the one hand, and pressures resulting from normative obligations pertaining to other roles, on the other. Verbal protestations to the contrary, they do not fully value the U code; secretly, they are likely to value the P code instead, which is linked in their minds with values which do receive social support.[1]

In Type II societies, typically, the socialist societies, the public has internalized the U code, theoretically; individuals know that P strategies are illegitimate, but develop rationalizations as to why it is all right to use them. As a consequence, in these societies, institutionalization of the U code becomes eroded and its use is less and less prized for its own sake. At the same time, there may come a time when the erosion process comes to a halt, when a *modus vivendi* has arisen, whereby the two codes have become intertwined inextricably. Could it be that in these societies, biculturalism eventually becomes so routinized that rationalizations for it are no longer necessary? Even if this is so, I shall assume, for the purposes of this study, that the gap between attitudes and behavior in these societies should be explained in terms of citizens' perceptions of how their system works.

II. DISCONTINUITY BETWEEN ATTITUDES AND BEHAVIOR

Price argued that in transitional societies exposure to Western education, urban life, modern occupations, and the like teach modernity of attitudes but not of behavior.

> Much of (the mobilization) research . . . has focussed on individual orientations rather than behavior, while tacitly making the inference that the latter will follow from the former. Such an inferential leap is unjustified, since there are powerful theoretical and empirical reasons for suspecting that the two need not be closely correlated. Since there are material and social costs to the individual for his behavior, his own orientation toward action is only one of a number of factors determining the final "behavioral event." At least as important as the individual's own orientation are the orientations of those he considers his "significant others." (Price, 1975: 84)

As mentioned in chapter 2, students of administration in developing countries have called this discrepancy between attitudes and behavior *formalism* or *polynormativism* (cf. Riggs, 1964). Empirically, this pattern was already identified for the Israeli case in my 1968 study of Israelis' attitudes and experiences with public bureaucracy. I found that Israelis overwhelmingly condemned the use of personal connections, yet, at the same time, very high proportions admitted to having used them. The more or less standard correlates of social-psychological modernization, such as education and occupation, were associated with many attitudinal aspects of universalism, but other findings suggested that exposure to Israeli society, and experience in organizational encounters, taught people to use P strategies (Danet and Hartman, 1972a; 1972b).[2]

This discontinuity between attitudes and behavior is, of course, by no means unique either to new or developing countries, or even to the particular substantive area studied. It is well established in social psychology that in a wide range of areas in life (e.g., income tax payment, driving practices, marital fidelity), people hold attitudes which conflict, or at least appear to conflict with their behavior (Fishbein and Ajzen, 1975; Ajzen and Fishbein, 1980). It is no small theoretical challenge to show that the discrepancy is not random, but systematic.[3]

The social mobilization hypothesis formulated by Price was intended to apply to all of Africa and to all new states undergoing industrialization. I suggest that a variation of the same hypothesis can be found to hold for all societies which reveal a gap between norms and behavior. It seems likely that in all societies, including Type I societies with only a small gap between attitudes and behavior, formal education and high-status occupations promote internalization of the U code on the attitudinal level. In the other types of societies, however, the two sets of variables discussed in chapter 2, objective difficulties in obtaining resources and sociocultural constraints toward particularism, will, in different constellations, depending on the type of society, encourage behavior to depart from this code. Individuals' perceptions of these difficulties and of pressures deriving from other roles or interests will, singly, or in combination, move behavior away from conformity with the U code.

To recapitulate the basic hypothesis: In all organizational cultures, social mobilization variables predict attitudinal socialization to the U code, and perhaps even participation in the system, but, at the same time, in Types II, III, and IV societies, four sets of countervailing social-psychological factors promote choice of strategies falling within the P code. These are the rewards and costs that individuals perceive for using U versus P strategies; their perceptions of the legitimacy of P strategies; their perceptions of what others are likely to do in similar situations; and finally, their perceived access to, or control of resources necessary for the use of P strategies. The hypothesis is displayed schematically in Figure III.1.

The behavioral part of this hypothesis resembles theory and research on the situational determinants of deviance. In particular, the hypothesis strongly resembles that of Cressey (1953) in his classic study of embezzlement:[4]

Figure III.1
Factors Promoting Systemic Biculturalism

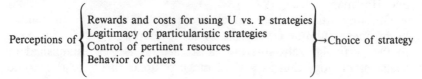

Trusted persons become trust violators when they conceive of themselves as having a financial problem which is non-shareable, are aware that this problem can be secretly resolved by violation of the position of financial trust, and are able to apply to their own conduct in that situation verbalizations which enable them to adjust their conceptions of themselves as trusted persons with their conceptions of themselves as users of the entrusted funds or property. (Cressey, 1953: 30)

Stated more generally, the hypothesis focusses on (1) perception of a need to engage in an officially deviant act; (2) having an opportunity to engage in that act without incurring the risk of sanctions; and (3) being able to rationalize the act.

Like the so-called situational control theories of deviance (cf. Downes and Rock, 1982: chap. 9), the view of rule-violation in organizational settings developed here sees individuals not as buffeted about by strains in culture and social structure, but as acting in a rational manner, making choices. People who break these rules are ordinary folks, respectable citizens—not the sort of people ordinarily thought of as criminal or as offenders.

III. FACTORS PROMOTING BICULTURALISM

A. Rewards and Costs for Using U versus P Strategies

Of the four types of objective difficulties discussed in chapter 2, probably two, and perhaps three, can fruitfully be asked about. Individuals can be asked to what extent they perceive public bureaucracy to be rigid or inefficient. It is also possible to ask people whether they perceive goods and services to be relatively plentiful or not. It does not, on the other hand, make much sense to ask individuals about monopoly; this is a structural condition whose influence can be taken as given.

I assume that choice of a U or P strategy, or the switch from U to P, is a rational act, based on a more or less explicit evaluation of the relative rewards for using the one or the other, on the one hand, and the sanctions to be incurred for using them, on the other. Briefly, if the rewards of using a U strategy, minus the costs of using them, exceed the net rewards of using a P strategy, clients will choose a U strategy. Conversely, if the net rewards for using a P strategy exceed those for using a U one, clients will choose, or switch to, a P one.

1. System support. Other things equal, I hypothesize that people who affirm the system and believe that it is usually fair, efficient, and responsive to legitimate needs and requests, will choose U strategies, whereas those who are highly critical of the system will be pushed toward P strategies. Several studies have demonstrated that such perceptions affect behavior. For example, beliefs about fairness of the system were found to be important determinants of income tax evasion in three studies (Strumpel, 1969; Vogel, 1974; Spicer and Lundstet, 1976), though Mason and Calvin (1978) failed to confirm this finding. In my 1968 study I found a relation between criticism of administrative functioning and use of protektzia. This relationship was again investigated in the 1980 study (see chapters 6 and 7).

2. Perceptions of general public need for P strategies. Besides general orientations toward the functioning of the system, directly measured beliefs about the necessity of using P strategies should be predictive of behavior. Thus, in the Israeli context, I had already found, in the 1968 study, that people who believe citizens cannot manage without protektzia were more likely to use P strategies, both generally, and in pursuit of redress, than were people who believe they can manage without it (Danet and Hartman, 1972a; 1972b).[5]

3. Problems experienced in past encounters. The above two variables pertain to general perceptions of prevailing conditions: People's own personal experiences should also have an effect on their choice of strategies. People who have encountered many problems in past organizational encounters should be more disposed to go outside the official code and to make use of P strategies than would those who have encountered few such problems.[6]

4. Personal need for P strategies. Besides problems actually experienced in past encounters, individuals' specific tendency to see themselves as needing to use P strategies to cope successfully should also be predictive of their use. In the 1968 study I had found that self-defined need for protektzia was strongly associated with actual use (see Danet and Hartman, 1972a). However, some findings suggested that reported need was not merely an objective indicator of problems encountered, but at the same time a sensitive measure of the perception that it is allowed to see oneself as needing protektzia. The more widespread the use of P strategies, the less such perceptions of so-called need for them will reflect objective difficulties alone and the more they will be contaminated by a culture of deviance.

5. The effectiveness of P strategies. When the official system is inefficient or unresponsive, clients will lack support for it, and will prefer P strategies. A simple and obvious hypothesis is that people will prefer P strategies if they believe them to be more effective than U ones.

6. Perceived lack of sanctions for choosing particularistic strategies. If clients believe that they enjoy social support for activating particularistic obligations, or for making small payments to officials for services rendered, whether before or after the event, they will do so. More important, other things equal, they will choose P strategies unless there are sanctions discouraging them from doing so, and, moreover, they know about these sanctions. Even if sanctions exist on the books, if the public knows they are not enforced, there will be little incentive to refrain from using them. I know of no empirical studies of the extent to which awareness of sanctions prevents organizational violations of the type in which "it takes two to tango." There are, however, many studies of the how sanctions affect conformity with rules generally.[7] For example, Schwartz and Orleans (1970) conducted a field experiment of the effects of appeals to conscience versus threats of sanction on compliance with income tax procedures. Despite some complexity of the results, they concluded that compliance can be increased by threat of punishment. In a later study of tax evasion, Mason and Calvin (1978) reported that of five independent variables, the one most highly correlated with admitted tax evasion was the belief in the probability of not being apprehended. Tittle and Rowe (1973) found that making children aware of sanctions was more effective in reducing cheating than stressing a moral appeal to refrain from it. Farrington's (1979) experiments on dishonesty found more dishonesty when the rewards were greater, and when the threat of punishment was less.

Perceptions about the presence or likelihood of surveillance also affect behavior. People are more likely to engage in an officially deviant act if it can be carried out in full privacy. Thus, Mason and Calvin (1978) cited two studies claiming indirect evidence that the affluent are more likely to avoid tax because part of their income is from sources where tax is not automatically deducted (Barlow, et al., 1966; Groves, 1958). However, Mason and Calvin (1978) themselves, found greater evasion among lower-income persons; they speculated that such people also receive much income from which no tax is automatically deducted, e.g., a waiter's tips. Embezzlement is often easy because embezzlers are in a position of trust and of freedom from surveillance (Cressey, 1953). In one study about 20 times as much damage was found on the upper deck of British double-decker buses as on the lower, better-supervised ones (Downes and Rock, 1982: 195–196).

At the same time, the issue of surveillance may not even be relevant in cultures where monetary payments or gifts are so widespread as to be culturally expected. In such situations, there may be little need for secrecy, because expressing gratitude is an act which enjoys social support.

7. Perceptions of covert prestige for using P strategies. Even if sociocultural pressures toward particularism are lacking, people may be aware that there is covert prestige for using P strategies: Successful users of such strategies may be secretly, if not openly admired.[8] As I suggested earlier, in bicultural societies, using at least some kinds of P strategies does not necessarily damage the individual's respectability; the most respectable people do it all the time.

When rule violations are extremely widespread, it may be an instance of what Pitts (1963: 254–259) has called "the delinquent community": Members of the group recognize the legitimacy of the official rules, yet constantly violate them, and are therefore in a perpetual state of delinquency. Just as Pitts showed how the peer group in a French high school operated in this fashion, so I suggest that there is a conspiracy of silence in hybrid organizational cultures—organizations enjoy a basic legitimacy as models of what ought to be, while at the same time, particularistic practices enjoy a second-order *sub-rosa* legitimacy.

In the context of Israeli society, this can be studied indirectly by examining the effects of length of residence in an immigrant society. Other things equal, people who have been exposed to, or have internalized a norm of covert prestige for P strategies, will be more likely to use them, alone or in combination with U ones, than people who are unaware of the secret prestige of being a P user, or those whose past socialization to U values prevents them from yielding to temptation. Thus, in Israel, the longer immigrants have lived in the society and hence the longer they have been exposed to local ways and to this norm of covert prestige for using P channels, the more likely they should be to use them.

B. Perceived Legitimacy of Particularistic Strategies

1. Perceptions of the legitimacy of expecting particularistic help.
Different kinds of questions need to be asked, depending on whether
one is interested in the perceived legitimacy of asking for favors, or
in attitudes toward monetary payments and gifts to bureaucrats. To
tap whether there are bases of legitimacy for expecting favors, questions could be asked about the right to expect help from specific
persons, such as a friend, a close relative, a distant relative, a
neighbor, a friend one hasn't seen for 10 years, an old army buddy,
and so on. The following hypothetical situation and its accompanying
question are illustrative of the kinds of information that could be
elicited: "Consider the following situation: A client of the agency
dispensing unemployment compensation was refused an extension
of his monthly payments. His uncle happens to be the manager of
the agency where he was refused. *Does the client have a right to
expect his uncle to intercede on his behalf?*" The relation between
the client and the third party could be varied, keeping the situation
constant. How the strength of the tie to the third party (uncle versus
second cousin, close friend versus acquaintance) affects perceptions
of the right to expect help from that person could also be tested.
Thus, people would probably be more skeptical about the right to
expect help from a friend not seen for 10 years than from a friend
seen regularly. The general hypothesis should be clear: In strongly
bicultural societies, expectations for such help should be widespread;
moreover, people who believe they have a right to expect help from
third parties should be likely to use them, even if they know they
are breaking the official rules.

2. Monetary payments and gifts. Although I have emphasized the
legitimacy of normatively grounded expectations, where suitable,
situations could also be devised to tap whether individuals think it
is all right to offer small (or large) sums of money to speed things
up, or to obtain benefits like driving licenses or customs exemptions.
It is also desirable to ask whether respondents think officials expect
such benefits. I know of no study in which this kind of research
has been attempted, although Price (1975) and Sebba (1983) have
both studied other aspects of the response to bribes.

C. Control of Resources

People cannot employ P strategies unless they control the resources
required for using them. Thus, they cannot offer a bribe unless they

have the funds to do so. Similarly, people cannot threaten physical violence if they are small and weak, or threaten blackmail if they do not control information which is potentially damaging to recalcitrant officials. Similarly, personal connections cannot be activitated unless one is integrated into viable social networks. Better off people tend to be better connected, as well. Recent research on the "small world" phenomenon (when two strangers meet and discover a close common link, causing them to comment "Isn't it a small world!") has suggested that better educated people of relatively high socioeconomic status (SES) tend to know more people than poorly educated people of low SES, and, in addition, tend to know relatively more people who are also of high status (cf. Gurevitch, 1961; Pool and Kochen, 1978; Travers and Milgram, 1969).

But people must not only be linked to relevant persons, *they must see these persons as a valuable social resource, willing and able to help, and waiting to be mobilized.* Similarly, having the funds necessary to offer someone a bribe is obviously insufficient, in and of itself, to encourage a client to offer one. Rather, the client must perceive that it is possible to offer the money.

Personal influence is a form of social credit, upon which people can draw in time of need. The differential distribution of this type of social credit was documented in my 1968 study, where I analyzed sub-group differences in access to protektzia. Highly educated, high status persons, and native Israelis of both European and Middle Eastern parentage all reported more access to protektzia than their lower-status counterparts (Danet and Hartman, 1972a). A theme which emerged from that research and which is elaborated in the present study is the double advantage of high status groups: they both have a better command of the U code than do lower-status groups, and they have better access to the connections with which to circumvent it, in practice. But again, I must reiterate, it is not only the fact of being well-connected, but the perception that these connections are available for use, that gives the stronger groups their double advantage.

D. Perceptions of the Behavior of Others

Individuals do not make reward-cost calculations or assess the likelihood that people will help them in isolation: They are aware of what goes on around them. Consequently, their perceptions of what others do in similar situations are themselves an important variable. Other things equal, individuals will be more constrained toward use of P strategies if they believe that most people use them, and conversely, if they believe that most people refrain from using them, they will tend to avoid them even when tempted. It has been shown in small group experiments that if an individual believes that the majority of a group do not have the same relation to a social object as he or she does, the person will conform to what he or she perceives as the group's judgment of correct relations to that object (Brown, 1965: 669).

This situation is quite different from those in which individuals engage in deviant acts themselves while believing that others refrain from them. In such situations of multiple ignorance, there may be many instances of rule violation, but not because of the belief that others do it too. Data from my 1968 survey provided initial support for this hypothesis in the context of organization-client dealings (see chapter 4, section IV.B.4).

IV. BICULTURALISM AND REDRESS

The Random House College Dictionary lists three meanings of the term *redress:* "(1) the setting right of what is wrong; (2) relief from wrong or injury; (3) compensation or satisfaction for a wrong or injury." Common to all three meanings is the idea that the individual has been wronged or harmed. But the response to it may highlight compensation or satisfaction on the one hand, or an explicit concern with rights on the other. The latter implies more clearly that an individual instance is analyzed in relation to some rule. Thus, in principle, people who seek redress have their case adjudicated in the loose sense—decided as to who is right or wrong, in accordance with an existing rule.

This is, however, too much of a top down view of redress. From the viewpoint of clients, the machinery of redress may simply be a means to get what they want. As I began to suggest in chapter 1, clients may not care particularly whether they get justice—they may just want some benefit or other. True, they may sometimes care passionately about being vindicated, but in some unknown proportion of the cases they may merely mouth the rhetoric of justice because that is what a client needs to do to get his or her way.[9]

In bicultural environments the less-than-full commitment to justice is expressed in another way: Citizens who switch from U to P strategies are *opting out, abdicating from the demand for universalistic justice.* They give up the right to receive a principled decision about their case. In this most basic sense, the U code is under-institutionalized for such persons: It is not infused with sufficient value for them to prize the decision in itself, apart from whatever benefits are involved. In societies where people readily switch to P strategies, socialization to U values therefore tends to be skin deep, undermined rather easily by situational constraints of the type I have outlined earlier.

Within societies there is also variation in the degree of internalization of the U code. Consequently, people should vary in the degree to which they will be vulnerable to social-psychological constraints. Those for whom the U code is most fully suffused with value will be least swayed by these factors, whereas those whose commitment is only skin deep will more readily yield to situational constraints. In our 1968 study Hartman and I found that believing bureaucracy to be unfair led to inconsistency of attitude and behavior primarily among the least socialized to U values: immigrants of Middle Eastern background and persons of low education (Danet and Hartman, 1972b). In the current study, a host of findings will demonstrate the continuing resistance to temptation by immigrants to Israel of European, especially Western European, background.

V. A TYPOLOGY OF CLIENT STRATEGIES

Thus far, I have spoken of P strategies in global fashion. Actually, I wish to be able to compare users of different types of P strategies. With that goal in mind, I now present a classification of the types of strategies clients may use, in both the public and private sectors. This typology classifies strategies according to three basic dimensions: (1) the legitimacy of the strategy; (2) whether or not it has been formally institutionalized; and (3) the motivational base underlying its use. Figure III.2 shows the various combinations of the three dimensions. In addition, the particular set of channels my collaborator and I chose to investigate in this study are displayed. A fourth distinction has also been added, to separate channels used in the public sector from those in the private sector. If this typology were applied to socialist societies, where there is no private sector, this distinction would of course not apply.

A. Legitimacy

First and foremost, does the strategy fall within the U frame, or is it within the P frame? Is it an attempt to activate some officially

Figure III.2

Classification of Channels of Redress in the Public and Private Sectors by Power Base, Legitimacy, and Institutionalization

Legitimacy	Institutionalization	Inducements		Threats		Norms	
		Private	Public	Private	Public	Private	Public
Legitimate	Institutionalized	—	—	consumer organization, lawyer, small claims court, TV program, radio, newspaper	lawyer, TV program, radio, newspaper	seller higher offical organizer representing seller	higher official ombudsman
	Spontaneous	—	—	negative publicity	petition demonstration	—	—
Illegitimate	Institutionalized	—	—	—	—	—	protektzia MK Minister political party trade union
	Spontaneous	—	(bribe)	threats of violence	threats of violence	—	—

recognized normative obligation of the organization, or is it an attempt to receive special treatment because of some non-U consideration, such as a bribe? All strategies which attempt to activate principles recognized by the U code will be called legitimate, and those which do not will be called illegitimate.

B. Institutionalization

Second, I distinguish between strategies which activate some previously institutionalized device or norm and those which are the spontaneous initiative of the client, as is the case in a demonstration. Studies of complaint-handling usually are focused on formally constituted, institutionalized devices like Better Business Bureaus or ombudsmen. I believe it is equally important to study the use of strategies which are the spontaneous, informal creation of complainants.[10]

C. Motivational Base

Finally, and perhaps most important, I classify strategies according to the type of motivational base, or the interactional principle underlying them—the type of influence attempt involved. There are three main classes of motivational or power bases: inducements, i.e., the offer of a reward of some kind in exchange for compliance; threats, i.e., of physical violence or other undesirable outcomes for the official or the organization; and, finally, appeals to norms of all kinds. In the first instance, activation of the strategy implies more or less explicitly "If I get what I want, I will reward you or the organization." The second implies or states explicitly, "If I do not get what I want, I will deprive you or the organization of something desirable." And the third says "You owe it to me," in one way or another. Classification of strategies by these three dimensions yields 12 possible theoretical types.

D. Five Main Types of Strategies

1. Legitimate institutionalized threats.   An important type of strategy is the appeal to some device which has the possibility of legitimately sanctioning the organization if the client does not obtain satisfaction. I chose to study two main variants of this type, the media and legal means. Public exposure of offending organizations through the media can be an obvious and powerful sanction (cf.

Mattice, 1980; Hannigan, 1977; Palen, 1979). In Israel the most salient example is a television program called "Kolbotek," which specializes both in the processing of complaints and in general socialization of citizens to consumer awareness. But letters to the editor, Action Line columns in newspapers, as well as a radio program investigating complaints also exist.

My collaborators and I asked our respondents about their experiences with lawyers, in both the public and the private sectors; and in the latter, we also asked them about small claims courts, which, as was pointed out in the Introduction, are new on the Israeli scene. Another device which is classified under this rubric is the appeal to consumer organizations, of which there are two major ones in Israel— one run by the Histadrut, Israel's gigantic conglomerate of trade unions, and the other by the Ministry of Tourism, Commerce, and Industry. Consumer organizations may be empowered to apply sanctions or they may not. Some may be primarily normative in character. The classification of any individual consumer organization must be decided upon analysis of the types of sanctions available to it, if any. In the case of Israel, the small claims courts were created to offer tougher sanctions than those the organizations could themselves offer—mainly those of public exposure.

2. Legitimate spontaneous threats. To represent the category of threats that are legitimate but spontaneous, we included the circulation of a petition or the organization of a demonstration, for the public sector, and the threat of spreading negative publicity about the offending organization, in the private sector. In both instances, clients are looking for what Buckle and Thomas-Buckle (1982) have termed "self-help justice," a form of do-it-yourself pressure, for which they need no official third party.

3. Illegitimate spontaneous threats. Threatening to turn the office upside down or to hit the official are obvious examples of illegitimate, spontaneous threats. Most studies of complaint-handling in organizational settings in the West have not typically included illegitimate threats as a client strategy. Certainly outside the West, and perhaps in the West as well, in theory at least, room should be left for the possibility that clients will choose threats of this kind.[11]

4. Legitimate institutionalized norms. The classic appeal in a universalistic bureaucracy is to a normative obligation of the organization: "You owe it to me; I demand my rights." Whether implicitly or explicitly, clients are communicating this message when they approach a higher official in the organization to appeal a refusal, or when they contact an office like that of the ombudsman.

   5. Illegitimate institutionalized norms. The varieties of patronage and brokerage which involve particularistic treatment all attempt to activate a non-universalistic, yet institutionalized, recognized normative obligation on the part of the addressee to provide help to the client.[12] Although these strategies may enjoy a certain legitimacy, from the viewpoint of the universalistic rules, they are illegitimate. In the Israeli setting we chose to study five such strategies.

   a. Protektzia. First, the interviewees were asked about their use of protektzia, both as a general strategy for getting their way in routine encounters, and then as an alternative to universalistic redress when they have been treated unjustly. The term protektzia generally implies approaching a person with whom one is already acquainted. The four other types of particularistic strategies I chose to study do not.[13]

   b. Personalized political brokerage. To contact a member of Israel's Knesset (MK) or a government Minister (including the Prime Minister) is to approach a specific, known person—though not necessarily one known personally. I will call these two types "personalized political brokerage." On first examination, I might have called them forms of patron/brokerage, like Boissevain's (1974) middle type (see chapter 1). Unlike his patron/brokers, however, in most cases these brokers are not personally known to clients—rather, they are familiar figures to them from the mass media.

   c. Organizational brokerage. Approaching a political party or a trade union differs from the above channels because in the latter cases, a specific person is not sought out at all. On the contrary, any well-placed member of the relevant organization should be able to pull the right strings, all within the framework of the common goals to which the client and the organization are committed. Political parties provide help in exchange for loyalty and votes; trade unions supply help as part of the network of mutual help of unions, and also expect loyalty from members (in time of strikes, for example—they are very common in Israel). To distinguish the latter two from personalized brokerage, I call them organizational brokerage.[14]

   Some may take issue with this classification of the various forms of political and organizational brokerage as illegitimate. Certainly, they may be quite well institutionalized, and within the framework of, say, party relationships, it is, of course, legitimate for one party member to approach another for help. But the critical issue is whether the appeal is legitimate vis-a-vis the universalistic criteria of the organization which the client ultimately wants to influence. Still, there are gray areas.

Consider a disabled veteran who appeals to an MK for help in getting the Ministry of Defense to grant special services to which this veteran has a clear, unequivocal right. The client may be bogged down in slow, complicated procedures, and his health problems may make it imperative to obtain these services as soon as possible. All he wants is to speed up things, not to get something to which he is not entitled. Is it justified to call this appeal to an MK illegitimate? This is, after all, the classic kind of casework which politicians do (cf. Uslaner, 1985; Gellhorn, 1966b; Karikas, 1980). If the intervention is primarily procedural, most people would probably say that it constitutes nothing more than friendly, humanitarian help and is therefore entirely legitimate.

If the intervention is *substantive,* however, rather than procedural, the situation is very different. Suppose the Ministry has refused the veteran's request, deciding that he is not eligible, say, because his disability, as previously determined by a Ministry-approved physician, is less than the percentage required by the rules. Would a phone call by an MK still be called friendly help? I think not. Even after taking account of the caveat that rule-application is not a matter of simple arithmetic, and even after recalling the basic premise of the study laid out in the Introduction—that decisions cannot always be neatly categorized as correct or incorrect in positivistic fashion. I suggest that the MK's phone call is at best quasi-legitimate. For the question is not whether it is legitimate to ask the organization to reconsider, but rather on what basis the organization will change its mind, if it does so? If it is difficult to refuse pressure from a political figure, if the official is flattered or derives status from having spoken personally with a celebrity, considerations leading to a change of heart are clearly not universalistic at all.

Yet another complication is that even if the help is only procedural, if it is effective, it may be at the expense of others—waiting their turn, say, for a telephone to be installed in their homes, to mention again that sore point in Israeli life. The line between favoritism and flexibility will always be fuzzy; it is simply not possible to draw a razor-sharp line between mere help and preferential treatment. There are, then, inevitable gray areas in the application of rules to cases.

6. Other types of strategies. The preceding typology has obviously left out some types of strategies, notably monetary payments and gifts. According to the typology, such payments would be classed as illegitimate, spontaneous inducements. Because it was the impression of our research team that bribery is still relatively rare in bureaucratic encounters in Israel,[15] it was not included in the list of strategies studied. My hunch is that unlike protektzia, there is no covert prestige for using bribery, and that therefore people would not be willing to admit to having offered bribes, in which case an interview conducted by a stranger would not very likely elicit much information. But in the many countries where payments and presents are quite routine, it might be possible to ask people about them directly.

Extending the biculturalism hypothesis to the specific topic of redress, Kies, Haas and I predicted that the same social-psychological variables which predict use of P strategies in routine encounters will also encourage people to choose avenues of redress which are based on some particularistic criterion. Six predictions were made: (1) people who perceive that the net rewards for using P channels are greater than those for U channels of redress will opt out of the latter, choosing P channels instead, at least some of the time; (2) the perception that there will be no punishment for using P channels will foster their use; (3) those who think citizens have a right to expect particularistic treatment from key individuals will be likely to use P strategies instead of U channels of complaint; (4) those who believe that P channels are widely used will be more likely to choose them themselves; (5) those seeing themselves as having the opportunity to use P channels will do so; (6) in addition, persons who use P strategies as a regular way of doing business in bureaucratic encounters, thereby violating others' right to U justice, will tend also to opt out of U justice when they themselves are aggrieved, and will use P channels instead.

VI. THE NEUTRALIZATION
OF RULE-VIOLATIONS

How do people live with the discrepancy between their own professed attitudes and their behavior in organizational encounters? The beginning of an answer lies in the techniques of neutralization which people may use, implicitly or explicitly, either to salve their consciences, or to persuade others that they may continue to be regarded as respectable members of the group.

There is a tradition of research on strategies for neutralization of deviance, beginning with the work of Sykes and Matza (1957) on how juvenile delinquents neutralize their behavior. Alternatively conceptualized as "accounts" (cf., e.g., Scott and Lyman, 1970a;

1970b), "justifications and excuses" (Austin, 1970), or "techniques of neutralization" (Sykes and Matza, 1957; Henslin, 1970), and, in an early formulation by Mills (1940) as "situated motives," these statements—for they are statements—generally claim either that the person was not responsible for the wrongdoing (classically, these are what are called excuses), or that the person was responsible, but the act is really a positive one, or at least a neutral one, on some other grounds (these are justifications).[16]

Figure III.3 identifies at least five basic types of techniques of neutralization which can be used in situations of violation of universalistic rules. No claim is made that this list is complete, and I have not tested its usefulness empirically. On the face of it, however, the various types seem to be natural extensions of the general theoretical approach taken in this book.

A. Neutralization of Responsibility

The first general technique available to the public is to disclaim responsibility for the act. There are several ways to do this.

Figure III.3
Techniques of Neutralization of Violations of Universalistic Rules

Technique	Example
I. Neutralization of responsibility	
a. Scapegoating	"The organization is so inefficient—this is what you have to do to get your rights."
b. Minimization of investment in deviance	"I didn't look for protektzia; it fell into my lap."
c. Duress	"I had to give him the bribe, or he wouldn't do what I asked, even though I had a right to what I wanted."
II. Neutralization of injury	"It didn't hurt anyone."
III. Detachment from investment in the moral value of a rule	"So what if someone else had to wait?"
IV. Denial of untowardness of the act.	"Everyone does it."
V. Appeal to other norms, values	
a. ultimate values	"It was a matter of life and death."
b. particularistic norms	"He had to help me—he's my cousin."
c. deference to high-status persons	"I shouldn't have to wait—I'm the mayor."

1. Scapegoating. As Scott and Lyman (1970a) suggested, the principle behind scapegoating is that a person alleges that his or her behavior is a response to the behavior or attitudes of others. Thus, people who say "It's the only way to get what you want from such an inefficient organization," or "That's what you have to do, in order to cope" claim, in one way or another, "I'm not to blame—it's the system."

2. Minimization of investment in deviant behavior. A variation on the theme of neutralization of responsibility is the claim that, in effect, the opportunity to break the rule "fell into one's lap." Consider a client who says, "I didn't look for protektzia—someone offered to help me." This type of claim implies that unsolicited favors are less deviant than those which are actively sought out by recipients. Such statements minimize, but do not totally neutralize, responsibility.

3. Duress. The claim of duress is often heard in criminal trials—in cases of self-defense, for example—"I had to kill him—he was about to stab me to death." In the context of client-official encounters, strict duress is probably extremely rare. But there are situations in some countries where officials refuse to carry out a request unless the client pays a bribe, or where they will take so long to fulfill it if no bribe is paid, that in effect the client is forced to pay it.[17]

B. Neutralization of Injury

Another basic technique of neutralization is to deny that the victim was harmed, or to minimize the extent of harm. Just as a person accused of assaulting someone can claim, "But he only has some cuts and bruises," so a client trying to salve his or her conscience about using pull behind the scenes may try to persuade himself or herself that no one was hurt by the act.[18]

C. Denial of the Moral Value of the Rule

People who say, simply, "I don't care about the fact that I broke a rule" are denying the moral value of the rule for them. A ruder version of the same kind of thinking would be comments like "So what if someone else had to wait while I got in?"

Still another variation would be the argument that it is not important to conform to this particular rule—that some rules are more important than others. Here, the person does not reject the moral value of the rule altogether, but claims the right to conform differentially to different ones.

D. Denial of the Untowardness of the Act

Normally when people are asked to provide accounts for their behavior there is a fair amount of consensus that people who commit such acts are in fact violating some rule. Alleged offenders can deny carrying out the act at all, but this is not the point. Here, offenders, clients, in this case, simply say, "There's nothing unusual about dashing the official (in Ghana), or using protektzia" (in Israel or Eastern Europe). The claim that "Everyone does it" would also fall in this category.

E. Appeals to Other Norms and Values

An important category of techniques of neutralization is the appeal to other norms and values, to transform the meaning of the act from something negative into something neutral, or—even better— into a positive act. This is the process of justification (cf. Austin, 1970).

1. Sacredness of human life. A person trying to have a close relative operated on without waiting his or her turn can say, "It's a matter of life and death"—thereby arguing, implicitly, that there is a higher-order norm stressing the value of human life which justifies violating routine bureaucratic regulations.

2. Particularistic norms. Just as I have shown that particularistic norms are experienced in many societies as a form of pressure on individuals to deviate from the rules, so individuals who do so can justify their behavior in the name of these norms. Thus, a client can rationalize, "He has to do me this favor—he's my cousin." And of course the official can say to himself or herself virtually the same thing—"I had to do him this favor—after all, he's my cousin."

3. Deference. A variation on this theme would be the justification of rule-violation as an act of deference to high-status persons, e.g., "I owe it to him because he is a VIP, the mayor, a famous physicist, etc. . . . How can I keep him waiting?" Or, "Because he's the mayor, he doesn't have time to wait around—I have to serve him first so he can get back to his job." The mayor, for his part, would think to himself, "I'm a busy man—I deserve special treatment so I can get back to my important work," or "I deserve special treatment because I'm a VIP."

F. Distribution of Techniques of Neutralization in Organizational Cultures

Type II, Type III, and Type IV cultures should differ radically in the techniques of neutralization which are predominantly used by clients and officials to rationalize violations. In Type II cultures, which are mainly characterized by the presence of objective difficulties, and by consequent efforts to circumvent the rules, the public will make heavy use of techniques of neutralization of responsibility for violations. In Type III societies, on the other hand, there should be heavier use of appeals to other norms and values, especially to particularistic norms enjoying continuing legitimacy. At the same time, the less people have internalized the U code in the latter societies, the less they will feel the need to engage in neutralization of their behavior at all. They will attempt to neutralize rule-violations only to the extent that their behavior is untoward in their own eyes, or in the eyes of significant others, or if explicitly challenged by others. If Type II societies excuse rule-violations, and Type III ones justify them, in Type IV societies individuals would use a mixture of justifications and excuses to rationalize their behavior, reflecting the presence both of objective difficulties and of legitimation for particularism.

VII. From Biculturalism to Diculturalism

At the end of chapter 2, I suggested that by studying the attitudes and behavior of individuals, it may be possible to find a way to return to the macro-sociological level of analysis maintained throughout that chapter. My next task is to show how that might be done.

To be able to characterize both individuals and societies as monocultural or bicultural, I distinguish societal diculturalism from individual biculturalism. The inspiration for this distinction comes from work in sociolinguistics over the last 20 years. Ferguson (1964) introduced the concept of diglossia to pertain to situations where one communication code is superposed on another. The superposed variety is not the primary native variety for speakers, but is learned in addition to it. Originally, Ferguson was interested in developing an analytical means to study the relation between, say, classical and colloquial Arabic or Greek.

Consider the fact that, as with H (high) and L (low) varieties of language, U is a formal, elaborated, written code, ideally used for communication in public settings, whereas P is an informal, unsystematized code, the natural code for communication among family and friends. Ferguson noted that when H and L are perceived to come into conflict, the proponents of H argue that it is superior because it is more beautiful, more logical, more expressive, and so forth. Proponents of L, on the other hand, argue that it is closer to the real thinking and feeling of the people. To extrapolate from Ferguson's discussion, when U and P conflict, the proponents of U argue that it is more just, more efficient, more logical, more modern; proponents of P can argue that it is more human and more flexible, again "closer to the real thinking and feeling of the people."

Fishman (1967) pointed out that societies can show varying combinations of diglossia with and without bilingualism. These terms can be adapted for macro- and micro-analysis of organizational culture, drawing important distinctions between situations of biculturalism with and without diculturalism.

A. Diculturalism without Biculturalism

If different sub-groups are found to use U and P, each staying within its own code quite stably over time, this would be an instance of a society with diculturalism but without individual-level biculturalism. This could be the state of things in developing countries where elites have internalized universalistic values and behave according to them, whereas the masses relate to officials in public organizations in ways which are governed by more primordial criteria.

B. Biculturalism without Diculturalism

If there is a pattern of two or more codes in use by individuals, with seemingly random switching, but with no stable pattern at the macro-level, this would be a society with biculturalism but without diculturalism. Fishman (1967) noted that the latter state of things characterizes immigrant societies in flux where patterns of behavior have not crystallized.

C. Both Biculturalism and Diculturalism

In contrast to each of the above two situations are those having both biculturalism and diculturalism. In such situations there is widespread use by individuals of both the U and the P codes, in fact so widespread as to justify generalizing about the society as a whole as one in which biculturalism is a stable, institutionalized, dominant pattern. In such situations, no analyst could claim that biculturalism is concentrated solely in a deviant or marginal subculture.

But just how widespread does biculturalism have to be to claim that societal-level diculturalism exists as well? It is, of course, quite arbitrary to establish a particular empirical criterion as critical. I propose that if one-third or more of those coming into contact with officials within a given time period use a particularistic strategy (whether bribery or personal connections) at least once, this is a pattern so widespread as to justify the label of societal diculturalism. In the second half of this book I show that this label is appropriate in the case of Israel.

D. Neither Biculturalism nor Diculturalism

The fourth logical combination of the societal and individual levels is that in which neither biculturalism nor diculturalism is found. This category, of course, would pertain to all societies whose organizational culture is homogeneous—theoretically, either homogeneously U, or homogeneously P.

VIII. Summary and Discussion

In this chapter I have attempted to translate many of the variables discussed in macro-sociological terms in chapter 2 to the level of the individual. In the approach developed here the individual is conceived of as a rational being, making choices which the structure of the situation makes available. Even if these choices are not necessarily viewed as fully conscious or calculated, in retrospect, it is possible to come away from this formulation with an image of what is perhaps an overly rational being—one for whom principle is far less important than interest. Like the control theories of deviance, this formulation can perhaps be faulted for implying that people obey the rules only when the lid is kept on, and that when no one is looking they will always try to get away with violating them (cf. Downes and Rock, 1982, chapter 9).

At least two points can be made in response to this criticism. First, by including in the list of techniques of neutralization the possibility of appealing to other norms and values, I leave room for principle-mindedness. Second, inclusion of the technique of disclaiming moral attachment to a rule is a way of making room for negotiation about the importance of particular rules in society.

A final note about biculturalism: This formulation may appear to suggest that an individual who offers a bribe or uses personal connections even once in a lifetime has become bicultural. This would be too literal an interpretation. Clearly, this way of conceptualizing the problem is meant to help characterize patterns of behavior which have become so regular as to have become a discernible feature of organizational culture. The formulation should be taken as a heuristic device to further understanding of the phenomenon under investigation.

The case for biculturalism is most easily made for those living in societies where particularistic norms compete with universalistic ones. Can it be claimed equally persuasively that, say, an Eastern European family that guarantees its members a kilo of beef every week by bribing the butcher is therefore bicultural? I would argue that the answer is yes, taking the position that the content of norms making them bicultural is simply different from that fostering biculturalism in the Third World. In socialist countries statements that start out as individual techniques of neutralization crystallize as unofficial norms. The propositional content of one such norm might be something like, "When people find themselves in situations where organizations do not respond to their needs or interests, they may break whatever rules constitute blocks to the pursuit of these needs and interests, in a manner which will avoid punishment." This would be a strategic meta-rule which would link the official and unofficial codes.

But enough of theorizing. It is time to move on to the Israeli case study.

IV
Israel's Organizational Culture
Prologue to the Case Study

Like the industrialized countries of the West, Israel defines itself as a pluralist democracy. Its political system, is, at least in theory, of the consociational variety, resembling the Netherlands or Switzerland (cf. Daalder, 1974; Eisenstadt and Roniger, 1980), though the continuing occupation of territories conquered in the Six Day War increasingly calls this self-definition into question. Like Western societies, it has a mixed capitalist and socialist economy. In other respects Israel strongly resembles the socialist countries. Its public sector is the largest of any democracy in the world—so large as to create quasi-monopolistic conditions. Second, its public bureaucracy is known to be quite inefficient. And at least some resources, like telephones and public housing, are scarce enough to create competition and consequently to encourage circumvention of official regulations. Thus, objective difficulties in obtaining benefits—one of the two major sets of factors which foster violations of universalistic rules—are present in Israel.

Like many developing nations, Israel is a new society, founded in 1948, with a colonial past, and salient primordial ties. But unlike these nations, in the Israeli case it makes no sense to speak of pre-existing primordial ties among a traditional population already resident in the area. Instead, Israel is an immigrant society, created on previously undeveloped soil.[1] The pioneering socialist ideology which brought the first groups of settlers to Palestine in the 1880's was in large part a response to anti-Semitism. Pressure for the creation of a Jewish state was greatly increased by the extermination of 6 million

Jews by the Nazis during World War II. The Holocaust profoundly strengthened Jewish identity, both among those who survived it, and among Jews in other parts of the world. A form of artificially revived, attenuated familism thus characterizes modern Jewry. This, too, is a major factor shaping organizational culture in Israeli society. In Hebrew it is called *mishpachtiut*—from the word for family, *mishpacha*.

Dr. I.E. Nebenzahl, a past State Controller and the first national ombudsman, summarized the first 25 years in public administration in the following way:

> In Israel, public administration is not exactly the favorite child. The administrative atmosphere of Israel is characterized by pragmatism and an intuitive approach; its merits are flexibility and improvisation. One of its shortcomings is that our administrators do not give sufficiently high priority to strict obedience [to] rules and regulations. . . . The resulting gap between the State as it would be, according to its own laws and rules, and the administration as it is, has its dangers. . . . Some of the values of regular and proper administration are sacrificed on the altar of action for its own sake. . . . A lack of respect for proper administration or at least indifference to the contribution which law and order can make to civilization, is among the traits of our national character. (Nebenzahl, 1974: 9–10, cited in Caiden, 1980: 13)

To trace the sources of these and other characteristics of Israel's organizational culture, it is necessary to take account of developments over a period of 100 hundred years or so. Three main time periods must be considered: the *Yishuv* (literally, the "Settlement"—the name given to Jewish colonization before 1948), between 1880 and 1948; (2) the early years of the State, from 1948, the year the State was declared, to 1967, the year of the Six Day War; and (3) the period from 1967 to the present.

I. THE ROOTS OF ISRAEL'S ORGANIZATIONAL CULTURE

A. Biblical Law

First among the influences shaping organizational culture in Israel is Biblical law. Caiden (1970) suggested that parts of the Old Testament resemble an administrative manual, which was followed by the First and Second Jewish Commonwealths. At least on the normative level, Biblical law continues to be a source of inspiration, though "less in [matters of] form and content than in spirit and ethics" (Caiden, 1970: 10). The values of justice, public morality, respect for legitimate authority,[2] compassionate administration, and social equality can all be traced back to the Bible.

B. The Ottoman Empire

A later source of influence, which again predates the years of settlement and statehood, is the Ottoman Empire, which ruled the area of Palestine for 4 centuries, until late in World War I. It was an empire that ruled from afar, and in which influence flowed only from above, not from below. Officials maintained law and order, exacted taxes, provided minimal services, and left local communities to manage their religious and sociocultural affairs (Caiden, 1970; Werner, 1983b).

Although Palestine was ruled from afar, there was no less despotism than in the Balkan countries ruled by the Ottoman Empire (see chapter 2). Caiden spoke of

> an indigenous Middle Eastern style . . . found particularly in Arab areas in which business is transacted at a regal pace, in a charming, courteous, if exasperating, fashion. Traditional institutions place a premium on deference to authority and status, bargaining skills and displays of bureaucratic officiousness. (Caiden, 1970: 17–18)

Nepotism was endemic among the Turks, offices were commonly bought and sold, and small payments to officials of *baksheesh,* "a form of Levantine extortion," to use Werner's (1983b: 623) phrase, were routine.

The early years of Jewish settlement took place against this backdrop of Ottoman rule. The first *aliya* (wave of immigration) during the years 1882–1903 saw 20,000–30,000 Jews arrive from Russia. In the second aliya, from 1904 to 1914, another 35,000 to 40,000 came from Russia and Poland.[3] The encounter with Turkish rule was not altogether a cultural shock, because these immigrants had spent their formative years under similarly autocratic Tsarist Russian and Eastern European regimes, in which hostile conditions had fostered the search for ways to circumvent the law (Werner, 1983b).

C. The British Mandate

When the British conquered Palestine, they turned the area into a Mandate, which lasted from 1922 until declaration of the State in

1948. They found a grossly underdeveloped area without adequate police or postal services and with a good deal of desert and swamp, disease and poverty, primitive transportation and communications (Caiden, 1970). The largely Arab population of approximately 750,000 at the start of the Mandate was unfit for self-rule. The British embarked on public works, set up basic services, introduced new laws. Order and efficiency were emphasized.

> The British pattern is still discernible in the legal system, in police organization, in post office, customs and railways administration, and, to a lesser extent, in local government, public utilities, banking and port control. It is a no-nonsense, orderly, condescending,[4] bureaucratic approach, with little room for bargaining, local initiative or disruption. (Caiden, 1970: 18)

With minor deviations, then, the British imprint on Palestine was largely that of an organizational culture of the first type outlined in chapter 2.

D. The Eastern European Imprint: the Import of Protektzia

During the period in which the Jews flocked to Palestine from Eastern Europe, the Arabs failed to develop national self-governing institutions. The Jews, on the other hand, having a strong tradition of communal organizations and self-help in the Diaspora, began to develop their own institutions—even before the British Mandate began. These came to include an Elected Assembly (*Asefat Hanivcharim*), and a body drawn from it called *Va'ad Leumi,* or National Council, the Jewish Agency (in charge of immigration, land settlement, and economic development), and the Zionist Organization, in charge of relations with Jews in the Diaspora.[5] These institutions came to have what I call the Eastern European imprint.

Institution-building activities were carried out with a pioneering sense of mission—settlers saw themselves as "building something out of nothing," and in a hurry, much as Nebenzahl (1974) wrote in the passage cited at the beginning of this chapter. They combined idealism and pragmatism, a combination which has left its mark to this day:

> Equally condescending towards expertise, theoretical analyses and detached rationalistic calculation, yet colliding when Utopian values have to be translated into feasible and operational policies, the interplay and changing relative weight of pragmatism and idealism determine much of the basic

tone in Israeli administration, including some of its best and some of its weakest features. (Dror, 1965: 13–14)[6]

The evolution of a Jewish polity and bureaucracy took place parallel to and independently of the British government and bureaucracy, and no attempt was made to emulate the formal regulations and hierarchical structures of the latter (Werner, 1983b). Jewish institutions were especially responsive to demands of clients because of common Jewish identity of officials and clients.

Solidarity among Jews was expressed by several popular phrases.[7] One was *Kol Yisrael chaverim*—literally, "All Israel are friends." Another phrase is still more explicit: *Kol Yisrael arevim ze laze:* "All Jews are responsible for one another, are guarantors for one another." Still another is *shmor li v'eshmor lecha:* "You take care of me, and I'll take care of you," or, as the phrase is sometimes rendered in English, "You scratch my back, I'll scratch yours."

In effect, then, protektzia was imported from Eastern Europe. To get things done, it was often enough to say "Moshe sent me." People related to one another on a particularistic basis, much as they had in the hostile environment of their countries of origin. What had begun as a form of self-defense against hostile Gentiles in Eastern Europe in time became comfortable habit in the new setting.

This pattern coincides strikingly with the definition of familism offered by Theodorson and Theodorson:

A form of social organization characterized by familial values that emphasize the subordination of the interests and personality of individual family members to the interests and welfare of the family group. It is characterized by a strong sense of family identification and loyalty, mutual assistance among family members, and a concern for the perpetuation of the family unit. (Theodorson and Theodorson, 1969: 146)

E. The Influx of Immigrants

The enormous heterogeneity of cultural origins of the various immigrant groups has clearly been one of the most important constraints on Israel's emergent organizational culture. Immigration from Eastern Europe continued over the years, and eventually, immigrants from other parts of the world also began to pour into Israel. The third aliya, from 1919 to 1923, saw 35,000 Russian Jews arrive. Between 1924 and 1931, the period of the fourth aliya, 82,000 came, mainly from Poland, though some came from America and the Middle East.

Then, in a final burst before World War II, in the years between 1932 and 1938, over 200,000 came, from Poland, Germany, Russia, Austria, and Rumania, and between 1939 and statehood in 1948, another 145,000 arrived, again mainly from Eastern Europe. Large numbers of Jews from African and Asian countries began coming only after statehood. Whereas they had constituted as little as 4%, and never more than 12% of any of the *aliyot* before statehood, they constituted 48% of all immigrants arriving in the period from 1948 to 1975. In absolute numbers, 751,000 Sephardic Jews came during this period (Smooha, 1978: Table Appendix, Table 9). Although Eastern Europeans and Sephardic Jews dominated in terms of absolute numbers, small groups from Western European and English-speaking countries also came.

II. THE FUNCTIONING OF PUBLIC BUREAUCRACY

In chapter 4 I suggested that four aspects of the functioning of public bureaucracy may cause difficulties for the public in obtaining goods and services: the presence of monopoly, scarcity of resources, inefficiency, and lack of flexibility in the application of rules. There is ample evidence that at least the first three of these factors are present in Israel. As for the matter of flexibility, almost no solid information is available, though in my study I found that Israelis perceive bureaucrats to be somewhat inflexible (see chapter 5).

A. Monopoly

It was suggested in chapter 1 that the public sector in Israel is unusually large for a democracy. It is time now to document that claim in more detail.

1. Government expenditures. Consider, first of all, that the proportion of total investments financed by the public sector is higher than in any Western country (Etzioni-Halevy, 1975; Barkai, 1964: 59–65). In the mid-1970's government expenditures totalled between 37% and 41% of the gross national product (United Nations, 1982). For the 1979 fiscal year, for example, government expenditures totalled 33% of the gross national product, as compared with, say, 29% for Sweden, the social welfare state par excellence, or 17% for the United States. In part these expenditures are high because of the extremely large proportion of the total budget spent on defense. Thus, in 1978–79, Sweden spent only one-tenth of its government budget on defense, whereas Israel spent a huge two-thirds on defense.[8]

2. Range of public services. But public expenditures are also high because of a commitment to provide many services which would be supplied by the private sector in other countries.

For various reasons the demand for social services is higher in Israel than in other countries of a similar level of economic development. The norms for social services are determined according to criteria used in the developed countries . . . the unusual demand for services derives from needs associated with the absorption of immigrants and social integration of population groups coming from a large number of countries and from different cultures. (Ofer, 1983: 2)

3. Large cooperative sector. One of the reasons that the public sector is so large is that in addition to the governmental and nongovernmental components, there is an extremely large cooperative component, which emerged in the 1920's, when collectives of workers were joined to create the Histadrut—a complex of trade unions— and the *Hevrat Ovdim,* or Workers' Society. Elazar has summed up the unusually broad range of economic activities subsumed by this cooperative component:

While the cooperative sector has diminished greatly in importance since the establishment of the state, it remains the biggest nongovernmental owner and operator in the country. The largest industries, including the largest conglomerate in the country, are under its ownership. The internal public transportation companies, with the exception of the state railroads and the miniscule internal airline . . . are workers' cooperatives. . . . The largest department store chain is Histadrut-owned. The Histadrut operates Kupat Holim (the Workers' Sick Fund), the largest health maintenance organization in the country, which serves over two-thirds of the population, and through it controls a network of hospitals and old-age and rest homes. . . . The Histadrut has become considerably bureaucratized over the years, so that . . . it has . . . become at least as distant from its own members as the government is from the man in the street. . . . (Elazar, 1985: 58–59)

These conditions of monopoly, quasi-monopoly and bureaucratization and their concomitants on such a large scale have made citizens unusually dependent, not just for small everyday services like telephones and electricity, or even for health care, or for educational and social services traditionally associated with the welfare state, but for weightier matters—e.g., for government-built apartments and for bureaucratically managed loans to pay for them.

B. Scarcity of Resources

As was noted in chapter 1, Israel is best characterized, paradoxically, as a "developed developing society" (Ben-Dor, 1974). Neither as affluent as many countries in the West, nor as poor as Third World countries, she lies roughly in between, or, more exactly, close to the less affluent of the Western countries.

1. **Pressure to provide services to immigrants.** As an immigrant society Israel has been under tremendous pressure to supply services to waves of newcomers. As a result, public administration has been on a crisis footing for most of its existence. Even though Israel has received financial assistance from other governments over the years, as well as from Jewry in the Diaspora, public administration has always been strapped for funds—even before the dizzying levels of inflation reached in the mid-1980's, and before the arrival en masse of Jews from Ethiopia in 1984–85. It should be stressed that scarcity is in part indirectly felt—in the lack of funds to hire, train, and house sufficient staff to do the work necessary to supply the goods and services that government is committed to make available.

2. **Standard of living.** At the same time, in other respects Israel is a relatively affluent society, so that the significance of scarcity for the quality of functioning of public administration should not be exaggerated. To compare the standard of living in Israel with that in other countries, I have assembled data on 20 selected countries; these data are presented in Table IV.1.

Inspection of the data on per capita income, reveals that the figure for Israel—$5,052 for 1980—is a good deal lower than the comparable figures for the first three countries in the list, the United States, Canada, and Sweden, all of which report a figure of about $11,000 per capita. Israel resembles the United Kingdom and Italy, among Western countries, and Czechoslovakia, among socialist ones. In contrast, the range among poor countries is between $202 for India and $576 for the People's Republic of China.

Table IV.1

The Standard of Living in 20 Countries

Country	Population	Per Capita Income	Life Expectancy	Infant Mortality*	Illiteracy	Passenger Cars*	Telephones*
United States	226,547,346	$11,596	74	12.5	negligible	545	775
Canada	24,343,181	$11,519	74	10.9	—	564	679
Sweden	8,323,033	$11,111	74	6.7	negligible	—	—
West Germany	61,703,000	$10,509	71	13.5	"	344	401
Denmark	5,123,989	$9,868	74	8.8	"	218	567
France	53,963,000	$9,479	72	10.0	"	322	368
Australia	14,574,488	$9,115	74	10.7	"	468	458
Austria	7,555,338	$7,127	73	13.9	"	270	323
Czechoslovakia	15,314,000	$5,542	70	16.6	"	129	195
United Kingdom	55,618,791	$5,340	73	11.8	"	264	417
Italy	57,197,000	$5,300	73	14.3	2%	286	299
Israel	3,921,700	$5,052	72	14.1	10%	83	253
USSR	268,800,000	$4,820	70	27.7	negligible	—	78
Hungary	10,709,536	$3,665	70	23.1	"	78	107
Poland	36,062,000	$3,513	71	21.2	"	51	86
Iraq	12,767,000	$2,666	62	30.6	49%	13	25
P.R. China	982,550,000	$576	68	N.A.	45%	N.A.	5
Egypt	42,930,000	$573	54	73.5	56%	8	11
Indonesia	147,490,298	$417	48	125.0	36%	36	24
India	683,810,051	$202	54	130.0	64%	12	31

* Per 1000 persons
Source: Hammond Almanac, 1983

Figures on life expectancy and infant mortality similarly reveal that Israel competes well with Western standards, with an average life expectancy of 72 and about 14 cases of infant mortality for every 1000 births (this rate being about the same as that for Austria or Italy). At 10%, illiteracy has not been wiped out in Israel, as it has in Western or socialist countries (excepting the People's Republic of China), but it is a far cry from figures of 36% to 64% for the poor countries (Indonesia, Iraq, Egypt, India, China).

Material well-being is also indexed by the prevalence of passenger cars and telephones. Data from the Hammond Almanac show Israel to have had about 80 cars per thousand persons in 1978. This figure is, in fact, very low compared to most of the other countries which it resembles on other measures (cf. 264/1000 for the United Kingdom and 286/1000 for Italy); however, it is very likely that in the years since 1978 Israel has begun to catch up. As for telephones, only in Canada and the United States are there as many as two telephones for every three persons in the population. Even other relatively affluent European countries have proportionately fewer telephones. Israel has reported about 253 per 1000 persons for 1978, again resembling Italy (for which the rate is about 300/1000).

In short, Israel is a relatively affluent country, in which only selected resources continue to be scarce. In the past, housing was scarce, as were loans to purchase apartments; popularly priced public housing for young couples is still in great demand today, though much housing is now privately built. Today parents may also compete to obtain preferential assignments for their daughters in the army, or to get their children into the more prestigious high schools. And increasingly, there will be competition to get aging parents into nursing homes, as Israel's population ages—thé forecast is for a severe shortage of such services in the future.[9]

C. Inefficiency

Israeli public bureaucracy is notorious for its inefficiency and lack of a service ethic. Some attribute the lack of a service ethic to the idea that, now that Jews are on their own turf, they do not have to kow-tow to anyone. The notion that being a civil servant could be a calling, as in the British tradition, is only poorly institutionalized. Lower-level officials who deal with the public rarely smile, often fail to look up, and establish eye contact when clients enter the room, and are frequently downright rude—or are out drinking tea or coffee, much like the Balkan officials described by Seton-Watson (1967; see chapter 2).

In Caiden's view, the symptoms of "bureaupathology"

> include the rate at which the best products of society seek other careers. Administrative activities have inadequate resources, and bureaucrats make do with unsuitable accommodation, poor equipment and depressing work conditions. The bureaucrat—the *pakid*—is a figure of fun, demoralized by hostile criticism, hard-pressed, overstrained and underpaid. He lacks incentives for better work performance and is seemingly unaware of the concept of service. Many have been thrust into positions beyond their abilities. (Caiden, 1970: 38–39)

Several types of empirical evidence can be used to document the problematic nature of Israeli public bureaucracy, data on public opinion, statistics on complaints to the ombudsman, and the reactions of immigrants from efficient, Type I countries to the workings of local bureaucracy.

1. General public opinion. In a 1968 survey (Danet and Hartman, 1972b), respondents were asked about levels of satisfaction with service, overall, and with three specific aspects of contacts—the laws and regulations, procedures, and the manner of officials. Of these, procedures were most often cited as problematic. An index which was used to integrate the replies to all four questions yielded a figure of almost 50% as dissatisfied with the functioning of public bureaucracy. Second, of those who had come into contact with it during the past year, two-thirds reported having had at least one negative experience.

Asked to state what disturbed them most when interacting with civil servants, a 1973 sample of the public interviewed by Nachmias and Rosenbloom cited wasted time, being sent from one clerk to another, long lines, and "non-understanding" civil servants, in that order (Nachmias and Rosenbloom, 1978: 49). Both of their samples— of the public and of bureaucrats—also rated the image of the bureaucrat on a series of 7-point scales. Both groups rated bureaucrats lowest on speed (though highest on honesty). As might be expected, the overall image held by the public was more negative than that held by the civil servants, though the general shape of the two profiles was quite similar.

2. Reactions of North American immigrants. Katz and Antonovsky (1973) asked nearly 1700 immigrants from the United States and

Canada to what extent each of 85 issues falling into six areas (work, housework, family, country generally, Hebrew, social life) had been problematic. Four of the 85 questions referred directly to bureaucracy, such as getting effects cleared at customs and the courtesy of officials. Of all matters investigated, those pertaining to bureaucracy were experienced as most problematic.

In a similar vein, Jubas (1974) presented 553 North American immigrants who had arrived after the Six Day War in 1967 with a list of 21 hypothetical factors which might lead to a decision to leave Israel. "Red tape and bureaucracy" was ranked first (Jubas, 1974: 189 ff., cited in Avruch, 1981: 137). Finally, in another study of American immigrants to Israel, 97% of those interviewed said that Israeli bureaucracy was "more difficult to deal with" than American bureaucracy (Avruch, 1981: 138).

3. Complaints. In a study Peled and I conducted of letters to the Jerusalem municipal ombudsman (Danet and Peled, 1973) the main problem complained about typically had something to do with procedures. In a comparison of the rate of complaining to the national ombudsman in nine countries (New Zealand, Canada, the four Scandinavian countries, France, and Britain, as well as Israel), there were only between 1 and 4 complaints per 100,000 population in France and Britain, and from 26 to 80 per 100,000 in all the others except Israel, where an extraordinarily high 250 per 100,000 persons petitioned the ombudsman (Danet, 1978; see also Table II.1, chapter 2). Similarly, the proportion of justified complaints is far higher than in the other countries and has remained quite stable at just under 50% in the last decade (Danet, 1978). Despite problems of comparison due to differing jurisdictions, differing efforts at publicity about the ombudsman's services, and so forth, there can be little doubt that the high figure for Israel reflects genuine difficulties encountered by the public.

D. Politicization

The functioning of public bureaucracy in contemporary Israel cannot be understood without taking into account the tendency to politicization which has characterized it from its inception. In the 1930's and 1940's, political parties, rather than the central government, came to supply most of new immigrants' needs, from housing to employment to education and medical care (Werner, 1983b; Elon, 1972). Werner (1983b) claimed, however, that political clientelism remained embryonic until 1948, because the machinery of a national government was not yet available. Thus, parties could not call in their debts until formal elections could take place. In the view of Eisenstadt and Roniger (1984), clientelism nearly took over in the 1950's, but incurred a long-lasting setback when a U-based system of public administration was established.

Still, recruitment to civil service positions has always been to some extent a matter of party patronage. In part this has derived from the history of the emergence of political and administrative structures in the pre-State, Yishuv period, during which various political factions and movements vied for recognition as the group best qualified to realize the Zionist, collective ideology. With statehood, a formula of allocation of jobs by party "key" became established.

In large part, politicization has been a function of the process of coalition formation in Israeli politics (Nachmias and Rosenbloom, 1978: 51). The electoral system is one of proportional representation based on party lists, rather than direct election of candidates. Because no party has ever obtained a large enough majority to control the Knesset, Israel's Parliament, coalitions have always been critical. As Nachmias and Rosenbloom (1978: 52) noted, "One of the central payoffs to coalition partners has been the distribution of public offices."

Pre-State administrative functions were performed by persons of little or no professional training in frameworks where party loyalty was more important than skills in the performance of administrative roles (Eisenstadt, 1967; Shapiro, 1977; Etzioni-Halevy, 1979; Medding, 1972, chapter 2; Sprinzak, 1984). Over the years, professionalization has greatly increased. In 1959 and in 1961, legislation was passed to require recruitment based on impersonal, universalistic merit-based criteria and to limit political activities of civil servants (Nachmias and Rosenbloom, 1978). Although recruitment is probably a good deal more universalistic today than in the past, there is ample evidence of a persisting gap between these laws and actual practice. For instance, 31% of senior appointments in the years 1960–66 were made without the required public announcement of a vacancy (Globerson, 1970, cited in Etzioni-Halevy, 1979). Despite the prohibition against political activity of civil servants, more than half of the senior civil servants were active in politics; moreover, the higher the rank, the greater was the tendency to be active (Globerson, 1970). Politicization also extends to promotions of civil servants, according to Etzioni-Halevy (1979).

In 1973 Nachmias and Rosenbloom (1978) asked a sample of bureaucrats whether they believed recruitment to be primarily patronage-oriented and ascriptive, or universalistic and achievement-oriented. Secondary analysis of their data has shown that 37% believed that ascriptive or patronage criteria are most important in recruitment, whereas the other two-thirds believed it to be universalistic.[10]

Although political influence has been harnessed to some extent in government bureaucracy, it remains more pervasive in the allied public institutions, the Histadrut, Israel's federation of trade unions, with its elaborate network of economic and political institutions, and in the Jewish Agency. Medding (1972) showed that even in the late 1960's and early 1970's party control of the Histadrut administration was viewed as entirely legitimate. Today, top-level posts considered legitimate avenues for party patronage are the personal staff of ministers, ambassadors, directors-general, advisors, accountants-general, budget directors, among others (Nachmias and Rosenbloom, 1978). The number of government ministries also expands and contracts, according to the interests of the reigning parties or coalitions (Nachmias and Rosenbloom, 1978: 52).

Etzioni-Halevy (1979) argued that two main factors produced such a politicized bureaucracy. First, the lack of a commonly accepted state framework in the pre-State period forced the national institutions, which did not have a monopoly over physical force—a basic characteristic of a truly sovereign state—to yield some of their authority to various political bodies. As noted earlier, these bodies, and not central, national institutions, organized immigration, settlement, and other services and doled out benefits to the public in exchange for political support (Etzioni-Halevy, 1979: 176–179). The contemporary consociational structure of public life is thus inherited from pre-State times.

The ideology of socialism was a second predisposing factor to politicization. The founding fathers and mothers had mainly come from Russia, as young people in their 20's, and were thus exposed to trends in Russian political culture of the time. The socialist ideology urged, among other things, collective control of administration and the economy. Although the founders were not in favor of a one-party state, they were clearly predisposed toward a very considerable degree of centralization of decision-making in the emergent society. Given this general background of politicization of public administration, in the relations between bureaucrats and politicians, it is no wonder that protektzia has flourished in client-bureaucrat transactions.

III. FAMILISM AND PRIMORDIALIZATION: A CLOSER LOOK

A. The Continuing Salience of Familism in Israeli Life

Familism continues to be a salient feature of contemporary Israel. The writer Amos Elon went so far as to claim that

> (There is) . . . a basic fact about Israeli life, without which nothing can be understood, that Israel is at base a community of faith. It is a *mishpacha*, not a state. (Elon, n.d., cited in Avruch, 1981: 123)

For Avruch, an anthropologist who studied the changes undergone by American immigrants in the mid-1970's, to immigrate to Israel is to invest

> in an image of a certain kind of society. This is a society whose template is *mishpacha* (the family). It is a society where (American immigrants) believed relations among Jews . . . would be, as in a family, warm, intense, face-to-face, diffuse, multiplex, and moral. The image of the society in which they invested is that of a gemeinschaft, not a gesellschaft. Members of this society are expected to relate to one another as something more than *chaverim* (comrades). (Avruch, 1981: 120)

As a result of investment in this kind of society, these immigrants have become primordialized, or traditionalized, to use Avruch's phrase.

1. Mishelanuim. However strong it may be, mishpachtiut is not activated simply by approaching another Jew. Things are more complicated than that. In a novel about the period of transition between the Yishuv and the state, Netiva Ben-Yehuda explained about the concept of *mishelanuim:* a slang neologism based on the word *mishelanu*—"from ours, one of us:"

> This matter, this strong feeling of "*shelanu*" is so characteristic of us in *Eretz* (in Israel). When we are in *Chutz-l'aretz* (abroad)—then *kulanu chaverim* (we are all friends). Without difference of religion, race, sex, party. Every Israeli abroad is *mishelanu*—in contrast to the *Goyim* (the Gentiles). But here, inside the country, there are millions of *mishelanu-*

im, of all kinds. And every one of us belongs to several, at least to one. There isn't a person who doesn't belong to at least one *mishelanu,* or who at least belonged at least once in his life to a *mishelanu.* And within our *mishelanu*—there is a division into still more, smaller sub-*mishelanuim.* And because none of us has a sign on his chest, which will tell who we are, and because apparently we don't have enough permanent customs which will identify us from afar, as older nations probably have, with great *chutzpah,* they ask you to which *mishelanu* do you belong, and every answer is accepted. Only one is not: in response to the answer "I don't belong to any *mishelanu*" they will tell you: "What do you mean? It can't be! Here in *Eretz?*" You can't be a non-conformist, and you can't be an agnostic. There's no such animal. If you want to say that you are an agnostic, you have to lecture about it for a whole hour. They don't believe you that such a thing can exist. (Ben-Yehuda, 1981: 53–54)

2. Anshei shlomenu. There is still another Hebrew phrase which vividly reflects the flavor of familism in Israel. In the decade before the state and the first decade or so following it, the phrase *anshei shlomenu* was commonly used in organizational and political transactions. Literally, *anshei shlomenu* means "people of our well being." More loosely, it means "those whose interests coincide with ours, who belong to us, who are loyal to us." Folklore has it that in certain circles all one had to do to obtain protektzia was to equip oneself with a slip of paper, duly signed by a key person, on which was written *hanal mianash. Hanal* is the abbreviation for "the person mentioned above," a phrase typical of bureaucratic writing style. *Anash* is an abbreviation for *anshei shlomenu,* the phrase just mentioned. It is as if one wrote, in English, "T.P.I.O.O.O."—for "This Person Is One Of Ours."[11]

B. Sources of Familism: Past and Present

There are at least four sources of familism among Jews in Israel, of which three probably continue to be operative to this day.

1. History of persecution of the Jews. As suggested earlier, the history of the persecution of the Jews has probably been the prime source of encouragement of in-group solidarity. This tendency to perceive the world in terms of "we" and "they" means, among other things, that people tend to trust only those who are insiders, or those with whom they have an established personal relationship. A typical instance of this phenomenon in the present context is the reaction of many Israelis to a problem with a bureaucratic agency— their first response may be to ask, "Now whom do I know in that office?"

2. Jewish ethics. A case can be made that solidarity among Jews was more than the product of a ghetto mentality—that it has not been merely a defensive reaction to negative forces, but also a positive expression of ancient Jewish ethical tradition. Rotenberg (1983) has argued that among the Hasidim, one of the orthodox Jewish streams prominent in pre-modern Eastern Europe and still thriving in Israel today, although a tiny minority, interpersonal relations have been dominated by what he calls the Issachar-Zebulun model, in which salvation is obtained through doing for others. In the ancient Biblical story of Issachar and Zebulun, one brother, Zebulun, worked as a merchant and supported his scholar brother Issachar, who was thus able to devote his time to religious study. In contrast to notions of instrumental exchange, according to which Issachar would feel uncomfortably indebted to his brother, the Jewish view, or at least the Eastern European Hassidic view, so argued Rotenberg, is that non-repayable giving to others is the road to salvation and that therefore both brothers could feel entirely comfortable with their arrangement. Thus, however aware or unaware the mainly secular, assimilated settlers from Eastern Europe in Palestine may have been of these ethical roots of solidarity among Jews, the saying *Kol Yisrael chaverim* probably expresses a positive, and not merely a defensive social value.

3. Size of the country. A third factor which has probably fostered familism is the small size of the country, though size *per se* may no longer be relevant today. In a past publication, I had speculated that in the early years, the small size of the country encouraged the feeling that "everyone knows everyone else" (Danet and Hartman, 1972a). And indeed, the probability that any given official and client would know each other in some context besides the organizational one was rather high in small communities, in the early years.

But today things have changed considerably. Although by world standards Israel is still a small country, with a population of only about 4 million, it has become a country of quite large cities. Today's Israel is highly urbanized; in fact, remarkably so for a new country. In the year 1980, over 90% of the Jewish population resided in urban localities, including smaller satellite settlements surrounding the three big cities (Central Bureau of Statistics, 1981, Table II/14, 48). The probability that any given citizen will be personally acquainted with a bureaucrat in his or her place of residence is therefore very small.

Even members of elites do not know one another, contrary to popular myth. In Gurevitch and Weingrod's (1978) research on patterns of acquaintance among Israeli elites they found that although politicians and media elites did tend to know members of other elites besides their own to a larger extent than the other elites studied (administrative, academic, arts and cultural, business), in general, elite members do not know one another, and moreover, family ties— often cited because of certain well-known cases of marriage between prominent families—are a statistically insignificant source of acquaintanceship.

Recent research on the small world phenomenon in Israel also suggested that size of locality may no longer be a factor. Recall that there are two ways to activate particularistic obligations, either to appeal directly to the official involved, or to go to some third party. The question is: How easy or difficult is it for any given citizen to think of someone who can provide the missing link to the official he or she wishes to influence?

This question is a special case of that studied in research on the small world phenomenon. Weiman (1983) investigated acquaintance networks in Israel, using a variant of the small world technique originally introduced by Milgram (see, e.g., Travers and Milgram, 1969). Participants in these studies are asked to provide a link to a named stranger; researchers then analyze the number of links required, on the average, to complete the chain to the target person. Seventy percent of all attempted chains were completed in the Israeli study, with the average length of chain being just over five persons, a result which is, surprisingly, virtually identical with that obtained in the original Travers and Milgram study, carried out in the huge United States. In short, this finding too suggested that although small size of locality may once have been important, this factor has declined in importance over the years. At the same time, the subjective feeling that everyone knows everyone may well persist.

4. Common enemy. The continuing danger to Israel's security promotes in-group solidarity in a number of ways. Although the pioneering ideology has become eroded over time, there is still a strong feeling of "being in this together," fostered by the frequent wars, by compulsory army service, and by the extensive reserve duty for all men up to the age of 50 and for women until age 24. Regardless of political views, the fact that Israel is surrounded by countries of varying degrees of hostility and that incidents of terrorism are an almost daily occurrence both reinforce the "we-they" view of the world. Nearly everyone has either lost one or more relatives or friends in the various wars, or knows someone who did so. Moreover, persons of vastly different social and educational backgrounds are thrown together in *miluim,* the reserves. Personal ties are often formed between individuals who do reserve duty together. Beyond the general sense of solidarity thus generated, such ties can prove a useful resource when protektzia is sought.

IV. INHERENT CONTRADICTIONS BETWEEN FAMILISM AND THE DEMANDS OF CIVIL SOCIETY

A. Medinat Yisrael versus Eretz Yisrael

From the inception of the Zionist movement, there have always been contradictions between the tendency toward familism and the demands of a universalistically grounded civil society, to which Israel is supposedly committed. Two analysts of these contradictions reached very similar conclusions. In Cohen's words:

> One of the salient features of political Zionism is that it purported to be not merely a "nationalist" ideology, but strove to integrate two, in principle, conflicting, value premises: the collective particularism of Jewish aspirations to an independent national state, and the universalism of modern Western civilization. The Jewish state was to be an enlightened one, in which the secular values of freedom, justice and equality for all citizens without difference of race, nationality, or religion would be fully realized; though a national state, it was to be a fully democratic one, in which universalistic principles would govern the relations between all citizens. In the high expectations of Zionist idealists, it was to be an ideal state, a "light unto the Nations." Both sets of premises, the particularistic and universalistic ones, became fundamental components of the legitimation of the State of Israel. In political practice, however, they necessarily clashed. (Cohen, 1985: 322)

In Kimmerling's (1985) formulation of tensions between civil and primordial definitions of the collectivity in Israel, these tensions are symbolized or epitomized by the two Hebrew phrases, *Medinat Yisrael* and *Eretz Yisrael,* meaning, literally, "the State of Israel," and "the Land of Israel." Whereas Medinat Yisrael locates the collectivity in a physical space, defined primarily by the 1949 cease-fire lines (with the addition of East Jerusalem after the Six Day War), Eretz Yisrael is a land whose borders are divinely promised, or, alternatively, are the boundaries of Mandatory Palestine, before partition in 1948. The social boundaries of Medinat Yisrael are defined by criteria of objectively defined citizenship; in contrast, those of the collectivity belonging to *Eretz Yisrael* are ascribed via kinship and spill over the geographical borders; they include all Jews everywhere, inside Israel as well as in the Diaspora. In the former, membership is based on a balance of rights and obligations to the state; in the latter, being born a Jew is a necessary and sufficient condition for membership.

B. The Effect of Events Since 1967

Cohen (1985) and Kimmerling (1985) concurred in their reading of events since 1967 as reinforcing the particularistic tendencies in Israeli society.

> The occupation (of the territories of the West Bank and Gaza) . . . exacerbated tensions between the particularistic and universalistic premises of Zionism . . . the particularistic tendency gradually gained the upper hand. This could be seen principally in the growing conviction among many Jewish citizens that the whole of biblical *Eretz Yisrael* belonged to the Jews, to the exclusion of the rights of others; in the settlement of a growing number of Jews in the occupied areas; and in the hardening of the opposition to the return of those areas to Arab sovereignty. (Cohen, 1985: 323)

The other major trend marking a shift in the direction of particularistic tendencies is the rise to power of the *Likud* in 1977. This was the culmination of new trends which had emerged since 1967, and especially since 1973, toward a revival of nationalist feeling and of religious belief and practice. What better expression of the weakening of civil ties could one hope to find than the slogan chanted by Menachem Begin's followers: *Begin, Begin, Melech Yisrael!*— "Begin, Begin, King of Israel!" The phrase is a direct copy of the line *David, David, Melech Yisrael* from a well-known Hebrew song. The phrase was further recycled when Ariel Sharon was the object of debate over his part in the massacres at the Sabra and Shatilla refugee camps in Lebanon—supporters with strong nationalist tendencies shouted *Arik, Arik, Melech Yisrael!* at demonstrations.

C. Research Evidence for the Persistence of Familism in the 1980's

To my knowledge, no empirical study has taken as a central goal the investigation of the nature and extent of familism in Israeli society. There are, however, a number of studies which provide strong indirect evidence of its continued salience.

1. Low social distance between superiors and subordinates. Hofstede (1979) interviewed employees of the same multinational corporation in 39 countries. Employees were asked to say (a) whether their superior had an authoritarian or democratic style of leadership; (b) whether they were afraid to disagree with him or her; (c) which style they themselves preferred. Answers to these questions were combined to create a "power distance" scale. Israel ranked thirty-eighth out of the 39 countries. Thus, in a hierarchical work situation, Israelis experience feelings of considerable closeness to their superiors, despite the difference in formal status.

2. Directness in communication style. Recent sociolinguistic research also points to the importance of in-group solidarity in explaining certain aspects of communication style. Blum-Kulka, Gherson and I (1985) studied the way Israelis word requests: Compare the blunt "Close the door," cast in the imperative, with the indirect, polite "Would you mind closing the door?" or with the still more indirect hint, "Gee, it's cold in here!" Think of a person shopping in a grocery store. Whereas in English the person might say, "Could I have a kilo of coffee, please?" an Israeli might say, with typical directness, *"Ten li kilo kafe"*—"Give me a kilo of coffee." No "please," and a blunt imperative! Such direct forms are used frequently, even among strangers, and are not generally perceived as rude.

Analysis of 500 requests actually made in family, social, and work settings, in person, as well as in writing or on the telephone, revealed that about half the time Israelis choose quite direct forms. Moreover, contrary to what is found in most research on this topic in other countries, the social status of the speaker vis-a-vis the hearer and the degree of acquaintance between them each had only a marginal effect on the choice of request form. Multivariate analysis showed these two variables to be far less important than others, such as the relative ages of the interlocutors (Blum-Kulka, Danet et al., 1985). We interpreted the results to mean that, unlike many countries where politeness requires one to be indirect, in Israeli society directness is positively valued and interpreted as expressing solidarity.

Complementary conclusions emerged from Katriel's (1986) study of *dugriyut* in Israeli society. The term *dugriyut*[12] comes originally from colloquial Arabic, and refers to an ethos of speaking frankly and directly, which Katriel found characteristic of *Sabra*[13] culture (that is, the culture of native-born Jews). Having undergone considerable transformation in the move from Arabic to Hebrew, the term *dugriyut* has come to carry five interrelated clusters of meaning for Sabras: to speak *dugri* is (1) to be sincere; (2) to be natural, simple and spontaneous; (3) to be assertive and active; (4) to express *communitas*—solidarity with others regardless of their place in the day-to-day hierarchy; (5) to give expression to an attitude of devaluation of language and speech, vis-a-vis action—in short, to be pragmatic (Katriel, 1986, chapter 2).

3. Continual reinforcement of solidarity in school, army, and kibbutz. Another study by Katriel, together with her collaborator Nesher, showed how feelings of social solidarity among peers are recreated daily in contemporary Israel. They analyzed the meanings and uses of the term *gibush*—"crystallization" or "consolidation." In school classrooms, in army units, and on kibbutzim talk is heard of *gibush hakvutza*—consolidation or integration of the group. The researchers pointed, for example, to the extreme normative pressure on school children giving parties to invite everyone in the class. Individualistic preferences for smaller gatherings of only personal friends are frowned upon (Katriel and Nesher, 1986).

V. Illegalism

Another aspect of public life in Israel which strongly influences its organizational culture is what Sprinzak (1986) called the trend toward illegalism. Just as universalism and particularism are countervailing trends, so forces pushing for legalism—respect for the rule of law— conflict with those pushing in the direction of illegalism, an instrumental attitude toward law.[14]

Sprinzak defined illegalism as

an orientation which does not view respect for law or respect for the idea of rule of law as a basic value. . . . a form of behavior governed by considerations of utility . . . a citizen or ruler guided by this orientation will not necessarily be hostile to the legal system. . . . Rather, he will be characterized by an instrumental attitude toward law. . . . He will obey the law . . . when it is in his interest to do so—unless there is clear danger of efficient sanction—(and) will ignore it whenever possible. (Sprinzak, 1986: 22)

Sprinzak argued that the rule of law has never been fully institutionalized in Israel and that illegalism is a basic characteristic of
political culture. In such a cultural climate, people break rules without
guilt.

A. Sources of Illegalism

There is considerable consensus among observers of Israeli society
as to the sources of this illegalism. In part it quite obviously derives
from the same sources as familism: the need to close ranks and to
fight for group survival, vis-a-vis hostile persecutors. Sprinzak divided
the phenomenon into three stages: the Yishuv period, during which
illegalism was blatant but the law was someone else's (i.e., British);
the period during which illegalism was in a state of latency; and,
finally, the post-Ben Gurion period of mature illegalism (Sprinzak,
1981; 1986). In support of his thesis, he noted that extremist political
groups have always enjoyed covert support for illegal activities, while
members of the Establishment overtly condemned them. The parallel
with the status of protektzia could not be greater.

Like Sprinzak, Kahane (1984b) and Werner (1983b) saw the roots
of this illegalism in the historical struggle for survival, under circumstances where circumventing the law could literally be a matter
of life and death, and, later on, in the activities of the pioneers
during the Yishuv. Circumvention of British law was patriotically
motivated. The settlers stole guns and building materials, smuggled
in arms and illegal immigrants, and created unauthorized settlements,
all in the name of *hamedina shebaderech,* the state-on-the-way or
in-the-making. The guiding spirit was *litzor uvdot*—a phrase meaning
to "create facts," to hurry up and get things done, solve problems,
making do with resources available, even if the activity had not yet
been, or would not be authorized. In contrast to these altruistically
motivated forms of rule-violation, egoistically motivated ones are
thought to be more common today (cf. Werner, 1983b; Kahane,
1984b; Sprinzak, 1981, 1986).

B. Contemporary Examples of Illegalism

**1. Driver behavior; income tax evasion; padding of hours
worked.** A lack of respect for rules is found in many aspects of
everyday life in Israel. A well-known area of quite blatant violations
is in the behavior of drivers on the road. Both on the highway and
in town, drivers flout the law, frequently taking chances and en-

dangering the lives of others. Second, although self-employed tax payers have long been known to evade paying full income tax, this phenomenon and related ones are now on a scale large enough that Israel is considered to have a flourishing black economy. To take another example, the padding of hours worked is a longstanding practice—superiors of employees working on an hourly basis look the other way as this is done because the hourly wage is often so low that a worker is almost forced to add hours, to make the wage minimally worthwhile.

2. Illegal settlements. Since 1967, zealous nationalist and religious groups have been settling in the West Bank, often without official approval. The settlers have been outspoken in claiming the right to break the law. For instance, consider the following passage from a pamphlet published by *Gush Emunim,* a rightist religious group:

> Throughout the history of settlement we broke the rules of law and order in the struggle for immigration and settlement. We said that these rights have the validity of a Zionist constitution, and every injunction which prevents or limits them is illegal and immoral. Our right to settle in every place in the Land of Israel is a basic Jewish right; it does not end with the rise of the State, and every injunction which limits it is illegal and immoral—it is an obligation to cancel (such injunctions). (Sprinzak, 1986: 125)

3. The Jewish underground. In the 1980's altruistically or ideologically motivated illegal activity even extended to the organization of a Jewish underground in the West Bank. Members were to engage, and, in fact, did engage in acts of counter-terror against Arabs. Although members of the group were eventually prosecuted and sentenced, large proportions of the population were sympathetic to their motives and ideological zeal. Nationalistic groups for whom particularistic loyalties were predominant tended to excuse and even to condone their behavior and once they were convicted, these groups even called for pardons.

4. Illegalism and archaeology. Archaeology happens to be an extremely popular pastime among Israelis. Although there is a law on the books governing the activities of archaeologists, illegal digging and commerce in artifacts are, in fact, widespread. The most dramatic case is that of the archaeological collection of the late Moshe Dayan, which was purchased from his widow by the Israel Museum for the princely sum of $1,000,000, donated by patrons. Dayan was known to have acquired many objects in his collection through illegal excavations. Unable to obtain a license to excavate because he was not professionally trained as an archaeologist (Teveth, 1972), he nevertheless not only regularly dug himself, but even mobilized personnel and equipment available to him in his capacity as Minister of Defense. Moreover, he engaged in illegal sales and trading of archaeological objects. Although the archaeological community was aware of his activities there was never a serious attempt to stop him. When the exhibit of the spectacular collection was opened to the public in April, 1986, professional archaeologists demonstrated outside the Israel Museum, protesting that the museum was making a cultural hero of a person who had stolen booty from the nation.

5. The killing of terrorists after capture and the ensuing cover-up. Still another example of ambivalence about law was the response to the killing of two terrorists after their capture. The two terrorists had captured a bus, in 1984. In the spring of 1986 the then attorney-general, Yizhak Zamir, strongly called for investigation of the circumstances under which they were killed after capture. The issue was not merely who killed the terrorists, but who was party to a cover-up of the murders and just what illegal acts were committed. Politicians, including those holding the highest offices, tried unsuccessfully to suppress investigation of these events. Even though the investigation did eventually take place and ostensibly cleared the then Prime Minister, Yizhak Shamir, and others, public doubts about responsibility for the cover-up were never completely allayed. Moreover, Zamir's position cost him his job as legal adviser to the government.

6. Illegalism and protektzia. All of the instances just surveyed involved violations of formally enacted laws. In contrast, protektzia is merely a violation of administrative regulations, not punishable by law. Still, it is evident that it reflects the same spirit of pragmatism, of ambivalence toward rules, and easy capitulation to the temptation to break them. It is also worth noting that there has never been a serious attempt to eliminate protektzia, and no serious sanctions, even administrative ones, have ever been applied, either to those granting it or to those seeking it. Unlike many Third World countries which occasionally launch campaigns to wipe out corruption, Israel has never once launched a campaign to stamp out protektzia. Is it any wonder, then, that it flourishes?

VI. Summary and Discussion

This chapter has shown that there is a strong prima facie case for viewing Israel as a Type IV society, one in which both objective difficulties in the functioning of public administration and cultural constraints work together to foster behavior which departs from official rules. In chapter 2 I argued that monopoly, scarcity, inefficiency, and rigidity promote rule-violations. Although scarcity may once have been an important factor in Israel, a review of the evidence led to the conclusion that, except for certain specified resources, like beds for geriatric patients, or a prized assignment in the army, or having a telephone installed quickly, Israel is too prosperous a country to be viewed as characterized by scarcity today. As for rigidity, this aspect of the behavior of officials has not been studied, though rigidity is likely to go hand-in-hand with inefficiency. In the next chapter a small bit of evidence from my study will confirm the hunch that the public perceives officials to be more rigid than flexible. It is the conditions of monopoly and near-monopoly in a democracy with an unusually large public sector and of inefficiency which drive Israelis to cut through red tape.

This chapter has argued that on the cultural level, two sets of forces tend to predispose Israelis to break the rules—those of familism and of illegalism. In the Israeli context the two phenomena are related, though familism does not necessarily entail illegalism, nor does illegalism by any means entail familism. Obviously, people may be disposed to break rules in the pursuit of pure personal self-interest, without any concern for the welfare of the group. Similarly, people may have internalized a norm of strong commitment to the group, yet that commitment may not require them to go so far as to break the law.

Evidence is increasing that acts of all kinds which illustrate an instrumental attitude toward law—whether by elected officials, political extremist groups, or ordinary citizens—have proliferated since the Six Day War.[15] In such a climate of permissiveness, protektzia is not likely to weaken or disappear.

In their study of public bureaucracy Nachmias and Rosenbloom (1978) claimed to have found evidence that the role of protektzia had weakened since the 1968 study by Hartman and myself (1972a; 1972b). They asked respondents, among other things, what citizens could do to try to influence public bureaucracy about an unjust regulation. Only 4% of the public said they would look for protektzia and only 2% of the bureaucrats mentioned it. Nachmias and Rosenbloom concluded that "either the norm of impersonality has become even stronger, or . . . both the norm and the actual behavior associated with it have become increasingly congruent and dominant" (Nachmias and Rosenbloom, 1978: 97). Of course, a single question is hardly sufficient to tap Israelis' views of protektzia. And given the opportunity to ask only one, this may not have been the best question to ask. Nachmias and Rosenbloom asked people what they would do about a matter of principle, not one of immediate personal interest. To take any action at all in such a case calls for a high level of public-regardingness. My view is that if researchers want to assess the status of protektzia they must examine what people do *when their own interests are at stake*. To be fair, Nachmias and Rosenbloom did not set for themselves as a major goal of their study the assessment of the status of protektzia, as I did, both in 1968 and in 1980. Whether their claim is to be taken seriously or not, the evidence presented in the next three chapters documents just how well-rooted protektzia continues to be in contemporary Israel.

V

"Using Protektzia is Wrong, But It's O.K. to Need It"

Bicultural Attitudes

If Israelis' professed attitudes about the illegitimacy of using pro-tektzia were a reliable indication, theirs could be thought a highly universalistic culture: Verbal condemnation of the use of personal connections is nearly universal. Similarly, a superficial examination of the effects of education and occupation, at least on some indicators, appears to suggest that well educated persons of high occupational status set the tone for a universalistic organizational culture. Only when actual experience with public bureaucracy and perceptions of its functioning are examined does the other face of the local organizational culture become visible. Although the correlations to be reported in this chapter are not particularly high, in contrast to those reported in the following two chapters, they do reveal a clear pattern. But before I turn to an exposition of this pattern, a few words about the sample are in order.

I. SAMPLE

In chapter I the sample was described only in broad outline as consisting of approximately 1000 Israeli Jews living in the three largest cities. More specifically, 1021 persons residing in these three metropolitan areas were interviewed, using a closed questionnaire, in the summer and fall of 1980. Interviews lasted an average of one and a half hours. Respondents were asked about their experiences in dealings with public and private organizations during the year 1979–80, and about their general orientations toward the functioning of public bureaucracy and various aspects of the use of protektzia. Both the late Naomi Kies and Hadassah Haas participated in the design of the questionnaire and supervised the fieldwork, which was carried out by interviewers of the Israel Institute of Applied Social Research.

The sample was drawn up from residential lists maintained by municipalities for tax purposes. These lists are a viable base from which to draw a sample because most people in Israel own their own apartments, living in condominium arrangements where tenants share expenses for building maintenance. As mentioned earlier in this chapter, most Jewish Israelis live in cities and towns, and most are concentrated in the three largest cities. Thus to sample the population of these cities is in effect to sample the Jewish population. There was a slight tendency toward overrepresentation of women, of persons having post-high school education, and of persons of European origin, but by and large the sample greatly resembled the profile of the Jewish population in 1980.[1]

Residents of development towns and kibbutzim were not included in the sample. No doubt, residents of development towns, who are more likely to be immigrants than those in the big cities, have different experiences and attitudes toward the redress of grievances and how to obtain benefits. Residents of kibbutzim might be particularly efficacious in pursuing redress, or in getting what they want, given the cooperative nature of their living arrangements, which foster a sense of autonomy and control. Limitations of budget unfortunately precluded extending the sample to include these groups. The study did not include the Arab population either, for the reasons outlined in chapter 1. For further details on the construction of the sample, as well as on the creation of empirical indices and statistical methods used in the case study, see Appendix C. The questionnaire is reproduced in Appendix B.

II. OVERT CONDEMNATION
OF PROTEKTZIA

A. General Condemnation of the Use of Protektzia

It is clearly the norm to say that use of personal connections is wrong. Most people believe, or at least go on record as believing, that it is wrong. As in 1968, respondents were asked, "Is it all right to use personal connections in arranging matters in government and public agencies?" Only 11% of those interviewed said that it was always or usually all right. Twenty-two per cent said that it was sometimes all right, or it depended on the circumstances. Another 20% said it was usually wrong, and a high 46%—the modal category chosen among the five offered—said it was never all right to use them. The skewing of the answers toward the negative end of the continuum showed that overt condemnation is by no means luke-warm.

This pattern of strong normative condemnation was already present in 1968, when a virtually identical, low 10% claimed that it was usually or always all right to use protektzia. In a 1974 replication of three questions from the 1968 set, 14% of the sample legitimated its use. The similarity of the three results, for 1968, 1974, and 1980, strongly suggested that overt condemnation of the use of protektzia has become a stable feature of Israel's organizational culture.[2]

B. Increased Homogenization of Attitudes since 1968

Because most of the population rejects the use of personal connections on the normative level, there is, of course, little potential for vari-ation. Still, when data on attitudes are analyzed by ethnic origin and education, a change since 1968 is discernible. At that time, one group had legitimated protektzia somewhat more often than the others; among immigrants of Middle Eastern or North African origin and of low education (8 years or less), 26% had legitimated its use, compared to only 6% to 12% of all other groups, except the poorly educated natives, among whom 18% had legitimated it. In the 1980 study, poorly educated Middle Easterners were no longer culturally distinctive: today, all groups are even more alike than in the past. In other words, there has been a process of homogenization of attitudes, with a range of only 6%–15% of all groups now legitimating protektzia.

C. Residual Influence of Ethnicity

At the same time, there is still a small but discernible residual influence of ethnicity. The normativeness of the Western Europeans lingers even among those born in Israel to parents coming from these countries. Only 8% of natives of Western European origin legitimated protektzia, compared to 17% of native children of natives, and 17% of natives born to Middle Easterners. Among Western

European immigrants, the percentage legitimating protektzia does not rise in the second generation: In both generations the Western Europeans are least likely of all groups to legitimate it. And just as Middle Eastern immigrants are slightly more likely to legitimate it than the other immigrant groups, so Middle Eastern natives are a little more likely to do so than natives born to parents belonging to the other two immigrant groups.

In the 1980 study, no clear trend emerged for the joint effects of ethnic origin and length of residence in Israel, in contradistinction to the finding in the 1968 study that Middle Easterners appeared to become increasingly more universalistic in attitude over time. Although our categories of length of residence may be too crude to justify the following claim, the data suggest that increasingly, the basic distinction is between all natives and all immigrants, wherever they come from—that being born in Israel is what now makes the difference. This is true not only for declared attitudes about protektzia but for a number of other findings to be presented in the following two chapters.

D. Age and the Legitimacy of Protektzia

An unexpected finding was that younger respondents were more likely than older ones to say it was all right to use protektzia. Among those aged 18–29, 14% legitimated its use; thereafter, the proportion dropped off in strict linear fashion, with only 8% of those aged 65 or more doing so. Although the range of percentages is narrow and the value of the Pearson correlation rather low (0.15; see Table V.1), the relationship is statistically significant. This finding, along with a similar relation between age and perceived need for protektzia, to be presented shortly, may seem to suggest that young people simply haven't yet been fully socialized to the U code and will become so in time. When integrated with many other findings, however, these results are consistent not with the social mobilization hypothesis, but with the other part of the grand hypothesis of this study, that exposure to the local culture debureaucratizes people. According to the latter view, young people are more exclusively products of the local culture, particularly if born in Israel.

In contrast to the relative homogeneity of professed attitudes about the legitimacy of protektzia, there is considerable variation in attitudinal measures of other aspects of organizational socialization, as well as socialization to the role of citizen, more generally. This variation tends to follow the pattern predicted by the social mobilization hypothesis.

III. CIVIC AND ORGANIZATIONAL SOCIALIZATION: GENERAL ORIENTATIONS

A. Civic Socialization

1. **Civic knowledgeability.** To tap respondents' knowledge about civic affairs, they were asked to name their mayor, the Minister for Commerce, Industry and Tourism, the Foreign Minister, and the General Secretary of the Histadrut. In addition, they were asked to say how many members there are in the Knesset (120) and to give the date of the most recent national elections (1977). Ninety-two per cent correctly named the mayor of their city; 90% knew the name of the General Secretary of the Histadrut, and the lowest proportion getting the correct answer was that naming the Minister for Commerce, Industry and Tourism (66%). Respondents were assigned a quiz score, summing across the six items, with scores ranging from 0 to 6. The mean score was 4.7, with the modal score the highest possible one of 6 points. These results indicated that Israelis are quite well informed in the public sphere.

In line with the social mobilization hypothesis, a correlation of 0.36 was found between respondents' educational attainments and their scores on this quiz; the corresponding value for occupation was 0.27 (Table V.1). Quiz scores were, in fact, associated with every one of the predictor variables except one—respondents' age. Natives, persons living in relatively spacious apartments,[3] men and secular persons were also particularly well-informed, as expected.

2. **Civic efficacy.** Feelings of civic efficacy were measured by an index based on seven questions taken from the scale developed by Friedmann (1974). The questions were used to tap efficacy vis-a-vis government generally, political parties, bureaucrats and members of Knesset.[4] The results show that Israelis are quite cynical about their ability to influence the system. For instance, more than half (56%) chose the most negative of seven categories, saying that they have no influence on government at all. Low civic efficacy clearly stands in contradiction to the other components of the civic culture and therefore might be taken as a hint that influence attempts will be made via illegitimate means. As a result, contrary to what is found

Table V.1

Aspects of Civic and Organizational Socialization by Respondents' Sociocultural Background[1]

Socialization	Education	Occupation	Length of Residence	Ethnic Origin	Housing Density	Sex	Age	Religiosity
Civic Socialization								
Civic quiz	0.36***	0.27***	0.13***	0.10***	0.13***	0.20***	-0.02	0.08**
Civic efficacy	0.08**	0.06*	0.01	0.06*	0.01	0.02	0.02	-0.08**
Political participation	0.11**	0.13***	0.08**	0.04	0.08**	0.13***	-0.25***	0.04
Organizational Socialization								
Quiz	0.22***	0.17***	0.13***	0.13***	-0.02	0.10***	0.20***	0.02
Clear how officials should perform	0.21***	0.18***	0.04	0.07*	0.05	0.02	0.03	0.02
Frequency of Contact								
Public sector	0.17***	0.14***	0.02	0.02	-0.02	0.10***	0.08**	0.07**
Private sector	0.31***	0.22***	0.10***	0.20***	-0.03	-0.03	0.23***	0.06*

[1] All correlations in this table, as well as throughout chapters 5-7, are Pearson product-moment correlations. The asterisks in this and all tables indicate the standard levels of statistical significance:

*** $p < 0.001$; ** $p < 0.01$; * $p < 0.05$.

in other countries, education is only weakly related to efficacy. As indicated in Table V.1, the correlation is only 0.08 between the two. The corresponding correlation for occupation was also very low (0.06). Natives and religious persons are also slightly more efficacious than immigrants and secular persons, although in step-wise regression analysis the latter variables were eliminated, raising the association between education and efficacy to a still-low 0.10.

3. Political participation. A three-variable index was used to measure intensity of political participation. The three original questions asked were whether respondents had voted in the most recent national elections, and in the local elections which had taken place at the same time, and whether they had been active in public or neighborhood meetings, demonstrations, and the like. Although nearly everyone had voted, only 14% had participated in other political activities. The various predictors in Table V.1 showed only weak positive associations with political activity: educated, high-status people, natives, males, and those in low-density housing are a little more active than their counterparts.

B. Organizational Socialization

1. Knowledgeability. We created factual quizzes to assess general knowledge in the public and private sectors. Public-sector knowledge was measured by questions as to whom should be contacted in each of the following matters: a child support allowance (the National Social Insurance Institute); housing for young couples (Ministry of Housing); sanitation services and collection of rubbish (Municipality); a strange dog that bit a child in the neighborhood (Ministry of Health, police); the price of a regulated item (Ministry of Commerce, Industry and Tourism); unemployment compensation (National Social Insurance Institute). For the private sector, the members of the sample were asked to give the price of each of six items: a liter of milk, a bus ride in the city, a daily afternoon newspaper, standard subsidized bread, a kilo of sugar, a kilo of flour.

People did far better on the public-sector quiz. Nearly all respondents knew where to go for child support payments, sanitation services, and housing for young couples. The problem for which most people lacked information was unemployment compensation— a result, no doubt, of low unemployment in Israel at the time and consequent lack of salience of the issue. As for the private sector, people simply did not know prices in the inflationary economy of

1980. The only item generally known to people was the cost of a bus ride. As with civic quiz scores, those for public-sector knowledge correlated generally with all the independent variables in the manner predicted by the socialization hypothesis. The strongest associations were with education (0.22) and age (0.20). Thus, older, better educated persons are best informed, as expected, and, moreover, natives are better informed than immigrants, and men more than women.

2. **Subjective knowledgeability.** To find out whether Israelis feel knowledgeable, they were asked whether it was clear to them how public officials should perform their jobs. Forty-two per cent chose the first of five categories, claiming that it was absolutely clear to them. And another 39% chose the second category. Thus, Israelis generally felt cognitively competent to deal with bureaucracy. The association between this sense of subjective knowledgeability and the predictor variables again generally echoed the pattern for objective quiz scores, although in the present case it was somewhat weaker on some variables. The correlation with education was 0.21, a value which is virtually identical to that obtained for quiz scores. Similarly, that between scores and respondents' occupation was 0.18. Moreover, people who felt knowledgeable tended also to be knowledgeable: There was a 0.25 correlation between the measures of subjective and objective knowledgeability.

C. Frequency of Contact

Three-fifths of urban Israelis had had at least some contact with government or public bureaucracy in the year preceding the 1980 interview. A quarter had been in some government or other public agency within the preceding month and two-fifths had been in one within the past 3 months.[5] Better educated people of relatively high socio-economic status had more contacts; this was especially so for the private sector (Table V.1).[6] Natives and younger people also had relatively more private-sector contacts than immigrants and older people. Secular people also had more contacts than religious ones, as expected. A step-wise regression analysis was performed, entering all sociocultural variables which had yielded a zero-order correlation of 0.10 or more, confirming that education was the best single predictor of contacts in both sectors. Thus, the predictor variables predict participation in the system, as well as knowledge and attitudes consistent with socialization to the U code.

IV. REWARDS AND COSTS

A variety of findings emerging from the 1980 study illuminate how the reward-cost structure of bureaucratic encounters encourages Israelis to become bicultural. One set of findings has to do with what is usually called system support.

A. System Support

In their conceptualization of the civic culture, Almond and Verba (1965) saw the competent citizen as one who not only possesses the necessary skills to be a constructive participant, but one who has strong positive feelings toward institutions. The 1980 study found that people who otherwise "fill the bill" when it comes to social-psychological modernization are highly critical of the system and hold a large array of beliefs which provide justification for the use of protektzia.

1. General evaluation of officials' performance. The members of the sample were asked, "In your opinion, do most government and public officials do their job the way they are supposed to?" Answers fell into a nearly normal distribution, with 50% in the middle of five categories, 14% in the first two positive ones, and 35% in the last two negative ones. Answers did not vary with respondents' sociocultural background.

2. The image of Israeli bureaucrats. Israeli bureaucrats are perceived as rather benign, perhaps well-meaning, but inefficient and tending to rigidity. As mentioned in chapter 4, Nachmias and Rosenbloom (1978) had investigated the image of Israeli bureaucrats using a set of Semantic Differential Scales. Kies, Haas and I replicated their scales, and added some others of our own. By and large, the results were the same as those obtained by Nachmias and Rosenbloom. The ratings hovered around the middle of the 7-point scale, with a slight worsening since 1973 on 4 out of the 8 items—on the honest/dishonest, strong/weak, brave/cowardly, and speedy/slow scales. The most negative single rating, both in 1973 and in 1980, was on the speedy/slow scale. Among the 4 scales added, the most negative rating went to the flexible/rigid dimension.

Respondents were also asked to rank on a 5-point scale each of 4 aspects of contacts in public bureaucracy—office hours and conditions surrounding contact with the public; the manner of officials;

fairness of treatment; and expertise of officials. The proportions assigning the two lowest categories—"poor" and "very poor"—to the 4 aspects of contact ranged from 19% to 35%, with conditions surrounding encounters rated lowest. A parallel set of questions worded somewhat differently ("To what extent do each of the following constitute a problem for the public?") confirmed this result; nearly three-fifths of the sample said that problems of office hours, long lines, and so forth were frequent and nearly 50% said that the manner of officials was often or always a problem. These ratings of aspects of contact were all related to general evaluations of the performance of officials, but perceptions of the manner of officials were the most strongly related (the correlation was 0.52), another indication of the salience of this aspect of contact in the minds of the public.

B. Is the System Universalistic?

Three different questions tapped perceptions of the universalism of officials. One asked, "There are different ways to arrange matters in government or public agencies. Which of the following ways is best?" Respondents chose between "Knowing the rules and laws and using them," "Using protektzia," and "Threatening and using physical force." Seventy percent chose the universalistic response; 26% said using protektzia was best, and a small 4% said threats were best. Asked whether someone who had no access to protektzia could arrange all his or her affairs without it, 12% said the person could always manage, 30% said she or he could usually do so, 44% said sometimes, or it depends on the situation, 11% said usually not, and a small 3% thought citizens could never manage. Thus, nearly three-fifths thought citizens need protektzia at least sometimes. Asked whether a citizen who was completely within his or her rights would still need protektzia, 9% thought the citizen would always need it and another 23% thought she or he would usually need it. Only one-fifth said he or she would never need it, or not usually. These perceptions of public need for protektzia are so widespread that they are not related to respondents' sociocultural background, though two correlations consistent with the social mobilization hypothesis were found. Better educated people, and persons living in low-density housing were a little more likely to claim that the system can be activated without protektzia; no doubt, both correlations reflect citizens' own competence, more than the adequacy of the system.

Asked why they thought most people used protektzia, the majority chose the first of three answers: (1) "It is possible to arrange the matter without protektzia but it would require more time and trouble;" (2) "It is possible to arrange the matter but the solution would be less good;" (3) "It would be impossible to arrange the matter without it." Just under 50% cited time and trouble; 18% chose the third answer. These results thus supported the view that most use of protektzia is procedural rather than substantive—people use it mainly to speed things up rather than to gain access to resources to which they are not entitled.

C. Personal Experience and Estimation of Public Need for Protektzia

Table V.2 demonstrated that the more often people have personally encountered problems in dealings with public bureaucracy, the more likely they are to believe that the public needs protektzia to cope successfully with the various agencies. The more often people had had problematic encounters, the more likely they were to reject knowing and using the laws and regulations as the best way to do business (-0.32). There was also an association of 0.23 between perceptions of general public need and the tendency for individuals to see themselves as needing protektzia during the past year (see Section D). Weaker correlations were found with other variables: persons having many negative experiences were a little more likely to believe in the effectiveness of threats, to claim that citizens need protektzia even when they are fully within their rights, and to deny that citizens can generally manage without using protektzia.

Table V.2
Estimates of General Public Need for Protektzia and Frequency of Personal Negative Experience

Measures of Public Need

Legitimate channels best	-0.32***
Respondent needed protektzia during the past year[1]	0.23***
Threats are effective[2]	0.14***
Citizens need protektzia even if right	0.11***
Citizens can manage without protektzia	-0.08*

(1) Direct measure.
(2) Composite measure combining six items about perceived effectiveness, worthwhileness of threats in both public and private sectors.
*** $p < 0.001$; ** $p < 0.01$; * $p < 0.05$.

Although personal negative experiences no doubt push people toward illegitimate strategies, the direction of causality may at least in part be in the opposite direction as well: Citizens may rate their experiences more negatively than they deserve, either in their own minds, or vis-a-vis the interviewer, to justify their use of protektzia. Still, the main thrust of these findings is that the use of illegitimate strategies is at least partly a response to a poorly functioning system.

D. Personal Need for Protektzia

Patterns of variation in perceived need for protektzia suggested that these perceptions only partly reflect an objectively difficult reality; they also reflect the influence of cultural factors. We asked, "Did it happen to you during the past year that you were in a situation where you felt you had no choice but to use protektzia to arrange some matter in a government or public agency?" Three hundred and twenty-three persons, or one-third of the total sample, said that this had happened to them. Removing those who had had no contacts from the base increased the estimate to slightly more than half of all those having contacts. It is thus extremely common for people to see themselves as needing protektzia.

1. **The correlates of personal need.** Table V.3 indicates that there is no relation between the chief social mobilization predictors and ostensible need for protektzia, as indexed by answers to the above question: educated people and those in high-status occupations are just as likely to claim to need protektzia as uneducated ones or persons in low-status occupations. Analysis of the data by ethnic origin and immigrant status (not shown in Table V.3) revealed that European immigrants were less likely to see themselves as needing it than either natives or Middle Eastern immigrants—only a quarter of the former claimed to need it, as opposed to 43% of the Middle Eastern immigrants and 46% of the natives. In short, the lingering normativeness of the European immigrants works to suppress perceived need.

Just as the social mobilization predictors—mainly, education and occupation—showed no association with ostensible need for protektzia, so the measures of cognitive socialization were unrelated. Virtually no difference was found between persons scoring high or low on the bureaucratic quiz; knowledgeables were nearly as likely to see themselves as needing to use personal connections as the poorly informed. Moreover, those feeling subjectively knowledgeable were

Table V.3
Predictors of the Tendency to Define Oneself as Needing Protektzia

Predictors	
Sociocultural Background	
Age	0.15***
Length of residence	0.15***
Education	−0.05
Occupation	0.05
Sex	−0.04
Organizational Socialization	
Bureaucratic quiz	-0.06*
Knows how officials should perform	-0.03
Officials perform well	-0.13***
Fairness of officials	-0.18***
Manner of officials	-0.14***
Office hours, etc.	-0.13***
Expertise of officials	−0.10***
Amount and Quality of Contact	
Amount	0.18***
Quality	0.19***
Satisfaction with most recent contact	0.15***

*** $p < 0.001$; ** $p < 0.01$; * $p < 0.05$.

again no more likely to need protektzia than those feeling less knowledgeable (i.e., those saying they do not have a clear idea of how officials are supposed to perform their job).

Perceptions of personal need for protektzia were associated, on the other hand, with two other sets of variables. Table V.3 shows correlations of 0.15 with both age and length of residence in Israel. Examined more closely, the relation with age turns out to be curvilinear, taking the form of a J-curve: just over one-third of all respondents aged 18–29 said they had needed protektzia and 42% of those aged 30–39 did also; thereafter, the proportions dropped off in linear fashion. But the basic difference is between those aged 18–49 and those aged 50 or over. Precisely the same pattern was found for an indirect measure of personal need (the data in Table V.3 are all based on the direct measure).[7] As for the effects of seniority, a 4-way breakdown (natives, pre-1948 arrivals, those arriving 1948–1954, those arriving 1955 or later) showed that, as with age, the main difference is between one group—in this case the natives—and all the others. The data for both the direct and indirect measures of personal need revealed natives to be more likely than immigrants to need protektzia.

The effects of age and nativity are cumulative: the highest proportion of persons defining themselves as needing protektzia was found among natives aged 18–49 (47%), whereas immigrants aged 50 or more are least likely to see themselves as in need of protektzia (only 26%). Although the effect of age alone could reflect need to become established in young to middle-adult years, and consequently, greater contacts, generally, there is no reason to assume that natives have more contacts than immigrants: On the contrary, it is the immigrants who have to become established. At least in the case of age, the correlation with need for protektzia could be a spurious effect of frequency of contact or of negative experience.

In fact, however, the associations between age and nativity and need for protektzia held up even when amount and quality of contacts were held constant. Regardless of frequency of contacts, natives were more likely to define themselves as needing protektzia than immigrants, and, similarly, younger people were more likely to do so than older ones. Thus, frequency of contact cannot alone account for the ostensible need for protektzia among younger people. Another important result is that frequency of contacts makes less of a difference for natives than for immigrants, and the same holds true for the two age groups. Finally, natives and younger people are more likely to claim to need protektzia regardless of whether their experiences have been entirely positive or at least partially negative. The import of these findings is that natives and younger people are definitely less influenced by objective constraints deriving from the quality of service than their counterpart groups. The findings therefore confirmed that the groups most exposed to local ways are responding to the implicit norm that it is all right to use protektzia, and not merely to the objective character of their experiences.

A second set of findings shown in Table V.3 indicated that negative evaluations of the functioning of public bureaucracy, especially of the fairness of officials, as well as the amount and quality of personal experiences are related to self-defined need. The more contacts people had had, the more likely they were to say that they needed protektzia. And the more often they encountered problems in these contacts, the greater the probability that they would do so. Finally, the less satisfied they were with their most recent contact, the more likely they were, again, to see themselves as needing protektzia.[8]

2. 1968 and 1980 compared. Has the effect of negative experience on need strengthened with the years? Or, on the contrary, do people need less of an excuse to allow themselves to need protektzia? Table V.4 addresses this question using the indirect measure of need, the only one available for both 1968 and 1980, unfortunately.[9] In 1968, according to this measure, 40% of those having had only positive contacts nevertheless saw themselves as needing protektzia at some point during the past year, whereas a higher 61% of those reporting at least one negative contact did so. Thus, already in 1968, self-defined need was not wholly a response to ostensible objective difficulties—to reiterate, even among those reporting no negative contacts, 4 out of 10 persons having contacts nevertheless indicated needing protektzia.

In the 1980 data the relationship reappeared, but with the difference that both groups had, in the meantime, risen in need for protektzia. Among those with only positive experiences, the rate of self-defined need was now 58%, as opposed to 40% in 1968, a rise of 18%. And among those with negative experiences the proportion had risen from 61% to 72%, a difference of 11%. The difference between positive and negative groups in 1968 was 21%. in 1980 it was only 14%. Both the general rise in self-defined need and the weakened association with quality of contacts supported the interpretation of widespread, and even increased, permissiveness about needing protektzia.

V. BICULTURALISM AND ATTITUDES ABOUT REDRESS

Findings on the attitudinal aspects of redress follow the general pattern I have been describing in the preceding pages. The social

Table V.4
Personal Need for Protektzia by Quality of Contact, in 1968 and in 1980 (indirect measure, percentages)[1]

	Quality of Contact		
Year	Positive	Negative	Difference
1968	40 (300)	61 (615)	+21%
1980	58 (226)	72 (337)	+14%
Difference	+18%	+11%	

[1] See footnote 7.

mobilization predictors once again showed correlations with cognitive aspects of socialization.

A. Knowledge of Channels of Redress

1. General levels of knowledge. Interviewees were presented with lists of 12 channels of redress for the public sector, and of 10 for the private one. The two lists overlapped somewhat (see Table V.5 below). An indirect index of familiarity was built from a question whose main purpose had been to learn whether respondents had used each channel and how effective they perceived it to be, whether they had used it or not. On the assumption that willingness to express an opinion generally presupposes familiarity, the data were dichotomized into the two categories "expresses opinion" and "doesn't know." In addition to these two indirect measures of knowledge of channels in the two sectors, answers were elicited to a series of direct questions about five channels, the ombudsman, "Kolbotek"—the television program which processes complaints—a consumer organization, small claims court, and the Citizens' Advice Bureau. On the whole, people claimed to be familiar with these channels. For instance, on a direct question, three-quarters indicated that they were familiar with the ombudsman and as many as 96% knew about "Kolbotek." Sixty percent knew about small claims courts; least familiar was the Citizens' Advice Bureau (only 54% knew about it).

2. The correlates of knowledge of channels.

(a) Sociocultural background. Not surprisingly, education was the best predictor among background variables of knowledge of channels (Table V.5), although a number of other characteristics of respondents were also associated with knowledge. Thus, men knew more channels than women and secular persons were familiar with more channels than religious ones. Almost without exception, the direct measures of familiarity with channels worked better than the indirect ones. In some cases, only on the former were additional associations found; thus, at least on the direct measure, the longer people had been in the country and the older they were, the better informed they were.

(b) Frequency of contact. People who had had many contacts in each sector were predictably more likely to know about channels. The effect is sharper for private-sector contacts than for public-sector ones. People reporting many contacts as consumers were somewhat

Table V.5
Familiarity with Channels of Complaint, by Sociocultural Background,
Frequency of Contact, and Civic and Organizational Socialization

Predictors	Public Sector Indirect Measure	Private Sector Indirect Measure	Both Sectors Direct Measure
Sociocultural Background			
Education	0.13***	0.10***	0.28***
Occupation	0.06*	0.07*	0.19***
Ethnic origin	0.08**	0.02	0.14***
Length of residence	0.03	-0.01	0.14***
Religiosity	0.12***	0.12***	0.11***
Age	0.03	0.03	0.09***
Sex	0.08**	0.08**	0.06*
Housing density	-0.06*	0.03	-0.02
Frequency of Contact			
Public Sector	0.06*	0.06*	0.10***
Private Sector	0.16***	0.14***	0.27***
Civic and Organizational Socialization			
Civic knowledge quiz	0.18***	0.15***	0.35***
Civic efficacy	-0.07*	-0.05	0.00
Political participation	0.06*	0.06*	0.13***
Bureaucratic quiz	0.11***	0.07**	0.30***
Clear how officials should perform	0.16***	0.12***	0.22***

*** $p < 0.001$; ** $p < 0.01$; * $p < 0.05$.

better informed on all channels of redress, in the public as well as the private sectors.

(c) Civic and organizational socialization. People who were knowledgeable about public affairs were also knowledgeable about channels of complaint (the correlations are 0.18, 0.15, and 0.35 for public-indirect, private-indirect, and combined-direct indices, respectively). The politically active are also a little more knowledgeable. The intercorrelation among various aspects of cognitive competence was once again revealed in the association between scores on the bureaucratic quiz and knowledge of channels; the correlation between

bureaucratic quiz scores and the direct measure of familiarity with five channels was 0.30. Subjective feelings of knowledgeability about public bureaucracy (knowing how officials are supposed to perform) followed the same pattern, once again yielding the highest correlation with the direct measure—0.22.

(d) Multivariate analysis. Step-wise regression analysis further identified the best predictors of familiarity with channels of complaint. As is made clear in Table V.6, the single best predictor, on all three measures, is civic knowledge, as tapped by the 6-item quiz. Amount of private-sector contact consistently fell into second place (I take consumer activity to be an indirect index of SES, and hence this result is consistent with the social mobilization hypothesis). The measure of general subjective knowledgeability in public bureaucracy remained important in 2 of the 3 tests; it ranked third as a predictor of public-sector knowledge of channels, and fourth on the private-sector measure, dropping out, however, when the preferred direct measure of familiarity was used. It is intriguing that religiosity remained important, at least in 2 of the 3 multivariate analyses. Thus, being a secular person contributed a small but significant amount to the variance in knowledge of channels, at least on the two indirect measures. But the more important result of this multivariate analysis was the solid multiple correlation of 0.44 obtained in the step-wise regression analysis of familiarity with channels, using the direct measure.

B. Subjective Knowledgeability

1. Knowledgeability in 1968 and in 1980. Thus far, I have emphasized objective knowledgeability about redress. We had also asked, "Do you generally know to whom to turn in order to complain about inappropriate or unpleasant treatment on the part of officials in government or public agencies?" Fourteen percent claimed they always know to whom to turn; another 28% said they generally know. Nineteen percent said they sometimes know; 21% reported they usually didn't know, and 17% never knew to whom to turn. This distribution of feelings of subjective knowledgeability is almost identical to that obtained in 1968.[10]

2. Predictors of subjective knowledgeability. The sense of subjective knowledgeability was found to be associated with a remarkably large

Table V.6
Predictors of Familiarity with Channels of Complaint: Step-Wise Regressions

	Simple r	Multiple r
*Familiarity with Channels, Public Sector**		
Civic knowledge	0.180	0.180
Frequency of contact private sector	−0.172	0.226
Clear how officials should perform	0.164	0.250
Religiosity	−0.110	0.266
*Familiarity with Channels, Private Sector**		
Civic knowledge	0.154	0.154
Frequency of contact, private sector	0.143	0.190
Religiosity	−0.115	0.213
Clear how officials should perform	0.116	0.224
*Familiarity with Channels, Public and Private Sectors Combined***		
Civic knowledge	0.348	0.348
Frequency of contact, private sector	0.266	0.399
Bureaucratic knowledge	0.296	0.427
Education	0.281	0.444

* Indirect measure
** Direct Measure

number of predictor variables. Among background characteristics of respondents, educational, and occupational attainments once again yielded the best correlations (0.25 and 0.23, respectively; see Table V.7). Men felt more knowledgeable than women. Again, people scoring high on the civic and bureaucratic quizzes were especially likely to feel knowledgeable about the possibilities of redress. The values of the correlations were 0.32 and 0.24 for the two quizzes. And general subjective competence (as indexed by the question whether it is clear how officials are supposed to do their jobs) was also associated with feelings of knowledgeability about redress (the correlation in this case is 0.25).

Finally, all three measures of claimed knowledge of specific channels were correlated with subjective feelings of knowledgeability about channels generally. And once again the correlation was strongest for the direct measure (0.29). Step-wise regression analysis identified civic knowledge quiz scores as the single best predictor, accounting for 10% of the variance. Scores on the direct measure of familiarity with channels were second in importance and general feelings of subjective competence were third; the three predictors together yielded a mutiple correlation of 0.41.

Table V.7
Predictors of Subjective Knowledgeability about Channels of Complaint

Predictors	Correlation
Sociocultural Background	
Education	0.25***
Occupation	0.23***
Sex	0.12***
Frequency of Contact	
Public sector	0.12***
Civic Socialization	
Civic quiz score	0.32***
Efficacy	0.10***
Political participation	0.07**
Organizational Socialization	
Bureaucratic quiz score	0.24***
Clear how officials should perform	0.25***
Officials perform properly	0.10***
Can manage without protektzia	0.13***
Familiarity with public channels—indirect measure	0.17***
Familiarity with private channels—indirect measure	0.13***
Familiarity with channels—combined direct measure	0.29***

*** $p < 0.001$; ** $p < 0.01$; * $p < 0.05$.

C. Positive Orientations toward Complainants and the Act of Complaining

1. The right to complain. Israelis claim to have a generally positive orientation both toward people who complain through formal channels and toward the act of complaining itself. Respondents were asked, first of all, "Do you feel that you have a right to complain in every instance that in your opinion you were treated unjustly by a government or public agency?" Just under three-fifths said they always have a right to complain and another 20% said they generally did.

2. The efficacy of complaining in the public and private sectors. Asked to what extent it helps to complain about problems encountered in each sector, sizable numbers gave positive replies in both cases. Thus, only 30% thought it was not helpful or not at all helpful to complain in the public sector and a still lower 16% chose these categories for the private sector. In line with the hypothesis that the client is stronger in the private sector, because of bargaining power—

the ability to take business elsewhere—a higher proportion thought it would be very helpful or helpful to complain in the private sector. Fifty-three percent chose these two categories when asked about the private sector, as compared to only 30% choosing them to estimate the efficacy of complaining in the public sector.

3. Perceptions of complainants. Five questions were used to probe attitudes toward complainants; here, too, the answers revealed a generally favorable orientation. For instance, only 18% agreed with the statement that, "People who complain are 'nudniks' who are never satisfied," and only 4% thought that "People who complain are people who want to destroy society." Four-fifths agreed that "People who complain are constructive citizens who care, who want to make things better."

4. The responsiveness of officials. In contrast to these favorable orientations, attitudes about the responsiveness of officials were quite another matter. Only a little more than one-third of the sample felt that officials generally pay attention to complaints and investigate them. A little under one-third actually believed that officials usually or always ignore complaints. Less than one-fifth believed that they "treat complainants with respect, and with appreciation for their display of good citizenship." Still, Israelis are not intimidated by officials: only one-tenth agreed that officials tell complainants that it is not in their interest to complain. These results suggested not a Kafkaesque bureaucracy which strikes terror in the hearts of citizens, but—consistent with findings presented earlier—an indifferent, inefficient one.

D. Perceptions of the Effectiveness of Channels of Complaint

I mentioned earlier that respondents were presented with lists of 12 channels of complaint in the public sector and 10 in the private one. They were asked to rate the likely effectiveness of each channel, on a scale from 1 to 3. The results are displayed in Table V.8. The first five channels were asked about in connection with both sectors; the next seven pertained only to the public sector, and finally, the last five pertained only to the private sector.

The main finding shown in Table V.8 is that particularistic channels are perceived to compete with universalistic ones. Although the television program received the highest ratings within each sector,

Table V.8
Perceived Effectiveness of Seventeen Channels of Redress in the Public and Private Sectors (percent "very helpful")*

Channel	Public	Private
TV program	76.5 (912)	65.6 (876)
Newspaper	40.2 (883)	28.6 (849)
Lawyer	39.3 (883)	29.8 (778)
Higher official	30.5 (875)	25.8 (850)
Threats	15.3 (801)	7.0 (759)
Personal connections	66.7 (893)	—
Ombudsman	32.9 (697)	—
Trade union	25.7 (758)	—
Prime Minister, Minister	20.7 (773)	—
Knesset Member	17.1 (780)	—
Public pressure	16.2 (803)	—
Political party	11.5 (712)	—
Small claims court	—	30.5 (702)
Consumer organization	—	22.9 (725)
Negative publicity	—	20.0 (768)
Seller	—	19.0 (886)
Organization representing seller	—	17.7 (722)

* N's vary because those not familiar with each channel have been excluded.

personal connections were perceived to be almost as effective (77% versus 67% choosing the category "very helpful").

1. Public sector. Israelis believe that among public channels, only the television program can compete with protektzia as an effective way to obtain what one wants. Just over three-quarters of the sample said it would be very helpful to contact this program, whereas two-thirds said that protektzia would be very helpful (Table V.8). All other public-sector channels received far lower marks: for example, only 30% to 40% believed that the other media, a lawyer, the ombudsman or simply appealing to a higher official would be very helpful. One-quarter thought appealing to the trade union is effective and one-fifth believed in contacting a government Minister or the Prime Minister. Slightly fewer people believed in the effectiveness of public pressure, like circulating a petition or organizing a demonstration. Note the high 15% who thought threats are effective. Turning to the political party was least highly evaluated. In Chapter 8 I will show that there are considerable gaps between these general public guesses as to the effectiveness of complaint channels and the experiences of those who had actually used them.

2. Private sector. The data for the private sector showed that again the television program is rated highest. Other media ombudsmen come second (with a considerable drop from 65% "very helpful" for "Kolbotek" to 29% for the other media). Lawyers are ranked somewhat lower for private-sector problems than for public-sector ones. Small claims courts received similar ratings (31% "very helpful"). Appealing to an organization representing the seller, spreading negative publicity, or going to a consumer organization or to a higher official were rated highly by only about one-fifth of the sample. Threats were again close to the bottom of the ranks, with 7% believing in them.

3. Sociocultural background and the effectiveness of threats. For the most part, perceived effectiveness of specific complaints channels did not vary with the sociocultural background of respondents. One exception was a finding of small but consistent ethnic differences in the belief in illegitimate threats. In the private sector, native children of natives were twice as likely to express support for threats as the other groups, although the actual size of the percentages is quite small (13% versus 6% to 7% for all other groups). Similarly, 21% of native children of natives affirmed the use of threats in the public sector, compared to 13% to 16% of all other groups. These results mirrored those indicating that protektzia is the province not of the marginal or the alienated, but of those most integrated into the society.[11]

4. Effectiveness of channel types. In Table V.9 the data from Table V.8 have been rearranged according to the typology of motivational bases presented in chapter 3. It is evident that Israelis believe that the best way to get justice, or at least to get what they want in the public sector, is to use some form of legitimized threat. The media are perceived as more powerful than legal means, primarily because of the extraordinarily high rating given to the television program. Note also the extremely low rating given to public pressure, a find which reflected the lack of a strong tradition of spontaneous voluntary association in Israel. On the average, the activation of non-U norms in the various forms of patronage and brokerage is believed to be about as effective as the appeal to U norms (higher official, ombudsman), but unspecified, apparently symmetrically based protektzia clearly stands out as more effective than the asymmetrically based ones asked about.[12]

Table V.9
Perceived Effectiveness of Channels of Redress in the Public and Private Sectors, by Power Base, Legitimacy, and Institutionalization

A. *Public Sector*		Average percent "very helpful"
Legitimate institutionalized norms		
Higher official	(30.5)	
Ombudsman	(32.9)	31.7
Legitimate institutionalized threats		
Media	(58.4)	
Legal	(39.3)	52.0
Legitimate spontaneous threats		
Public pressure	(16.2)	16.2
Illegitimate institutionalized norms		
Unspecified protektzia	(66.7)	
Personalized political brokerage	(18.9)	28.3
Organizational brokerage	(18.6)	
Illegitimate spontaneous threats		
Threats of physical force	(15.3)	15.3
B. *Private Sector*		
Legitimate institutionalized norms		
Seller	(19.0)	
Higher official	(25.8)	
Organization representing seller	(17.7)	20.8
Consumer organization	22.9)	
Legitimate institutionalized threats		
Media	(47.1)	
Legal	(30.2)	35.5
Legitimate spontaneous threats		
Negative publicity	(20.0)	20.0
Illegitimate spontaneous threats		
Threats of physical force	(7.0)	7.0

The data on the private sector in Table V.9 suggested that Israelis feel rather inefficacious vis-a-vis the private sector, too. Although legitimate institutionalized threats were once again rated most highly, an average figure of 36% does not appear to be very high at all. This result echoed one from an early pilot study of persuasive appeals in organizations (Katz and Danet, 1966). Katz and I had found that in a situation of appealing to a bank manager for a loan, people chose altruistic appeals ("I need the money badly") at an unexpectedly high rate, preferring them either to activation of a norm of reciprocity ("I have been a customer of this bank for twenty years") or either inducements or threats ("I will have my son open an account;" "If you don't grant the request, I'll transfer my account to another bank"). What we wrote then of these results may apply equally well to the private sector generally, even 20 years after that study was conducted:

Retrospectively, it seems likely that we have overrated the power of the client vis-à-vis the . . . Israeli bank. The reality of the Israeli situation is such that the client's power to bargain with the bank is probably quite limited. The existence of tight controls on credit makes it rather less likely than we originally thought for a client to take his business elsewhere. Indeed, it appears that clients perceived the bank as having a large amount of power and perceive themselves as relatively limited in their ability to bargain. (Katz and Danet, 1966: 187)

VI. PERCEPTIONS OF THE BEHAVIOR OF OTHERS

The second of the three social-psychological factors hypothesized in chapter 3 to predict behavior in hybrid organizational cultures was individuals' perceptions of the behavior of others. For purposes of prediction of patterns of behavior in Israel, all that is needed in this chapter is to document that most Israelis think that most people use protektzia.

The members of the 1980 sample were asked, "In your opinion, do most people in Israel seek out protektzia when they need to arrange something in a government or public agency?" A very high 70% thought most people always or usually look for protektzia. One-quarter thought most people do this sometimes, or said that "It depends on the situation." Only a tiny 6% said most people either never look for protektzia or do not usually do so. These figures were virtually identical with those obtained in 1968. Thus, another stable

feature of organizational culture in Israel—like the avowed illegitimacy of protektzia—is the widespread belief that "Everybody does
it."

These perceptions were totally unrelated to respondents' education
or occupation, or, for that matter, to any of the other sociocultural
background variables, with one minor exception. People over 65
were less likely than the other age groups to think that use of
protektzia is common. This no doubt reflects the lesser involvement
of older people in public life—some of them have gotten out of
touch with what goes on. In short, assessments of what goes on in
the real world have nothing to do with socialization to the U code—
those who have a good command of it are just as likely as those
who do not to believe that use of protektzia is widespread.

VII. Summary and Discussion

The findings of this chapter demonstrate unequivocally that Israelis
are strongly bicultural in their orientations. They are reasonably well-
informed, at least about the basic kinds of matters tapped by the
public-sector and civic indexes. They claim familiarity with the array
of universalistic channels of redress that are available and claim to
feel knowledgeable about them. A number of findings illustrated the
common maxim that "Knowledge is power." Those who are well
informed also feel knowledgeable subjectively.

Israelis are positively oriented toward the possibility of complaining
about injustice or poor service. But they also have reservations about
the efficacy of U channels. The fact that protektzia was rated more
effective than any other channel suggests that U channels must
compete for clients with the interpersonal networks that Israelis
mobilize when the route to some desired benefit is blocked.

One of the most important findings of this chapter was the mass
of evidence, on the one hand, for the belief that people must resort
to protektzia, at least some of the time, and yet, on the other hand,
the firm rejection of protektzia on the normative level. Thus, the
phenomenon of formalism (Riggs, 1964), already identified in the
1968 study, is firmly rooted in the local organizational culture and
has probably become a permanent feature of it.

In this chapter the ground-work has been laid for analysis of
patterns of organizational behavior. I have shown that social mobilization variables predict socialization to the U code, and that, at
the same time, at least 2 of the 3 sets of social-psychological variables

predisposing individuals to P behavior are amply present—cynical assessments of the rewards to be gained by staying within the U code and widespread perceptions that everyone uses protektzia. The third social-psychological factor discussed in chapter 3 was control of pertinent resources, especially the perception that such resources are available and may be mobilized. The critical resource in the Israeli context is access to key persons who can motivate officials to circumvent official regulations. Because patterns of variation in perceived access to protektzia greatly resemble those for actual use of it, I have delayed presentation of them until the next chapter. I will examine evidence suggesting that reported access to critical networks, like perceptions of personal need for protektzia, is not simply a report of an objective state of things. Rather, at least some of the findings suggested that—like perceptions of need for protektzia—reports of access are also affected by the prevailing cultural climate and by past organizational socialization in citizens' country of origin.

As for actual use of personal connections, it is obvious that asking people about their actions is by no means the best way to find out about them, especially if their actions are by their own declared criteria deviant. Still, although some people may have hesitated to speak frankly about their use of particularistic ties in organizational encounters, enough people evidently did so that this study yielded a remarkably rich set of findings on actual use of protektzia and how it relates to other aspects of organizational encounters. It is time to turn to chapter VI.

VI
Protektzia and Social Integration

The current mayor of Tel Aviv, Shlomo Lahat, affectionately known as "Chich," is reputed to have remarked, *"B'drom Tel Aviv merimim kisaot; b'tsfon Tel Aviv merimim telefon."* Literally, this sentence means, "In south Tel Aviv they lift/pick up chairs; in north Tel Aviv they lift/pick up the telephone." *L'harim*—to lift or pick up—is used idiomatically in both halves of the sentence. In Hebrew, *l'harim kisei,* literally, to pick up a chair, means to threaten— *l'harim yad* is to raise the hand to strike, or more directly, to strike. The message should be clear enough: In southern Tel Aviv there are large concentrations of relatively poor Jews of Sephardic, or Middle Eastern and North African origin; north Tel Aviv is a bastion of well-heeled Ashkenazic, or European old-timers and natives. In this chapter I will show that it is indeed people like those living in north Tel Aviv who most often pick up the telephone to circumvent official arrangements. At the same time, large numbers of all social groups in Israel do so.

I. ACCESS TO, AND USE OF PROTEKTZIA: ESTIMATES OF GENERAL INCIDENCE

A. Access

To tap access to protektzia, following the question about need for protektzia ("Did it ever happen to you during the past year that you felt you had no choice but to use protektzia to arrange some matter?"), respondents were asked, "Did you have someone you could approach to ask for protektzia?" Three hundred and fifty-four people claimed they had access, or 37% of the general sample (see Table VI.1). This proportion rose to 57% when those who had had no contact with public bureaucracies were removed from the data.[1]

How do these results compare with those for 1968? Unfortunately, because this direct question about access was not asked in 1968, comparison is possible only via a less satisfactory indirect measure, based on answers to the basic question about use of protektzia in routine encounters. Respondents were asked, in both years, "Did it happen during the past year that you sought protektzia from someone, in order to arrange some matter in a government or public agency, on your own behalf or on behalf of friends or family?" Apart from three categories of intensity of use ("many times," "a few times," "once or twice," those not having used protektzia could choose from three reasons for not having done so: "No, because I didn't need it;" "No, because I didn't want to ask for protektzia," and "No, because I didn't have anyone to approach." Just as the data on this question were rearranged to create an indirect index of need for protektzia,[2] so they were regrouped in still another way to tap access. First, those who said they hadn't needed protektzia were removed, because they were unclassifiable as to access; then the remaining persons were dichotomized—those saying they did not have anyone to approach versus all the others.

According to this indirect measure, the proportion of the population claiming access rose considerably, from 40% in 1968 to 64% in 1980 (Table VI.1). Generally, then, people are more likely to claim access to personal connections today than in the past.

Table VI.1
Access to and Use of Protektzia in 1968 and in 1980

Access and Use	1968 (N=1886)	1980 (N=1021)
Access: percent having access		
a) Direct measure	—	34.7%
b) Indirect measure	40.0%	64.0%
Use: percent using at least once		
a) General sample	20.0%	23.3%
b) Those having contact	37.8%	38.1%
c) Those having need, access	69.1%	59.3%

B. Use of Protektzia

As is demonstrated in Table VI.1, at least one-fifth of all Israelis admit to using protektzia in routine bureaucratic encounters. The measure of use is a simple dichotomy of answers to the question about use: All those using personal connections at least once, versus those saying they hadn't used them, whatever the reason. There is little difference between the two time periods; the figures are 20% for 1968 and 23.3% for 1980 (Table VI.1).

These are, of course, low first estimates. For one thing, the percentages rose dramatically when contact and need were held constant. In both years, the proportion using personal connections nearly doubled when persons having had no contacts were removed. And when the base was further narrowed to those having contacts, needing protektzia, and reporting access, the proportions rose still further, in 1968 to 70% and in 1980 to 60%. Despite the ostensible 10% drop in use since 1968, the basic finding, then, is that *given the opportunity, most people use protektzia.*[3]

Actually, even these more precise estimates are in all likelihood too low. First of all, if the general norm is to say that using protektzia is wrong, some persons, especially those of Western European and Anglo-Saxon origin, will probably not admit to having used it. Second, it is reasonable to assume that for many persons using protektzia is so much the normal, habitual way of arranging things that they do not even think of their behavior as using it. Third, in these figures no account is taken of multiple use by individuals.

The fact that about one-fifth of the sample admitted to using protektzia, whereas only one-tenth legitimated it (chapter 5) means, quite obviously, that many people are living with inconsistency between their attitudes and behavior. Later in the chapter I will look at findings which identify these persons and elucidate the sources of their hybridization. But let us begin with a more basic question: Who are the people who routinely use protektzia? How do they come to join the delinquent community (Pitts, 1963; see chapter 3)? What leads them to become bicultural in their behavior?

II. SOCIAL-PSYCHOLOGICAL PREDICTORS OF USE

To review the grand hypothesis of this study, I have predicted that although social mobilization variables predict U attitudes, they do not predict U behavior, but that, rather, perceptions of (1) the reward-cost structure of the situation; (2) the behavior of others; and (3) control of pertinent resources will predict P behavior. The Israeli data conform to the prediction quite well, although some variables are far more important than others.

A. Perceptions of the Reward-Cost Structure of the Situation

Although three measures of perceptions of the reward-cost structure yielded roughly similar low, positive correlations with actual use of protektzia, a fourth proved far more successful in predicting it (Table VI.2). People who rejected the proposition that legitimate channels are the best way to arrange personal affairs were a little more likely to have used protektzia themselves (the correlation is −0.15). Second, those who claimed that even if citizens are entirely within their rights, they still need protektzia were a little more likely to have done so than people who are more sanguine about the official system (this correlation is 0.14). Finally, the more problems people have encountered in the past (the measure called "quality of contacts" in Table VI.2), the more likely they were to have used protektzia, although this correlation too is quite low—only 0.14.

The fourth measure, that of perceived personal need for protektzia, is quite another matter. People who see themselves as needing protektzia are extremely likely to have used it. Individuals were

Table VI.2
Predictors of the Use of Protektzia (general sample)

Predictors	
Perceptions of Reward-Cost Structure	
Legitimate channels best	−0.15***
Even if right need protektzia	0.14***
Quality of contacts	0.14***
Personal need for protektzia	0.47***
Perceptions of Behavior of Others	0.12***
Perceived Access to Protektzia	0.52***
Legitimacy of Using Protektzia	0.16***
Sociocultural Background	
Age	0.18***
Generation	0.16***
Length of residence	0.17***

*** $p < 0.001$; ** $p < 0.01$; * $p < 0.05$.

asked whether they had found themselves in a situation where they
felt they had no choice but to use protektzia (see chapter 5). Answers
to this question correlated at the level of 0.47 with actual use. I
showed in chapter 5 that these perceptions of need are influenced
by a climate of permissiveness—that they are not simply a subjective
report of an objective state of things.

B. Perceptions of the Behavior of Others

What of the belief that "everyone does it?" Does it, too, predict use
of protektzia? Only to a degree: The measure of perceptions of the
behavior of others yielded a low but statistically significant correlation
of (0.12; Table VI.2). Those believing that most people use protektzia
all or most of the time were a little more likely to admit having
used it themselves. The correlation turned out to be low because
the belief that everyone uses it is so widespread—we saw in chapter
5 that about two-thirds of the sample thought most people use it
most or all of the time.

C. Control of Resources: Access to Protektzia

The single best predictor of actual use of protektzia is the measure
of whether individuals had access. Answers to the direct question
about access ("Did you have someone to approach?") produced the
highest correlation with actual use of any variable in the study.
Thus, people who say they had someone to ask for help in time of
need are extremely likely to go ahead and mobilize that person or
persons. The correlation is a striking 0.52 (Table VI.2), a little higher
even than that for perceived need for protektzia, which is 0.47. Thus,
knowing whether or not a person claimed access to brokers who
could intervene in a bureaucratic decision enables us to predict
correctly in 27% of the cases that that person will in fact use
protektzia.

D. The Legitimacy of Protektzia.

In line with the grand hypothesis that social mobilization variables
predict attitudes but not behavior, little or no correlation should be
found between people's attitudes as to whether using protektzia is
legitimate and whether they admit using it. In fact, as is indicated
in Table VI.2, the correlation is a low but positive 0.16. This
correlation means that people who go on record as believing pro-

tektzia legitimate were a little more likely to have used it, and conversely, those who say it is not legitimate were a little less likely to have used it. But the fact that the correlation is so low shows that (1) many people who said it is wrong nevertheless admitted to having used it, and that (2) most of those having used it are living with inconsistency between their attitudes and behavior.

III. WHO HAS ACCESS TO PROTEKTZIA?

If perceived access to protektzia is the best predictor of actual use of it, the next question is: Who, then, has access? How great an advantage is it, in an immigrant society, to be a native? How much of a disadvantage is it to be a Jew of Middle Eastern or North African origin? Do differences disappear in the second generation? How rapidly does access grow with increased number of years lived in the country? How much of an advantage do old-timers have over newcomers? How does education interact with these variables?

The distribution of access is highly skewed and mirrors other aspects of stratification in Israeli society. At the same time, we will see that even among the "have-nots," sizable numbers reported access. In my view this is because sometimes it is an advantage to know the people at the bottom, or to be able to influence them, rather than those at the top, and less well integrated people are more likely to know people at the bottom than are the better integrated. But I am getting ahead of my story. I begin with the general distribution of access in the sample.

A. Sociocultural Background: The Importance of Education and Occupation

Most sociocultural characteristics of respondents investigated are related to access, but primarily their education and occupation—the same two variables which best predict mobilization to U values.

The better educated one is, and the more prestigious and high-paying one's occupation, the more likely a person was to report access (Table VI.3; the respective correlations are 0.26 and 0.21). There are weaker but nevertheless statistically significant effects for length of residence, ethnic origin, age, and—to introduce a variable not previously discussed—generation, i.e., first, second or third generation in the country. The results therefore confirmed that the "haves" by other criteria—those who are best integrated because they were born in Israel or came to the country a long time ago,

Table VI.3
Predictors of Access to Protektzia (total sample, direct measure)

Predictors	
Sociocultural Background	
Education	0.26***
Occupation	0.21***
Length of residence	0.18***
Ethnic origin	0.12***
Generation	0.08**
Age	0.08**
Civic and Organizational Socialization	
Knows to whom to complain	0.17***
Bureaucratic knowledge quiz	0.16***
Civic knowledge quiz	0.14***
Everyone gets the same treatment	−0.14***
Familiarity with combined channels, direct measure	0.14***
Frequency of contacts	0.14***
Clear how officials should perform	0.12***
Civic efficacy	0.06*

*** $p < 0.001$; ** $p < 0.01$; * $p < 0.05$.

are well educated and have high-prestige and high-paying jobs—are also most likely to have the connections to get around the rules when they wish to do so.

B. Length of Residence in the Country

Access to protektzia rises in nearly perfect linear fashion with increased length of stay in Israel. The Pearson correlation is 0.18 (Table VI.3). A closer look at the data showed that among natives needing protektzia, 53% reported access; among those who had arrived in Palestine before 1930 the figure is a virtually identical 50%. In contrast, among those arriving in 1966 or later, only 26%—half the proportion for the others—had someone to approach.

C. Access to Protektzia and the Debate about Israel's Ethnic Gap

One of Israel's most persistent social problems is what is usually known as *hapa'ar ha'adati,* the "ethnic gap," or *haba'aya ha'adatit,* "the ethnic problem." Jews of Middle Eastern and North African origin are not only concentrated in low-paying, low-status occupations, but complain of active discrimination against them. The recurrent question is whether over time, Jews of these backgrounds, who started out with relatively fewer resources, are approaching parity with Jews of European origin.[4]

Students of inequality everywhere look at variables like material well-being, including income, patterns of consumption, ownership of property; at occupational and educational status; and at power indicators like representation in political institutions. May not self-reported access to protektzia be used as a symbolic indicator of equality? Middle Eastern Jews commonly complain that, unlike Europeans, they lack protektzia (Bensimon-Donath, 1970; Shama and Idris, 1977; Smooha, 1978). In Bensimon-Donath's study of North African immigrants, for example, 50% complained about the use of protektzia by others, to their detriment (Bensimon-Donath, 1970: 461; cited in Smooha, 1978: 192).

To use protektzia is to wield power, or at least to influence someone in a manner which promotes personal interests.[5] Generally speaking, researchers have shown that Middle Eastern Jews are heavily underrepresented when it comes to more conventional measures of power. For instance, summarizing his study of ethnic leadership in 1970–71, Smooha wrote:

> Oriental origin handicaps access to power, especially power beyond the middle or lower-middle ranks; ethnic particularism is perhaps highest in politics and in assignment to positions of trust, and ethnic quotas prevent free competition for power. . . . Our analysis of power disparities documents the pyramidal form of Oriental representation. Such distribution patterns strongly suggest the existence of barriers against Oriental upward mobility, and the Orientals do receive less than their proportional share of patronage, dispensed by their respective political parties. (Smooha, 1978: 193–194)

Because protektzia is a form of social credit, it is also appropriate to compare its distribution in the population with that of income. In Smooha's summary of the evidence on income and other aspects of material well-being it was concluded that despite improvement in the standard of living of all groups, material well-being of Oriental Jews had improved less than that of Europeans (Smooha, 1978: 153–154).[6] Using somewhat more recent data, Bernstein and Antonovsky (1981) analyzed degree of integration over time of European and Middle Eastern Jews on three socio-economic variables, one of which was income. Although the income gap between the two immigrant groups narrowed in the 1960's, it was considerable and stable in the 1970's. Moreover, they argued that it was underestimated because of the greater size of Middle Eastern families.

What, then, do the data on access to protektzia tell us about Israel's ethnic gap? Do they mirror other forms of inequality? The short answer to these questions is that an ethnic gap is discernible, but other variables are more important.

1. Ethnic origin. Whether the direct or indirect measures of access to personal connections were used, I did find that immigrants of Middle Eastern origin were least likely of five ethnic groups to report access to protektzia and native children of natives were most likely to do so (Table VI.4). Moreover, among the three groups of natives, those born to Middle Eastern fathers were lowest on access. Thus, both among immigrants and among natives, Middle Easterners consistently reported somewhat less access than did persons of European origin.

2. Ethnic origin and education. Because there is known to be a high correlation between ethnic origin and education in Israel—Europeans are better educated, on the average, than are those of Middle Eastern origin—and because these two variables so clearly place Israelis in the social structure, it is important to analyze how they jointly affect access to protektzia. Table VI.5 shows that for all ethnic groups, education made a difference, although it made more of a difference for native children of natives, for native children of Europeans, and for European immigrants. That is to say, education increases the probability that one has, or believes one has, access at a greater rate for those who are already in a stronger position, in terms of prestige. Compare the increment added by education for

Table VI.4
Access to Protektzia by Ethnic Origin (percent having access)

Ethnic Origin	Direct Measure*	Indirect Measure*	N
Native children of natives	52.2	76.6	67
Native children of Europeans	47.8	75.0	197
Native children of Middle Easterners	42.0	64.8	141
European immigrants	32.2	62.8	422
Middle Eastern immigrants	26.8	52.1	185

* See note 3.

the two Middle Eastern groups with those gained by the others: for the former, the gain is only 7% to 9%; for the latter it is 22% to 36%.

Among those with at least some high school education, the numbers fell into a neat, linear pattern: Native children of natives were highest, with 61% reporting access, and Middle Eastern immigrants lowest, with 30%. Although this pattern did not recur for those with only elementary schooling, the joint effect of education and ethnicity was generally cumulative. Being native or European and of high education greatly increased the probability of access to protektzia. But the point worth stressing is that education matters more than country of origin.[7]

3. **Persistence of a small ethnic gap into the second generation.** A small but discernible ethnic gap also persists into the second generation, although generation per se matters more than ethnicity: Among all first generation immigrants, 31% reported access (direct measure); among children of immigrants, the figure was 45%, whereas 52% of native children of natives did so (Table VI.3 shows that the value of the Pearson correlation for generation is a low but statistically significant 0.08). Using the direct measure of access, I found that within each generational group, 5% more European Jews than Middle Eastern Jews reported access. When the indirect measure was used, the difference was again the same within each generation, though the size of the difference was a little larger (10%–11%). Thus, controlling for generation weakens ethnic differences—whether or not

Table VI.5
Access to Protektzia by Ethnic Origin and Education (percent having access)[a]

Ethnic Origin	Education		Difference	Pearson's r
	0–8 years	9+ years		
Native children of natives	33.3 (15)	61.2 (49)	+27.9	−0.24*
Native children of Europeans	15.4 (13)	51.5 (169)	+36.1	−0.19**
Native children of Middle Easterners	37.0 (27)	45.9 (27)	+8.9	−0.07
Europeans	15.7 (89)	37.5 (299)	+21.8	−0.20***
Middle Easterners	23.0 (74)	30.3 (99)	+7.3	−0.08

[a] Among the total sample, direct measure.
*** $p < 0.001$; ** $p < 0.01$; * $p < 0.05$.

an individual is born in Israel is more important for access to protektzia than specific country of origin.

4. The gap in 1968 and in 1980. In the 1968 study, important effects of ethnicity, generation, and education on access to protektzia were found (Danet and Hartman, 1972a). Have the effects of these variables strengthened or weakened over time? Has the gap between the haves and have-nots grown or diminished? Table VI.6 shows that although all groups reported greater access in 1980, the rate of growth is greater for thé haves than for the have-nots.

In this table I revert to the less satisfactory indirect measure of access since the direct question was not asked in 1968. According to the indirect measure, both among educational groups, and among ethnic groups, the haves have risen in access a good deal more than the have-nots. Thus, whereas 45% of natives reported access in 1968, by 1980 71% of them did so; in 1968 37% of European immigrants had access, as compared with 62% in 1980; among Middle Eastern immigrants the proportion rose from 40% to 52%. Computation of the differences between years shows that the rate of growth for Middle Easterners is only half that for natives and European immigrants.

A very similar pattern emerged for education (the lower half of Table VI.6). The proportion reporting access among the poorly educated rose from 36% to 49% over the 12-year period. Among those with at least some high school education it rose from 42% to 69%. Once again, the rate of growth for the advantaged group is

Table VI.6
Access to Protektzia in 1968 and 1980 by Ethnic Origin and by Education (percent having access) [a]

	1968	1980	Difference
Ethnic Origin			
Natives	45% (332)	71% (249)	+26%
Europeans	37% (892)	62% (218)	+25%
Middle Easterners	40% (401)	52% (121)	+12%
Difference between natives and Middle Easterners	+5%	+19%	
Education	36% (496)	49% (139)	+13%
0–8 years			
9+ years	42% (1203)	69% (442)	+27%
Difference	+6%	+20%	

[a] Indirect measure, among those having contact and need.

double that for the disadvantaged one. Moreover, whereas there was only a 6% difference between educational groups back in 1968, today the gap has increased to 20%.

The effects just reported would no doubt be less sharp if the direct measure of access were available for both years. Still, these results reliably illustrate a general phenomenon known in studies of gaps between groups over time: Invariably, the group (or groups) starting out with an advantage maintains that advantage or even increases it.

D. Civic and Organizational Socialization

As the correlations between access to protektzia and education and occupation would suggest, persons holding a good command of the U code were also most likely to report access (see Table VI.3). People who scored high on the civic and bureaucratic quizzes were familiar with channels of redress, and, in addition, felt subjectively competent (thought they know how officials are supposed to do their job, felt they know to whom to complain) and were especially likely to report that they had someone to whom they could turn in time of need. Moreover, they were also likely to be people who do not believe that everyone gets the same treatment—on the contrary, they knew best that some people get better treatment than others.

People who had many encounters with public bureaucracy reported a little more access than did those having few contacts (Table VI.3). This finding is probably in part a product of the association between education and occupation and contact—educated people of high socio-economic status have more contacts (see chapter 5). But it is also likely that having many contacts helps to get to know people personally and therefore to have access to protektzia, whether through direct influence attempts or via the mobilization of third parties. We shall see shortly that regression analysis removes frequency of contact from the list of variables contributing significantly to variance in access.

I had expected a stronger relationship between feelings of civic efficacy and access than that shown in Table VI.3 (only 0.06). I would have thought that personal belief in having access to key persons would foster feelings of general efficacy. Evidently, widespread cynicism about government and politics is almost as common among those reporting access as among those without access. This means that efficacy within organizations is virtually unrelated to feelings of general political efficacy.

E. Multivariate Analysis

Step-wise regression analysis eliminated all but four predictors of access to protektzia. The single best predictor was subjective knowledgeability about channels of complaint—the personal belief that one knows where to go when one wants to complain. Actually, rather than seeing these feelings as a predictor, the two variables are probably better seen as co-varying. People who have access feel subjectively competent and those who feel competent tend also to have access to protektzia. Even after these feelings of subjective knowledgeability have been taken into account, scores on the civic knowledge quiz, length of residence in the country, and rejection of the belief that the best way to proceed is to know and use the U code each make a statistically significant contribution to the variance. The four variables yield a multiple correlation of 0.33 with access to protektzia and thus account for 11% of the variance. It is evident that the four together tap aspects of being an insider—having been around long enough to know how the system works.

IV. ETHNIC ORIGIN AND USE OF PROTEKTZIA

Chapter 5 demonstrated that the various ethnic groups bring with them to Israel differing orientations toward the use of protektzia and that the Western European immigrants consistently reject protektzia on the normative level more than the others. What happens to the Western Europeans and so-called Anglo-Saxons when they begin to see "how the system really works?" How does being born in Israel modify the effect of country of origin? Do native Israelis of Western European or Anglo-Saxon origin still reveal traces of the normativeness of their parents?

To tease out the answers to these questions, I examine patterns of use of protektzia, using a 7-way breakdown by ethnic origin. In Table VI.7 four groups of natives are distinguished—native children of native fathers, native children of Western European fathers, native children of Eastern European fathers, and native children of Middle Eastern fathers. Similarly, I compare three groups of immigrants, separating the Western Europeans from immigrants from Eastern Europe.

A. The Lingering Normativeness of Western Europeans

Table VI.7 examines, first of all, rates of intensive use of protektzia in the sample as a whole. Answers on the question about use are dichotomized so as to contrast those using it many times or a few times with those using it only once or twice, or not at all. These data revealed that Western European immigrants are lowest on intensive use, not only among all immigrants, but among all ethnic groups (only 3.4%).

Moreover, the Western European immigrants are most likely of all groups to resist temptation, when both need and access are present—although even about half of *them* yield when temptation knocks at the door (third column, Table VI.7). Similarly, they continue to display traces of universalism even when they are born in Israel, at least insofar as frequent use is concerned. They show a smaller gain in frequent use in the second generation than do either Eastern Europeans or Middle Easterners (first column, Table VI.7).

But the most important finding is that among those having contact, need, and access, natives of Western European origin no longer show traces of normativity; they are even second highest among the four groups of natives on use of protektzia (third column, Table VI.7). Having crossed the psychological threshhold into the local organizational culture, they no longer refrain from activating personal connections. The critical factor thus appears to be the willingness to see themselves as needing protektzia. If this willingness and perceived access are both present, then Western European natives are about as likely as anyone else to use protektzia.

B. The Importance of Being Native

By far the most important contrast shown in Table VI.7 is that between all natives and all immigrants. The more variables that are held constant, the sharper the difference between immigrants and natives. In the total sample, an average of 10% of all immigrants have used personal connections more than once or twice, compared to 4.5% of all immigrants. Among persons having had contacts with public bureaucracy, 34% of natives have used them at least once, twice as high a proportion as that for all immigrants combined (17.5%). Finally, among persons reporting contact, need, and access, three-quarters of all natives have used protektzia at least once in the last year, compared to nearly 52% of all natives.

C. 1968 versus 1980

The findings reported in the preceding section constitute a change from those found in the 1968 study. That study had identified a cross-over effect of apparent bureaucratization of attitudes among

Table VI.7

Use of Protektzia among Seven Ethnic Groups

Ethnic Origin	Total sample: % using more than once or twice	Those having contact: % using at least once	Those with contact, need, access: % using at least once
Native children of native fathers	13.8	39.7	70.8
Native children of Western European fathers	4.8	33.3	80.0
Native children of Eastern European fathers	11.7	32.1	71.0
Native children of Middle Eastern fathers	9.8	29.3	83.3
All natives	10.0	33.6	76.3
Western European immigrants	3.4	16.9	47.4
Eastern European immigrants	4.4	14.9	51.3
Middle Eastern immigrants	5.7	20.7	56.3
All immigrants	4.5	17.5	51.7

the Middle Eastern and North African immigrants, over time, and of concomitant de-bureaucratization of behavior, over time, of European, particularly Western European, immigrants. As has just been seen, this pattern did not recur in 1980. In chapter 5 it was shown that there is increased homogenization of attitudes—today, all ethnic groups uniformly say that using protektzia is wrong. As for actual use, we have just seen that the important distinction is now between natives and immigrants. There was no clear association between ethnicity and use of protektzia in relation to length of residence in Israel.

D. Multivariate Analysis

To identify the most important predictors of use of protektzia, a log-linear analysis was performed, using the logit version, in which a dependent variable is specified.[8] Only four variables turned out to be important: age of respondents, perceived need for protektzia, claimed access to it, and perceived legitimacy of its use. Table VI.8 presents the distribution of the data on routine use of protektzia cross-tabulated by these four predictors.

Table VI.9 goes on to display data on the goodness-of-fit of 18 different models for the figures in Table VI.8; for each model, its terms, the value of L^2, and p values are presented. I shall concentrate on those models which yielded a probability of a Type I error at about 0.25.[9]

As can be seen from Table VI.9, three models yielded p values of from 0.230 to 0.267 (nos. 15, 16, and 17). Although all are therefore candidates as causal explanatory models of routine use of personal connections, the next task is to identify the model which is easiest to interpret theoretically, and which offers the most parsimonious explanation. In fact, the three models resemble each other considerably; they share the term {UCN}, referring to the three-way interaction between use, access, and need. They differ in the way in which they account for the relation between attitude (legitimacy of protektzia) and behavior. In the case of model no. 15, age is linked both directly and indirectly to use, through need for protektzia. But no direct link between age and legitimacy is posited. Only the term {UL} is present, positing a zero-order link between attitudes and behavior.

In contrast, in model no. 16, age is posited to affect use both directly and indirectly, through attitudes about legitimacy. Finally, in model no. 17, in addition to the term {NCU}, the interaction of

Table VI.8
Cross-Tabulation of Use of Protektzia in Routine Encounters by Personal Need for Protektzia, Age, Access to Protektzia, and Legitimacy of its Use

Personal Need	Age	Access	Legitimacy*	Routine Use	
				no	yes
no	−35	no	no	94	1
no	−35	no	?	44	6
no	−35	no	yes	19	2
no	−35	yes	no	32	9
no	−35	yes	?	10	7
no	−35	yes	yes	3	0
no	35–49	no	no	79	4
no	35–49	no	?	18	2
no	35–49	no	yes	12	2
no	35–49	yes	no	24	5
no	35–49	yes	?	9	2
no	35–49	yes	yes	2	1
no	50+	no	no	145	1
no	50+	no	?	33	1
no	50+	no	yes	13	0
no	50+	yes	no	48	2
no	50+	yes	?	6	2
no	50+	yes	yes	2	0
yes	−35	no	no	30	8
yes	−35	no	?	7	3
yes	−35	no	yes	8	1
yes	−35	yes	no	7	36
yes	−35	yes	?	1	24
yes	−35	yes	yes	0	15
yes	35–49	no	no	20	2
yes	35–49	no	?	8	0
yes	35–49	no	yes	2	0
yes	35–49	yes	no	12	28
yes	35–49	yes	?	3	10
yes	35–49	yes	yes	2	9
yes	50+	no	no	27	3
yes	50+	no	?	3	1
yes	50+	no	yes	5	2
yes	50+	yes	no	3	18
yes	50+	yes	?	1	9
yes	50+	yes	yes	0	6

* no = It is always or usually wrong to use protektzia;
  ? = It depends, sometimes;
  yes = It is usually or always all right to use protektzia.

Table VI.9
Models Fitted to the Four-Way Cross-Tabulation of Data on Use of Protektzia in Table VI.8

Model*	L^2	d.f.	p
1 [LCAN] [U]	487.90	35	0.000
2 [AN] [CA] [UL] [UA] [UN]	325.42	55	0.000
3 [LAN] [ULC] [UA]	297.70	43	0.000
4 [UL] [UC] [UA] [UN]	90.21	58	0.004
5 [ULCA] [ULN]	57.42	30	0.002
6 [ULC] [UAN]	75.38	50	0.012
7 [CAN] [UL] [UC] [UA] [UN]	75.89	51	0.013
8 [UAN] [UC] [UL]	78.87	54	0.015
9 [ULA] [UC] [UN]	73.68	50	0.016
10 [CN] [LA] [UL] [UA] [UN] [UC]	73.08	53	0.035
11 [LA] [CA] [AN] [UL] [UC] [UN] [UA]	69.34	50	0.036
12 [LA] [CAN] [UL] [UC] [UA] [UN]	63.28	47	0.057
13 [ULCN] [UA]	56.33	44	0.107
14 [ULCN] [AN] [UA]	51.30	42	0.154
15 [UAN] [UCN] [UL]	59.20	52	0.230
16 [UCN] [ULA]	54.01	48	0.256
17 [NCU] [LA] [UL] [UA]	57.92	52	0.267
18 [UCAN] [UL]	46.15	44	0.383

* Key to abbreviations of predictor variables: N=need, A=age, C=access,
L=legitimacy, U=use.

need/access/use, three other terms occur: the zero-order link between
age and legitimacy of protektzia ({AL}), the relation between attitude
and use ({UL}), and a direct link between age and use ({UA}). Models
no. 16 and 17 are nearly identical and are hierarchically related; no.
17 is the simpler of the two because it excludes the indirect effects
of age on use, via perceived legitimacy, and of legitimacy on use,
via age. Theoretically, nos. 16 and 17 are preferable to no. 15 because
they coincide with the spirit of previous analyses, which had suggested
that there are two separate phenomena in the data, the need/access/
use complex and the separate secondary effect having to do with
younger persons tending to legitimate protektzia more often than
older ones.

   The next task, then, is to decide which of the two latter models,
nos. 16 or 17, is preferable. This can be done by computing the
difference in L^2 between the two and testing to see whether the
difference is statistically significant. The difference between L^2 for
the two is 57.92–54.01 = 3.91. Because there are 52 degrees of
freedom in model no. 17 and 48 in model no. 16, there is a difference
of 4 degrees of freedom between them. The probability of obtaining

a value of 3.91 at 4 d.f. is p = 0.40; hence the addition of the higher-order interactions does not significantly improve the prediction. Accordingly, it is model no. 17 which most parsimoniously represents the data. This model is presented graphically in Figure VI.1.

The two separate triangular relationships are clearly displayed, although it is not possible to show graphically the difference between the two triangular relationships: In the case of need/access/use, the indirect effects are included, as well as the direct, zero-order ones. In the case of age/legitimacy/use, as has just been seen, they are not.

V. CONSISTENCY OF ATTITUDES AND BEHAVIOR

By combining information on respondents' attitude and behavior with respect to use of protektzia, a new variable can be created called "consistency of attitude and behavior." Dichotomizing people as legitimating or not legitimating (the latter including those saying "it depends"), and as using or not using protektzia (or at least willing to use it, had they had access) produces four possible types. In practice the combination of favoring protektzia but not using it, given opportunity, was so rare that it was eliminated. I shall speak, then, of three main types: (1) the consistently U person; (2) the inconsistent person who uses protektzia though he or she rejects it on the normative level; and (3) the consistently P person.

A. 1968 versus 1980

The proportions of these three types among those having contact have hardly changed since 1968. About one-quarter in both years

Figure VI.1
A Model of the Routine Use of Protektzia*

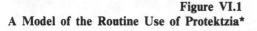
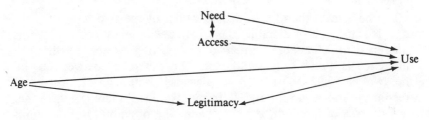

* Based on Model no. 17 in Table VI.9.

were U purists, resisting temptation to use protektzia. Another 30% were fully P types. The modal category, in both years, is the inconsistent group—fully 45% in 1968, and a slightly higher 48% in 1980 condemned protektzia but used it, or would have done so, had they had the chance. The stability and size of this group confirmed that this is the pattern most encouraged by the forces operating in Israeli society.

B. Predictors of Consistency

We found a relation between respondents' age and consistency of attitude and behavior. In line with many previous findings, younger people were less likely to be consistently universalistic. The correlation was of an order similar to others examined in chapter 5 and earlier in this chapter—a low but significant 0.17. Similarly, old-timers and natives were less consistently universalistic than relative newcomers.[10] On the other hand, the highly educated and those in professional and managerial positions are more likely to be consistently U. Will the U purists eventually disappear from the Israeli scene? Immigration has all but stopped in recent years. As younger natives grow up and become educated professionals or white collar workers, which forces will have the greater influence on them— normative socialization or exposure to local ways? All the evidence points in the direction of the latter.

VI. REASONS FOR USE AND NON-USE OF PROTEKTZIA

A final set of findings relates to the reasons people give for using or for not using protektzia. To some extent, I have, of course, been exploring this very question by looking at what I have been calling "perceptions of the reward/cost structure of the situation." But, in addition, data are available on the responses to some direct questions about reasons for use.

A. Justifying Protektzia: A Comparison of General Public Opinion and the Justifications of Users

Members of the general sample were asked, "What is the main reason, in your opinion, that people like you use protektzia?" Users were asked, "What was your main reason for using protektzia?" In both cases, respondents were offered three categories from which to choose: (1) "without protektzia it would have been impossible to arrange the matter;" (2) "without protektzia it would be possible to arrange the matter, but it would take more time and trouble;" (3) "without protektzia it would be possible to arrange the matter, but the solution to the problem would be less good" (if respondents insisted on a combination of categories, they were coded in a fourth category).

It is evident from the data in Table VI.10 that there is a difference between general public opinion and the reasons given by users. In both sets of answers, the modal reason is that people use protektzia to save time and trouble; the claim that it is impossible to manage without it falls second in both sets of answers and the claim that one obtains a less satisfying solution without it falls into third place. But on closer inspection, the first and second categories are drained of a small proportion each. Users were thus twice as likely as the general sample to claim that one can't manage without it (37% versus only 18%). I am led to two conclusions. First, these results support the contention expressed at several points in this book that much use of personal connections in Israel is procedural—to cut through red tape and get goods or services with less agony or stress. At the same time—whether or not it is objectively true that sometimes people can't get their entitlements without protektzia (and there is no reliable way of estimating how often this happens)—a sizable

Table VI.10
Reasons for Use of Protektzia by Ethnic Origin and by Education

Sociocultural Background	Time & trouble	Solution less good	Impossible without	Combin- ation		
Ethnic Origin						
Native children of natives	44.0	20.0	24.0	12.0	100.0	(25)
Native children of Europeans	51.7	15.0	20.0	13.3	100.0	(60)
Native children of Middle Easterners	39.0	7.3	46.3	7.3	100.0	(41)
Europeans	33.3	10.5	49.1	5.3	100.0	(57)
Middle Easterners	37.1	17.1	42.9	2.9	100.0	(35)
Education						
0–8 years	27.0	8.1	62.2	2.7	100.0	(37)
9–12 years	40.2	14.7	36.3	8.8	100.0	(102)
13+ years	49.4	14.3	26.0	10.4	100.0	(77)
All respondents						
General sample	49.2	16.2	18.3	16.3	100.0	(996)
Users	41.5	13.4	36.9	8.3	100.0	(217)

proportion of users justify, or perhaps rationalize, their behavior as not a matter of choice at all—they simply had to go the illegitimate route.

B. Sociocultural Background and Justifications of Use

If both objective difficulties and subjective feelings of deprivation are involved in the claim that there was no choice, given the many findings about the difficulties of the have-nots in coping with Israeli bureaucracy, then Middle Easterners and the poorly educated should be most likely to cite this as a reason for using protektzia, whereas Europeans and natives of European origin would more often cite time and trouble as the reason. On the other hand, if the erosion of universalism is so great as to encourage everyone to feel that protektzia must be used, then perhaps differences between haves and have-nots will not be so great.

1. Ethnic origin and generation. As is indicated in Table VI.10 the results for ethnic origin and generation do indeed conform quite closely to the first set of expectations. Native children of natives and natives of European origin were most likely to cite time and trouble as the main reason for using protektzia, whereas both groups of immigrants did so less often. And native children of natives and natives born to European fathers were only about half as likely to say they couldn't manage without protektzia as all immigrants and native children of Middle Eastern fathers. In short, for the haves, using protektzia is a luxury, a time-saver; the have-nots believe they couldn't cope without it.

2. Education. The results for education followed exactly the same pattern. The higher the level of education of respondents, the more likely they were to cite time and trouble as the main reason for seeking connections; complementarily, the lower the educational attainment, the more likely people were to say that they couldn't manage without them. Whereas 62% of those with up to 8 years of schooling said they couldn't manage without, only 26% of those with post-secondary schooling did so. These results suggest that stronger groups enjoy a greater sense of freedom and choice—whatever the decision they make about a problem in a bureaucratic encounter, to act or not to act, to go the legitimate route or to use personal connections, they perceive their decision as a matter of choice.

Weaker groups, in contrast, perceive their decision as more constrained by forces beyond their control.[11]

C. Reasons for Not Using Protektzia

As for the reasons people do not use protektzia, considerable evidence
has already been presented that persons of European, especially
Western European, origin tend to refrain from using protektzia for
normative reasons, even though by their own self-definition they
needed it and had someone to approach. Readers will recall that
the question probing use of protektzia gave three choices for never
having used it: (1) "No, I didn't use it because I didn't need it;"
(2) "No, because I didn't want to ask for protektzia;" and (3) "No,
because I didn't have anyone to approach." In the sample as a
whole, 376 persons said that they had had no need, 154 said that
they didn't want to use protektzia, and 211 said that they had had
no one to approach. Thus, among those needing but not using it,
people were far more likely to say they lacked access than that they
chose not to use it. There was also an association between professed
attitudes toward the legitimacy of protektzia and the reasons given
for non-use. Predictably, the more unequivocally people rejected the
legitimacy of using protektzia, the less likely they were to say they
had no one to ask, and the more likely they were to say that they
didn't want to use it.

VII. SUMMARY AND DISCUSSION

The short and simple answer to the question, "Who uses protektzia?"
is: *nearly everyone*. Given perceived need and access, and even if
experiences with bureaucracy have generally been quite positive,
people readily use personal connections. Beyond this basic result,
which confirms general impressions of the society, this chapter has
yielded a number of less obvious, important findings.

First, it is intriguing that more people claim access to protektzia
today than in 1968. There is no way of assessing whether more
people really do have access, for access is not simply "have something
in a bottle." The term has been used so often in this chapter that
it may appear unintentionally reified—It is not a static thing at all,
but an ephemeral, shifting phenomenon. People may have viable
personal connections in one problematic situation, but none at all
in another. The main point about this rise in reported access is that
Israelis seem to feel, more than ever, that it is important to be able

to say that they have connections. Thus, the importance of such connections as a status symbol has increased, over time. Although this longitudinal comparison was based on the inferential indirect measure of access, rather than the preferred direct one, I am confident that the basic finding of more frequent claims to access is reliable, and would have emerged, had I had data on the direct measure for 1968.

Second, perceived access to protektzia was consistently though moderately related to attributes of respondents which tap their social integration into Israeli society. Interviewees' education and occupation—the same two variables which best predicted mobilization to the U code—also proved to be the best of the sociocultural predictors of access to protektzia. Weak effects of ethnicity were also discernible. But the important distinction today is not country of origin, but simply whether or not individuals were born in Israel.

Third, as the grand hypothesis predicted, social-psychological factors, rather than sociocultural ones, predicted use of protektzia. Least important among the former were perceptions of the behavior of others; the belief that everyone uses protektzia is too widespread to serve as a predictor variable. Need, access, and use are so interrelated that it may be best to think of them as reflections of one variable: it might be called "the threshhold for deviance," or "the threshhold for biculturalism."

One surprise was that despite the relatively low correlation between overtly expressed attitudes toward the legitimacy of protektzia and actual use, attitudes are important enough, after all, to remain in the equation in multivariate analysis. Even after access and need were held constant, individuals' professed attitudes were of some help in predicting their behavior, after all.

Fourth, the hybrid nature of Israel's organizational culture was further revealed in the finding that those claiming access to personal connections are also those displaying both subjective and objective competence in the U code. Those enjoying access both felt they knew to whom to complain and commanded basic knowledge about organizational affairs.

Fifth, the general rise in perceived access to protektzia observed between the years 1968 and 1980 is not evenly distributed in the population. Although for all groups a gain over time was indicated, haves showed double the gain of have-nots. This finding emerged for both education and for ethnic origin.

Sixth, just as country of origin has become less important today than in 1968 in affecting access to personal connections, so it is also less important in relation to actual use of them. The basic distinction today is again between all immigrants and all natives: Three-quarters of all natives having contact, need, and access reported using protektzia, compared to one-half of all immigrants in a similar position. Note that, at the same time, the rate of use is high even among immigrants having the opportunity.

Detailed analysis of the reasons people give for using protektzia showed that for the haves using it is a matter of choice, a means to make life easier, a luxury, whereas for the have-nots, it is more often seen as a necessity, a commodity without which they cannot manage—providing, of course, that they have access.

A. Protektzia Flourishes

Putting all these findings together, it is clear that Nachmias and Rosenbloom (1978) are completely wrong: protektzia is not dying out in Israel. On the contrary, the rich mosaic of findings revealed in this and the preceding chapter vividly and unequivocally demonstrate that protektzia is alive and well. Social-psychological variables accounted quite well for patterns of use of personal connections, much as the grand hypothesis had predicted. The analysis has also shown that access to personal connections is quite unevenly distributed in the population and is closely associated with the degree of integration of individuals into the society.

B. Diculturalism as Well as Biculturalism

In chapter 3 I noted the difficulties in establishing an empirical criterion of societal diculturalism. I suggested that if one-third of those coming into contact with public bureaucracy during a given time period were found to use particularistic strategies at least on one occasion, that society could be classified as dicultural. In the Israeli case study, as reported in this chapter, three-eighths of all persons having contacts admitted to using protektzia at least once. By this criterion, then, Israel is a society not only in which organizational biculturalism is prevalent at the individual level, but one in which this phenomenon is widespread enough to justify labelling the society as dicultural.

C. Protektzia and the Ethnic Gap

Although evidence of ethnic differences was found in access to and use of protektzia, these differences were small. Other variables are far more important than ethnicity in Israeli society today: Even among deprived groups, in this case the Middle Eastern and North African immigrants, access to and use of protektzia are now quite common. But how does it happen that there are not greater disparities between European and Middle Eastern Jews than those found?

At least in part, the answer probably has to do with the fact that, as Smith (1976) noted was the case for Russia (see chapter 2), it is often enough to know or to have access to relatively low-ranking employees of organizations to circumvent the system. Sometimes it is even better to know or have access to the people at the bottom than at the top. Thus, persons of Middle Eastern or North African origin could do fairly well in activating personal connections, and not much less well than Europeans, because they have better access to low-ranking bureaucrats than do persons of European origin.

There is indirect support for this argument in Weiman's (1983) study of the small world phenomenon in Israel. He showed that ethnicity affects acquaintance networks in an important way: Individuals asked to provide links to a target person were far more able to do so when the target person and the starter were of the same ethnic origin. Because Middle Easterners tend to be concentrated in the lower ranks of organizations, clients of Middle Eastern origin may thus have an advantage when trying to influence them. Weiman's results therefore suggest that intra-ethnic networks mitigate inequalities in access to protektzia.

D. Protektzia and Organizational Competence

In his study of American immigrants in Israel, Avruch suggested that for Americans to adapt to Israeli bureaucracy, they must learn (1) that rules are not necessarily applied universalistically; (2) that role specificity, or single-strandedness, is not necessarily maintained, and neither is affective neutrality; (3) that "by invoking particularism through protektzia, by seeking multiplexity and affective valence, they can manipulate the system to their advantage" (Avruch, 1981: 141). As I argued in chapter 4, then, to be organizationally competent in Israel is both to know the official code and to know how to get around it.

Because the findings of this study showed that the normativeness of Western European and Anglo-Saxon immigrants tends to suppress use of protektzia among them, it is extremely interesting to compare these results with Avruch's research. Here is his summary of what his 100 American immigrants had to say:

> The almost universal idiom for insuring bureaucratic success in the eyes of *olim* (immigrants) is the possession and use of protektzia. Eighty-two per cent of the Jerusalem sample attached at least "fair" importance to it—of whom half thought it was "very important." Only 3 percent believed protektzia was "not at all important." Close to three-fourths of the sample said that they had used protektzia at least once; 15 percent said they use it often; 26 percent said they have never used protektzia . . . Finally, 65 percent . . . thought protektzia was important but "a bad thing, morally wrong." (Avruch, 1981: 144)

Avruch's findings that three-fourths of his sample had used protektzia at least once since time of immigration, and that 15% had used it often are not incompatible with my result that roughly half of all immigrants had used it in the last year, given need and access.

E. Southern Italy and Israel Compared

Although in some ways Israel presents a unique constellation of factors, as is true for any country, in a more basic sense it is probably not terribly different from many other countries. The review in chapter 2 showed that personal connections are used to some extent in every country, and in most countries they are used quite often. To provide some perspective on the Israeli case, I have chosen to compare it with another, seemingly similar organizational culture.

The Israeli situation reminds me of the notions of "official system" and "real system," as used by Galt to analyze public administration in southern Italy, specifically, in the island of Pantelleria, off the coast of Sicily:

> It is useful to postulate an ideal type model with two systems of action for obtaining scarce resources from bureaucracy . . . We can call one the *official system* and the other the *real system* . . . the official system consists of the procedures a person should go through *by regulation* when dealing with both government and private bureaucracies . . . the official system . . . is codified. Official system procedures are defined by written . . . sets of laws or regulations . . . the official system is viewed as either corrupt or extremely inefficient . . . Stacks of dog-eared papers in offices confirm the impression of inefficiency. Clerks are hopelessly slow . . . Unlike the official system, the real system is not codified . . . (it) is not based on statute, but on personal linkages within networks . . . what are herein called the real system and the official system are together a set of "parallel structures" . . . The codified official system can be viewed as the permanent and rigid trellis around and through which the real system grows. The former is fixed and difficult to change, the latter is always changing and flexible. (Galt, 1974: 191–193)

Both Galt and Smart (1983) wrote of *furbi* and *fessi,* two social types familiar to locals in Southern Italy. The *furbo* is a wily, clever, crafty person, who knows how to get ahead, to get what he (not usually she) wants. A *fesso* is a fool, a person easily duped, naive. The "art of *arrangiarsi* (of getting by in adverse economic circumstances) referred to by Smart (1983: 130) seems similar in feeling to the Israeli notion of *lada'at l'histader*—literally, to know how to arrange oneself, more idiomatically, to know how to manage, to get what one wants:

> Few words are heard in Israel as often as *lehistader.* Although it is the reflexive verb of *seder* ("order"), it means quite the opposite of formal order. In the vernacular, the meaning of *lehistader* is "to take care of oneself," "to fix oneself up," to steer through life by bending the rule to one's purpose, to organize oneself as best one can . . . In Israel, as in Italy . . . *lehistader* is a vital element to the art of living. It is the Israeli's password through the maze of authority, the thicket of law, the confines of impersonal regulations. Regulations are "objective" and thus theoretically just; but the needs of the individual, his private concepts of right and wrong, are superior. The average Israeli recognizes few regulations of universal applicability. In his dealings with the authorities he invariably demands, firmly and loudly, exceptional treatment . . .
> There are many ways to take care of oneself, *lehistader:* the intimate phone call to a friend, or a friend of a friend, the help of one's political party . . . an imperious pounding of official tables, a high tone of outrage, a demanding wail . . . (Elon, 1972: 310)

There are similar parallels between the Italian notion of raccommandazioni and that of protektzia. Literally, raccommandazioni are recommendations, or letters of recommendation. It is not necessary to have such letters; sometimes it is enough to be known as a person who has connections.

I might even compare the Italian notion of fesso with the Israeli term *freier,* an expression taken over from the Yiddish and increasingly heard these days. In their World Dictionary of Spoken Hebrew, a gold mine of colloquial expressions unacknowledged by compilers of standard Hebrew dictionaries, Dahn Ben-Amotz and Netiva Ben-Yehuda (1972) defined a *freier* as "a person who is a candidate to fall into a trap, or be victimized by a trick." They quoted, for example, an expression a newspaper once attributed to Ezer Weizmann, a popular and colorful public figure, among other things once head of the air force: "They were convinced that an air force person is a kind of *freier,* running around in the clouds" (Ben-Amotz and Ben-Yehuda, 1972: 191).

Despite all the apparent similarities, there is an important difference between Israel's organizational culture and that of southern Italy: *In the latter bribery is important, as well as personal connections; in Israel it is not.* According to Smart (1983), a furbo gets ahead by preying on the weaknesses of fessi, who cannot actively differentiate between the real and official systems. I believe that the Machiavellian connotation implied in the furbo-fesso dichotomy is alien to Israel. To explain why it is lacking is to explain why personal connections are so often mobilized but bribery is so rare.

Two of Avruch's immigrants were quite explicit about the rarity and inappropriateness of bribery in Israel. One said:

> . . . there's always some guy . . . who can get you a license. And I'm not talking about bribery. The system works on protektzia, not on money changing hands. Protektzia is based on reciprocity; on trading favors; on personal contacts. In a way it's more primitive than bribery. We're not talking about cash credit but about social credit. Protektzia is to bribery what barter is to cash. (Avruch, 1981: 141)

Another immigrant got himself into trouble for trying to bribe an official:

> When I first tried to get (an import) license . . . I made the big mistake of trying to offer that *pakid* (official) some money—to bribe him. Boy, did I land on my ass! I thought he'd call the Marines in! In the States a little cash to grease the wheels always worked, but I learned then and there you can't do that, by and large, in Israel. In fact, I think that because I tried to bribe him, the *pakid* really had it in for me. What did I learn? *People* grease the wheels here, not just money. (Avruch, 1981: 147–148)

A study by Sebba (1983) on perceptions of the degree of seriousness of various offenses, including bribery and protektzia, among native Israelis and Russian and North American immigrants, is very pertinent here. He found that natives were about as lenient as the Russians when it came to protektzia, in contrast to the North Americans, whereas the reverse was true for bribery. Although the Russians were lenient toward bribery too, native Israelis were even more likely to condemn it than the North Americans.

The cynicism of southern Italians undoubtedly has to do with center-periphery disparities in economic development, which create a strong sense of "we/they." Locals feel alienated, suspicious, even exploited. As for socialist countries, alienation of citizens from government is probably more widespread than in countries like Italy.

In addition, bribery may flourish alongside exchange of favors because need exceeds the resources that seekers of scarce benefits can offer in return for mere favors. Given citizens' dependence on government for all goods and services and the large size of socialist countries, both geographically and in population, people are not likely to know many persons who can open the gates to desired resources. The role of trust in these societies is ambiguous. As I noted in chapter 2, on the face of it, no trust is necessary in obtaining benefits via bribes: one pays cash on delivery . . . however, persons engaging in bribery must trust one another not to inform the authorities.

In Israel constraints toward solidarity make bribery largely unnecessary and inappropriate. For Israelis (for Israeli Jews, that is), the "they" in the "we/they" contrast is the enemy, the Arabs, or the Gentiles—not the bureaucrats! When protektzia is talked about, Israelis generally smile. This is not the cold smirk of the cynic, but the warm, expansive smile of "We know how it is," and "We are all in this together" (at least among Jews, of course).

I am suggesting, then, that Israelis do not perceive the use of protektzia as a zero-sum game. Competition in the pursuit of interests is mitigated by feelings of solidarity and trust and by the perception of low social distance between persons, even those of differing social status. In chapter 4 I reviewed three studies which in different ways brought out the salience of egalitarian solidarity among Israeli Jews. We saw that Hofstede's (1979) research on social distance between supervisors and employees, Blum-Kulka, Danet and Gherson's (1985) study of the language of requests in Israeli society, and Katriel's (1986) analysis of *dugri* ("straight," direct) speech in Israel, all pointed in the same direction. The findings presented in this chapter clearly converged with these three studies.

One final comment is in order before moving on to chapter 7. This chapter may have given an inflated impression of just how often protektzia is actually used in Israel. We should not forget that this study lacks adequate data on all the myriad matters arranged, day after day, in routine fashion, following U procedures completely—all the times when the system really does work without intervention. It would be a tall order to try to estimate what proportion of all contacts are purely U in all aspects (probably such minor transactions as buying stamps should be omitted from the estimate). But no such estimate is needed to proffer the guess that, despite the vast array of findings presented in this chapter, most people, of all sociocultural backgrounds, manage most of their organizational dealings without protektzia.

I turn to a more specific question: How does the use of protektzia interrelate with the use of universalistic redress channels? It will come as no surprise that devices like ombudsmen and letters to the editor compete for customers with the purveyors of personal influence. Just how the two types of channels are interrelated is discussed in chapter VII.

VII
Abdication from Justice
Biculturalism and Redress

In a society which reveals deeply entrenched biculturalism in its attitudes and beliefs about organizational life, and in which the use of personal connections is extremely widespread in routine encounters, the probability of biculturalism in the response to injustice is inevitably very high. This chapter will show, first of all, that there is once again prima facie evidence in partial support of the social mobilization hypothesis—social mobilization variables do discriminate fairly well between those who are highly active in the pursuit of redress (or at least what appears to be redress) and those who are not. However, data on the choices people make reflect widespread biculturalism once again. Thus, the social mobilization hypothesis successfully predicts *quantitative, but not qualitative* aspects of redress behavior. The findings show that a significant portion of the time, Israelis opt out of the pursuit of universalistic justice, abdicating their right to principled, universalistically grounded decision-making. Moreover, the system is self-perpetuating because protektzia is a more effective route to satisfaction than any other channel. Most important of all is the finding that groups best socialized to the U code on the normative level are precisely the persons most likely to be hybrid in the response to injustice, to use both U *and* P channels.

179

I. The Tendency to Take Action

A. General Trends

1. The proportion ever using channels of redress. Readers will recall from chapter 5 that members of the sample were asked about their experiences in connection with 12 channels of complaint in the public sector and 10 of them in the private sector. For each sector the following general question was asked: "I will read to you a list of devices that people use *in cases when they have been treated unjustly.* Have you ever used each of them, and if so, did it help? Even if you have never used each one, how helpful are they, generally?"

Four hundred and nineteen persons, or 41% of the sample, had, at some time in the past used at least 1 of the 12 public-sector channels (Table VII.1). And 381 persons, or 37%, had used 1 or more of the 10 private-sector channels. Thus, 4 out of every 10 persons claimed to have made at least one attempt at some time in their lives to appeal some organizational decision or to complain about poor service, and 6 out of 10 had apparently never done so.[1]

The proportion of persons having used at least one public-sector channel of redress appears to have doubled since 1968, when only

Table VII.1
Distribution of the Sample by Number of Channels of Complaint Used in the Public and Private Sectors

Total Channels Used	Sector			
	Public		*Private*	
	%	N	%	N
0	59.0%	602	62.7%	640
1	20.1	205	19.5	199
2	9.0	92	10.7	109
3	5.8	59	3.4	35
4	2.5	26	1.7	17
5	1.2	12	0.7	7
6	0.9	9	0.2	2
7	0.2	2	0.3	3
8	0.3	3	0.5	5
9	0.6	6	0.1	1
10	0.1	1	0.3	3
11	0.2	2	—	—
12	0.2	2	—	—
	100.0%	1021	100.0%	1021

20% reported having used any channel. However, this conclusion is probably not fully justified. In 1968 Hartman and I had asked about only 5 channels, whereas in the more recent study 12 were investigated. Four of the channels were identical in the two studies— appeals to a higher official, letters to a newspaper, use of a lawyer, and use of personal connections. In 1968 "Kolbotek" and the ombudsman could not have been investigated because they did not exist at the time. The fifth channel asked about, back then, was the State Controller—the precursor of the ombudsman. Thus, the higher rate of channel use in 1980 may have been in part an artifact of the greater number of channels asked about. Still, it is also likely that since 1968, consciousness of the possibilities of redress has also increased, to no small extent because more channels have come into existence. Probably, then, use of channels of complaint has increased over time, but not as much as the data seem to indicate.

Table VII.2
Intensity of Use of Channels of Complaint in the Public and Private Sectors, by Predictor Variables

Predictors	Public Sector	Private Sector
Sociocultural Background		
Education	0.15***	0.14***
Occupation	0.15***	0.13***
Sex	0.11***	0.04
Age	0.03	0.12***
Sector	0.08**	0.06
Civic and Organizational Socialization		
Civic quiz score	0.14***	0.10***
Political efficacy	0.08*	0.02
Political participation	0.09***	-0.07
Bureaucratic quiz score	0.17***	0.12***
Clear how officials should perform	0.16***	0.12***
Familiarity with public/ private channels (direct measure)	0.14***	0.11***
Knows to whom to complain	0.25***	0.11***
Amount and Quality of Contact		
Amount-public sector	0.21***	0.13***
Quality-public sector	0.20***	0.19***
Amount-private sector	0.18***	0.20***
Quality-private sector	0.12***	0.29***

*** p < 0.001; ** p < 0.01; * p < 0.05.

2. Intensity of channel use. Table VII.1 also documents that it is extremely rare to have used more than one channel. The proportions having used anywhere from 1 to 12 channels in the case of the public sector, and from 1 to 10 in the private one, decreased sharply in almost perfect linear fashion. Only about one-tenth of the sample had used two channels, in each sector, and only about another one-tenth claimed to have used three or more. Thus, hyperactive complainants are extremely rare—only 1 in 5 persons in the original sample reported ever using two or more channels.

B. Predictors of Intensive Channel Use

As indicated in Table VII.2, intensive users of channels of complaints are generally those predicted by the social mobilization hypothesis. The better educated and the higher the occupational status of complainants, the more channels they were likely to have used. Moreover, men were a little more likely to be intensive users than women, at least in the public sector. And those working within the public sector were a little more likely to be active channel users in that sector than those employed in the private sector.

The results for the measures of organizational and civic socialization also generally followed the pattern: People who scored high on the bureaucratic (public-sector) and general civic quizzes, who are familiar with channels of complaint, and who feel subjectively knowledgeable, both in general and with respect to redress, were especially likely to be multiple users. And again, the politically active and those feeling politically efficacious were somewhat more likely to be multiple users than their counterparts. Many of these findings recurred in the data for the private sector as well. Also, quite reasonably, the more contacts people have had, the more channels they have used; this finding also recurred for both sectors.

But these findings in support of the social mobilization hypothesis are, in fact, misleading. The more important question is: Which channels do people choose?

II. THE CHOICE OF CHANNELS OF COMPLAINT: BICULTURALISM ONCE AGAIN

In the following pages I examine data on the choice of channels of complaint first, at a purely descriptive level, and then in an increasingly analytical manner. I start by looking at the empirical distribution of use of each of the channels asked about in the public and private sectors.

A. The Incidence of Use of Seventeen Channels

Table VII.3 is a master chart of the incidence of use of seventeen different channels of complaint in the two sectors. In the first column within the sections devoted to each sector are displayed the general results in the sample as a whole. For the public sector I also display the percentages using each channel with the total number of persons reporting negative experiences as the base. For the private sector separate data are available for three situations, problems with spoiled groceries, faulty products, and faulty services.

1. Public sector. The single public channel most used by the sample as a whole is the one that requires least effort—appealing to a higher official. Twenty-nine percent of the total sample had tried this strategy. Expressed as the proportion of those reporting one or more negative contacts, this proportion is a high 70%. Note that this channel remains within the framework of a two-party relationship between the client and the organization. It is of greater interest to analyze which types of three-party channels are approached. Only if a third party is approached would most researchers classify the situation as a true dispute (see Felstiner and Sarat, 1980–81). *The single most popular third-party choice in response to perceived injustice is protektzia.* Thirteen percent of the total sample, and 31% of those reporting at least one negative contact had made use of personal connections in response to a situation in which they had been treated unjustly. The ombudsman comes fairly close, but only second, with 8% of the total sample, and 19% of those experiencing problems having contacted him. These results strongly suggest, then, that the ombudsman must compete with protektzia as an address for redress of grievances. As for use of other channels, about 7% of respondents, and 17% to 18% of those experiencing problems, had approached either a lawyer or a trade union. All other public-sector channels were used even more rarely. Threats of physical violence or other illegitimate trouble-making were cited by only 3% of the sample and by 6% of those having negative contacts.

2. Private sector. In the private sector, 22% of respondents claimed they had approached a person of higher authority in some place of business at least once in the past; another 38% had gone back directly

Table VII.3

Use of Seventeen Channels of Complaint by Sector and Type of Situation or Problem (percent using each channel)

Channels	Public Sector			Private Sector			
	Total Sample N = 1021	Negative Contacts N = 426	Specific Negative Contacts N = 613	Total Sample N = 1021	Groceries N = 374	Products N = 114	Services N = 99
1. Seller	—	—	—	37.9	76.5	—	—
2. Higher official	29.0	69.5	17.5	22.0	—	7.9	2.0
3. Organization representing seller	—	—	—	—	—	—	—
4. Ombudsman	8.1	19.0	3.1	6.1	1.0	—	2.0
5. Consumer Organization	—	—	—	3.6	—	0.9	—
6. Lawyer	7.4	17.8	1.1	4.8	—	—	1.0
7. Small claims court	—	—	—	3.0	—	0.9	—
8. TV program	4.4	10.6	1.0	3.8	—	0.9	—
9. Radio, newspaper	6.1	14.6	1.0	3.7	—	0.9	—
10. Negative publicity	—	—	—	4.9	—	0.9	—
11. Prime Minister	4.5	10.8	1.5	—	—	—	—
12. Member of Knesset	4.0	9.6	1.0	—	—	—	—
13. Political party	1.9	4.5	—	—	—	—	—
14. Petition, demonstration	3.5	8.5	—	—	—	—	—
15. Union	7.0	16.7	1.1	—	—	—	—
16. Protektzia	12.7	30.5	2.0	—	—	—	—
17. Threats	3.0	6.3	1.0	1.9	—	0.9	2.0

to the person with whom they had dealt in the first place; and 6% had approached an organization representing the seller, such as a wholesale distributor. All of these are basically two-party channels, in which the dispute is kept more or less "in house." Relatively speaking, third-party channels were used even more rarely in the private sector than in the public one.[2] No third-party channel was used by more than 5% of the sample, though if lawyers and small claims courts are combined, 8% had used legal means.

The last three columns of Table VII.3 present the use of the various channels in connection with specific types of private-sector problems. There are some noteworthy differences in the three columns. Three-quarters of all persons having problems with groceries claim to have gone back to the seller—the easiest thing to do. This may also indicate that corner grocery stores and supermarkets are fairly responsive to complaints about spoiled goods. Little special effort is required to return to the seller because people tend to patronize the same place fairly regularly. This is, in fact, virtually the only thing people with grocery problems do.

The figures for products and services are very different and in particular reflect the difficulties of consumers in knowing what to do about problems with services. Eight percent of those having problems with products appealed to a higher official, whereas only 2% of those having problems with services did so—presumably at least in part because there is no higher official to whom one can appeal, in the latter case, where service providers work in solo fashion. Another reason for the lower rate of complaining about services is the greater difficulty in the latter case in determining adequate standards of quality.

C. The Motivational Bases Underlying Channels of Redress

1. Incidence of the motivational types. Reclassification of the various channels according to the typology presented originally in chapter 3, and later discussed in chapter 5, produces a theoretically more satisfying picture of the incidence of the various types of channels. Table VII.4 displays the empirical distribution of channel use according to the six categories of motivational base identified. Here, I take as the N the total of all incidences of use of channels, a total of 761 instances.

Forty-two percent of all appeals in the public sector were to universalistic-normative channels, that is, to a higher official within the organization or to the ombudsman. Another 18% were to channels

Table VII.4

Incidence of Use of Basic Channel Types in the Public and Private Sectors

Channel Type	Sector	
	Public	Private
Universalistic-normative	41.9%	74.2%
Legitimate threats	18.4	21.9
Personalized political brokerage	8.5	—
Organizational brokerage	9.6	—
Unspecified brokerage	17.1	—
Illegitimate threats	4.5	4.0
	100.0%	100.0%
	(761)	(480)

based on legitimate threats—a lawyer, the media, a demonstration. Note that *a very high 40% of all actions taken, in response to the experience of injustice were particularistic.* Although the use of illegitimate threats was quite rare (only 5%), the various forms of particularistic brokerage combined (personalized appeals to the Prime Minister or an MK; organizational appeals to a political party or trade union; protektzia) constituted 35% of all channel use. Thus, the ratio of use of U versus P channels is 3:2.[3]

2. Interrelations among the various types: Patterns of multiple use. Although use of more than one channel is rare, there is discernible patterning in multiple use. Table VII.5, a matrix of intercorrelations among the various motivational types, asks, for example, whether users of channels based on legitimate norms tend also to use those based on legitimate threats (e.g., a lawyer) or those based on particularistic norms (protektzia, organizational brokers—union officials, party workers, political personalities).[4]

This table shows that, first of all, people who appeal to a higher official or contact the ombudsman are about as likely to have used a particularistic strategy as well, as they are to have used channels based on legitimate sanctions, like a lawyer or the media. The correlations are most alike for legitimate threats and for the use of illegitimate political brokers—members of the Knesset or the Prime Minister or some other government minister (0.36 and 0.37, respectively). Second, users of channels based on legitimate threats are far more likely to have used, in addition, a non-U organizational broker (a union official, a party worker), than they are to have contacted the ombudsman or approached a bureaucrat's supervisor

Table VII.5
Use of Channels of Redress: Intercorrelations Among Six Motivational Types*

Channel Type	1	2	3	4	5
1) Legitimate norms	—				
2) Legitimate threats	0.36	—			
3) Illegitimate personalized political brokerage	0.37	0.35	—		
4) Illegitimate organizational brokerage	0.25	0.51	0.30	—	
5) Protektzia	0.34	0.39	0.26	0.33	—
6) Illegitimate threats	0.15	0.22	0.10	0.21	0.23

*All correlations, $p < 0.001$.

(the respective correlations are 0.51 versus 0.36). Third, all three strategies based on particularistic norms are intercorrelated; here, the correlations range from 0.26 to 0.33.[5] Although there are no detailed data on the sequence of channels chosen in connection with particular problems, these data strongly suggest that people easily move from the normatively based universalistic channels to protektzia or patron/brokers, skipping over the possibility of using one or more channels based on legitimate sanctions in connection with the same problem. In other words, the findings suggest that Israelis refrain from escalating legitimate normative pressure within the U frame, opting instead to switch to a particularistic strategy.

Another interesting finding was that users of illegitimate threats seem to be a somewhat distinctive group. Just now, I asked what users of a particular type of channel were likely to do, in addition. Here, I ask, what are they least likely to do? Regardless of the channel type examined, the least likely choice for users of each type is illegitimate threats. For instance, users of channels based on legitimate norms are most likely to have approached political VIPs (0.37) and least likely to have threatened violence (0.15); similarly, users of protektzia are most likely also to have activated one or more channels based on legitimate sanctions (the correlation is 0.39) and least likely also to have threatened an official (the value of the correlation is 0.23). Even users of legitimate threats are more likely to have used any other type of channel than they are to have tried an illegitimate threat as well.

III. THE PERVASIVENESS OF BICULTURALISM: HYBRIDIZATION

A. "Pure" versus "Hybrid" Complainants

In the discussion thus far, the unit of analysis has been the instance of channel use. I moved from a consideration of the original data on individual channels to analysis of variation in channels classified by motivational type. A still more general way to examine the data is to characterize respondents as "pure" versus "hybrid" complainants, as monocultural or bicultural in their behavior. To pursue this approach, they were classified as falling into one of three basic categories: (a) used only U channels; (b) used both U and P channels; (c) used only P channels.

1. **Incidence of pure and hybrid types.** Purely U types are the most common group (Table VII.6). Just over half of persons making one or more influence attempts used only U channels. Thirty-seven percent were hybrid types, having used at least one U channel and at least one P one. The rarest type, then, is the one who reported having used only P channels.

Actually, this estimate of the incidence of purely universalistic types is somewhat misleading because it does not separate those using only one channel from those using two or more. The more interesting question is, given use of at least two channels, how often do people remain universalistic, and how often do they in fact report use of at least one U and one P channel? I return to this question later.

Table VII.6
Use of Universalistic and Particularistic Channels of Complaint In 1968 and in 1980: "Pure" and Hybrid Types of Complainants

Channels of Complaint	Year	
	1968: Ever used any of 5 channels	1980: Ever used any of 12 channels
Universalistic only	47.0%	50.8%
Universalistic and particularistic	38.0	36.6
Particularistic only	15.0	12.5
	100.0%	99.9%
	(381)	(419)

2. Comparison of 1968 and 1980. There are fairly comparable data on channel use in 1968 and 1980. On the face of it, in Table VII.6 it appears that the distributions of complainants in the two time periods are strikingly similar and that the basic pattern of response to injustice has not changed at all. However, the absolute numbers for each year show that the number of persons is roughly the same in the two years: 381 persons had used at least one channel in 1968, and 419 in 1980. But recall that the 1968 sample contained 1886 persons, whereas the 1980 sample contained 1021. If the proportions of these three types of persons *in each sample as a whole* are recalculated, quite different results emerge. In 1968, 138 persons were hybrid, a figure which constitutes 7.3% of the sample as a whole. In 1980, 152 persons were hybrid, or 14.9% of the sample as a whole. In short, these data suggested that *the proportion of hybrids, of bicultural complainants, in the population as a whole, has doubled.*

This increase can be attributed to any or possibly all of four different factors. For one thing, on the average, people reported somewhat more contacts in 1980 than they did in 1968. In the latter, 49% of the sample reported at least one contact; in 1980 the figure was 61%. More contacts mean more problems, and therefore more action to solve them. Second, as I mentioned earlier, consumer consciousness and awareness of client rights have increased, in the meantime, so people are probably better informed of the possibilities of fighting City Hall than in the past. A related factor is that, because there are more complaint-handling devices available, complaint-handlers have to drum up business to justify their existence, in effect competing in a market for customers. This is as true of complaint-handling devices as of any organization offering a service.

The fourth factor is methodological, rather than substantive, and refers to the fact mentioned earlier that in 1968 only five public-sector channels had been asked about, whereas in 1980 12 were investigated. In a 1972 paper on results for channel use in the 1968 study, it was reported that in the sample as a whole, respondents reported little use of channels of complaint. Only about one-fourth of them had appealed to supervisors in the office where they had trouble, whereas less than one-tenth appealed to the State Controller, wrote letters to the editor, or hired a lawyer. One-fifth had used personal connections (Danet and Hartman, 1972b: 16).

If the State Controller is taken as the precursor of the ombudsman, as indeed he is (and today the two roles are filled by the same person, in the Israeli system), all five of the channels originally studied in 1968 are used with virtually identical frequency as in

1968. Thus, the additional instances of channel use in the 1980 data were probably picked up by the questions both on channels which could not have been asked about in 1968, because they did not exist ("Kolbotek," the ombudsman), and on channels which *did* exist then, but which were not asked about (the various forms of political and organizational brokerage). Thus, by not having asked about these forms of brokerage, we may have under-estimated use of P channels in 1968.

Because of all these complications, it is not possible to say to what extent each of the four factors just discussed accounts for the increase in redress activity since 1968. It is unlikely, however, that methodological differences alone account for the increase. These difficulties aside, the key finding is clear: *The basic pattern of hybridization in redress behavior was already present in 1968 and has been spreading in the population.* At the same time, the fact should not be overlooked that in both time periods, 85% of all complainants had made some use of U channels. Thus, despite the trend toward hybridization, U channels are hardly disappearing from the scene.

IV. PREDICTORS OF BICULTURALISM

In the first three sections of this chapter, only general distributions of various phenomena connected with redress in the sample as a whole have been discussed. It is time to move on to the next task—to identify the sociocultural and social-psychological profiles of complainants.

A. Variation in Motivational Types

1. Sociocultural background.

(a) Social mobilization: education and occupation. If the social mobilization hypothesis were to predict choice of channel sub-types, better educated, high-status persons should use channels based on legitimate norms (e.g., the ombudsman) and those based on legitimate sanctions, like the television program or a lawyer; they should refrain from using particularistic channels. In fact, these persons use both U channels and P ones. Thus, the groups best socialized to the U code use both the ombudsman and protektzia, if not in connection with the same problem, then in connection with different problems on different occasions.

(b) Ethnic origin. As for the effects of ethnic origin, consistent with the social mobilization hypothesis, Western Europeans are highest in the use of channels based on U norms. Among Western European immigrants, 52% had either written to the ombudsman or appealed to a person of higher authority than the official originally dealt with (or both), compared to only 28% to 29% of the Eastern European and Middle Eastern immigrants (Table VII.7). The same effect is discernible in the second generation, although it is weaker: 40% of natives of Western European origin used U-normative channels, compared to 28% to 34% of the other three groups of natives.

Interestingly, controlling for access to protektzia, I found that the rate of use of U-normative channels is particularly high among Western Europeans reporting access to protektzia. Fully two-thirds of both the natives and the immigrants from these countries reported appealing a decision to a supervisor or contacting the ombudsman, compared to only 32% to 45% of all other ethnic groups reporting access. Among those not reporting access, the distinctiveness of the Western Europeans disappears, at least for the second generation. This finding showed that the sophisticated person who has an especially good command of the rules, who knows how the system works in practice, and who is well-connected, by no means abandons the U-based channels he or she was taught to use.

This distinctiveness of the Western Europeans recurred only partially in the data on the other type of U channel—those based on legitimate sanctions. Among immigrants, it is once again the Western Europeans who were highest in use of these channels, although only by a small margin; whereas 19% of them had used one or more of them, only 11% to 12% of the other two immigrant groups had done so. Among natives, however, this time, the Western Europeans were *lowest:* Only 10% of them had used channels invoking legitimate sanctions, compared to 15% to 18% of the other three groups of natives.

This latter discrepancy is a strong hint of the de-bureaucratization of Western Europeans. Consider the data in Table VII.7 on the use of protektzia as a redress channel: Among both natives and immigrants, the Western Europeans are once again the highest. Among immigrants, 24% of them had used protektzia, whereas only 11% of Eastern Europeans and 14% of Middle Easterners had done so. The distinctiveness of the Western Europeans is even more apparent among natives though they are small in numbers. Fully one-third of the Western natives born to Western European fathers had used protektzia, but only 14% to 18% of the others. The pattern recurred,

Table VII.7
Choice of Channels by Motivational Base and Ethnic Origin (percent of persons using each channel)*

Ethnic Origin	Motivational Base						N
	Universalistic Norms	Legitimate Threats	Protektzia	Political Brokerage	Organizational Brokerage	Illegitimate Threats	
Native children of natives	28.4	17.9	18.0	4.5	9.0	—	(67)
Native children of Western Europeans	40.0	10.0	33.3	10.0	10.0	11.8	(20)
Native children of Eastern Europeans	33.9	15.8	16.1	8.7	7.1	4.0	(183)
Native children of Middle Easterners	29.9	15.3	14.0	7.3	6.6	0.9	(137)
Western European immigrants	51.9	18.5	24.0	11.1	7.4	2.3	(54)
Eastern European immigrants	28.1	11.4	11.1	4.5	7.4	3.4	(377)
Middle Eastern immigrants	29.3	12.2	14.0	5.5	5.5	5.0	(181)

* Differences significant $p < 0.05$ for universalistic-normative channels and for *protektzia*; all other differences not significant.

but in much paler form for at least 1 of the 2 forms of brokerage, that of organizational brokerage.[6] Although there is hardly any variation in the rate of use of this channel, it is once again the native children of Western Europeans who are highest.[7]

These results pertaining to the Western Europeans are in part the product of another aspect of their behavior, which is consistent with the social mobilization hypothesis: They are generally very active, so they use all channels relatively frequently. Among immigrants the Western Europeans showed the highest rate of use on 4 out of the 6 types of channels; among natives, they are highest on 5 out of the 6. Once again, intensity of activity is consistent with general socialization to the U code, although the content of behavior is not. These results dovetailed nicely with the more general ones about the correlation between social mobilization variables and total number of channels used, discussed earlier in this chapter.

There is intriguing evidence that Western Europeans need a higher threshhold of frustration before crossing over to the use of protektzia. When those reporting access to protektzia in routine encounters are separated from those not doing so, among persons *not* reporting access in routine encounters, Western Europeans were much more likely to admit to using protektzia in response to an injustice than any other ethnic group. A high 30% of natives born to Western European and Anglo-Saxon fathers, but not reporting access in a routine matter, admitted using protektzia as a channel of redress, compared to only 7% of native children of natives and native children of Eastern Europeans, and a tiny 3% of natives born to Middle Eastern fathers. The discrepancy was no smaller among immigrants: Nearly a quarter of Western Europeans not claiming access to protektzia in a routine matter nevertheless used it in response to the experience of injustice. In contrast, only 4% of Eastern European immigrants, and 8% of Middle Eastern ones did so. A X^2 test revealed that the probability of obtaining such a distribution by chance alone was a tiny 0.0004.

Among persons who did claim access in routine matters, on the other hand, there were no differences between ethnic groups. Twenty to 25% of each group said it had used protektzia as a way to deal with injustice. In brief, then, these findings are consistent with the finding in chapter 5 that Western Europeans are slower to define themselves as needing protektzia than other groups.

It is also illuminating to read the numbers horizontally, that is, to examine the rank order of choice of channels within each ethnic group. For all groups, use of those based on universalistic normative power is the first choice. For the Western Europeans, but not for any other group, the number 2 choice is clearly protektzia. All the others are about as likely to use protektzia as channels based on legitimate sanctions.

2. Social-psychological predictors. The set of four social-psychological predictors generally correlated with choice of channel subtypes in a manner consistent with the findings presented in chapter 6.

(a) Perceptions of reward-cost structure. In chapter 6 I reported that of two measures of perceptions of reward-cost structure, the frequency of negatively evaluated experience and self-defined need for protektzia, the latter was the better predictor of behavior. Here, in contrast, the two measures are about equally successful in predicting redress behavior.

Not surprisingly, routine use of protektzia is related to its use as a channel of redress (0.16) and also to use of well-known political brokers (0.12). But note that people seeing themselves as needing protektzia are also likely (albeit less so) to have used a legitimate U channel (whether based on norms or on sanctions). People reporting frequent negative experiences are most likely to have appealed to a supervisor or to have contacted the ombudsman (the correlation is 0.26, the highest shown in Table VII.8) and are also likely to have used protektzia as an alternative to U redress (here the value of the correlation is 0.14).

(b) Perceptions of the behavior of others. Perceptions of what others do are not generally predictive of redress behavior, again because there is too much consensus in the population—everyone knows that everyone uses protektzia some of the time. In Chapter 6 we saw that these perceptions correlated with use of protektzia only at the level of 0.12 and that of the four sets of social-psychological measures, they were least successful in predicting behavior. Here, in Table VII.8, there is a similar low but statistically significant correlation of 0.09 between perceptions of others' behavior and the use of protektzia as an alternative to U-based redress.

3. Control of resources: Access to protektzia. Predictably, claimed access to protektzia in routine encounters is more strongly related to its use as a channel of redress than to any other motivational type of channel investigated (the correlation is 0.24; see Table VII.8).

Table VII.8

Social-Psychological Predictors of Channel Use by Motivational Type

Social-Psychological Predictors	Motivational Type					
	Legitimate Norms	Legitimate Threats	Personalized Political Brokerage	Organizational Brokerage	Protektzia	Illegitimate Threats
Need for protektzia	0.10***	0.09**	0.12***	0.04	0.16***	0.02
Negative experience	0.26***	0.09**	0.10**	0.07*	0.14**	0.07
Perceptions of the behavior of others	0.01	0.03	0.02	0.01	0.09**	0.01
Access to protektzia	0.17***	0.05	0.06*	0.09**	0.24***	0.04

*** p < 0.001; ** p < 0.01; * p < 0.05.

The second highest correlation is with use of U-normative channels, yet another hint that it is the same people who use both.

B. Hybridization

These results strongly suggest but do not demonstrate directly that the same persons who use U channels also use P ones. They only show that the same groups that used U ones also used P ones. Turning to analysis of the sociocultural and social-psychological profiles of hybrids, I can now confirm trends which began to emerge in less abstract forms of analysis; in addition, some new insights emerge.[8]

1. Sociocultural background.

(a) Education and occupation. Table VII.9 confirms that better educated persons and professionals and high-level administrators are more likely to be hybrid than those who are poorly educated or in blue-collar occupations. Thus, 47% of professionals and high-level administrators are bicultural, compared to only 26% of blue-collar workers. And again, among educational groups the highest proportion of hybrids (47%) is among those having completed a B.A. At the same time, these differences among educational and occupational groups are weaker than the ones found in the 1968 study, indicating that a process of homogenization is probably under way.[9]

(b) Ethnic origin. As for ethnic origin, given the myriad findings in chapters 5 and 6 which showed the centrality of being born in Israel, I had expected all natives to be distinctively more hybrid than all immigrants. This is what had been found in the 1968 study. At that time, 50% of natives, but only 32% of European immigrants, and 38% of Middle Eastern immigrants, were bicultural in their use of redress channels. Today the difference between natives and immigrants is a little smaller. On the average, 46% of natives, and 36% of immigrants were hybrids according to the 1980 study, another finding which indicates that homogenization is taking place. Also, contrary to the expectation that the longer people had been in the country, the more likely they were to be hybrid, there was no clear association in the 1980 data with the number of years immigrants had spent in Israel.

At the same time, intriguing differences among ethnic groups persist: Despite the general process of homogenization, the Western Europeans continue to be distinctive (Table VII.10). Western Eu-

Table VII.9

Predictors of Hybridization

Predictors	Hybridization				
	Only U	Both U & P	Only P		
Social Mobilization					
Occupation*					
Professional, administrative	48.2	46.5	5.3	100.0%	(114)
Clerical, sales	53.3	34.6	12.1	100.0%	(107)
Blue-collar, services	60.9	26.1	13.0	100.0%	(46)
Housewives, students	50.0	31.7	18.3	100.0%	(142)
Education*					
No schooling	[42.9]	[14.3]	[42.9]	100.0%	(7)
1–4 years	[50.0]	[50.0]	—	100.0%	(2)
5–8 years	58.8	23.5	17.6	100.0%	(68)
9–10 years	45.3	35.8	18.9	100.0%	(53)
11–12 years	53.3	34.1	12.6	100.0%	(135)
Partial post-high school	47.8	44.8	7.5	100.0%	(67)
B.A. or more	47.7	46.5	5.8	100.0%	(86)
Social-Psychological Variables					
Need for protektzia*					
Needed	43.8	43.1	13.1	100.0%	(160)
Didn't need	56.3	31.6	12.1	100.0%	(247)
Negative experience**					
Many negative experiences	36.7	51.7	11.7	100.0%	(60)
A few negative experiences	60.8	34.2	5.0	100.0%	(120)
One or two	58.2	38.2	3.6	100.0%	(55)
None	47.4	35.8	16.8	100.0%	(137)

Predictors of Hybridization (*continued*)

Table VII.9

Predictors	Hybridization			
Perception of others' behavior				
Most people always use protektzia	45.3	36.8	17.9	100.0%	(106)
Most people usually use it	53.9	35.6	10.5	100.0%	(19)
Most people use it sometimes	51.8	37.3	10.8	100.0%	(83)
Most people usually don't use it	55.2	31.0	13.8	100.0%	(29)
Most people never use it	[50.0]	[50.0]	—	100.0%	(2)
Access to protektzia***				
Yes	42.6	46.3	11.1	100.0%	(190)
No	59.2	28.6	12.1	100.0%	(206)

*** p < 0.001; ** p < 0.01; * p < 0.05.

ropean immigrants are almost twice as likely as immigrants from either Eastern Europe or North Africa and the Middle East to be hybrid. Sixty-four percent of them are hybrid, compared with only 32% to 33% of the other two immigrant groups. Among natives, children of Western European fathers are again most hybrid; 50% of them are hybrid, compared to 31% to 40% of the other three groups of natives (though it should be noted that there are only 10 Western European natives in the table). It is also interesting that both groups of natives born to European fathers are even more hybrid than the third generation Israelis. No doubt, this is the result of differences in occupational status: Third generation natives and natives of Middle Eastern origin have lower occupational status, on the average, than those of European origin and hence are less well connected.

In the lower half of Table VII.10 the same data are exploited in another way; it combines the hybrid and purely P categories to see which groups show the strongest incidence of use of P channels as an alternative to U-based redress. It is evident that among both immigrants and among natives, the Western Europeans are the most likely to use P channels. The lower half of Table VII.10 also shows that at least four-fifths of all immigrant groups made some use of

Table VII.10

Hybridization by Ethnic Origin

Ethnic Origin	Hybridization				
	Only U	*U & P*	*Only P*		
Native children of natives	53.1	31.2	15.6	100.0%	(32)
Native children of Western Europeans	30.0	50.0	20.0	100.0%	(10)
Native children of Eastern Europeans	49.4	39.3	10.4	100.0%	(77)
Native children of Middle Easterners	55.4	33.9	10.7	100.0%	(56)
Western European immigrants	35.7	64.3	—	100.0%	(28)
Eastern European immigrants	54.5	32.9	12.6	100.0%	(143)
Middle Eastern immigrants	49.3	32.4	18.3	100.0%	(71)

	Used U channels	*Used P channels*
Native children of natives	84.3	46.8
Native children of Western Europeans	80.0	70.0
Native children of Eastern Europeans	92.5	64.5
Native children of Middle Easterners	89.3	44.6
Western European immigrants	100.0	64.3
Eastern European immigrants	87.4	45.5
Middle Eastern immigrants	81.7	50.7

U channels. But even here there are discernible differences: Among immigrants, every single one of the Western Europeans used some U channel (among natives, however, it is persons of Eastern European origin who are most likely to have used U channels).

The distinctive pattern of the Western Europeans becomes clear only when all the important findings about their attitudes and behavior can be examined simultaneously. Data from chapters 5 and 6 are now integrated with those from the present chapter, as shown in Table VII.1. To review, in chapter 5 it was shown that Western Europeans are clearly the least likely of all ethnic groups to legitimate protektzia, and least likely to see themselves as needing it, though even one-fifth to one-quarter of them come to need it. Second, as was seen in chapter 6, they are least likely of all groups to report using protektzia in routine encounters and least likely to use it more than once or twice. This is true both for natives and for immigrants of Western European origin.

From the data on access a different story begins to emerge. Among immigrants, we saw that Western Europeans were highest on access; and among natives they were second only to native children of natives. Moreover, once need and access are held constant (column f in Table VII.11), Western Europeans were just as likely to use protektzia as other groups. In other words, once they have made the psychological leap to deviance or biculturalism, they become as deviant as the others.

But the full extent of the unique transformation of the Western Europeans becomes apparent only when redress behavior is examined (the last two columns in Table VII.11, in which data from Tables VII.7 and VII.10 are summarized). We have seen that second-generation Western Europeans are most likely of all groups to use protektzia as a complaint channel. Even among immigrants—those who ostensibly still carry with them the influence of past socialization in their country of origin—Western Europeans are most likely to do so (24%, compared with 11% to 14% of the other groups).[10] Finally, the results showed that they are head and shoulders ahead of the others in hybridization: Fully half of all second generation Western Europeans and nearly two-thirds of immigrants from these countries are hybrid. Although the full distribution of hybridization by seven categories of ethnic origin is not statistically different from chance, the contrast between Western Europeans and all the others is, at p < 0.01. Despite their small numbers in the population, *Western Europeans are, in short, the leading hybrids.* It looks like, of all immigrant groups, they have changed the most as a result of integration into Israeli society.[11]

2. Contact. Several other findings on the association between hybridization and predictor variables are worth noting briefly. For one, frequency of contact was clearly associated with biculturalism. Among people reporting many contacts, 59% were hybrid, as compared with 40% of those reporting almost no contacts, or only a few. And only about one-quarter of those having many encounters reported using only U channels, as opposed to about one-half of those reporting few contacts. Thus, those who have many dealings with the system, and who therefore come to know how it works, learn to use P as well as U channels in the search for redress of grievances.

3. Redress culture. Second, knowledgeable people are especially likely to be hybrids. This finding is entirely consistent with those I have just presented for sociocultural background. Whereas about one-third of those scoring 0 to 3 on the bureaucratic quiz were hybrids, the proportion was 44% among those scoring 4 to 6. Similarly, the more channels people know about, the more hybrid they are: Among those knowing about only one of the five U channels asked about directly (the ombudsman, "Kolbotek," Citizens' Advice Bureau, appealing to a higher official, small claims court), only 29% were hybrids, whereas nearly one-half of those familiar with all five channels were hybrids. Moreover, measures of subjective and objective knowledgeability worked the same way, just as was seen in earlier chapters. Those who feel knowledgeable tend to be hybrids. Over one-half of those who claimed always to know to whom to complain were hybrids; the proportion descends in orderly linear fashion with decreasing subjective knowledgeability, until only a little over one-quarter of those saying they never know where to go are hybrids.

A composite redress-proneness score,[12] which was compiled from the preceding data on subjective knowledgeability, as well as on perceptions about people's right to complain, and the perception of complainants as constructive citizens, are also linearly related to hybridization. Three-fifths of those receiving the highest possible score on the redress-proneness scale were hybrid in their use of channels; at the same time, even among those scoring very poorly,

Table VII.11
A Summary of Attitudes and Behavior by Seven Categories of Ethnic Origin

Ethnic Origin	(a) Legitimacy: % saying legitimate	(b) Need: % "needing"	(c) Routine use: % using more than once or twice	(d) Access: % having access	(e) Routine use, given need, access	(f) Use of protektzia as channel: % used	(g) Hybridization: % hybrid
Native children of natives	17.1%	43.3%	13.8%	53.8%	70.8%	18.0%	31.4%
Native children of Western Europeans	8.3%	21.4%	4.8%	48.5%	[80.0%]	33.3%	50.0%
Native children of Eastern Europeans	11.0%	40.2%	11.7%	44.4%	71.0%	16.1%	40.3%
Native children of Middle Easterners	16.9%	37.8%	9.8%	43.2%	83.3%	14.0%	33.9%

Table VII.11 (*continued*)

A Summary of Attitudes and Behavior by Seven Categories of Ethnic Origin

Ethnic Origin	(a) Legitimacy: % saying legitimate	(b) Need: % "needing"	(c) Routine use: % using more than once or twice	(d) Access: % having access	(e) Routine use, given need, access	(f) Use of protektzia as channel: % used	(g) Hybridization: % hybrid
Western Europeans	7.3%	24.5%	3.4%	49.0%	47.4%	24.0%	64.3%
Eastern Europeans	7.5%	22.0%	4.4%	29.9%	51.3%	11.1%	32.9%
Middle Easterners	12.1%	43.4%	5.7%	27.6%	56.3%	14.0%	32.4%

a) n.s.; difference between Western Europeans and others significant, p < 0.01.

b) p < 0.001.

c) n.s.; difference between Western Europeans and others significant, p < 0.01.

d) p < 0.001.

e) p < 0.05.

f) p < 0.05.

g) n.s.; difference between Western Europeans and others significant, p < 0.01.

as many as one-third were also hybrids. In short, *to be positively oriented toward the pursuit of redress in this society is to be a hybrid.*

Moreover, to be an active user of channels is to be hybrid. It is now possible to diagnose precisely what people using one, two, three, four, or more than four channels did. Among those using one channel only, three-quarters used a U channel and only one-quarter used a P channel. Already, among those having used only two channels, more than half (56%) are hybrid, having used one U channel and one P channel. Thereafter, virtually every activist, using three or more channels, is bound to have used both U and P channels. Among those using three channels, a very high 93% are hybrids; among those using four, the figure jumps still higher to 96%, and among those using five channels or more (there were 36 such persons), *every single one was a hybrid.*

The above data now enable us to qualify the discussion of the proportions of purely U and hybrid types in Section III.A.1 above. There, we saw that, when single and multiple users of channels are both included in the calculation, 42% were hybrids. As I pointed out, strictly speaking, it makes sense to calculate the proportion of hybrids only among those using at least two channels, because people cannot be hybrids unless they use more than one channel. Recalculating this proportion, after elimination of the one-time users, I arrived at the remarkably high figure of 79% hybrid. In other words, *4 out of every 5 persons having used two or more channels are bicultural.* The value of the Pearson correlation between total channels used and hybridization is 0.66.[13]

4. Social-psychological predictors.

(a) Perceptions of reward-cost structure. The highest proportion of hybrids was found among those reporting many problems (52%). At the same time, as indicated in Table VII.9, the association is not neatly linear; the probability of being a hybrid is about as high among those reporting only positive contacts as it is among those having only one or two problematic encounters, or some such encounters.[14] Self-defined need for protektzia also predicts hybridization with some degree of success: 43% of those saying they needed to use protektzia in routine encounters were hybrid complainants, compared to 32% of those not needing protektzia routinely. X^2 tests for both of these predictors indicated that the distributions were significantly different from chance.

(b) Perceptions of the behavior of others. I did not find a significant relation between perceptions of the behavior of others and the tendency to hybridization, again because the belief that everyone uses protektzia is so widespread. However, those thinking most people never use protektzia or usually avoid it are a little less likely to be hybrid, as the grand hypothesis would predict (Table VII.9).

(c) Perceived control of resources: Access to protektzia. On the other hand, perceived access to protektzia did prove to be fairly important. People who reported access to personal connections in time of need in bureaucratic encounters were significantly more likely than those without access to be hybrid complainants (the value of the Pearson correlation was 0.18). There may be partial redundance here, as some of those reporting need and access in routine encounters may have been thinking of instances where they experienced an injustice.[15]

5. Routine use of protektzia and hybridization in redress. Earlier in this chapter, I formulated the hypothesis that people who use protektzia as a general mode of doing business in bureaucratic encounters will also use particularistic channels as avenues to redress when they experience injustice. This hypothesis was confirmed at the highest level of significance: 51% of those routinely using protektzia were hybrids, compared to only 29% of those not reporting routine use. This association may have again been somewhat inflated, because of the problem of partial overlap between answers on the two sets of questions, just noted above. As was seen, however, when the data on Western Europeans versus the others were examined, not all hybrid complainants necessarily used protektzia in routine encounters.[16]

6. Multivariate analysis. We have seen that a very large number of predictor variables are associated with hybridization. To isolate the more important ones and to probe more deeply into the way they interrelate with hybridization, a log-linear analysis was performed, again using the logit model, as in chapter 6. Seven predictor variables were entered: education, nativity (native versus immigrant), Western European origin versus all other origins, self-defined need for protektzia, claimed access to it, presence or absence of negative experience in bureaucratic encounters, and use of protektzia in routine encounters. Early in the analysis nativity and the contrast between Western Europeans and all others were eliminated. This is theoretically satisfying because these variables are of interest primarily to students of Israeli society or to students of immigrant societies.

The basic data set prepared for logit analysis is presented in Table VII.12. Respondents were dichotomized into hybrids versus all others. Hybridization was cross-tabulated with routine use, access, need, negative experience and education; three educational levels were analyzed: completed 8 years of elementary school or less; completed 1 or more years of high school; and obtained at least one year of post-high school, typically, university education.[17]

(a) A comparison of thirteen models. Thirteen different models to account for the interrelations among these six variables were tested. The results are displayed in Table VII.13. Following the criterion of Knoke and Burke (1980), to which I referred in chapter 6, namely, that a model whose p value ranges between 0.10 and 0.35 should be chosen, three models emerged as candidates to explain variation in hybridization, nos. 8, 9, and 10.

Model no. 8 contains four terms: the interaction of education with the complex of negative experience/need/access/routine use; and the zero-order relationship between hybridization and each of three variables: education, access, and routine use, respectively. Model no. 9 closely resembles no. 8, to which it is hierarchically related. In both, the first and second terms are identical; the third term in model no. 9 contains higher-order interactions, as well as all of the zero-order relations included in model no. 8. It includes, for example, the association between need for protektzia and hybridization via experience, access, and routine use.

Unlike the other two models, no. 10 contains no term positing a direct relationship between education and hybridization. There are terms positing direct zero-order effects of education on assessments of experience, on perceived need for protektzia, and on access; second, a set of four terms stipulates the importance of zero-order associations between experience, need, access, and routine use and hybridization, respectively.

(b) Choosing a model. The decision as to whether model 9 is or is not preferable over no. 8 is simple. The difference in their respective values of L^2 is 15.43, a figure which, at 13 d.f. (the difference in degrees of freedom between the two models), would result at a probability of 0.25; hence the addition of the interaction effects included in model no. 9 does not significantly improve the

Table VII.12

Cross-Tabulation of Hybridization in Use of Complaint Channels by Routine Use of Protektzia, Access to It, Need for It, Quality of Experience, and Education

Routine Use	Access	Need	Negative Experience	Education	Hybridization no	Hybridization yes
no	no	no	no	elementary	49	1
no	no	no	no	high school	78	7
no	no	no	no	university	39	2
no	no	no	yes	elementary	23	2
no	no	no	yes	high school	57	8
no	no	no	yes	university	31	1
no	no	yes	no	elementary	13	1
no	no	yes	no	high school	13	1
no	no	yes	no	university	5	0
no	no	yes	yes	elementary	19	0
no	no	yes	yes	high school	20	6
no	no	yes	yes	university	10	5
no	yes	no	no	elementary	6	0
no	yes	no	no	high school	28	4
no	yes	no	no	university	14	8
no	yes	no	yes	elementary	1	2
no	yes	no	yes	high school	15	2
no	yes	no	yes	university	21	8
no	yes	yes	no	elementary	2	0
no	yes	yes	no	high school	3	0
no	yes	yes	no	university	0	0
no	yes	yes	yes	elementary	0	1
no	yes	yes	yes	high school	7	0
no	yes	yes	yes	university	3	3
yes	no	no	no	elementary	2	0
yes	no	no	no	high school	2	1

Table VII.12

Cross-Tabulation of Hybridization in Use of Complaint Channels by Routine Use of Protektzia, Access to It, Need for It, Quality of Experience, and Education *(continued)*

Routine Use	Access	Need	Negative Experience	Education	Hybridization	
yes	no	no	no	university	0	1
yes	no	no	yes	elementary	2	0
yes	no	no	yes	high school	2	0
yes	no	no	yes	university	0	1
yes	no	yes	no	elementary	0	0
yes	no	yes	no	high school	3	0
yes	no	yes	no	university	1	1
yes	no	yes	yes	elementary	1	1
yes	no	yes	yes	high school	5	0
yes	no	yes	yes	university	2	1
yes	yes	no	no	elementary	0	1
yes	yes	no	no	high school	1	1
yes	yes	no	no	university	5	1
yes	yes	no	yes	elementary	0	1
yes	yes	no	yes	high school	3	0
yes	yes	no	yes	university	3	3
yes	yes	yes	no	elementary	7	0
yes	yes	yes	no	high school	20	5
yes	yes	yes	no	university	5	3
yes	yes	yes	yes	elementary	5	4
yes	yes	yes	yes	high school	28	8
yes	yes	yes	yes	university	19	19

Table VII.13
Models Fitted to the Data for Hybridization Displayed in Table VII.12*

Model	L^2	d.f.	p
1 [EXNAZ] [H]	112.28	47	0.000
2 [EXNA] [HE]	93.75	45	0.000
3 [NAZ] [EX] [EN] [HE] [HA] [HZ]	142.55	76	0.000
4 [XN] [AZ] [EX] [EN] [EA] [HX] [HA] [HN] [HZ]	271.27	76	0.000
5 [XNAZ] [HE] [HX] [HN] [HA]	117.00	72	0.001
6 [NAZ] [EXN] [HE] [HA] [HZ]	104.95	73	0.009
7 [NA] [NZ] [AZ] [EX] [EN] [EA] [XN] [HE] [HA]	101.57	75	0.022
8 [EXNAZ] [HE] [HA] [HZ]	55.17	43	0.101
9 [EXNAZ] [HE] [HXNAZ]	39.74	30	0.110
10 [XNAZ] [EX] [EN] [EA] [HX] [HA] [HN] [HZ]	79.25	67	0.145
11 [NAZ] [EX] [EN] [EA] [XN] [HE] [HA] [HZ]	74.41	73	0.432
12 [NAZ] [ENA] [EX] [HE] [HA] [HZ]	71.61	71	0.457
13 [NAZ] [EX] [EN] [EA] [XN]	20.24	30	0.910

* Key to variables:
N = need for protektzia
A = access to protektzia
Z = routine use of protektzia
E = education
X = negative experience
H = hybridization

prediction of hybridization. The simpler model is thus the preferable one.

The next step is to choose between models no. 8 and no. 10. Here, the decision is again relatively simple, but this time primarily on theoretical grounds, rather than empirical ones. The original theoretical formulation elaborated in chapter 3 had predicted that in hybrid organizational cultures social mobilization variables would not predict behavior. Accordingly, a model which eliminates this direct association is clearly preferable. On this account, then, model no. 10 is to be preferred.

But might it be that model no. 8 provides a better empirical account of the Israeli data than no. 10? The answer turns out to be comfortingly negative. The two models are empirically just about as powerful. The value of L^2 obtained by subtracting that for model no. 8 from the one for model no. 10 does not even begin to approximate statistical significance. Therefore, each model can serve as an empirically adequate account of the Israeli data. This result surely reinforces the decision to choose model no. 10 on theoretical grounds.

Figure VII.1
A Model of the Road to Hybridization of Redress Behavior (Model No. 10 in Table VII.11)

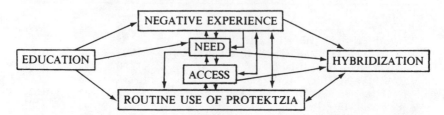

In Figure VII.1 the structure of model no. 10 is laid out. It provides an elegant summary of the entire Israeli case study. It shows clearly that the complex experience/need/access/use is the heart of the model. The various zero-order associations as well as the higher-order interactions of these variables predict hybridization, much as predicted by the grand hypothesis. But the model specifies the relationships in a degree of detail which was not anticipated in the grand hypothesis.

At the same time, there is an obvious and important difference from the grand hypothesis, namely, the persistence of education in the model. The zero-order associations between education and negative experience, need, and access nicely sum up the role that education plays in fostering entrance into the delinquent culture. They indicate that the theory must be revised to stipulate that in hybrid organizational cultures the social mobilization variables simultaneously promote socialization to universalistic values and entrance into social circles which regularly violate them.

V. OUTCOMES: NOTHING WORKS LIKE PROTEKTZIA

The pattern of hybridization documented in this chapter is self-perpetuating, because no other channel of redress, universalistic or particularistic, can compete with protektzia, and because organizational brokerage turns out to be at least as effective as official channels having the capacity to sanction offending officials or organizations (e.g., a lawyer, the media). Fully four-fifths of all users of protektzia in routine matters reported that it was either "very helpful" or "helpful;" only one-fifth said it was not helpful. The 130 users of protektzia as a channel of redress were even more effusive: 71% said it had been "very helpful," and another 23% said it had been "helpful." Thus, taking these results as rough estimates of the efficacy of activating personal connections, I suggest that only about one-tenth to one-fifth of the time does protektzia fail. Apparently, not only do people rarely refuse to intervene, but their efforts almost never fail.

A. Protektzia Compared with Other Channels

In Table VII.14 the ratings given by users and non-users of 12 public-sector channels, including protektzia, are compared. The channels are arranged in order of actual effectiveness reported by users, with protektzia in first place, and appeals to an MK coming in last. The results indicated that although the general public tended somewhat to under-estimate the effectiveness of channels, *it makes no mistake about protektzia.* Non-users rated it second in effectiveness, to be outdone only by the television program. Sixty-six percent of non-users thought it would be very helpful, about 11% less than the proportion predicting that "Kolbotek" would be very helpful (note also that users of the program are not so rosy in their assessments of it; only half of users said it had actually been very helpful).

Table VII.14
Effectiveness of Twelve Channels in the Public Sector: The Experience of Users Compared with the Estimates of Non-Users*

Channel	Users		Non-Users		Difference
	%	N	%	N	
Protektzia	70.8	(130)	66.2	(763)	+ 4.6
Lawyer	57.9	(76)	37.4	(757)	+20.5
Trade Union	56.3	(71)	22.6	(687)	+23.7
TV program	55.5	(45)	77.6	(867)	−22.1
Political party	52.6	(19)	10.4	(693)	+42.2
Newspaper, radio	38.7	(62)	40.3	(821)	− 1.6
Ombudsman	38.6	(83)	32.1	(614)	+ 6.5
Higher official	36.5	(296)	26.8	(579)	+ 9.7
Public pressure	36.3	(36)	15.6	(767)	+20.7
Illegitimate threats	33.3	(27)	14.7	(774)	+18.6
Prime Minister, minister	23.9	(46)	20.5	(726)	+ 3.4
Knesset Member	14.6	(41)	17.2	(739)	− 2.6
Average % "very helpful"	42.9		31.8		+11.1

* Percent of respondents who answered "very helpful". N's vary because those not familiar with each channel have been excluded.

Of the other two types of particularistic strategies, personalized political brokerage (appealing to an MK or to the Prime Minister or another government minister) turned out to be ineffective in most cases, just as non-users had correctly estimated. But organizational brokers, on the other hand—party hacks and trade union officials—turned out to be very good bets. Although non-users grossly underestimated their effectiveness, users found them very helpful about half the time—just as effective as hiring a lawyer or contacting "Kolbotek." The largest error made by the non-users in guessing the effectiveness of the various channels was in connection with political party workers; the non-users were off by a remarkably high 42.2%. And the second biggest error was in connection with the other type of organizational brokerage, contacting trade union officials. Thus, a small group of persons having the capacity to do so obtains satisfaction via the mobilization of organizational brokers.

Consider also the differences between the experiences of those using the ombudsman, the U channel par excellence, and those using protektzia. The ombudsman ranked only seventh: Only a little over one-third of those who had contacted the ombudsman said he had been very helpful. Of course, in part this difference also reflects several other factors. One is the lack of "teeth" available to the ombudsman, compared to legitimate channels based on threats; indeed, 3 of the 4 types of channels based on legitimate institutionalized threats (lawyer, TV program, newspaper/radio, pressure/petition) ranked higher than the ombudsman. At the same time, effectiveness of channels does not just depend on the channel, of course—with regard to U-based channels, it also depends on whether the client has a case: Consider the fact that about half the complaints handled by the ombudsman are found to be unjustified (cf. Danet, 1978). Protektzia works better than U-based channels like the ombudsman precisely because it cancels or suspends the U-based norm involved. For the purposes of diagnosis of how the system works, what is important is that people were 1.5 times as likely to have activated personal connections as to have contacted the ombudsman and were far more likely to report success using the former than the latter.

B. Predictors of Success with Channels

The double advantage of educated people, professionals, and others working in high-status occupations, which has recurred throughout this study, reappeared in the data on outcomes. Educated persons and those of high occupational status generally tended to report greater success when seeking redress, in the public as well as the private sectors, than did those of low educational attainment and occupational status. The highest correlation between education and success was in use of protektzia, not in the search for redress generally. This finding suggests, then, that it is not quality of socialization to the U code, but—once again—promixity to elites and general social integration that promotes success.

At the same time, the advantage of the stronger groups, vis-a-vis the weaker ones, is not a large one. Comparing natives to immigrants, for example, I found that although about four-fifths of all natives and of all European immigrants using protektzia in routine matters found it very effective, fully two-thirds of Middle Eastern immigrants did so. Thus, the underdog group is somewhat disadvantaged, but only relatively so, vis-à-vis natives.

VI. Summary and Discussion

This chapter has demonstrated conclusively that the response to injustice is heavily bicultural and that the best integrated persons are most likely to be bicultural. Better integrated, better connected persons also tend to obtain somewhat better outcomes, although everyone does well, using protektzia.

Among the many important findings that emerged in this chapter, some of the more outstanding are the following: First of all, it is now clear that the single most frequently used channel, in response to the experience of injustice, is not the ombudsman, but protektzia. Strictly speaking, of course, to use protektzia is not to complain at all, since to complain means to demand redress within the universalistic frame. Second, a high 40% of all channels used—more precisely, of all reported instances of channel use—were particularistic—whether protektzia or the four forms of patron/brokerage studied.

Third, striking evidence was found that persons well integrated into the system are more likely to combine universalistic-normative channels with particularistic ones than with universalistic channels with teeth—those based on legitimate sanctions. These data suggested strongly, although they did not directly prove, that when people want to do something besides write to the ombudsman or see a supervisor, they opt for what they know to be extremely effective channels, that is, the particularistic ones.

Although data were not collected on the sequence in which people used the various channels, I interpreted these findings to mean that people skip over the channels based on legitimate sanctions. Further support for this inference was found in several forms of consistency in multiple channel use, e.g., that people who tend to use one type of particularistic channel also tend to use the others (moreover, those who do use channels based on legitimate threats in the public sector tended to do so also in regard to private-sector problems).

This pattern of hybridization in redress behavior was already found to be present in the 1968 study, and is at least as strong today, and has probably spread still further in the population. Counter to the grand hypothesis, social mobilization variables did predict at least the quantitative aspects of redress behavior fairly well. Better educated persons, and persons of high occupational status did use more channels of complaint that their counterparts. But once the focus was shifted to the content of channels chosen, social mobilization variables either became unimportant, or the correlations found were in quite the opposite direction, such that the relatively stronger groups were the most hybrid.

Another significant finding was that, in Israeli society, to be an active complainant, frequently taking action in response to perceived injustice, is to be a hybrid. *A remarkably high 4 out of every 5 persons having used at least two channels had employed at least one universalistic one in combination with one particularistic one.*

The logit analysis of hybridization provided a concise summary of the basic elements in the entire case study. It is worth noting the differences between the model accounting for hybridization in redress (this chapter) with that accounting for routine use of protektzia (chapter 6). Both logit analyses forced me to alter the predictions generated by the grand hypothesis, but in different ways. The analysis of routine use of personal connections showed that attitudes about the legitimacy of their use could not entirely be eliminated, contrary to the prediction. In contrast, data on attitudes about the legitimacy of protektzia did drop out in the log-linear analysis of use of channels of complaint. Another difference is that the two key dependent variables in the study, routine use of protektzia and hybridization, are associated with different background variables. In chapter 6 respondents' age remained surprisingly important. The trend for younger people to legitimate protektzia was important enough to survive the test of multivariate analysis. Here, in the analysis of hybridization, respondents' education persisted.

Readers who are not particularly interested in Israeli society or in the problem of social change in immigrant societies may have found the analysis of the behavior of Western Europeans in this chapter too detailed for their taste, especially since ethnicity as a whole proved not to be an important predictor variable. May I suggest in response that the findings on this group are of a general theoretical importance which bears no relation to their small number in the Israeli population and which goes beyond issues of immigration and social change.

The transplantation of this group to a bicultural environment constitutes a natural field experiment. I have tried to interpret the findings on their behavior as indicating change over time. Of course, this is not a longitudinal study and, strictly speaking, I have not been able to compare the behavior of the same persons over time.[18] Still, recall the pair of findings on (1) the apparent reluctance of Western Europeans to use protektziá routinely on the one hand, and (2) their crossing over to the other side, their becoming more bicultural than all the others when it comes to redress, on the other. These findings suggest not only that there is a threshhold for rule-violation, for conversion to biculturalism, for induction into the delinquent community, but that *the stronger a person's initial internalization of the U code, the stronger the provocation must be to violate that code.* They echo and elaborate a finding from the 1968 study. There, Hartman and I examined the effect of perceptions that public bureaucracy is unfair on consistency of attitude and behavior (Danet and Hartman, 1972a). A zero-order correlation between the belief that bureaucracy is unfair and the tendency to be inconsistent proved to hold, on closer analysis, only for immigrants of Middle Eastern origin and for those of low educational attainment. In other words, persons who had more thoroughly internalized the U code were better able to resist the temptation to become inconsistent.[19] While we had established in the 1968 study that for those of European origin bureaucratization is more than skin deep, we did not probe the breaking-point for them when situational constraints would overtake the restraining effects of past socialization. Here, in the data on hybridization in redress behavior, I have taken that next step.

The panoply of findings on hybridization in use of channels indicates that the U culture of redress is under-institutionalized in Israel. Evidently, people do not care enough about universalistic justice to value the pursuit of satisfaction through official channels. They abdicate the right to a universalistically grounded decision— even a decision that may go against their own interests. In contrast, I have argued, where the culture of redress is more fully internalized, individuals will prize, or at least respect the right to a universalistically grounded decision, *even* if that decision goes against their interests.

Even if protektzia does work like a charm, might it disappear if the system were more responsive? I suspect not. My hunch is that even if the organizational factors that foster rule-violations—monopoly and near monopoly and inefficiency (and probably rigidity, too)—were to recede in the near future, the patterns identified in this study would probably persist. For one thing, as I showed in Chapter IV, the forces of both familism and illegalism have been reinforced in the period since the 1967 war. But even if factors promoting covert legitimation for particularistic expectations were completely neutralized tomorrow—an unlikely development—the pattern of hybridization might still persist, albeit in a somewhat weakened form, simply because in the interim this pattern has become comfortable, unthinking habit, the routine way of handling routine trouble.

The findings of this chapter, and indeed, of the two preceding ones, as well, bear a striking resemblance to the results of Wolfsfeld's (1988) study of the politics of protest in Israel. He examined the tendency to take political action through institutionalized or conventional channels—such as being active in a political party—or through mobilized or unconventional ones—strategies in which the individual goes outside the institutional system, e.g., signs a petition or participates in a demonstration (cf. Barnes, Kaase et al., 1979). Wolfsfeld's three types of activists, Conformists, Dissidents and Pragmatists, parallel the purely U, purely P, and hybrid organizational types distinguished in this book. Conformists were those using only institutionalized channels; Dissidents were those using only mobilized channels outside the system. The political action repertoire of Pragmatists combined institutional and mobilized strategies, just as organizational hybrids both appeal to ombudsmen and mobilize personal connections.

As Wolfsfeld wrote,

> Israelis are more likely than citizens from other countries to use mobilized action as an alternative to institutional actions. A quarter of all Israelis who are active confine themselves to protest (mostly demonstrations), a figure unequaled in any other country studied. (Wolfsfeld, 1988: 33)

In addition, when those using at least one channel outside the institutional system are contrasted with the conformists (e.g., Dissidents and Pragmatists combined), Israel had a high 46% of nonconforming activists; only one other country among the eight others investigated, Italy, came close, with 44% choosing at least partially non-conventional strategies (Wolfsfeld, 1988: Table 1-5).

Moreover, like the organizational hybrids described in this chapter, Dissidents and Pragmatists, tend to be relatively well educated (Wolfsfeld, 1988: Figure 3-4). Thus, just as this book has shown that protektzia is primarily used not by marginal, weak or deviant groups in Israel, but by the best educated, highest-status persons, so Wolfsfeld concluded:

> The results stand traditional theories of protest on their head. Mobilized action was seen as a refuge for the downtrodden and the ignorant; in fact, it is the educated who dominate this mode of action. (Wolfsfeld, 1988:81)

Even Wolfsfeld's results on the unimportance of ethnicity for political behavior dovetail with those of the case study reported in this book. He found that ethnic origin had little to do with either institutional or mobilized political action. The two sets of negative findings give support to the interpretation that Jews of Sephardic origin have become better integrated into the society by the late 1980's, and thus participate more in public life than they did in the past.

There is a final similarity between our two studies—the most important one of all: in both, psychological factors predicted behavior more successfully than did sociocultural characteristics of individuals (compare Wolfsfeld, 1988: Table 3-8). The striking similarities in the results of these two studies, which were independently carried out, should add validity to the claims that each of us has made.

VIII
Biculturalism versus "Modernity"

The patterns of organizational culture identified in the preceding three chapters are a far cry from what a group of researchers based at the Hebrew University expected to develop when they first began to study the encounter between Israeli bureaucracy and immigrants, back in 1958, just 10 years after the founding of the State. In that year Elihu Katz and S.N. Eisenstadt led a research seminar on "Bureaucracy and New Immigrants." Katz and Eisenstadt and their students, many of whom are today well-established sociologists in their own right, certainly recognized that there were countervailing forces pushing toward bureaucratization, on the one hand, and toward debureaucratization, on the other. They were aware that bureaucratic agencies were officially committed to universalism, but that a variety of constraints tended to undermine this commitment. At the same time, a look back at the publications of the 1950's and 1960's which dealt with this topic reveals that the researchers tended to believe that Israel was well on the road to becoming a society which was universalistic in practice, as well as on paper.

I. The Absorption-Modernization Paradigm

A. Particularistic Behavior as Temporary Aberration

In an earlier book on the absorption of immigrants in Israel, Eisenstadt (1954) had already pointed to the co-existence of contra-

218

dictory universalistic and particularistic trends in the new society, dating from the Yishuv period, and acknowledged that it was much too early to predict what shape the society would take. As for the matter of absorption of immigrants via bureaucratic agencies, he summarized research indicating that officials sometimes went beyond purely bureaucratic relations and established direct personal relations with clients:

> In these cases the official tried to perform, beyond his formal functions, some more personal ones—protective and advisory—as well, and to enlarge to some extent the immigrants' field of participation and feeling of active belonging. (Eisenstadt, 1954: 174)

A related phenomenon was the tendency for officials to turn themselves into members of the immigrants' own group, to help them transform its structure and pattern of behavior "according to the roles inherent in the new social structure" (Eisenstadt, 1954: 175). Thus, officials were stepping out of the narrowly universalistic definition of their roles, or at least broadening them to accommodate the needs of immigrant clients. These observations implied that the bureaucrats stepped out of their roles only because *they had to*— that it not for the pressures to respond to the needs of unsocialized immigrants, they would have behaved in a universalistic manner.

Bar-Yosef, a member of the original 1958–59 seminar, continued the analysis of the absorption of immigrants via bureaucratic frameworks, in a paper produced in the 1960's. Focusing on processes of "desocialization and resocialization," she suggested that "the bureaucratic situation per se has effects of degradation and desocialization," because it tends to ignore the status adults usually enjoy as a result of age and experience—"The universalistic approach of the Israeli bureaucracy does not distinguish between age groups"— and because it treats clients as members of universalistically defined categories (Bar-Yosef Weiss, 1968, 1980: 27). Note that both of these statements make no clear distinction between the official, normative commitment to universalism and actual practice.

She reported that to relieve "bureaucratic stress," i.e., the unpleasantness or unsatisfying nature of universalistic treatment, clients developed a number of strategies. One was to develop a distinctive manner of presentation of self to reduce the anonymity of the client categories. She noted, for example, that Yemenite immigrants cultivated a romanticized image which helped them to gain special status. European immigrants, on the other hand, tended to elaborate what she called a "personal myth," to display themselves as interesting individuals who rated special consideration, either as members of high ranking groups or because of personal charisma. A third strategy was to manipulate the interaction, either by exploitation of opportunities offered within the universalistic rules, or by personalization and the activation of loyalties based on "family and friendship ties, local ties, old associational membership, or the partly institutionalized party bosses and influentials of voluntary associations" (Bar-Yosef Weiss, 1968, 1980: 31).

The use of personal connections was thus portrayed as an *aberrant* phenomenon—among immigrants, but not among absorbing officials. Bar-Yosef suggested that "The myth of 'important contacts' is the strongest collective myth of the immigrant subculture" (italics supplied; Bar-Yosef Weiss, 1968, 1980: 31). Only a few lines later she went on to write that "Some behavior patterns are guided by a veridical perception of the social reality while others are elicited by *distorted and mythical images*" (italics supplied; Bar-Yosef Weiss, 1968, 1980: 32). The implication, once again, is that, left alone, the bureaucracy is universalistic and that it is immigrant clients who "don't know any better," who try to personalize contacts with officials. In other words, to activate U norms is to be veridical, to seek protektzia is to be influenced by "distorted and mythical images."

In a paper which shifted the focus to the response of officials to clients of differing immigrant backgrounds, Katz and Eisenstadt acknowledged that prior to the influx of non-Western immigrants, Israeli organizations were not close approximations of the Weberian model. Nevertheless, the implicit premise in this paper, too, was that Israel was on the road to becoming a modern, Western-style society, and that ultimately, the forces of bureaucratization would probably win the day (Katz and Eisenstadt, 1960).

Katz and Eisenstadt and their students were well aware that immigrants of differing sociocultural backgrounds brought differing expectations to encounters with immigration and other officials. Indeed, one of the foci of the research stimulated by their seminar was precisely the nature of these differing expectations. It was assumed that those coming from Europe, or at least from Western Europe and the English-speaking countries, would not have to change very much, since their expectations for behavior were consistent with the premises of a universalistic civil society. They would simply transfer patterns learned from past socialization to the new society.

Research interest was concentrated on immigrants from Middle Eastern and North African societies who lacked exposure to bureaucratic ways and who would therefore have to learn the norms of a modern bureaucratized society. For instance, the researchers speculated on what would happen to a new immigrant from, say, Morocco or Yemen, who was observed to bargain with a bus driver over the fare (cf. Katz and Eisenstadt, 1960; Katz and Danet, 1973a, Introduction). They identified with the notion that people like this bus passenger had to be re-socialized, to be taught the rules governing interaction in a universalistic, hierarchical organization like the bus company, where the driver did not pocket the fare or determine its cost. Once again, de-bureaucratization occurred because officials had to step out of their role to teach immigrants how to be clients. By implication, de-bureaucratization was therefore *temporary*.

B. Two Working Hypotheses

In 1963 a team of researchers headed by Elihu Katz undertook a series of empirical studies of bureaucratic encounters in which they aspired to go beyond the preliminary observations of the earlier exploratory studies.[1] Working within the absorption-modernization paradigm, the group formulated two working hypotheses: (1) immigrants from Western, bureaucratized backgrounds will display behavior which conforms with the U code, whereas those of Middle Eastern, non-bureaucratized backgrounds will display behavior which corresponds to the P code; (2) exposure to Israeli bureaucracy will transform the Middle Easterners, making them like Westerners.

The three main studies carried out by the project team in the 1960's addressed themselves to different combinations of these hypotheses. Once again, the same assumption, that Israel was on the road to becoming a modern society, implicitly guided the work. For instance, we wrote of "bureaucratic competence," assuming that to be a competent client was to conform with the norms of universalism and specificity (Danet, 1971; Danet and Gurevitch, 1972). It was only when the third study produced evidence too extensive to "write off" as a temporary aberration that we began to pay serious attention to the cultural patterns then taking shape, although even in the papers in which the results of this study were reported (Danet and Hartman, 1972a; 1972b), we continued to equate bureaucratic socialization with modernization, as Avruch (1981: 134) correctly points out.

1. A pilot study of persuasive appeals. The first study undertaken by the project team was a study of the persuasive appeals clients would use to influence officials in four hypothetical situations. This study mainly addressed itself to the first hypothesis, of differences between individuals of differing sociocultural backgrounds. In each of the four situations, clients were asked what they would say to persuade officials to grant a request. In accordance with expectation, persons of Western background and of high educational attainments appealed in the language of norms, whereas those of Middle Eastern background and of low educational attainment appealed to the altruism of officials, thus using a strategy which was inappropriate in a bureaucratic setting (Katz and Danet, 1966).

2. The Customs study. Like the pilot study, in a larger, full-fledged study on the same topic, a content analysis of letters to Israeli Customs officials (from the years 1959 and 1962), analyzed the reasons clients gave to persuade officials to grant a request. It too focused primarily on the effects of sociocultural background of immigrants on their attitudes and behavior. As in the pilot study, in the Customs study persons hypothesized to be modern in background—coming from the West, of high education or occupational status—conformed with U norms to a greater extent than their less modern counterparts (Danet, 1971; Danet and Gurevitch, 1972).

C. First Hints of De-bureaucratization as a Feature of the Host Society

There were, in fact, strong hints in both the pilot study and in the Customs study that exposure to Israeli bureaucracy de-bureaucratized persons of European origin. Thus, in the pilot study, whose data were gathered in 1962–63, Katz and I found that "part of the data support the idea that clients learn through experience that it pays to ask for a favor" (Katz and Danet, 1966: 188). We reported that

> those with experience in the police and in the workers' committee situations tend to give *fewer* normative responses (and correspondingly higher altruistic responses). . . . Even more surprising is the finding that it is the respondents of Western origin who change most as a result of experience, rather than the Easterners. It seems that the levelling among those with experience . . . is a product of the *debureaucratization* of the Western group rather than the socialization of the Easterners to bureaucratic ways. (Apparently) . . . newcomers, particularly those from traditional backgrounds, do tend to learn that norms are the appropriate rhetoric of communication in organizations, but . . . actual experience at the same time creates an opposite constraint. Possibly newcomers simultaneously

learn both the rules and how to get around them! (Katz and Danet, 1966: 185)

II. THE 1968 SURVEY: RECOGNITION OF FORMALISM AS A SYSTEMIC FEATURE OF PUBLIC BUREAUCRACY

The 1968 study of Israelis' attitudes and experience with regard to the use of protektzia afforded the first opportunity to examine the effects of exposure to Israeli bureaucracy in depth. Findings from this study have been cited in the preceding three chapters to provide a comparison with findings from the present one.

The Customs study had necessarily been focused on persons requiring the services of Customs officials, mainly quite recent immigrants. The pilot study was also too limited to allow for a thorough examination of the attitudes and behavior of old-timers and natives. There, the sample of only a little over 100 army reservists was too small for any but the simplest, generally dichotomous cross-tabulations. Thus, for different reasons, neither of these studies could provide data adequate to the task of assessing how exposure to Israeli bureaucracy influenced individuals.

In contrast, the 1968 attitude survey worked with a large enough sample (1886 persons) to enable us to look closely at old-timers and natives for the first time. This survey began to uncover the phenomenon of de-bureaucratization among these groups. The generalizations the team was prepared to make at the time were extremely tentative, not only because the scientific stance traditionally requires caution, or because one-time examination of a phenomenon provides a less than fully satisfactory basis for generalization, but also, I suspect, because we still found it difficult to acknowledge that the pattern becoming institutionalized was so different from that in the West (cf. Danet and Hartman, 1972a, 1972b).

III. REJECTION OF THE ABSORPTION-MODERNIZATION PARADIGM

The results of the 1980 study make it eminently clear, if it was not clear before,[2] that the absorption-modernization paradigm did not predict the shape of organizational culture as it evolved in the 1970's and 1980's. Biculturalism is widespread among all ethnic groups, not just the supposedly unsocialized immigrants of North African or Middle Eastern background. The evidence of the present study has confirmed what the 1966 pilot study could only suggest: That it is, in fact, the immigrants from the Western European and English-speaking countries who have undergone major change as a result of adapting to Israeli society—perhaps even more than the Middle Eastern and North African immigrants, although the latter groups have undoubtedly changed a great deal as well. Rather than focusing on the Middle Eastern and North African immigrants, on the one hand, and on the Western European and English-speaking immigrants, on the other, far more attention should have been paid to the groups from Eastern Europe, from the beginning. For it is clearly they who have had the strongest influence on Israeli bureaucracy.

The question now arises, why were we so wrong? Why did we continue to believe in the absorption-modernization paradigm for so many years, even when some of the research evidence began to suggest that it did not fit the emerging reality? It appears that several factors were involved. Some have to do with our own biases as researchers; others have to do with a failure to assess important features of the emerging society. In some cases, the relevant data were available and not enough attention was paid to them. In others, developments of the 1970's simply took a turn which could not have been anticipated, in the late 1960's.

IV. WHY WE WERE SLOW TO IDENTIFY BICULTURALISM

A. Ethnocentric Bias

One reason why our research group was so slow to recognize that biculturalism was becoming a basic feature of the society had to do with ethnocentric bias on our part. In retrospect, it now appears quite possible that the research team made an implicit and unwarranted assumption that Middle Eastern immigrants would become like *us*. The members of the team over the years have all been either natives of the United States, or native Israelis of European origin who were educated in the United States.[3] Thus, we may have assumed, unwittingly, that people like us—the supposed carriers of modernity—would have a strong impact on Israel's emergent organizational culture. But demographic developments alone made it unlikely that Israel would become a society of the kind I characterized in chapter 2 as Type I—one with little gap between U norms and behavior.

B. Effects of Numbers

As pointed out earlier, in the work on bureaucracy and the public in Israel, we have generally thought in terms of three cultural groupings of Jews: the Western Europeans and those from English-speaking countries, the Eastern Europeans, and immigrants from North Africa and the Middle East. One unanticipated consequence of thinking in terms of these three groups, I suspect, is that the tendency was to give the three groups equal weight, ignoring the potential impact of differences in size of the three groups. In fact, immigrants from the most universalistic countries and their offspring are, and have always been only a tiny minority in Israel's population.

1. Composition of the population in 1980. As indicated in Table VIII.1, Jews from classically bureaucratic countries, Germany and Austria, constituted only an insignificant 2.9% of the 1980 population of Israel (including both immigrants and children of immigrants). And persons from North America and Oceania (United States, Canada, Australia, New Zealand), locally called Anglo-Saxons, constitute only another 1.7%. As for immigrants from other countries of Western Europe, such as, say, Belgium, France, or Sweden, they are so few in numbers that in official statistics they are relegated to a residual category. Among those born abroad, the total percentage for Germans, Austrians, and Anglo-Saxons combined is only a slightly higher 5.0%. Those hailing from Asia and Africa constitute over 44% of all immigrants; when immigrants and children of immigrants are combined, the percentage remains just about the same. The Eastern Europeans constitute about 45% of all immigrants, and 33% of the total Jewish population (the drop is the result of the lower birth rate among Europeans than among Middle Easterners).

Thus, if size of group is any indication of potential influence in a society, the Eastern Europeans and Middle Easterners both had a very large and more or less equal chance of shaping organizational culture in Israel, whereas those from Western Europe and the English-speaking world had only the slightest probability of doing so.

2. Composition of the population during various periods of immigration. But the more important question is: Which groups dominated in the early, formative years? Table VIII.2 shows that immigration of persons from strongly U countries has just about always been marginal in terms of absolute numbers, so that they were not likely to have been able to set the tone in earlier periods. Immigration

Table VIII.1
Jewish Population of Israel by Country of Origin, 1980*

Country/Continent	Born abroad	Born in Israel	Total
Asia-Total	*21.0*	*23.7*	*22.5*
Turkey	3.1	2.7	2.8
Iraq	7.2	8.9	8.1
Yemen, Southern Yemen	3.6	6.2	5.0
Iran	3.6	3.4	3.5
India and Pakistan	1.3	0.9	1.1
Other	1.6	1.7	1.6
Africa-Total	*23.2*	*21.8*	*22.4*
Morocco, Tangier	14.9	13.3	14.0
Algeria, Tunisia	3.6	3.6	3.6
Libya	1.9	2.7	2.4
Egypt, Sudan	2.1	2.0	2.0
Other	0.5	0.2	0.3
Europe-Total	*51.1*	*27.9*	*38.2*
USSR	14.2	4.8	9.0
Poland	12.0	8.6	10.1
Rumania	12.7	5.7	8.8
Bulgaria, Greece	2.4	1.8	2.1
Germany, Austria	3.1	2.7	2.9
Czechoslovakia	1.5	1.2	1.3
Hungary	1.7	1.3	1.5
Other	3.0	1.7	2.3
America, Oceania-Total	*4.7*	*1.5*	*2.9*
North America, Oceania	1.9	0.7	1.7
Latin America	2.1	0.9	1.4
Israel-born father born in Israel		25.0	14.0
TOTAL	100.0%	99.9%	100.0%
GRAND TOTAL	1,447,400	1,835,300	3,282,700

* Computed from Central Bureau of Statistics (1981), Table II/24, p. 58.

during the first aliya (1882–1903) was entirely from Russia, and that of the second aliya (1904–1914) was from Russia and Poland.

Although Jews from Germany and Austria and from English-speaking countries began to arrive after 1919, immigrants from the two German-speaking countries have never constituted more than 3% of immigrants in any time period, except in the years 1921–1945 when they fled the Nazis or sought a haven after the Holocaust. And so-called Anglo-Saxon immigrants have never constituted over 5% of immigrants arriving in any time period except after the Six

Table VIII.2
Percentage of Immigrants to Israel from Universalistic Countries by Period of Immigration*

Period	% of immigrants from Germany and Austria	% of immigrants from America, South Africa, Oceania	Total immigrants
1919–1923	3.3	2.3	35,100
1924–1931	1.8	2.9	81,600
1932–1938	20.2	2.4	197,200
1939–1945	21.5	0.2	81,800
1946–1948	3.5	0.3	56,600
1948	2.0	0.7	101,819
1949	3.0	0.8	239,576
1950	0.8	0.6	170,215
1951	0.4	0.3	175,129
1952–1954	1.4	3.8	54,065
1955–1957	0.3	1.7	164,936
1958–1960	0.7	3.5	75,487
1961–1964	0.4	4.7	228,046
1965–1967	1.1	8.8	60,793
1968–1973	1.5	18.7	247,802
1974–1975	1.0	19.5	52,007

* Source: Friedlander and Goldscheider (1979), Tables 2.8 and 2.11.

Day War, by which time cultural patterns in Israel had undoubtedly become fairly fixed. Thus, the Eastern Europeans who settled in Palestine during the period of the Yishuv had the double advantage of getting there first and of reinforcing their early influence with a steady influx of immigrants in later years.

C. Composition of Elites

Despite their tiny numbers, the universalistic types *have* made their mark on Israeli culture. It is not hard to think of persons of Anglo-Saxon origin who have held prominent positions. Israel's current president, Haim Herzog, was born in Ireland. And Israel's famous woman prime minister, Golda Meir, although born in Russia, grew up in the United States. Moshe Arens, former Minister of Defense, is a native of the United States. Abba Eban, former ambassador to the United Nations and former Foreign Minister, was born in South Africa. Might it not be that persons in elite positions, influential decision-makers, have disproportionately come from universalistic backgrounds? Could it not be that, although small in number as a

whole, Western Europeans and persons from English-speaking backgrounds came to dominate the elites? In fact, this is not the case.

Weingrod and Gurevitch (1977) analyzed the ethnic origin of six
types of Israeli elites: administrative, political, economic, academic,
professional, and artistic-cultural. As is shown in Table VIII.3, by
1972, persons born in Western Europe and the English-speaking
countries constituted only between 13% and 26% of all elites except
the academic one, where they were a very high 44% of all full
professors in Israel's universities. Persons from universalistic backgrounds were clearly overrepresented in the bureaucratic elite, if we
compare their proportion of 24% with the tiny proportion of persons
of this background in the country as a whole but not enough to
dominate it. Middle Easterners were grossly underrepresented; although they constituted 27% of the total population in 1972, they
occupied a tiny 3% of elite positions at best, except in the political
sphere where they have made some headway—with nearly 9% of all
elite positions.

Eastern Europeans continue to dominate all of Israel's elites except
the academic one. The lower half of Table VIII.3 also shows that
all the elites except the academic one are dominated by people who
immigrated to Israel quite early, before 1948. This general picture
is confirmed by Raphaeli's (1970) analysis of the ethnic background
of civil servants, senior civil servants, and members of the Knesset
in 1967 (Table VIII.4). Eastern Europeans constituted 38% of all
civil servants, 47% of all senior civil servants, and 58% of all MKs.
Moreover, persons from the Americas constituted only 0.8% of all
civil servants and 0.9% of all senior civil servants in 1967.

D. Unanticipated Importance of Familism and Illegalism

Taken together, all of the factors just discussed suggest that we
grossly over-estimated the strength of universalistic tendencies, and
that, ultimately, universalism "never really had a chance" in Israeli
society. In fact, it may even make sense to argue that biculturalism
is over-determined in Israel.[4] Although a malfunctioning bureaucracy
may be a necessary and sufficient condition for endemic rule-violations, as in the case of the socialist societies (Type II societies
according to the typology developed in chapter 2), in the Israeli
case, cultural factors are probably at least as important. As I argued
in chapter 4, two sets of cultural factors have also been critical—
familism and illegalism. I will not review here the discussion of each
of these phenomena; both were discussed in considerable detail in

Table VIII.3
Distribution of Six Israeli Elites by Country of Origin and Period of Immigration in 1972 (in percentages)

Feature	Admin-istrative	Political	Economic	Academic	Profes-sional	Artistic-Cultural	Total Elites	Total** Population
Country of Origin								
Israel	31.4	24.4	27.9	17.9	32.8	32.4	26.7	47.9
Central/E. Europe	38.9	48.3	41.5	28.7	50.8	40.5	39.6	
W. Europe	20.1	11.9	18.0	26.0	6.6	21.6	18.9	27.2
English-speaking	3.4	1.7	5.5	17.9	6.6	1.4	6.7	
(W. Europe + English-speaking subtotal)	*23.5*	*13.6*	*23.5*	*43.9*	*13.2*	*25.6*	*25.6*	*27.2*
Middle East and North Africa	2.7	8.5	1.6	2.2	1.6	0.0	3.2	24.9
Others	2.7	2.8	4.9	—	1.6	0.0	3.4	—
No data	0.7	2.3	0.6	2.2	0.0	4.0	1.5	—
Total	99.9	99.9	100.0	99.8	100.0	99.9	100.0	100.0
Period of Immigration								
Before 1920	3.0	3.0	2.3	0.5	0.0	2.0	2.0	
1921–1933	22.4	36.8	30.3	15.7	24.4	37.3	25.8	
1934–1939	41.3	25.6	35.6	28.7	29.3	23.5	32.4	
1940–1948	13.3	15.8	11.4	10.2	22.0	13.7	13.2	
(Before 1920 – 1940–1948 subtotal)	*80.0*	*81.2*	*79.6*	*55.1*	*75.7*	*76.5*	*73.4*	
1949–1956	9.0	6.0	6.8	14.6	14.6	3.9	9.4	
1957–	4.0	2.3	5.3	15.7	4.9	7.8	7.1	
No data	7.0	10.5	8.3	14.6	4.8	11.8	10.0	
Total	100.0	100.0	100.0	100.0	100.0	100.0	99.9	

* TYPE OF ELITE

* Source: Weingrod and Gurevitch, 1977, Tables 2 and 3.

** Source: Central Bureau of Statistics (1974), Table 2/19, p. 45.

chapter 4. And there I also reviewed evidence and analyses by other researchers suggesting that both have been greatly reinforced since the 1967 war and since the rise of the Likud to power in 1977.

Suffice it to say that when designing the questionnaire for the 1980 study, my collaborators and I failed to realize the importance of developing empirical measures of familistic tendencies in individuals. The work of Berger (1959) on Egypt, and of Price (1975) on Ghana shows that this can be done.[5]

As for illegalism, the importance of this factor also became clear only after data analysis was already well under way, and in particular, after coming to know the work of Sprinzak (1981; 1984; 1986). Haas, Kies and I should have developed operational measures of illegalism, focusing on perceptions of the violability of rules. We assumed that the question tapping attitudes about the legitimacy of protektzia would provide an adequate measure of an instrumental attitude toward rules. But in retrospect, it would have been preferable to develop measures of this kind which are independent of specific attitudes toward the use of protektzia.

V. A REVISED MODEL OF BICULTURALISM IN ISRAEL

Because the case study lacked measures of familism and illegalism, there is a regrettable gap between the theoretical explanation of biculturalism in Israel, as developed in this book, and the evidence for that explanation in the survey data. I conclude this chapter with a brief look at two revised models which I believe provide a good account of biculturalism in Israel, first at the macro-sociological level and then at the level of the individual. The validity of these models awaits further testing.

A. A Model of Macro-Level Diculturalism[6]

A revised model of macro-level diculturalism posits that constraints on public administration and constraints on collective identity work together to produce three phenomena, which in turn, promote diculturalism. Constraints on public administration (reviewed in chapter 4) lead to objective difficulties for the public in obtaining benefits. Historical and social constraints on the collective identity of Jews everywhere, and in particular on that of Jews in Israel (also reviewed in chapter 4), promote illegalism and familism. Finally, these three

Table VIII.4

Distribution of Civil Servants, Senior Civil Servants, Members of Knesset, and the Total Population in 1967, by Ethnic Origin*

Country of Origin	Civil Servants		Senior Civil Servants		Members of Knesset	
Israel	22.3		22.8		27.2	
Middle East	15.3		4.7		10.8	
North Africa	12.3		1.9		1.7	
Eastern Europe	23.3	38.1	37.9	47.0	56.6	58.3
Balkans	14.8		9.1		1.7	
Other European countries	11.2		22.7		5.0	
Americas	0.8		0.9		0.0	
	100.0%		100.0%		100.0%	
	(40,382)		(1552)		(120)	

* Source: Raphaeli, (1970).

Figure VIII.1

A Macro-Level Model of Diculturalism in Israel

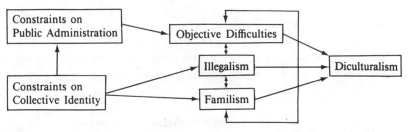

sets of factors, objective difficulties, illegalism, and familism together produce diculturalism.

Some new hypotheses are generated by this model. For example, it suggests that there is an empirical correlation in Israeli society between familism and illegalism (I noted in chapter 4 that they do not necessarily go together). Second, the model proposes that familism and illegalism promote societal diculturalism independently of the presence of objective difficulties caused by malfunctioning of public administration.

B. A Final Model of Individual-Level Biculturalism

In Figure VIII.2 the macro-level model shown in Figure VIII.1 is translated into one appropriate for the prediction of individual behavior. Comparison with the general individual-level model developed in chapter 3 (see Figure III.1) will show that it differs in several respects. First of all, given the importance of education in the empirical results—contrary to the grand hypothesis, it persisted in multivariate analysis—it is here retained, but now generalized as "location in the social structure."

Two of the original three sets of social-psychological variables included in the general model developed in chapter 3, perceptions of the reward-cost structure of contacts, and control of pertinent resources are retained. The variable "perceptions of the behavior of others" is removed because, as we saw in chapter 5, the belief that everyone uses protektzia is too widespread to constitute a useful predictor variable. Finally—and this is the critical change—instead of speaking of "perceptions of the legitimacy of particularistic strategies," as I did in chapter 3, as a step in the direction of breaking down the notions of familism and illegalism into variables which are meaningful in the present context, I have entered (1) perceptions of the right to expect particularistic help (familism); and (2) perceptions of the violability of rules (illegalism).

Like the macro-level model in Figure VIII.1, in the micro-level model some new hypotheses are suggested beyond the basic one that adding operational measures of familism and illegalism will improve the prediction of biculturalism. For instance, it suggests that we will find that persons who claim access to protektzia are especially likely to show evidence of familistic orientations and of an instrumental

Figure VIII.2
A Final Model of Micro-Level Biculturalism in Israel

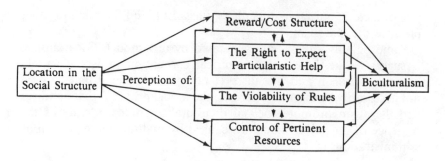

attitude to rules (Figure VIII.2). Which of the two is the more important in predicting access to protektzia or biculturalism in the response to injustice?

The model also helps to formulate new questions about the transformation of persons from Type I societies. Do immigrants from English-speaking or Western European countries use familism as a rationale for biculturalism, as Avruch's (1981) analysis of their primordialization would suggest? Might it be that their strong internalization of values upholding the rule of law leads them to resist adoption of an instrumental attitude to rules and that in their case it is familism more than illegalism that explains biculturalism?

C. Assessing the Relative Weights of Objective Difficulties, Familism and Illegalism

Because the 1980 study invested heavily in studying perceptions of the reward-cost structure of contacts with public agencies and did not investigate familism or illegalism adequately, it is not possible to make a conclusive empirical generalization about the relative weights of each of these factors in shaping organizational culture. Nevertheless, there are clues in the 1980 data which enable one to speculate on fairly firm ground.

Readers will recall that in chapter 5, much attention was devoted to a variable called "perceived personal need for protektzia." I argued that findings on variations in need for protektzia reflected not only perceptions about the malfunctioning of public administration, but also something I called there, rather vaguely, "cultural constraints," or "a climate of cultural permissiveness." It is clear now that these cultural constraints are none other than familistic tendencies and illegalism.

We had found a high correlation of 0.47 between need for protektzia and actual use in routine encounters. Recall that need was indexed by the question, "Has it ever happened to you during the past year that you were in a situation where you felt you had no choice but to use protektzia?" If measures of familism and illegalism were available, and held constant, how would this correlation be modified? In my opinion, it seems quite likely that it would be drastically lowered. Probably, perceptions of need for protektzia are spuriously inflated by familistic expectations and an instrumental attitude to rules.

Some support for this prediction is available in the finding from the 1980 study that the incidence of problems encountered and actual routine use of protektzia were correlated only at the level of 0.14. Those reporting many problems were only a little more likely than those reporting few or none to use protektzia in routine encounters. Thus, this question on negative experiences is probably a more reliable indicator of actual problems encountered than the question on ostensible need for protektzia, and actual problems encountered may have very little to do with whether people either consider themselves to need or actually use protektzia.

But all of this is only speculation. Definitive assessment of the relative weights of objective difficulties, familism, and illegalism in explaining biculturalism awaits further research. At the very least, it is no longer possible to speak of organizational socialization as a form of social-psychological modernization. That view has unequivocally been laid to rest.

IX
Conclusions

I. THE ARGUMENT OF THE BOOK

It is time to pull together the various strands of the argument of
this book and to sum up what we have learned from the Israeli case
study. In the initial statement of the thesis of the book, I proposed
that in hybrid organizational cultures, the universalistic culture of
redress is likely to be under-institutionalized. Where routine behavior
is bicultural, the response to injustice will also be bicultural: Aggrieved clients easily opt out, or abdicate their right to universalistic
justice, turning a good deal of the time to particularistic channels
of patronage and brokerage, or bribing officials, instead of using the
services of ombudsmen or media complaint-handlers. Instead of
prizing the right to receive a universalistically grounded decision—
even if they are wrong—clients forego this right—so I argued—
sacrificing principle for interest. Contrary to the view that it is the
unsocialized, marginal groups who engage in deviant behavior, in
these societies it is the respectable citizens who routinely break the
rules.

A. Patterns of Organizational Culture: The Typology

1. Factors promoting hybrid organizational cultures. In chapter 2
I proposed that either or both of two sets of factors promote hybridization in clients' behavior in organizational encounters. First,
any or all of four types of objective difficulties experienced by clients
in obtaining goods and services may promote what I have called

235

"code-switching"—changing from the U code to the P one. To be bicultural is to be a person who switches from U to P channels— easily, often, and without guilt. The four types of factors causing difficulties were: (1) scarcity of resources; (2) inefficiency; (3) rigidity in the application of rules to cases; and (4) monopoly. Second, I argued that the persistence of traditional forms of particularism in a society may also encourage deviations from the rules. I distinguished between asymmetric and symmetric forms of particularism, the former referring to various forms of patronage and brokerage in which the client is in a condition of dependence on a person who commands greater control of critical resources than he or she does. By symmetrical particularism I meant forms of exchange among relative status equals, primarily family and friends.

2. The typology. In chapter 2 a typology of four theoretically possible types of organizational culture was presented. In Type I, neither objective difficulties nor the persistence of bases of legitimacy for particularism are present; patterns of behavior strongly conform to the U code. Obvious examples of such cultures are the United States, the United Kingdom, the Scandinavian countries, and other Western European countries. Type II countries abound in objective difficulties but lack traditions giving legitimacy to particularism; we saw that the socialist societies of Eastern Europe and the People's Republic of China fall into this category.

Type III countries are those where tradition gives legitimacy to particularism but objective difficulties are not present. It was hard to think of examples, perhaps because countries legitimating particularism nearly always also have objective difficulties surrounding the dispensation of goods and services. Or it may be that even if forms of particularism flourish in other institutional areas, they do not affect official-client encounters unless objective difficulties are also present. I speculated that Japan might by a Type III country, moving toward Type I. The last theoretical type, Type IV, refers to countries displaying both objective difficulties and persisting legitimacy for particularism in bureaucratic encounters. Probably, most developing countries fall into this category.

B. The Grand Hypothesis: the Importance of Social-Psychological Factors

In chapter 3 I switched to a micro-sociological, or social-psychological perspective, and developed a theoretical framework for the analysis of citizens' attitudes and behavior in hybrid organizational cultures. I proposed to focus on four sets of social-psychological variables as predictors of behavior in such cultures. The notion of "objective difficulties" was translated into "perceptions of the reward-cost structure of the situation." The idea of persistence of bases of legitimacy for particularism was translated into the notion of "perceptions of the right to expect particularistic treatment from key persons." To these two groups of factors two other variables were added: Perceptions of control of critical resources, e.g., access to persons who can intercede on an individual's behalf, or control of financial resources necessary for bribery, and perceptions of the behavior of others, the idea being that those who believe others engage in particularistic behavior will be likely to do so themselves.

The grand hypothesis of the study was then specified: It was divided into two parts. I hypothesized (a) that in hybrid organizational cultures the so-called social mobilization variables—those which mobilize citizens to modernity—will predict attitudes but not behavior of citizens, and that (b) in such cultures the social-psychological variables just reviewed will better predict behavior than the social mobilization ones. A way of classifying various U and P channels of redress was proposed, using three features of these channels: Whether or not they are institutionalized; their legitimacy; and the underlying motivational base (norms, threats, inducements). I also developed some hypotheses about the techniques of neutralization of deviance which people living in hybrid organizational cultures will use to excuse or justify their behavior.

II. RESULTS OF THE ISRAELI CASE STUDY

At the end of chapter 2 I laid out a four-part research agenda for the student of client behavior in hybrid organizational cultures: (1) to diagnose the extent of biculturalism in the population of a society; (2) to assess perceptions of objective difficulties and of the legitimacy of particularistic strategies; (3) to analyze the extent to which these factors can be used to explain biculturalism in individuals; (4) to use micro-level data to make some generalizations about the society. In the Israeli case study answers were sought to these questions in relation to two chief dependent variables: the use of personal connections in routine bureaucratic encounters, and the tendency toward hybridization in the response to injustice. Here is a summary of what we have learned about organizational culture in Israel:

A. The Diagnosis

1. The gap between the rule and routine behavior. There can be no question that Israelis are strongly bicultural. Nine-tenths of the sample went on record as saying that using protektzia is wrong—they know the rule—yet one-fifth of the general sample, and, more important, one-half of those having had contact with government and public bureaucracy admitted to having used it at least once in the last year. This is a good deal higher than the criterion of one-third of those having contact which I proposed in chapter 3. The proportion rose still higher, to three-fifths, among those having had contacts, *and* having seen themselves as needing protektzia and having access to it. Typologizing individuals as to whether their professed attitude and behavior are consistent, (or, whether their behavior is consistent with what they know to be the rule), my collaborators and I found that the modal category was the inconsistent—48% of those having contact said that using personal connections was wrong, yet admitted to having used protektzia in the last year, or would have used it, had they had access.

2. Protektzia and redress. As for the relation between protektzia and redress, many striking findings indicated that the two are inseparable. Readers will recall that respondents were asked about their use of 12 channels of complaint in the public sector, including 7 U ones and 5 P ones. First of all, the single most used channel after appeals to a higher official is protektzia. Notably, there were more instances of use of protektzia than of the ombudsman. The next most frequently used channel after the ombudsman was again a particularistic one—going to a trade union official. Of the 761 instances of channel use reported by the 374 persons claiming to have taken action at least once in the past, fully 40% were concentrated in the five particularistic channels, protektzia, political party, trade union, member of the Knesset, Prime Minister or other government minister. In other words, *4 out of every 10 instances of action taken to obtain redress of grievances were outside the U frame.*[1]

Most persons (602, or 59%) had never used any of the channels, a finding which is consistent with studies of redress behavior in other countries.[2] The majority of the other 41% of the total sample who did take action had used only one channel; they constituted another one-fifth of the total sample. Thus, persons having used two or more channels were rather rare. There were 214 of them in the sample. Three-quarters of single-channel users had used a U channel rather than a P channel. But among those using two or more, *4 out of every 5 persons were hybrids, combining at least one U channel with at least one P one. Moreover, the more channels complainants reported having used, the more likely they were to be hybrids.* Thus, activists, those who actively pursue redress in Israeli society, are inevitably hybrids. The zero-order correlation between number of channels used and hybridization was a high 0.66. As for the comparison with the 1968 data, I concluded that the proportion of hybrids in the population at large has grown and may even have doubled.

B. The Social-Psychological Predictors

1. Perceptions of the reward-cost structure of the situation. A large number of aspects of what I have called "perceptions of reward-cost structure" were discussed in chapters 3 and 5.

(a) Public need for protektzia. Nearly three-fifths of the Israeli sample thought citizens need protektzia at least sometimes. About half of those having had at least one contact with public bureaucracy in the past year had encountered a problem at least once. And the more problems people had themselves experienced, the more likely they were to believe that the public needs protektzia to cope successfully.

(b) Personal need for protektzia. Israelis easily define themselves as needing protektzia. When asked "Did it ever happen to you in the past year that you were in a situation where you felt you had no choice but to use protektzia to arrange some matter in a government or public agency?" one-third of the total sample and a little more than one-half of those having had contacts said that it had happened to them. To some extent the distribution on this question may have been influenced by its wording. In effect, respondents were given permission to say that they had had no choice. But the distribution cannot be an artifact of question wording alone. The correlates of need for protektzia indicated that this social-psychological variable is no mere reflection of objective difficulties, but is also influenced by what I termed the "climate of cultural permissiveness," fostered—as I argued—by the two cultural constraints of familism and illegalism. The data showed that those best integrated into the society, most in the know as to how it works, are quickest to give themselves permission to need protektzia.

2. Control of resources: access to protektzia. Three-hundred and fifty-four people claimed to have had access to protektzia when they needed it. This constituted 37% of the general sample and 57% of those who had contact. These figures pertain to a direct question about having someone to approach. Because an indirect measure of access was the only one used in the 1968 study, only this less satisfactory measure could be used to compare the incidence of access in the two studies. Although comparison based on the direct measure would have been preferable, the indirect one is probably reliable enough to tap the general trend over time. It suggested that access has risen, or, to be more precise, that more people claim to have access to protektzia today than in 1968. Being able to use protektzia has become more of a status symbol than ever.

The better integrated into the society people are, the more likely they are to claim access. Well educated persons, those employed in high-status occupations, and natives to the country are highest on access to personal connections. Minor differences among ethnic groups were gleaned, but in general ethnicity is not a very important variable in the 1980 data. Comparing the data for 1968 and 1980, I found that among the haves (the educated, natives, immigrants of European origin) the rate of growth in reported access appears to be double that for the have-nots (the poorly educated, immigrants of Middle Eastern origin). The single best predictor of access was subjective knowledgeability about channels of complaint; alternatively, the two variables can be seen as co-varying—people who see themselves as having access to protektzia also feel they know to whom to turn when they want to complain. No doubt, the causal relationship is also partially in reverse: Having access fosters feelings of competence.

3. Perceptions of the behavior of others. A single question tapped perceptions of what others do in bureaucratic encounters. Respondents had been asked: "In your opinion, do most people in Israel seek out protektzia when they need to arrange something in a government or public agency?" A very high 70% thought that most people always or usually look for protektzia; this figure was virtually identical with that obtained in 1968. Thus, most people believe that most people use protektzia frequently. To put it crudely, everybody knows that everybody does it.

C. Success in Predicting Biculturalism

Of the four research tasks I laid out in chapter 2, the most central was that of predicting who will be bicultural and who will not. The grand hypothesis stated that social mobilization variables would predict attitudes but not behavior, that instead behavior would best be predicted by the social-psychological variables. Let me summarize the results for each part of the hypothesis, in turn.

1. The social mobilization variables. Removed from the larger context of this study, a number of findings could mistakenly be interpreted as indicating that Israel's is a universalistic organizational culture. Thus, in chapter 5, we saw that educated persons and those of high occupational status tended to have the best command of cognitive aspects of organizational culture: They scored best on quizzes of factual information about public and government bureaucracy and about general civic matters. Moreover, they displayed most familiarity with channels of complaint and had the strongest feelings of subjective knowledgeability.

Counter to the grand hypothesis, the social mobilization variables did predict at least some aspects of behavior in the manner they would in Type I organizational cultures. In chapter 7, they predicted intensity of use of channels of complaint, the quantitative aspect of redress behavior, with some degree of success. Among background characteristics of individuals, their education and occupation best predicted how many channels of complaint they had used. However, the size of the correlations with total channels used was lower than that found for the cognitive variables just reviewed.

At the same time, the best predictors among sociocultural variables of access to protektzia were precisely the two social mobilization variables I have just been discussing. In chapter 6 I reported correlations of 0.26 and 0.21 between access and education and occupation, respectively. Thus, the very persons who are best socialized to the U code are also the most likely to be in a position to mobilize personal connections. At the same time, it is evident that these correlations are not especially high, because *even among relatively disadvantaged groups,* large numbers also claim access to protektzia.

True to the grand hypothesis, these two variables did not predict whether individuals actually used protektzia in routine encounters. Whereas the social mobilization hypothesis in its narrow version would have predicted that educated persons of high occupational status would avoid using P channels, no relation was found between the two variables and actual use. On the other hand, other background characteristics—age, generation, and length of residence—did show some association, at the zero-order level, with use of protektzia. Moreover, respondents' age even survived the test of multivariate analysis: Younger people who legitimate its use on the normative level are especially likely to use it.

As for use of redress channels, the better educated were more, rather than less likely to use particularistic channels and to be hybrid than the poorly educated. In general, then, either the social mobilization variables did not predict behavior, as was expected, or, an inverse relation was found.

2. Social-Psychological variables.

(a) Use of protektzia in routine encounters. Of the two best operational measures of perceptions of the rewards and costs of using U versus P channels, self-defined need for protektzia was a far better predictor of routine use of it than was the frequency of problematic encounters. A high correlation of 0.47 was found between perceived personal need for protektzia and actual use of it. Reported access to protektzia predicted use even better than did perceived need: Here the correlation was 0.52. Need and access together yielded a high multiple correlation of 0.61 with use. In short, given that people see themselves as needing protektzia and having someone to approach, it is extremely likely that they will in fact use protektzia. The three are so inter-related that they may be interpreted as tapping a higher-order, more general variable, which might be called "induction into the delinquent community."

Of the three sets of social-psychological variables investigated, the least important was perceptions of what others do. These perceptions did not predict use of protektzia with any great success because too many people said that everyone uses it.

(b) Redress behavior. In general, people who use protektzia routinely are also likely to use it as a response to the experience of injustice. As demonstrated in chapter 7, however, there was an important exception to this finding. Persons of Western European origin exhibited clear hybridization only when it came to redress. This suggested that their threshhold for biculturalism is higher than among persons from less strongly universalistic backgrounds.

Multivariate analysis of hybridization showed that a rather large number of variables account for this phenomenon in Israel. Of seven predictor variables entered into a log-linear analysis, two—nativity to the country and being from Western Europe—were eliminated. This was a good result because the multivariate analysis sifted out those factors which are unique to Israel, or to immigrant societies, leaving those of more general theoretical interest. Hybridization was found to be the product of interrelations among respondents' education, their reported need for and access to protektzia, and their report of negative experience in bureaucratic encounters, as well as their routine use of protektzia. The model which best fit the data contained two major components. The main explanatory complex was in the group negative experience/need/access/ routine use. The model indicated no direct link between either general negative experience or self-defined need for protektzia and hybridization in redress. On the other hand, access to protektzia and use in routine encounters were both directly linked. A separate, secondary effect was the direct effect of education on redress behavior: For a small minority in the sample—no doubt, primarily those of Western European origin—high educational attainment worked to suppress the tendency toward hybridization, much as the simple version of the social mobilization hypothesis would predict.

Chapter 7 also showed that the trend toward hybridization is inevitably reinforced by the relatively greater efficacy of particularistic channels, especially protektzia and organizational brokerage (unions, political parties), in comparison with the average efficacy of universalistic channels. In a society in which nothing works like protektzia, and in which so many persons manage to use it successfully, there is little reinforcement for use of channels like the ombudsman.

D. Change Since 1968

Since comparative data were available for two time periods, 1968 and 1980, I have wherever possible attempted to compare 1980 findings with those for the earlier study. Most findings available for both years clearly indicated perpetuation of the status quo, if not a further strengthening of the place of protektzia in Israeli society. It is necessary to "scrape the bottom of the barrel" to locate findings indicating a possible weakening of the status of protektzia; and even these few are not persuasive. For example, there was a 10% drop in the proportion admitting to use of protektzia in routine encounters, among those reporting need and access, and there was a similar 10% drop in use among those reporting only positive contacts. Although 10% differences are no doubt significant in samples the size of the 1968 and 1980 samples (1886 and 1021, respectively), these findings surely pale in the light of the massive evidence that protektzia is solidly entrenched and possibly gaining in covert legitimacy.

For one thing, the basic pattern of formalism, of lip service to the rule that using protektzia is wrong, combined with actual use given opportunity and need, was exactly the same in 1980 as in 1968. Second, in 1980, as in 1968, social-psychological factors were the main determinants of use. The fact that self-defined need for protektzia has risen since 1968, coupled with the fact that natives and younger people are disproportionately likely to see themselves as needing it today, suggests that there is greater cultural permissiveness today surrounding its use, greater willingness to enter the delinquent community. The same is true of the evidence for increased hybridization in the use of complaint channels.

E. Israel as a Type IV Society

The results of this case study more than meet the criterion set earlier to determine whether macro-level diculturalism is present, as well as individual biculturalism, in a given society. In chapter 3 I had suggested that if one-third of those having contact showed evidence of biculturalism, the phenomenon would be considered stable enough to merit characterizing it as a feature of a society, and not just of individuals. Given the four findings that (1) one-half of those having had contacts had used protektzia routinely; (2) 45% of all complainants (including the single-channel users) were hybrids; (3) 4 of every 10 instances of channel use were particularistic; and (4) among multiple users of channels of redress, 4 of every 5 persons were bicultural, the generalization of profound societal diculturalism can hardly be contested.

Although the empirical study lacked solid measures of familism and illegalism, when combined with indirect evidence from other studies of Israeli society (Hofstede, 1979; Blum-Kulka, Danet, and Gherson, 1985; Katriel, 1986; see chapter 4), it generally supported the idea that the Israel of the 1980's is best characterized as a Type IV society, one in which both the presence of objective difficulties and cultural forces providing legitimation for particularistic expectations promote violations of universalistic rules (see Chapter 4). As was pointed out in chapter 8, further research is necessary to develop operational measures of familism and illegalism and to assess the relative weights of malfunctioning of public administration, familism and illegalism as constraints on organizational culture in Israel. In chapter 8 I speculated that a new study providing a full test of the revised model of individual biculturalism might well show that familism and illegalism are far more important in inducting people into biculturalism than is the malfunctioning of public administration.

III. PROTEKTZIA IN PERSPECTIVE: INSTRUMENTAL OR SYMBOLIC EXCHANGE?

There are some important theoretical questions about the nature of protektzia which did not receive their due in previous chapters. Earlier, I called it a form of social credit, but did not discuss how this credit works: Whether, for example, it is limited to two parties in an instrumental exchange relationship, or whether it is more global, rooted in group membership.

A. Anglo-Saxon versus French Theories of Social Exchange

Two quite opposite views of protektzia are possible, one that it is an expression of a form of exchange which is (1) instrumental or utilitarian, (2) contractual in nature, (3) involving low trust between the parties, and (4) restricted to the two parties involved, the other that it is (1) primarily a form of symbolic exchange, (2) non-contractual, (3) in which trust between the parties is high and (4) best viewed as a group phenomenon rather than a matter of private negotiation between two parties. As Ekeh (1974) has shown, these two views of social exchange are characteristic of two opposing theoretical schools of thought, the Anglo-Saxon school, whose best-known advocates are Homans (1950) and Blau (1964), and which emphasizes individual self-interest and psychological motivation, and the French school, associated mainly with Levi-Strauss (1949; 1969), which focuses on group processes and the relation between social exchange and social solidarity. Rather than argue that protektzia is either instrumental or symbolic in nature, I shall argue that it must be seen as *both*.

B. Symbolic More than Instrumental

Because the model developed in chapter 3 invested heavily in the importance of apparently rational calculations of reward and cost, I appear to fall in the instrumental camp of social exchange theorists, e.g., that of Homans (1950) and Blau (1964), rather than the symbolic one associated with Levi-Strauss (1949; 1969). But that would be an oversimplification. It is probably fairer to say that the theoretical perspective of the book is an implicit blend of the utilitarian and symbolic views of exchange.

To ask someone to intervene on one's behalf when the road to some benefit is blocked is to act out of self-interest; however, at the same time, the mobilization of particularistic help in client-official encounters is not narrowly instrumental, *at least not in the Israeli case*. Support for this contention comes from the work of my former student, Neta Ha-Ilan (1986), who collected protektzia stories, case histories, in three areas, (1) goods and services to the public; (2) employment (getting a job); (3) business transactions (whereby government agencies commission work in the private sector). Her informants were persons in a position to grant protektzia as members of organizations, rather than clients. She found that in the area of goods and services, individuals mainly mobilized horizontal ties (family and friends), which were specially improvised for the purpose, whereas in the areas of employment and business deals, the ties invoked tended to be vertical and to have continuity over time.

Although neither Ha-Ilan's data nor mine directly addressed the question of whether those providing help expect and receive reciprocal help or other benefits in return, the fact that horizontal ties predominated in client-official encounters suggests that, in addition, the form of exchange involved must also be viewed as generalized, to use Levi-Strauss's (1949; 1969) term. In matters of protektzia in bureaucratic encounters, A helps B, and on another occasion B may help—not A, but C or D. Therefore, protektzia transactions related to client-official encounters are not merely instances of restricted, specific, two-party exchange, but of generalized exchange among members of the group. If the recipient repays at all, he or she repays not the person who helped, but *the group*. Protektzia is, therefore, a kind of gift from the group to its members, with the difference that, unlike a true gift, it is solicited.[3]

IV. Afterthoughts

Reflecting back on the theoretical formulation and on the Israeli case study, I would like to address several topics before bringing this book to a close.

A. Exaggeration of Disregard for Justice

The approach developed in this book may exaggerate the extent to which bicultural individuals appear not to care about justice. It is not clear to what extent the apparent lack of concern with universalistic justice is a substantive finding about the particular society studied, or one which is characteristic of all societies, and to what extent the results may be a product of the method used. In the introduction I cited the article by Mayhew (1975) in which he reported that the group of Americans studied did not care about principle as much as might be expected. Because my own study did not compare Israel with a Type I society like the United States, it is not possible to make a firm generalization in this respect, although I believe that persons in Type I societies (at least educated, high status ones) do care more about universalistic justice than those in the other types of organizational culture.

Studies in which a different kind of methodology is used might show that on the whole, Israelis have perceptions about what is fair or unfair not radically different from those in other societies. At the same time, it is noteworthy that even among experimental social psychologists investigating the sense of injustice there is debate about (a) whether those perceiving injustice in a given situation actually experience distress; and (b) whether distress motivates behavior to reduce inequity (cf. Greenberg, 1984).

B. Lack of Information on the Conditions in which Various Strategies are Mobilized

Another limitation of the study is that no information was collected on the circumstances in which individuals mobilized personal connections, or, for that matter, when they used universalistic channels. It would have been illuminating to know when and why clients contacted the ombudsman, and when they chose instead, or in addition, to contact someone who knows someone. Is protektzia used mainly to cut through red tape, as I have argued, or is it to gain access to benefits to which an individual is not entitled? Ha-Ilan's (1986) study appears to confirm my hunch: The majority of her set of 92 protektzia stories involved simplifications or changes of procedure, rather than the granting of benefits to which the recipient was not entitled.

C. Inflated Incidence of Particularistic Behavior

As I noted at the end of chapter 6, an unintended result of the way biculturalism was operationalized in the case study is that it makes the use of particularistic strategies appear to be more frequent than it probably is, in practice. No attempt was made to measure the incidence of encounters in which clients routinely used universalistic strategies—in situations like getting a new passport, applying for a tax rebate, or for a child allowance from the Social Insurance Institute, and so on. It is very likely that even among persons who are bicultural according to the criteria developed in this study, most of their encounters are routinely universalistic. Only systematic comparative research, comparing Israel with, say, other Mediterranean or Latin American countries, where particularistic strategies are also common, can provide precise information on the relative incidence of biculturalism in Israel.

D. "Corruption" versus "Biculturalism"

Throughout the book I have attempted to make a virtue out of the decision not to use the term *corruption* for the phenomena studied. In that same spirit I have generally avoided the term *deviance,* except for an occasional reference to the notion of the delinquent community. The concept of biculturalism is an elegant solution to the problem that informal patterns of behavior are often treated, theoretically, as some form of step-child, of secondary status or interest. Although the term does have this advantage of giving equal weight to both, there is, nevertheless, a need to ask whether the term is widely applicable.

The term probably best fits those societies in which (1) most, if not all groups are able to use both the U and P codes successfully most of the time; (2) there are relatively few or relatively weak cleavages between elites and masses; (3) rule-violations are more functional than dysfunctional, although they may be both; and (4) possibly where the exchange of favors, rather than monetary payments, is the dominant informal pattern. If in a given society it is impossible or inordinately difficult for weaker groups to obtain their most basic entitlements, either through the official U channels or through bribes or personal connections, if official and unofficial ways of doing business heavily exploit these groups, it might appear naive to label a pattern of behavior as merely bicultural.

E. From Protektzia to Bribes?

If protektzia has gained in strength in the period since the Six Day War, might it be that bribery is also on the increase, in at least some kinds of client-official encounters? There was, for example, a major scandal in 1986 in which driving test examiners were charged with accepting bribes to pass persons being tested. The Department of Licenses has traditionally been a pocket of especially off-putting, probably excessively tough treatment of the public. For years, very high proportions of drivers have been failing their tests on the first or second try. When resources are this hard to come by, it may be a short step from voluntary solicitation of personal favors to coercive extortion of bribes.

Still another recent scandal surrounded the activities of a Jewish official who served as intermediary between Arabs in East Jerusalem and the West Bank and the Israeli authorities and who accepted illegal payments for his services. If payments are common in transactions between Arabs and Jews, might they spread to transactions between one Jew and another? Critics of the continuing occupation of the administered territories in the West Bank and Gaza speak of the corrupting influence of the occupation on various aspects of Israeli society. Could it be that another of the negative effects of the occupation will be to encourage Jewish bureaucrats controlling access to certain scarce or difficult-to-obtain resources to expect bribes—even from Jewish clients?

F. The Arab Population: A Very Different Experience

The results of an M.A. study by my student, Taher El-Makawi (1988), freshly available as this manuscript was completed, provided strong hints that the experience of the Arab population within Israel's borders is indeed of another order from that portrayed in this book. In interviews with 120 persons in the West Bank and within the pre-1967 borders, he found that, in both areas, nearly 100% believed that some kind of payment must be made, at least some of the time, to receive a service. Only one-fifth, both in the West Bank and even inside the so-called "Green Line" (the pre-1967 borders), thought that a Jewish official could be approached directly. Thirty percent thought the payment could be symbolic; 55% thought it would have to be a substantial payment, either a sum of money or an expensive gift; and 15% thought the payment would be an obligation to reciprocate. Educated citizens of Israel were the only group substantially to think that the payment could be in the form of non-material reciprocation, e.g., by voting for a party.

El-Makawi's thesis has begun to tap a complex set of relations in the Arab situation. *Waasta*—the Arabic term for mediation—among Arabs is no simple equivalent of protektzia among Jews. Important research questions are: (1) What cultural patterns characterize encounters between Arab officials and Arab clients, and between Arab clients and Israeli/Jewish officials, and in what ways are the two types of situations similar or different? (2) To what extent are these patterns determined, on the one hand, by traditional cultural legitimation for particularism in a modernizing society, by traditional forms of patronage and brokerage, and, on the other, by the political status quo, by the continuing occupation of the administered territories, by the subordinate status of the Arab minority within the pre-1967 borders?

A chilling picture is painted by Grossman in a recent book about the West Bank. In a chapter on *waastonerim,* a Hebraized term for purveyors of waasta, the go-betweens mediating between Arab residents and the Jewish authorities, he wrote:

> the most common cases, the everyday ones, are the most infuriating of all. In general the unholy alliance between the government and its middlemen[4] creates a situation where the residents (of the West Bank) have to pay good money for rights to which they are entitled by law, but they don't know it. The attitude of the population to the *waastonerim* is ambivalent: they despise them but they need them; they vilify them but they are afraid to harm them. (Grossman, 1987: 148)

Grossman even listed the prices charged by waastonerim for (1) a building license (250–300 dinars); a license to open a business (500–1000 dinars); for an authorization of reunification of a family (3000 dinars). To overstate the case somewhat, the picture emerging from El-Makawi's research and Grossman's reportage suggests that, whereas Jews use protektzia because they are "in," Arabs use waasta because they are "out." In short, the rather benign picture painted in this book, of Israelis, that is, Israeli Jews, doing each other favors is only half the story of organizational life in the Israel of the late 1980's. For Jews, protektzia is a luxury; for Arabs, apparently, waasta makes life possible.

V. UNIVERSALISM, PARTICULARISM, AND SOCIAL JUSTICE

To return to a more general level of discussion, some will want to ask: is biculturalism good or bad? The only possible answer, I believe, is, some of both.

A. The Price of Biculturalism

Particularistic allocation of benefits is obviously unjust. If the rules say that only certain categories of persons are eligible to receive a certain benefit, it is patently unfair for persons clearly not fitting these categories to receive them. And even the ostensibly lesser offense of using bribes or personal connections to simplify or speed up procedures—as in getting in to see an official ahead of turn in the line, or having a file moved up in the pile—are also unfair because they are at the expense of other persons waiting their turn. Intervention by go-betweens like political figures, to speed up work-in-progress on a matter already in the pipeline, is less likely to be labeled as unfair, because if work has already started on such matters, just when the work is completed is not necessarily a matter of fairness; more likely, it is a matter of efficiency.

A far more serious cost of biculturalism, in the long run, is the fact that favoritism and bribery prevent or retard administrative reform. With respect to redress of grievances, it is evident that where favoritism and bribery are prevalent, only the tip of the iceberg will reach official complaint-handlers, a non-representative sampling of the problems actually encountered by citizens. Large numbers of persons solve their problems under the table, in ways which leave no trace. Consequently, complaint-handlers cannot serve as adequate sources of organizational feedback, because they do not receive basic information on organizational functioning.

In such situations, persons who work for reform, or at least claim to do so, are not likely to be very successful, no matter how strong their commitment to it. As has been shown in this book, the major obstacle to reform is clearly the fact that violations of universalistic rules are systemic: They are not the random behavior of isolated, unsocialized individuals—they are engendered and perpetuated by the system.

As I began to speculate at the end of chapter 7, the forces that originally engendered biculturalism may become less important over time, as patterns of behavior simply become "they way we do things around here," comfortable, unquestioned habit, perhaps persisting even after they are no longer necessary. Whether these forces remain important or not, in hybrid organizational cultures persons who are responsible for reform are not likely to be strongly motivated to bring about change, even if they go on record as being deeply committed to it. Because they belong to the groups which most benefit from the status quo, to fight for change is potentially to undermine their own behind-the-scenes advantages. Where these conditions hold, except for occasional, perhaps token victories against corruption, made much of in the media, the same old patterns will persist.

Hybrid organizational cultures thus tend to be self-perpetuating. Given such a pattern of well-entrenched biculturalism, the introduction of devices like ombudsmen to such settings promises little in the way of serious administrative reform. Ombudsmen may serve other important functions, such as symbolizing the possibility of justice, socializing citizens to bureaucracy, fighting discrimination against minority groups, or providing catharsis for citizens' frustrations (cf. Scott, 1984), but in countries with enormous social problems, yawning gaps between elites and masses and few resources, they are even less likely to serve as catalysts for administrative reform than they are in the developed societies with an ostensible commitment to responsive service and to reform.

B. The Benefits of Biculturalism

But the picture is not all black. The first and perhaps most obvious advantage of biculturalism is that it oils the wheels of bureaucracy; it can keep a sluggish system moving. As Sampson (1985) suggested, at least in some circumstances biculturalism can therefore help organizations to fulfill their declared goals. As I wrote in an earlier paper (Danet and Hartman, 1972a), protektzia serves this function in Israel. For example, although the corporation responsible for installation of telephones is supposed to work according to a clear set of criteria as to who has priority and who must wait (e.g., heart patients and high government officials, versus ordinary citizens with no special claim), whoever has a telephone installed on a given day—a person who obtained it via protektzia or someone who patiently waited his or her turn—that day, the agency did its job—it installed some telephones. Under monopolistic conditions, activation of personal connections may actually improve efficiency; pressure on the organization may increase the average number of telephones installed per week.

A second, and very important positive function of biculturalism is that it humanizes bureaucracy. Although many have reflected on the dehumanizing consequences of bureaucratization for the individual, none has put it more eloquently than the social scientist whose name is so closely tied to the word *bureaucracy*. In a speech given in 1903 Max Weber gave expression to grave doubts:

Imagine the consequences of that comprehensive bureaucratization and rationalization which already we see approaching . . . each man becomes a little cog in the machine. . . . It is horrible to think that the world could one day be filled with nothing but these little cogs. . . . This passion for bureaucracy . . . is enough to drive one to despair. . . . That the world should know no men but these: it is in such an evolution that we are already caught up, and the great question is therefore not how we can promote and hasten it, but what can we oppose to this machinery in order to keep a portion of mankind free from this parcelling out of the soul, from this supreme mastery of the bureaucratic way of life. (Weber, in Mayer, 1943: 96–97)

Although Weber was thinking mainly of the effects of bureaucratization on officials, his reflections apply no less to the public.

In the pithy term invented by Berger et al. (1974), the price of modernity is "the homeless mind." Bureaucratization is one of the main contributors to this condition. The compensations of the private sphere are supposed to make up for the discontents experienced by the public. But the private sphere is what is "left over" after the public sphere has taken its due, and is found wanting. Youth cultures and counter-cultures are striving to create, or rather to recreate, some of the same social conditions as are found in countries like Israel, where the split between the private and the public is blurred.

There may be less universalistic justice in Israel than in the West, but *using personal connections makes people feel good*. Every time someone uses protektzia, he or she activates a chain of interaction between persons who might not otherwise have had occasion to come together. Other things equal, being able to affect one's outcomes is preferable to passivity, and being in touch with others is preferable to being alone and isolated.

All this is true, of course, only if pulling strings is a matter of *choice*. At least in the less exploitive, less coercive situations, using personal connections or even making monetary payments, humanizes bureaucracy. Negotiation is possible: There is a person behind the desk, not a mask or a machine. To use personal connections is to participate in the system. Similarly, at least in some circumstances, affordable bribes can promote a sense of autonomy and control.

At the same time negotiability can also have its price. If rules are negotiable, if they are applied with notorious flexibility, clients can never know where they stand. *No* is possibly not *no* at all; try again another day, see another official, make a few telephone calls, bring a note from the doctor . . .

Another important function of biculturalism is that it can promote social integration. In societies like Israel, where a very large proportion of the population are immigrants, the activation of personal connections can be seen as beneficial not only for the integration of the individuals involved, but for long-term integration in the society. Recall Weiman's (1983) study of the small world phenomenon in Israel, discussed toward the end of chapter 6. Although he found that Israelis have a harder time crossing ethnic boundaries than making contact with persons of the same ethnic origin as themselves, it *was* possible to do the former as well as the latter. If protektzia brings into interaction and helps create and maintain relationships between persons of radically different social origins and status (say, a carpenter from Iraq and a physician originally from Russia, who know each other from army reserve duty), it may undermine official organizational arrangements, but at the same time it promotes solidarity between sub-groups in the society.

In short, biculturalism is neither good or bad, across the board. Assessment of the balance between functional and dysfunctional aspects of the phenomenon must be made in the context of the particular society being investigated. Despite the fact that protektzia undermines universalistic justice and constitutes a formidable obstacle to administrative reform in Israel, for Israeli Jews, at least, the benefits of biculturalism may outweigh the costs.

This book has attempted to show that organizational cultures can develop stable patterns which, for all their contradictions and problematics, provide viable alternatives to those which characterize the Western democracies. In an exploratory article on the problem of how to evaluate the contribution of ombudsman, I proffered the tentative conclusion, on the basis of the limited evidence then available (mainly, Hill's [1976] study of the New Zealand ombudsman) that the ombudsman idea appears to be "an extraordinarily successful institutional innovation" (Danet, 1978: 363).

Since that time, Caiden has performed the mammoth task of assembling materials on the spread of the ombudsman idea around the world in a two-volume handbook (Caiden, 1983). In the initial chapter to this valuable handbook, Caiden, MacDermott and Sandler assessed the evidence that had come in, in the intervening years, and generally concurred with my assessment, though they noted the prevalence of a number of serious constraints on the functioning of ombudsmen: Some offices receive too few complaints because they are little known or discourage complainants; some offices have restricted jurisdiction or are reluctant to tackle big issues like corruption and waste. Sometimes they are unable to investigate problems themselves, or are not able to do so as freely as they should be, because they are denied resources, access, and so forth. Some offices are too formal—they have become another formidable bureaucracy; incumbents who challenge the system too openly tend not to be reappointed (Caiden, MacDermott and Sandler, 1983: 125).

To this list must now be added the generalization that the contribution of ombudsmen will also be severely constrained in societies whose cultural patterns contradict the basic premises of the ombudsman idea.

Appendices

Appendix A

Bureaucratic Encounters in Israel:
A Research Inventory

Appendix B

The 1980 Questionnaire

Appendix C

Methods

Appendix D

Glossary of Hebrew Terms Used in Talk
About Organizational Culture in Israel

Appendix A
Bureaucratic Encounters in Israel: A Research Inventory

Figure A.1

Studies of Bureaucratic Encounters in Israel: 1960–1987*

Study	Period Studied	Topic	Method & Setting	Ethnic Groups Emphasized	Main Dependent Variables
1. Katz & Eisenstadt (1960)	1958–59	response of officials to new immigrants	observations in busses, health clinics, well-baby clinics, encounters between Settlement Authority instructors & immigrants	Middle Eastern immigrants	bureaucratization, de-bureaucratization; teaching roles; cooptation as form of normative deviation
2. Bar Yosef & Schild (1966)	mid-1960s	officials' defenses against client pressures	structured interviews with officials in six agencies, development town	Middle Eastern immigrants	use of individual & group defenses against pressures for particularism
3. Katz & Danet (1966)	1962–63	influence of clients' sociocultural background on orientations	questionnaire, hypothetical official-client situations	Europeans vs. Middle Easterners	universalism/particularism in persuasive appeals
4. Amir (1967)	1960–65	violence in social welfare offices	statistical, qualitative analysis of court cases	social welfare clients	use of violence by clients; punishments given in court
5. Bar Yosef-Weiss (1968)	1948–68	desocialization/resocialization of clients	observations of immigrant-official interactions	Eastern European & Middle Eastern immigrants	status degradation in resocialization to Israeli clienthood

6. Danet (1971)	influence of clients' sociocultural background on orientations	content-analysis of letters to Customs authorities	Western European, Eastern European & Middle Eastern immigrants	universalism/particularism of motivating mechanisms in persuasive appeals
7. Danet & Gurevitch (1972)	presentation of self by clients	content-analysis of letters to Customs authorities	Western European, Eastern European, Middle Eastern immigrants	specificity/diffuseness in roles made salient in persuasive appeals
8. Danet & Hartman (1972a)	orientations of public toward use of protektzia	survey of Jewish population, 4 main cities	Middle Eastern, Eastern & Western European immigrants; Middle Eastern & European natives	legitimacy of use of protektzia; pressures on officials from superiors & public to grant protektzia
9. Danet & Hartman (1972b)	organizational competence of public	survey of Jewish population, 4 main cities	same as no. 8	perceived universalism of public administration; effectiveness of legitimate channels vs. protektzia
10. Danet et al. (1972)	official-client relations in telephone office	interviews with officials, clients	—	perceived prevalence of protektzia, pressures on officials from superiors & public to grant protektzia

Figure A.1 (cont.)

Study	Period Studied	Topic	Method & Setting	Ethnic Groups Emphasized	Main Dependent Variables
11. Marx (1972, 1973, 1976)	1964–66	social contexts of violence	ethnographic observation, case analysis in development town	immigrants from rural Morocco	rational violence in bureaucratic encounters
12. Katx & Antonovsky (1973)	1967	bureaucracy & immigrant adjustment	interviews with immigrants	North American immigrants	problematicalness of bureaucratic encounters; effect of perceived inefficiency, discourtesy of officials on immigrant adjustment
13. Danet & Peled (1973)	1967	complaints to the Jerusalem ombudsman	content-analysis of letters; interview with complainants	Middle class European vs. lower class Middle Eastern neighborhoods	problems complained about; form, content of letters; ind. vs. group letters
14. Danet (1973)	1959; 1962	response of Customs officials to client appeals	content-analysis of letters; materials in files	European/Middle Eastern immigrants	positive/negative response; latent particularism in relation to sociocultural background of client
15. Jubas (1974)	1967–71	immigrant adjustment	questionnaire	American & Canadian immigrants	motivation for immigration; immigrant adjustment

16. Dornstein (1976)	?	compliance of taxpayers	analysis of personal files in Income Tax Authority	Western European, Eastern European, Middle Eastern	compliance with tax regulations
17. Handelman (1976)	1950–65	official-client transactions over time	extended case analysis, relations between social welfare agency & one family; observations + analysis of files	Tunisian immigrant family	tactics, transactions which transformed short-term affiliation into long-term career as "social case"
18. Danet (1978)	1971–72	complaints to Israel national ombudsman	comparative measures based on data from ombudsman's annual reports	—	rates of complaining; % justified complaints
19. Nachmias & Rosenbloom (1978)	1973	bureaucratic culture; efficacy, competence of the public; images of officials	interviews with national stratified samples of public & of bureaucrats in 3 largest cities	—	perceived ability of public to influence bureaucracy; choice of channels; protektzia; evaluations of service
20. Maimon (1978)	1974	favoritism in civil service	questionnaire	European vs. Middle Eastern immigrants, natives	perceptions of prevalence of protektzia in recruitment, promotion
21. Caplan (1980)	1969–72	patterns of contact between East Jerusalem Arabs & Israeli officials	observation, unstructured interviews	East Jerusalem Arabs	expectation of personalized, diffuse treatment

Figure A.1 (cont.)

Study	Period Studied	Topic	Method & Setting	Ethnic Groups Emphasized	Main Dependent Variables
22. Shokeid (1980)	1960–78	accommodation to bureaucracy of immigrants' agricultural settlement	field research in 1 moshav	immigrants from 1 Moroccan village	factors leading to change from resistance to universalistically-based appointments to acceptance
23. Avruch (1981)	1975–77	social identity & immigrant adjustment, including to bureaucracy	in-depth interviews with 19 immigrant families; structured questionnaire to 100 immigrants	American immigrants	perceptions of prevalence of protektzia; use of protektzia
24. Shamgar-Handelman (1981; 1986)	1967–80	emergence of war widows as a bureaucratic category	interviews with 71 widows, social workers, bureaucrats	—	negotiation over category of "war widow" as moral, psychological, social welfare category
25. Weiman (1982)	1981	effectiveness of persuasive appeals	field experiment on responses to telephoned requests	—	effectiveness of appeals in relation to type of organization
26. Sebba (1983)	1981	attitudes toward white collar crime including protektzia & bribery	questionnaire	American, Russian immigrants, natives	perceived seriousness of offense; predisposition to report to authori-

					ties; perception that authorities should take tough line
27. Ben-Ezer (1985)	1982–85	sources of misunderstanding between officials & Ethiopian immigrants	observations	Ethiopian immigrants	Ethiopian attitudes toward authority figures; code of honor as affects interaction with officials
28. Ha-Ilan (1986)	1984	protektzia networks	protektzia stories analyzed for no. & types of links	—	frequency of horizontal vs. vertical ties, types relationships involved
29. Levenstein (1986)		use of protektzia as predicted by equity theory	—	—	—
30. El-Makawi (1987)	1987	use of waasta by Arabs	questionnaire	Arab citizens of Israel and residents of West Bank	legitimacy of waasta; perceptions about need for waasta; expectations for particularistic treatment

* A list of all studies, with full references, follows this chart; not all items appearing in this appendix were necessarily cited in the text; only those cited in the text also appear in the full reference list of the book.

REFERENCES TO APPENDIX A

Amir, Menachem (1967). *Report of the Commission on Violent Behavior in Government Social Welfare Offices.* Jerusalem: Szold Institute (Hebrew).

Avruch, Kevin (1981). *American Immigrants in Israel: Social Identities and Change.* Chicago: University of Chicago Press.

Bar Yosef, Rivka, and E.O. Schild (1966). "Pressures and Defenses in Bureaucratic Roles," *American Journal of Sociology, 75,* 665–673. Reprinted in Elihu Katz and Brenda Danet, eds. *Bureaucracy and the Public: A Reader in Official-Client Relations.* New York: Basic Books. 288–299.

Bar Yosef-Weiss, Rivka (1968). "Desocialization and Re-socialization: The Adjustment Process of Immigrants," *International Migration Review, 2,* 3, 27–42. Reprinted in Ernest Krausz, ed., *Studies of Israeli Society,* 19–37. New Brunswick, NJ: Transaction Books. vol. 1, *Migration, Ethnicity and Community.*

Ben-Ezer, Gadi (1985). "Cross-Cultural Misunderstandings: the Case of Ethiopian Immigrants," *Israel Social Science Research, 3,* 65–73.

Caplan, Gerald, with Ruth B. Caplan (1980). *Arab and Jew in Jerusalem: Explorations in Community Mental Health.* Cambridge, MA: Harvard University Press.

Danet, Brenda (1971). "The Language of Persuasion in Bureaucracy: 'Modern' and 'Traditional' Appeals to the Israel Customs Authorities," *American Sociological Review, 36,* 847–859.

——— (1973). " 'Giving the Underdog a Break:' Latent Particularism among Customs Officials." In Elihu Katz and Brenda Danet, eds., *Bureaucracy and the Public.* New York: Basic Books. 329–337.

——— (1978). "Toward a Method to Evaluate the Ombudsman Role," *Administration and Society, 10,* 335–370.

Danet, Brenda, and Michael Gurevitch (1972). "Presentation of Self in Appeals to Bureaucracy: An Empirical Study of Role Specificity," *American Journal of Sociology, 77,* 1165–1190.

Danet, Brenda, and Harriet Hartman (1972a). "On *'Protektzia:'* Orientations toward the Use of Personal Influence in Israeli Bureaucracy," *Journal of Comparative Administration, 3,* 405–434.

Danet, Brenda, and Harriet Hartman (1972b). "Coping with Bureaucracy: the Israeli Case," *Social Forces, 51,* 7–22.

Danet, Brenda, and Tsiyona Peled (1973). "Jerusalem's Municipal Ombudsman," *City and Region, 2,* 68–80 (Hebrew).

Danet, Brenda, Mira Ben Ari, and Pua Sczupak (1972). *The Telephone Services Authority: Attitudes of Staff toward Their Work, Communication with the Public.* Jerusalem: The Israel Institute of Applied Social Research, The Communications Institute, Hebrew University, and Management Sciences Branch, Ministry of Communications, State of Israel (Hebrew).

Dornstein, Miriam (1976). "Compliance with Legal and Bureaucratic Rules: the Case of Self-Employed Taxpayers in Israel," *Human Relations, 29,* 1976, 1019–1034.

El-Makawi, Taher (1988). *"Waasta:* Orientations of the Arab Population in Israel and in the Occupied Territories toward the Use of Personal Connections in Bureaucratic Encounters." Jerusalem: Unpublished M.A. thesis, Dept. of Communications, Hebrew University (Hebrew).

Ha-Ilan, Neta (1986). "With a Little Help from My Friends: Social Aspects of the Use of *Protektzia.*" Jerusalem: Unpublished M.A. thesis, Dept. of Sociology and Social Anthropology, Hebrew University (Hebrew).

Handelman, Don (1976). "Bureaucratic Transactions: The Development of Official-Client Relationships in Israel." In Bruce Kapferer, ed., *Transaction and Meaning: Directions in the Anthropology of Exchange and Symbolic Behavior.* Philadelphia: Institute for the Study of Human Issues. 223–275.

Jubas, Harry (1974). "The Adjustment Process of Americans and Canadians in Israel and Their Integration into Israeli Society." Unpublished Ph.D. dissertation, Michigan State University.

Katz, David, and Aaron Antonovsky (1973). "Bureaucracy and Immigrant Adjustment," *International Migration Review, 7,* 247–256.

Katz, Elihu, and Brenda Danet (1966). "Petitions and Persuasive Appeals: A Study of Official-Client Relations," *American Sociological Review, 31,* 811–822.

Katz, Elihu, and S.N. Eisenstadt (1960). "Some Sociological Observations on the Response of Israeli Organizations to New Immigrants," *Administrative Science Quarterly, 3,* 113–133.

Levenstein, Dov (1986). "Use of *Protektzia* and Perceptions of Equity." Unpublished M.A. thesis, Dept. of Labor Relations, Tel Aviv University (Hebrew).

Maimon, Zvi (1978). "Favoritism and *Protektzia* among Israeli Workers," *International Management Review, 19,* 85–99.

Marx, Emanuel (1972). "Some Social Contexts of Personal Violence." In Max Gluckman, ed., *The Allocation of Responsibility.* Manchester: Manchester University Press.

Marx, Emanuel (1973). "Coercive Violence in Official-Client Relationships," *Israel Studies in Criminology, 2,* 43–44.

Marx, Emanuel (1976). *The Social Context of Violent Behavior: A Social Anthropological Study in an Israeli Immigrant Town.* London: Routledge & Kegan Paul.

Nachmias, David and David H. Rosenbloom (1978). *Bureaucratic Culture: Citizens and Administrators in Israel.* London: Croom Helm.

Sebba, Leslie (1983). "Attitudes of New Immigrants to White-Collar Crime: A Cross-Cultural Exploration," *Human Relations, 36,* 1091–1110.

Shamgar-Handelman, Lea (1981). "Administering to War Widows in Israel: the Impact of Law and Bureaucracy on the Formation of a Category of Client," *Social Analysis, 9,* 24–47.

———— (1986). *Beyond the Glory of Heroism: Israeli War Widows.* Mt. Holyoke, MA: Bergin & Garvey.

Shokeid, Moshe (1980). "Reconciling with Bureaucracy: Middle Eastern Immigrants' *Moshav* in Transition," *Economic Development and Cultural Change, 29,* 1, 187–205.

Weiman, Gabriel (1982). "Dealing with Bureaucracy: the Effectiveness of Different Persuasive Appeals," *Social Psychology Quarterly, 45,* 136–144.

APPENDIX B
THE 1980 QUESTIONNAIRE

In this appendix, the questionnaire from the 1980 study of encounters in public and private agencies is reproduced. Questions which were also asked in the 1968 study are marked by an asterisk.

We are carrying out a study of contacts between the public and government or public agencies, and businesses and services in the private sector (such as stores, dentists, garages, etc.). We would like to learn about what people expect from such encounters. What are the main factors which lead people to be satisfied or dissatisfied in these encounters. What do people do when they feel they have been treated unjustly?

This questionnaire is anonymous (your name is not recorded). Your cooperation will help us a great deal in our efforts to make suggestions as to how to improve services of all kinds.

I. ATTITUDES AND EXPERIENCES IN PUBLIC BUREAUCRACIES

We begin with a series of questions on encounters the public has with government and public agencies.

*1. To what extent did you have an opportunity in recent months to come into contact with government or public agencies?

    1—I had many opportunities
    2—I had a few opportunities
    3—I had almost no opportunities
    4—I had no contacts at all

  2. When was the last contact you had with a government or public agency?

    1—I had no contacts with government or public agencies
    2—A year ago or more
    3—Six months to a year ago
    4—Three to six months ago
    5—Two to three months ago
    6—A month to two months ago
    7—Between two weeks and a month ago
    8—In the last week

  3. In which government or public agency did you have this contact?

    1—Social welfare services
    2—Employment agency
    3—Treasury, income tax authorities

267

    4—Ministry of Housing
    5—Police
    6—Ministry of Transportation, Registry of Motor Vehicles
    7—Ministry of Defense, Israel Defense Forces
    8—Ministry of Communications
    9—Prime Minister's Office
    10—Ministry of Health
    11—Ministry of Religious Affairs, Rabbinical Courts, Rabbinate
    12—Ministry of Education
    13—Ministry of Justice
    14—Ministry of the Interior
    15—Lands Authority
    16—Broadcasting Authority
    17—Municipal Authorities
    18—National Social Insurance Institute
    19—Ministry of Immigrant Absorption, Jewish Agency
    20—Customs
    21—Public transportation (bus companies)
    22—Ministry of Commerce and Industry
    23—Ministry of Agriculture
    24—Electric Company
    25—Other
    26—Doesn't remember

4. Was the matter you wanted to arrange in this government or public agency . . .

    1—A personal or family matter
    2—A matter pertaining to a group, neighborhood, street, city
    3—A matter pertaining to the Israeli public at large
    4—Doesn't remember

5. Who initiated the contact?

    1—I did, or a member of my family
    2—The group or organization whom I represent
    3—An office or agency
    4—Doesn't remember

6. In general, were you satisfied with your most recent encounter with a government or public agency?

    1—Very satisfied
    2—Satisfied
    3—Not so satisfied
    4—Not satisfied
    5—Not at all satisfied

7. Do you feel that you have a right to complain in every case where in your opinion you have been treated unjustly in some government or public agency?

   1—Yes, always
   2—Yes, usually
   3—Sometimes (depends on the situation)
   4—Usually not
   5—Never

*8. Did it ever happen to you in contacts with government or public agencies during the past year that you were treated in an inappropriate or unpleasant manner by officials? To what extent did this happen?

   1—It happened many times
   2—It happened a few times
   3—It happened only rarely (once or twice)
   4—It never happened
   5—I was never in a government or public bureaucracy

9. In what government or public agency did you encounter inappropriate or pleasant treatment by officials?

   1—Social welfare services
   2—Employment agency
   3—Treasury, income tax authorities
   4—Ministry of Housing
   5—Police
   6—Ministry of Transportation, Registry of Motor Vehicles
   7—Ministry of Defense, Israel Defense Forces
   8—Ministry of Communications
   9—Prime Minister's Office
   10—Ministry of Health
   11—Ministry of Religious Affairs
   12—Ministry of Education
   13—Ministry of Justice
   14—Ministry of the Interior
   15—Lands Authority
   16—Broadcasting Authority
   17—Municipal authorities
   18—National Social Insurance Institute
   19—Ministry of Immigrant Absorption, Jewish Agency
   20—Customs
   21—Public transportation
   22—Ministry of Commerce and Industry
   23—Ministry of Agriculture
   24—Electric Company

25—Other

26—Doesn't remember

10. Did you try to do something about it? (Interviewer: code up to four actions taken.)

    1—I didn't do anything, I told friends or family, I forgot about it

    2—I complained to a higher official in the same agency

    3—I complained to the ombudsman

    4—I wrote to a Ministry, the Prime Minister

    5—I wrote to a MK or other elected official

    6—I wrote a letter to the editor or a newspaper or to a radio program

    7—I wrote to the TV program "Kolbotek"

    8—I went to a lawyer

    9—I circulated a petition; organized a demonstration

    10—I used personal connections; sought *protektzia*

    11—I went to a trade union, the Histadrut, a workers' committee

    12—I went to a political party

    13—I tried to threaten, to use physical violence

11. Do you feel that what you did helped you to solve the problem?

    1—It helped me very much

    2—It helped me

    3—It didn't help me so much

    4—It didn't help me

    5—It didn't help me at all

12. Do you think that in every instance in the future in which you feel that you were treated unjustly you will complain?

    1—I'm sure I'll complain

    2—I'm almost sure I'll complain

    3—Maybe I'll complain

    4—I'm sure I won't complain

(To the interviewer: ask the following question only of those who answered 1—I didn't do anything, in question 10.)

13. Why didn't you complain? Please give the main reason.

    1—I didn't know to whom to turn

    2—It wouldn't have helped anyway

    3—I didn't have time, the matter wasn't important enough

    4—I was afraid to complain

    5—It's not nice, not appropriate for a person like me

6—Other
7—Doesn't know

And now we will ask you a few questions on your attitudes toward government and public bureaucracy.

*14. In your opinion, do officials in government and public agencies perform their jobs successfully?

1—Very successfully
2—Successfully
3—Not so successfully
4—Not successfully
5—Not at all successfully

*15. Is it clear to you how officials in government and public agencies are supposed to treat the public?

1—It's absolutely clear to me
2—It's clear to me
3—It's not so clear to me
4—It's not clear to me
5—It's not at all clear to me

*16. In your opinion, do officials in most government and public agencies do their job as they should?

1—To a very great extent
2—To a great extent
3—To a moderate extent
4—To a limited extent
5—To a very limited extent, or not at all

Now we will ask you to evaluate government and public agencies in different areas we will list, and to note how important each area is to you.

17. How would you evaluate office hours (times, queues, waiting rooms)?

1—Very good
2—Good
3—Mediocre
4—Poor
5—Very poor

18. How would you evaluate the manner and behavior of officials in government and public agencies?

1—Very good

2—Good
3—Mediocre
4—Poor
5—Very poor

19. How would you evaluate government and public agencies with respect to all that pertains to *fair treatment* to citizens with different problems?

1—Very good
2—Good
3—Mediocre
4—Poor
5—Very poor

20. How would you evaluate the *knowledge and professional training* of officials in government and public agencies?

1—Very good
2—Good
3—Mediocre
4—Poor
5—Very poor

*21. In your opinion, what is the best way for citizens to arrange matters in government and public agencies?

1—In person, orally
2—By telephone
3—By mail
4—There's no one way, it depends on the problem (do not read)

22. There are different ways of arranging matters in government and public agencies. Which of the following three ways is in your opinion the best way?

1—To know the rules and laws in government and public agencies and to use them
2—To use *protektzia*
3—To threaten and to use physical force

23. In your opinion, do all people receive the *same treatment* in government and public agencies, or do some people receive better treatment?

1—Everyone gets the same treatment
2—Some people get better treatment

24. Who, in your opinion, are the people who receive better treatment? Cite the main reason for this.

1—Some people get better treatment because they know the rules and procedures better

2—Some people get better treatment because they know the right people

3—Some people get better treatment because they are respected

4—Some people get better treatment because they use threats, force, or shout and make a scene

25. Do you know to whom to turn in order to complain about inappropriate or unpleasant treatment on the part of officials in government or public agencies?

    1—I always know to whom to turn
    2—I usually know to whom to turn
    3—Sometimes I know to whom to turn
    4—Usually I don't know to whom to turn
    5—I never know to whom to turn

Now I will read to you a list of things people do in cases where they have been treated unjustly. Have you ever used each of the following, and did it help? If you have never used each one, do you think that using it would help, if you tried it?

		Used			Didn't use			
		Very helpful	*Somewhat helpful*	*Not helpful*	*Very helpful*	*Somewhat helpful*	*Not helpful*	*Don't know*
26.	Higher official	1	2	3	4	5	6	7
27.	Ombudsman	1	2	3	4	5	6	7
28.	Minister, Prime Minister	1	2	3	4	5	6	7
29.	Member of Knesset	1	2	3	4	5	6	7
30.	Newspaper, radio	1	2	3	4	5	6	7
31.	TV program	1	2	3	4	5	6	7
32.	Lawyer	1	2	3	4	5	6	7
33.	Petition, demonstration	1	2	3	4	5	6	7
34.	*Protektzia*	1	2	3	4	5	6	7

	Used			Didn't use			
	Very helpful	*Some- what help- ful*	*Not help- ful*	*Very help- ful*	*Some- what help- ful*	*Not help- ful*	*Don't know*
35. Trade union	1	2	3	4	5	6	7
36. Political party	1	2	3	4	5	6	7
37. Threats, physical force	1	2	3	4	5	6	7

38. To what extent, in your opinion, does the public have enough possibilities and channels to complain about situations of dissatisfaction or poor treatment at the hands of government and public officials?

    1—There are very many possibilities
    2—There are many possibilities
    3—There are quite a few possibilities
    4—There are few possibilities
    5—There are very few or no possibilities at all

39. Do you think it helps to complain?

    1—Very much
    2—Somewhat
    3—To a slight extent
    4—Very little
    5—Only very little or not at all

There are different beliefs among the public about people who complain in government and public agencies. To what extent do you agree with each of the following opinions?

	Agree fully	*Agree*	*Don't agree or disagree*	*Don't agree*	*Absolutely don't agree*
40. People who complain feel they were treated unjustly	1	2	3	4	5
41. People who complain are "nudniks"	1	2	3	4	5
42. People who complain are troublemakers	1	2	3	4	5

	Agree fully	Agree	Don't agree or disagree	Don't agree	Absolutely don't agree
43. People who complain are concerned, good citizens	1	2	3	4	5
44. People who complain are people who want to destroy society	1	2	3	4	5

How, in your opinion, do public and government officials respond to people who complain?

	Always, almost always	Usually	Sometimes	Seldom	Never almost never
45. Threaten them that it's better not to complain	1	2	3	4	5
46. Ignore them, don't respond	1	2	3	4	5
47. Respond, investigate complaint	1	2	3	4	5
48. Treat them with respect for good citizenship	1	2	3	4	5

49. Sometimes people feel they have been treated unjustly by government or public officials. Do you think the reason for this is that the laws are not good, or that the laws are not carried out?

    1—The laws are not good
    2—There are good laws but they are not carried out
    3—Don't know

Now I will read to you a list of characteristics which people usually ascribe to government and public officials. You are to rank each characteristic on a scale from 1 to 7. The highest score on the scale is 7 and the lowest score is 1. How would you rank officials according to the following characteristics?

1	2	3	4	5	6	7
50. Inefficient						Efficient
51. Dishonest						Honest

	1	2	3	4	5	6	7
52.	Unpleasant						Pleasant
53.	Humane						Inhumane
54.	Weak						Strong
55.	Cowardly						Brave
56.	Slow						Fast
57.	Diligent						Lazy
58.	Active						Passive
59.	Bad						Good
60.	Don't try to help						Try to help
61.	Stubborn						Flexible

[Interviewer: beside each question the correct answer is listed; code (1) if the interviewee answers correctly; code (2) if s/he answers incorrectly; code (3) if sh/he doesn't know, doesn't try to answer.]

There are all sorts of reasons why difficulties and problems occur in encounters of the public with government and public officials. What is your opinion about the following?

		Always, almost always	Usually	Sometimes	Seldom	Never almost never
62.	To what extent do the *laws* cause problems?	1	2	3	4	5
63.	To what extent do *procedures* constitute problems?	1	2	3	4	5
64.	To what extent does the *behavior or manner* of officials cause problems?	1	2	3	4	5

It often happens that citizens have problems or questions about the jurisdiction of government and public agencies, but they don't know to whom to turn. Can you tell me, please, which government or public agency is responsible for the following matters:

	Correct	Incorrect	Doesn't know	Correct answer
65. Child benefits	1	2	3	Nat. Soc. Ins. Inst.
66. Housing for young couples	1	2	3	Ministry of Housing
67. Sanitation garbage collection	1	2	3	Local authorities
68. Strange dog biting neighborhood child	1	2	3	Ministry of health, police
69. Price of regulated goods	1	2	3	Ministry of Commerce and Industry
70. Financial aid to unemployed	1	2	3	Nat. Soc. Ins. Inst.

II. PROTEKTZIA

Sometimes citizens feel that it is possible to arrange matters in government or public agencies through use of *protektzia*. We would like to ask you a few questions about your attitude to this topic.

*71. Do you think it is all right to use *protektzia* in order to arrange matters in government and public agencies?

    1—Yes, always
    2—Yes, usually
    3—Sometimes, depends on the situation
    4—Usually not
    5—Never

*72. Do you think most people in Israel use *protektzia* when they need to arrange something in a government or public agency?

    1—Yes, always
    2—Yes, usually
    3—Sometimes, depends on the situation
    4—Usually not
    5—Never

73. What is the main reason, in your opinion, that people like you look for *protektzia*?

1—Without *protektzia* they can't arrange the matter at all

2—Without *protektzia* they can arrange the matter, but it takes more time and trouble

3—Without *protektzia* they can arrange the matter, but they obtain a poor solution

4—Combination of any of the above

*74. Can someone who has no possibility of obtaining *protektzia* arrange all of his/her affairs in government and public agencies in Israel, even without it?

1—Yes, always
2—Yes, usually
3—Sometimes, depends on the situation
4—Usually not
5—Never

*75. When a citizen is completely in the right *vis-à-vis* the law, does it still happen that s/he needs *protektzia* in order to arrange matters in government and public agencies?

1—Yes, always
2—Yes, usually
3—Sometimes, depends on the situation
4—Usually not
5—Never

76. There are different opinions about when people use *protektzia*. With which of the following two opinions do you agree?

1—Most people use *protektzia* only after they failed to arrange some matter in the accepted way

2—Most people use *protektzia* without trying to arrange the matter in the accepted way

77. Did it ever happen to you during the past year that you felt that you had no other choice but to use *protektzia*, in order to arrange some matter in a government or public agency?

1—Yes
2—No

78. Did you have someone whom you could approach to ask for *protektzia*?

1—Yes
2—No

*79. Did it happen during the past year that you sought *protektzia* from someone, in order to arrange some matter in a government or public agency, whether on your own or on behalf of your family or friends? How often did you use *protektzia*?

1—Many times
2—A few times
3—Once or twice
4—Never, because I didn't need *protektzia*
5—Never, I needed it, but didn't want to ask for *protektzia*
6—Never, because I didn't have anyone to approach

80. What was the main reason you sought *protektzia*?

1—Without *protektzia* I couldn't arrange the matter at all
2—Without *protektzia* I could arrange the matter, but it would take more time and trouble
3—Without *protektzia* I could arrange the matter, but I would arrive at a poorer solution
4—Combination (don't read)

81. Did using *protektzia* help you to arrange the matter?

1—It helped me very much
2—It helped me
3—It didn't help me so much
4—It didn't help me
5—It didn't help me at all

III. CONSUMER AFFAIRS

And now we will ask you a few questions about contacts the public has with businesses and private services. We are interested in knowing about your attitudes and experiences in stores, garages, doctors' offices, lawyers' offices, etc. We will begin with a few questions about your experience. When were you last in each of the following places?

	Up to a week ago	1–2 weeks ago	2–4 weeks ago	1–2 months ago	2–12 months ago	Over a year ago	Never
82. Grocery, supermarket	1	2	3	4	5	6	7
83. Clothing, shoe store	1	2	3	4	5	6	7
84. Bookstore	1	2	3	4	5	6	7

	Up to a week ago	1–2 weeks ago	2–4 weeks ago	1–2 months ago	2–12 months ago	Over a year ago	Never
85. Car agency, auto accessory shop	1	2	3	4	5	6	7
86. Furniture household goods shop	1	2	3	4	5	6	7
87. Electric household appliance shop	1	2	3	4	5	6	7
88. Dentist other private doctor	1	2	3	4	5	6	7
89. Lawyer, other professional	1	2	3	4	5	6	7

90. When did you last receive a service from a skilled worker like a plumber, electrician, television technician, etc.?

    1—Less than a week ago
    2—A week to two weeks ago
    3—Two weeks to a month ago
    4—A month to two months ago
    5—More than two months ago

91. Did it ever happen to you during the past year that in an encounter with a store or private service, you felt you didn't get what was coming to you?

    1—Many times
    2—A few times
    3—Almost never happened
    4—Never

I will read to you a list of problems that arise sometimes when we buy a product or a service. To what extent have you had any of the following problems?

	Many times	A few times	Almost never	Never
92. Product broken, faulty	1	2	3	4
93. Poor manner	1	2	3	4
94. Price, payment conditions unfair	1	2	3	4
95. Goods not supplied on time	1	2	3	4

		Many times	A few times	Almost never	Never
96.	Service, warranty poor				
97.	Product of less than promised quality	1	2	3	4

(*Interviewer:* Ask the following questions only of those who answered 1–3 in at least one of questions 92–97. If not, go on to question 108.)

Did you try to do anything in the cases where you felt you didn't get what was coming to you? Did you use any of the following channels, and did it help you? If you didn't use them, do you think that using them would help, usually?

		Used			Didn't use			
		Very helpful	Some-what helpful	Not helpful	Very helpful	Some-what helpful	Not helpful	Don't know
98.	Higher official	1	2	3	4	5	6	7
99.	Seller, provider of service	1	2	3	4	5	6	7
100.	Consumer organization	1	2	3	4	5	6	7
101.	Lawyer	1	2	3	4	5	6	7
102.	Small claims court	1	2	3	4	5	6	7
103.	Newspaper, radio	1	2	3	4	5	6	7
104.	TV program	1	2	3	4	5	6	7
105.	Negative publicity	1	2	3	4	5	6	7
106.	Threats, physical violence	1	2	3	4	5	6	7

(*Interviewer:* Ask the following question only of those who didn't complain, who answered categories 4–7 at least once in questions 98–106.)

107. Why didn't you complain in those instances in which you felt that you didn't get what you had coming to you? Cite the main reason you didn't complain.

    1—I didn't know to whom to turn
    2—It wouldn't have helped, in any case
    3—I didn't have time, the matter wasn't important enough
    4—I was afraid to complain
    5—It's not nice to complain, not appropriate for a person like me
    6—Other
    7—Don't know

108. Do you feel that what you did helped you to solve the problem?

    1—It helped me very much
    2—It helped me
    3—It didn't help me so much
    4—It didn't help me
    5—It didn't help me at all

And now we would like to ask you a few questions about daily purchases.

109. Sometimes it happens that we buy dairy products (milk, cheese, yoghurt) or some other foodstuffs and find that they are spoiled. What do you usually do when this happens?

    1—I don't do anything
    2—I go back to the place I bought it and complain
    3—I complain to the company which markets the product, or to the producer
    4—I write a letter to a newspaper or to a radio program
    5—I contact the Ministry of Health
    6—I write to *Kolbotek* TV program

(*Interviewer:* Ask the following question only if the respondent answered category 1 in question 109.)

110. Why didn't you complain?

    1—I didn't know whom to contact
    2—It wouldn't have helped anyway
    3—I didn't have time, the matter wasn't important enough
    4—I was afraid to complain
    5—It's not nice to complain, not appropriate for a person like me
    6—Other
    7—Don't know

(Interviewer: Ask the following question if the respondent chose categories 2–6 in question 109.)

111. Were you satisfied with the treatment of your complaint?

    1—Very satisfied
    2—Satisfied
    3—Not so satisfied
    4—Not satisfied
    5—Not at all satisfied

112. Did you buy any product during the past year which cost at least IL 4,000 (approximately $50), for example an electrical appliance, a piece of furniture?

    1—yes
    2—no

113. What was the most recent product which you bought which cost at least IL 4,000?

    1—A refrigerator, stove, washing machine, television, stereo, etc.
    2—Small household appliance, mixer, toaster, etc.
    3—Furniture, household equipment
    4—Books
    5—Clothing, shoes
    6—A car
    7—Other

114. In what store did you buy this item and where?

	In my neighborhood	*In my city*	*In another city*
Private store	1	2	3
Dept. store	4	5	6
Shekem	7	8	9
Factory, from producer	10	11	12

115. Before you bought this product, did you seek advice and compare prices and quality of the product in several places?

    1—Yes, to a very great extent
    2—Yes, to a great extent
    3—Yes, to a moderate extent
    4—Yes, but only to a limited extent
    5—Yes, but only a very limited extent

116. How much did you pay?

    1—IL 4,000 to 7,500
    2—IL 7,501 to 10,000
    3—IL 10,001 to 15,000
    4—IL 15,001 to 25,000

    5—IL 25,001 to 50,000
    6—IL 50,001 to 100,000
    7—IL 100,001 to 250,000
    8—IL 250,001 to 500,000
    9—More than IL 500,000

117. How did you pay?

    1—In cash or by check, the entire sum before receiving the product
    2—In payments, up to two months
    3—In payments up to a half year
    4—In payments up to a year
    5—In payments up to two years or more

We would now like to ask you about problems that arise sometimes in connection with the purchase of goods. To what extent have you encountered the following problems in connection with purchase of goods?

118. Did you receive the product more or less on time, as promised?

    1—I received the product at time of purchase
    2—I received the product more or less at the time promised
    3—I didn't receive the product at the time promised
    4—Don't know, product delivery time hasn't come due

119. When you received the product, was it in good condition, or was it faulty?

    1—The product was definitely of the quality promised
    2—The product was more or less of the quality promised
    3—The product wasn't at all of the quality promised
    4—Don't know

120. After purchasing the product did you find that the price and payment conditions were fair?

    1—Yes, the price and payment conditions were perfectly fair
    2—Maybe, I'm not sure if the price or payment conditions were fair
    3—No, the price and payment conditions were not fair
    4—Don't know

121. After using the product did you find that it was in good condition, or was it faulty?

    1—It was in good condition
    2—It had a few defects
    3—It had many defects

122. Did you have any problems in connection with service or the warranty?

    1—The product is new, I didn't need service yet
    2—The service and warranty are very good
    3—The service and warranty are good
    4—The service and warranty are not so good
    5—The service and warranty are not good at all

123. In general, are you or those who use the product satisfied?

    1—Very satisfied
    2—Satisfied
    3—Not so satisfied
    4—Not satisfied
    5—Not at all satisfied

(*Interviewer:* Ask the following question if the respondent mentioned at least one problem in questions 119–123).

124. Did you do anything about the problem which arose in connection with the purchase of a product? Whom did you contact?

    1—I didn't do anything
    2—I complained to a higher official
    3—I complained to the seller or provider of service
    4—I complained to the organization which represents the seller or provider of service
    5—I contacted a consumer organization
    6—I took a lawyer
    7—I submitted a complaint to the small claims court
    8—I wrote a letter to a newspaper or radio program
    9—I wrote to the TV program *Kolbotek*
    10—I spread negative publicity about the business or product among friends and family
    11—I used threats or physical force

125. What was the main problem about which you complained?

    1—The product didn't arrive on time
    2—The product was faulty
    3—The product was not of the quality promised
    4—The price and payment conditions were not fair
    5—The service and warranty were not good

126. Do you feel that what you did helped you to solve the problem?

    1—It helped me very much
    2—It helped me

3—It didn't help me so much
4—It didn't help me
5—It didn't help me at all

(*Interviewer:* Ask the following question if the respondent didn't complain in question 124).

127. Why didn't you complain?

1—I didn't know whom to contact
2—It wouldn't have helped anyway
3—I didn't have time, the matter wasn't important enough
4—I was afraid to complain
5—It's not nice, not appropriate for a person like me
6—Other
7—Don't know

And now we will ask you a few questions about your experience getting various services in the private sector.

128. Did you pay over IL 4,000 during the past year for services like repairs, improvements (house, car), or services like medical care, legal advice, etc.? If so, what sort of service was it?

1—No
2—Yes, household repairs
3—Automobile repairs
4—Furniture, other household products repairs
5—Medical treatment
6—Legal advice
7—Courses
8—Other

129. How much did you pay?

1—IL 4,000 to 7,500
2—IL 7,501 to 10,000
3—IL 10,001 to 15,000
4—IL 15,001 to 25,000
5—IL 25,001 to 50,000
6—IL 50,001 to 100,000
7—IL 100,001 to 250,000
8—IL 250,001 to 500,000
9—More than IL 500,000

130. How did you pay?

1—In cash or check, the entire sum, in advance

2—Cash or check, entire sum when the work was finished

3—Cash or check, in part at the beginning, the rest when the work was finished

4—In payments, I continued to pay after the work was finished

131. Before you received the service (household or car repairs, medical care, etc.) did you seek advice from friends and compare prices and quality of work?

1—To a very great extent

2—To a great extent

3—To a moderate extent

4—To a limited extent

5—To a very limited extent

132. Did they finish the work or the treatment more or less on the date promised?

1—Yes, more or less on the date promised

2—The treatment or work are not yet completed

3—They finished a little late

4—They finished very late

133. After you received the service, did you find that the price and payment conditions were fair?

1—Yes, the price and payment conditions were fair

2—Maybe, not sure

3—The price and payment conditions were not fair

134. Was the quality of the service or treatment on the level promised?

1—Yes, definitely at the level promised

2—More or less at the level promised

3—Absolutely not at the level promised

135. In general, were you satisfied with the service or treatment that you received?

1—Very satisfied

2—Satisfied

3—Not so satisfied

4—Not satisfied

5—Not at all satisfied

(*Interviewer:* Ask the following question only if the respondent mentioned at least one problem in questions 132–134.)

136. Did you do anything about the problems that arose in connection with a service or treatment?

    1—I didn't do anything, I told family and friends; I forgot about it
    2—I complained to a person of higher authority in the same organization
    3—I complained to the provider
    4—I complained to the organization which represents the seller
    5—I contacted a consumer organization
    6—I took a lawyer
    7—I went to small claims court
    8—I wrote a letter to a newspaper or radio program
    9—I wrote to TV program *Kolbotek*
    10—I spread negative publicity about the firm or product
    11—I threatened, used physical force

137. What was the main problem you complained about?

    1—The service was not completed on the date promised
    2—The price and payment conditions were not fair
    3—The quality of the work or service was not good

138. Did it help to complain?

    1—It helped me very much
    2—It helped me
    3—It didn't help me so much
    4—It didn't help me
    5—It didn't help me at all

(*Interviewer:* Ask the following question only if the respondent didn't complain in answer to question 136.)

139. Why didn't you complain?

    1—I didn't know whom to contact
    2—It wouldn't have helped anyway
    3—I didn't have time, the matter wasn't important enough
    4—I was afraid to complain
    5—It's not nice, not appropriate for a person like me
    6—Other
    7—Don't know

And now we will ask you a few general questions about your attitude toward business and providers of services.

140. In your opinion do employees in private businesses usually treat their customers well?

   1—Very well
   2—Quite well
   3—Not so well
   4—Not well
   5—Not well at all

Sometimes people claim that not everyone receives the same treatment in private businesses or offices which are *not* government or public. To what extent do you agree with each of the following opinions?

	Agree fully	Agree	Don't agree or disagree	Don't agree	Absolutely don't agree	Don't know
141. Some people get better treatment because they know a lot about products and service	1	2	3	4	5	6
142. Some people get better service because they know the right people	1	2	3	4	5	6
143. Some people get better service because they have high social status	1	2	3	4	5	6
144. Some people get better service because they bring pressure, threaten, shout, hit officials	1	2	3	4	5	6

145. In your opinion, does it help to complain about a product or service purchased in a private place of business?

   1—To a very great extent

2—To some extent
3—To a moderate extent
4—To a limited extent
5—To a very limited extent or not at all

There are several kinds of channels to which citizens can turn when they feel that they have received unfair treatment in a public or private agency. Are you familiar with each of the following channels, and how did you learn about them?

		Not familiar	Family friends	Users	Lawyer, other professional	Via mass media	Other	Don't remember
146.	Ombudsman	1	2	3	4	5	6	7
147.	Citizens' Advice Bureau	1	2	3	4	5	6	7
148.	Small Claims Court	1	2	3	4	5	6	7
149.	Consumers' Organization	1	2	3	4	5	6	7
150.	TV program	1	2	3	4	5	6	7

We are interested in learning whether people pay attention to the prices of different goods under present inflationary conditions. (*Interviewer:* If the interviewee answered correctly, code [1], if not, code [2]; if s/he doesn't know, code [3].)

How much does each of the following items cost?

		Correct	Incorrect	Doesn't know
151.	Liter of milk	1	2	3
152.	Bus fare	1	2	3
153.	Evening newspaper	1	2	3
154.	Subsidized bread	1	2	3
155.	Kilo sugar	1	2	3
156.	Kilo flour	1	2	3

157. There are people who claim that in conditions of inflation it is impossible to know prices of goods or services. To what extent do you agree with this?

   1—Agree strongly
   2—Agree

3—Don't particularly agree
4—Don't agree
5—Strongly disagree

158. How would you compare your behavior today (under conditions of inflation) with that in the conditions which prevailed 4–5 years ago? Do you know prices better, to the same extent, or less today?

1—Better
2—To the same extent
3—Less

IV. POLITICAL AND CIVIC ORIENTATIONS

And now we would like to ask you about your attitudes toward the political system. Before you is a scale; let's suppose that the number *seven* means that you agree completely and that the number *one* means that you disagree completely. Please tell us to what extent you agree with each of the following sentences.

159. People like me have no influence over government decisions.

160. The parties are only interested in my vote during elections, and not in my opinions.

161. Members of the government are not interested in the opinions of people like me.

162. When the government makes policy it takes into consideration voters like me.

163. Workers in public and government service care about the opinions of people like me.

164. Members of the Knesset don't care what people like me think.

165. People like me have influence over decisions in local government (municipality or local council).

		Correct	Incorrect	Doesn't know
166.	What is the name of the mayor in your city?	1	2	3
167.	Who is the Minister of Commerce and Industry?	1	2	3
168.	How many members are there in the Knesset?	1	2	3
169.	When were the last Knesset elections?	1	2	3
170.	Who is the Foreign Minister?	1	2	3

		Correct	Incorrect	Doesn't know
171. Who is the General Secretary of the Histadrut?

	Correct	Incorrect	Doesn't know
171.	1	2	3

172. To what extent did you participate in the last year in political or public activity (public meeting, home discussion group, demonstration, neighborhood meeting)?

  1—Never
  2—Once or twice
  3—3–4 times
  4—4–5 times

173. Did you vote in the last Knesset elections?

  1—Yes
  2—No

174. Did you vote in the last municipal elections?

  1—Yes
  2—No

V. BACKGROUND CHARACTERISTICS

175. Sex

  1—Male
  2—Female

176. Age

  1—18–24
  2—25–29
  3—30–34
  4—35–39
  5—40–44
  6—45–49
  7—50–54
  8—55–64
  9—65+

177. Education

  1—No schooling
  2—Up to 4 years
  3—5–8 years
  4—9–10 years

5—11–12 years
6—Some higher education
7—B.A. or more

178. Type of school in which last studied

1—Elementary
2—Technical (including agricultural)
3—Academic high school
4—Yeshiva
5—Seminar
6—University
7—Technion

179. Marital status

1—Single
2—Married
3—Divorced, separated
4—Widowed

180. Children

1—None
2—One
3—2
4—3
5—4
6—5
7—6
8—7
9—8 or more

181. Country of origin

1—Native of Israel
2—Central, Eastern Europe (Czechoslovakia, Hungary, Rumania, Poland, Russia)
3—Southern Europe (Yugoslavia, Bulgaria, Greece, Italy, Spain)
4—Western Europe (France, Belgium, Holland, Scandinavia, Germany, Austria, Switzerland)
5—English-speaking countries (America, England, Canada, Australia, S. Africa)
6—North Africa (Morocco, Algeria, Tunisia, Libya, Egypt)
7—Middle East (Iran, Turkey, Arab countries)
8—Far East
9—South America

182. Country of origin of father
     (same categories)

183. Country of origin of mother
     (same categories)

184. Religiosity

     1—Fully orthodox
     2—Quite observant
     3—Somewhat observant
     4—Non-observant, secular
     5—Non-Jew

185. Housing density (Formula: number of rooms, not including kitchen, divided by number of persons)

     1—Up to one person per room
     2—1.00–1.99
     3—2.00–2.99
     4—4.00 and higher

186. City

     1—Jerusalem
     2—Haifa
     3—Tel Aviv/Jaffa
     4—Ramat Gan
     5—Givatayim
     6—Bnei Brak
     7—Bat Yam
     8—Holon
     9—Other

Appendix C

Methods

In this appendix readers interested in further information about methodological aspects of the Israeli case study will find sections on (1) the construction of the sample; (2) the creation of composite indices from sets of questions in the original questionnaire; (3) response rates; and (4) the statistical methods used.

I. Construction of the Sample

The basic strategy for construction of the sample was chosen in consultation with the Statistical Advisory Service of the Department of Statistics of the Hebrew University. The goal was to create a sample of 1200 persons aged 18 or over, residing in Israel's three main cities, Jerusalem, Haifa, and greater Tel Aviv. My collaborators, Naomi Kies and Hadassah Haas, and I decided to sample the lists maintained by municipalities for city property tax purposes. Fortunately for us, these lists were updated to 1979–80, the year the study was to take place. Samples were created from the lists for Jerusalem, Haifa, and all 10 of the cities in what is known as the "inner ring" of metropolitan Tel Aviv, as defined by the Central Bureau of Statistics. Unlike many Western countries where significant proportions of the population live in rental housing, most Israelis, even of low income, own their own apartments, living in condominium arrangements, and very few, even middle class persons, own private homes. Property ownership was thus a feasible basis on which to create a sample.

The number of housing units to be chosen within each community was determined in proportion to the relative size of the community (in relation to the total population of the areas to be sampled) and to the average size of family in it. To obtain a sample of approximately 1,200 persons, 1,845 housing units were sampled, on the assumption that the drop-out rate at this stage would be about 30%. The intended size of the sample in each city was further adjusted in accordance with the known, specific drop-out rate for each one, as had been obtained in the latest survey of family expenses conducted by the Central Bureau of Statistics.

The interviews were conducted by the Israel Institute of Applied Social Research, in accordance with our instructions. Interviewers chose the specific individuals to be interviewed within each housing unit according to the method developed by Kish (1965). Of the original 1200 housing units to be sampled, we obtained interviews from persons in 1021, a drop-out rate at this second stage of 15%.

In Table C.1 the internal distribution of the final sample by city is compared with the relative proportion of each one within the total area sampled. Residents of Haifa and Givataim are slightly over-represented and those of Tel Aviv-Jaffa and Bnei Brak are slightly under-represented. But the two distributions are quite similar.

As for the demographic distribution of the sample, compared to the population, the relevant comparison is made in Table C.2. There is some under-representation of men and of persons of North African or Middle Eastern origin. Skewing is most noticeable with respect to education. Persons having post-high school education are notably over-represented and those with 4 years or less of education are under-represented. Except for apparent slight under-representation of young people aged 18–29, the age distribution is quite satisfactory. Actually, the representation of young people, particularly of those aged 18–24, is difficult to estimate, because exactly comparable data for the adult Jewish population are not available. As noted in footnote (a) in Table C.2, the first category in the data available from the Central Bureau of Statistics includes persons aged 20–24 and our

Table C.1

Internal Distribution of the Sample by City in Comparison with the Relative Size of the Population of Each City Included

City	Sample	Population of the 10 Sample Cities*
Jerusalem	20.5	21.2
Haifa	18.5	15.8
Tel Aviv-Jaffa	21.7	24.2
Ramat-Gan	9.2	8.9
Givataim	5.9	3.6
Bnei Brak	4.5	6.6
Bat-Yam	10.6	9.6
Holon	8.7	9.5
Other	0.4	0.5
Total	100.0%	100.0%

* Sources: Central Bureau of Statistics (1981).

category is 18–24. Similarly, the census data on sex distribution of the population are for persons aged 15 or more, whereas our sample consisted of persons aged 18 or over. In this case, of course, the discrepancy between ages of sample and population is not likely to be a problem, because at every age roughly half the population are males and half are females. Thus, women are somewhat over-represented, as often happens in surveys, because they are more often to be found at home. We did not think that the discrepancies between sample and population were of an order to require weighting in data analysis.

II. Composite Indices

A number of composite indices were created from the raw data, several of which are among the central dependent variables of the study. Although each one is explained, either in a footnote or in the text in the appropriate place, for the convenience of readers the composition of these indices is provided below. The indices appear more or less in order of appearance in the text of chapters 5–7.

A. Political Participation

Two measures of general political/civic orientations were created, and were used as predictor variables. These are a measure of political participation and of feelings of efficacy vis-à-vis the political system. The measure of political participation was based on questions 172–174 (see Appendix B):

172. To what extent did you participate in the last year in political or public activity (a public meeting, home discussion group, demonstration, neighborhood meeting)?
173. Did you vote in the last Knesset election?
174. Did you vote in the municipal elections?

We tallied up the total number of times individuals responded "yes" to questions about three kinds of political activity. Scores thus ranged from 0 to 3.

B. Civic Efficacy

An index of civic efficacy was created from answers to seven questions (numbers 159–165; see Appendix B). The items tapped feelings of

PULLING STRINGS

Table C.2
Demographic Composition of the Sample and of the Adult Jewish Population in Israel in 1980

Feature	Sample	Jewish Population
Age[a]		
18–24	10.6	13.7
25–29	12.8	14.5
30–34	14.7	13.0
35–39	10.3	8.1
40–44	8.1	7.5
45–49	7.9	7.4
50–54	8.7	7.2
55–64	12.5	13.0
65+	14.4	15.7
	100.0	100.0
Sex[b]		
Males	42.4	49.2
Females	57.6	50.8
	100.0	100.0
Ethnic origin[c]		
Native	40.1	39.0
Central, Eastern Europe	31.0	25.9
Southern Europe	4.7	1.5
Western Europe	3.2	3.8
English-speaking countries	2.1	0.8
North Africa	8.0	14.6
Middle and Far East	10.2	13.1
South America	0.8	1.2
	100.0	100.0
Education: Years of Schooling[d]		
0	2.3	6.4
1–4	2.8	3.9
5–8	18.6	21.3
9–12	47.2	47.6
13+	28.5	20.8
	100.0	100.0

[a] Source for age of Jewish adult population, Central Bureau of Statistics, *Statistical Abstract of Israel, 1981,* Table II/23; the first category refers to persons aged 20–24.

[b] Source for sex of Jewish adult population, Central Bureau of Statistics, *Statistical Abstract of Israel, 1981,* Table II/21; the figures refer to persons 15 years old or more.

[c] Data on ethnic origin of Jewish adult population compiled from Tables II/23 and II/25, Central Bureau of Statistics, *Statistical Abstract of Israel, 1981;* the data for the population refer to persons aged 15 and over. NB: in the Census data persons from the United Kingdom are included in the category Western Europe.

[d] Source for years of education of Jewish adult population, aged 15 and over, Table XXII/1, Central Bureau of Statistics, *Statistical Abstract of Israel, 1981.*

efficacy vis-à-vis government, political parties, and bureaucrats in civil service and local government. They are adapted from a scale developed by Friedmann (1974). Respondents were asked to rate on a 7-point scale the extent to which they agreed with each of seven propositions; answers were coded 1 if respondents completely disagreed and 7 if they agreed completely. The items are as follows:

159. People like me have no influence over government decisions.
160. The parties are only interested in my vote during elections, and not in my opinions.
161. Members of the government are not interested in the opinions of people like me.
162. When the government makes policy it takes into consideration voters like me.
163. Workers in public and government service care about the opinions of people like me.
164. Members of Knesset don't care what people like me think.
165. People like me have influence over decisions in local government (municipality or local council).

Scores on this composite index thus varied from 7 to 49. It is evident that some of the items are phrased so that agreement reflects efficacy and in other cases agreement reflects lack of efficacy. In creating the index, scores were reversed where necessary, so that low numbers were consistently given to answers reflecting feelings of efficacy and high ones to answers reflecting lack of efficacy.

C. Need for Protektzia

In the 1980 study self-defined need for protektzia was measured in two ways. Having realized the centrality of this variable from the results of the 1968 study, where need was only measured indirectly and in an inferential manner, we included a direct question in the 1980 study (number 77 in Appendix B): "Did it ever happen to you during the past year that you felt that you had no choice but to use protektzia, in order to arrange some matter in a government or public agency?"

To be able to compare perceptions of need for protektzia in 1968 and 1980, we also computed the indirect measure on the 1980 data, in the same manner as it had been computed in the 1968 study. The indirect index is based on a rearrangement of answers to the general question about use of protektzia in routine encounters: "Did it happen during the past year that you sought protektzia from someone, in order to arrange some matter—whether on your own behalf or on behalf of your family or friends—in a government or public agency? How often did you use protektzia?" (question number 79; Appendix B). Categories for this question were as follows:

(1) Many times
(2) A few times
(3) Once or twice
(4) Never, because I didn't need protektzia
(5) Never, I needed it but didn't want to ask for protektzia
(6) Never, because I didn't have anyone to approach

We coded individuals as needing protektzia if they answered (1)–(3)— on the assumption that anyone using it felt the need for it. In addition, those answering (5) and (6) were also coded as needing it. In effect, then, we dichotomized all respondents: All those answering this question but not choosing (4) were considered to have needed it.

D. Access to Protektzia

As with need for protektzia, access was measured directly in the 1980 study, via an explicit question. Following the question about need, individuals were asked, "Did you have someone to whom you could turn, to seek protektzia?" (question 78, Appendix B). Once again, to be able to compare access in 1980 and 1968, when only an indirect measure was used, we also computed the indirect measure for the 1980 data. This is based on yet another arrangement of the answers to the question about use (question 79, Appendix B; see above). Here we simply dichotomized all those saying "I didn't have anyone to approach" versus all the others saying that they had used protektzia or would have done so, excluding those who specifically said they hadn't needed it—they were omitted from this measure because we had no way of knowing if they would have had someone to approach, had they needed it.

E. Consistency of Attitude and Behavior

To classify individuals as consistently U, consistently P, or mixed in their attitude and behavior with regard to protektzia, we first dichotomized all persons as (1) either legitimating protektzia (saying it was always or generally all right to use it), or (2) not legitimating it (the remaining three categories in response to question 71, Appendix B). Second, we again dichotomized individuals as either having used protektzia or not having used it (question 79, Appendix B): Among those not using it, those who said they didn't have anyone to approach were classed with the users, on the assumption that had they had access, they would have used it.

This cross-classification produced four possible types: In practice the combination of legitimating protektzia but not using it was so rare that we eliminated it from the analysis. The remaining three types, then, are: (1) legitimates protektzia on the normative level and uses it; (2) rejects on the normative level but uses it; and (3) rejects it on the normative level and does not use it.

F. Quizzes of Cognitive Knowledge

Three quizzes of cognitive knowledge were included in the questionnaire, each consisting of six questions, with possible scores thus varying from 0 to 6 correct answers on each.

1. Knowledge of matters pertaining to public bureaucracy. The index of knowledge of matters pertaining to public bureaucracy was based on questions on to whom one should turn with a problem in each of the following areas: child benefits; housing for young couples; sanitation, garbage collection; a strange dog biting a neighborhood child; the price of regulated goods; and financial aid to the unemployed (questions 65–70 in Appendix B).

2. Private-sector consumer knowledge. In the private-sector index only prices were asked about—a salient matter in a period of very high inflation. Respondents were asked the price of a liter of milk, a bus ride, the evening newspaper, subsidized bread, a kilo of sugar, and a kilo of flour (questions 151–157 in Appendix B).

3. Civic knowledge. To measure general knowledgeability about civic affairs, we asked respondents to name their mayor, the Minister of Commerce and Industry, the Foreign Minister and the General Secretary of the Histadrut and to say how many members there are in the Knesset and when the last Knesset elections took place (questions 166–172; Appendix B).

F. Familiarity with Channels of Complaint

Three measures of familiarity with channels of complaint were developed, two of which indirectly tapped such familiarity with channels in the public and private sectors, respectively, and in one of which respondents were asked directly about five channels.

1. Familiarity with public-sector channels: indirect measure. We asked respondents about 12 channels in the public sector: going to a higher official, appealing to the ombudsman, to a Minister or the Prime Minister, contacting a newspaper or the radio, to the TV program "Kolbotek," getting a lawyer, signing a petition or organizing a demonstration, using protektzia, contacting a trade union official, a political party, or using threats (questions 26–37, Appendix B). We asked them to say whether they had used each channel or not; if so, did it help, and if they hadn't used any, did they think it would help to do so if they had a problem. Respondents who said they "didn't know" or who otherwise refrained from choosing any of the six substantive categories (see questions 26–37 in Appendix B) were coded 7—"don't know." We used these "don't know's" as an index of lack of familiarity. In short, we dichotomized all individuals as either giving an answer which we assumed reflected familiarity with the channel or as not being familiar with it. Scores thus ranged from 0 to 12 channels known.

2. Familiarity with private-sector channels: indirect measure. Respondents were asked about 10 channels in the private sector: appealing to a higher official or supervisor of the employee, to the seller or provider of a service, to a consumer organization, getting a lawyer, going to small claims court, contacting a newspaper or the radio, or "Kolbotek," spreading negative publicity, and threatening physical violence. As in the case of the public-sector channels, they were supposed to say if they had used each channel, if it helped, and if they hadn't used it, did they think that it would help? Once again, the "don't knows" were coded as not being familiar with each channel and all other answers were considered to reflect familiarity. Here scores on familiarity with channels ranged from 0 to 10 channels known.

3. Familiarity with channels in both sectors: direct measure. It is evident that both of the preceding measures are highly inferential, though the findings relating to them in chapter 5 provide indirect validity that they tapped what we wanted to tap. Fortunately, we also asked respondents directly about five channels of complaint (questions 146–150, Appendix B). We asked: "There are several kinds of channels to which citizens can turn when they feel that they received unfair treatment in a public or private agency. Are you familiar with each of the following channels, and how did you learn about them?" The five channels were: the ombudsman, a Citizens' Advice Bureau, Small Claims Court, consumer organizations, and "Kolbotek," the television program. All those not answering "not familiar" (category 1; see questions 146–150, Appendix B) were coded as being familiar with each channel. Thus scores varied from 0 to 5 channels known.

G. Redress-Proneness Index

A general index of orientations toward redress was created by synthesizing information on (1) the question about the right to complain ("Do you feel you have a right to complain in every case where in your opinion, you have been treated unjustly in some government or public agency?"; question number 7, Appendix B); (2) the question about subjective knowledgeability ("Do you know to whom to turn in order to complain about inappropriate or unpleasant treatment on the part of officials?"; questions 25, Appendix B); (3) a set of five items tapping perceptions of complainants (questions 40–44, Appendix B). Respondents were asked to say to what extent they agreed with each of the following:

40. People who complain feel they have been treated unjustly.
41. People who complain are "nudniks."
42. People who complain are troublemakers.
43. People who complain are concerned, good citizens.
44. People who complain are people who want to destroy society.

A scale of 5 points was presented, ranging from full agreement to absolute disagreement. The data on these five statements were eventually transformed so that a low number consistently represented a positive attitude toward complainants and a high one represented a negative one. Thus, persons with the most favorable orientation toward redress received a score of seven, and those with the most negative orientation received a score of 35.

H. Intensity of Use of Channels

We also developed two indices of intensity of use of channels, simply by summing up the total number of channels—12 in the public-sector case, and 10 in the private-sector one—that respondents said they had used. Scores on these two measures thus ranged from 0 to 12 in the former case, and from 0 to 10 in the latter.

I. Hybridization of Redress Behavior

One of the key variables in this study is what I have called "hybridization of redress behavior" (see chapter 7). The term refers to the mixed use of U and P channels. To create this index, the data on use of the 12 public-sector channels (questions 26–37, Appendix B) are used, once again, but in a different manner. Because each channel is classed as U or P (see chapters 3 and 7 in particular), I characterized individuals by the total repertoire of channels used: only U, both U and P, or only P. U channels are the ombudsman, appealing to a higher official, going to a lawyer, or to any of the media, organizing a petition or demonstration; P channels are using protektzia, contacting a trade union or party official, and using threats. Although the full three-way division of respondents into (1) using U channels only; (2) using both U and P channels; (3) using P channels only was used in cross-tabulations, in multivariate analysis, respondents were dichotomized into those using both U and P versus all the others (see chapter 7).

III. RESPONSE RATES

In general, response rates were very good. In a check of the responses to all the general questions in the study, about both the public and the private sectors, the average number of persons not responding to the question was only 32.1, or a low 3% of the sample. As indicated in Table C.3, there are some differences between the response to questions about the two sectors, although in all cases levels of response seem adequate.

Note that the general comparison omits from the check all questions to specific sub-groups, e.g., persons encountering a problem with a service and what they did about it. The average number of persons not responding to general questions in the public sector— a total of 71—was 39.5, or 3.9% of the sample. Response rates were slightly better to questions about consumer affairs; here, the average number of persons not relating to the question was only 24.7, or 2.4%. Not surprisingly, few people avoided responding to the quiz questions, where "I don't know" was an acceptable substantive answer.

Table C.3
Response Rates to Questions about Experiences in the Public and Private Sectors (average no. and percent of sample not responding to a question)

	Public Sector			Private Sector		
Type of Question	Total no. questions	Average no. persons not responding	Percent	Total no. questions	Average no. persons not responding	Percent
All	71	39.5	3.9	47	24.7	2.4
Quiz	6	2.5	0.2	6	1.5	0.2
Channels	12	32.1	3.1	10	73.7	7.2
Protektzia	9	25.4	2.5	—	—	—

Of special interest are the responses to the batteries of questions on public and private channels of complaint and on protektzia. It is evident from Table C.3 that people had a harder time relating to questions about private-sector channels than about those in the public sector. Whereas only 32 people, on the average, or 3.1% of the sample, failed to respond to questions about public-sector channels, 73.7, or 7.2%—more than double—failed to answer questions, on the average, about channels for the handling of consumer problems. In my opinion, this is a reflection of the rather slow development of consumer awareness of the right to complain in Israel.

As for the general questions about protektzia, response rates were excellent. On the average, 25 persons or only 2.5% of the sample failed to respond to the questions. It is pertinent to the substantive issues of the Israeli case study that people were more responsive to questions about protektzia than they were about channels of complaint.

IV. STATISTICAL METHODS

The basic technique of data analysis used in this study is the computation of Pearson product-moment correlations. Whenever nominal data were involved, as in a breakdown by respondents' ethnic origin, cross-tabulations were used. In addition, cross-tabulations were occasionally introduced as a supplement to correlations, even when purely ordinal data were involved, to give a more concrete sense of the data than is experienced when looking at a set of correlations.

Two techniques of multivariate analysis were used. In most cases, wherever quite a large number of predictor variables were found to be significntly related to a dependent variable, a step-wise regression analysis was performed, entering all such predictors. In the case of two important dependent variables, use of protektzia in routine encounters and hybridization of redress behavior, log-linear analyses were performed, using the logit version, in which a dependent variable is specified. For further details on this technique, see Knoke and Burke (1980) and Upton (1980).

APPENDIX D

GLOSSARY OF HEBREW TERMS
USED IN TALK ABOUT
ORGANIZATIONAL CULTURE IN ISRAEL*

anshei shlomenu. Literally, "People of our well being." More loosely, "people of our persuasion, those loyal to us, to party interests." Phrase commonly used by party workers in the 1950's, still occasionally heard today. See chapter 4.

avansim. Financial "advances" to officials, or taken by them, without later deducting from salaries. Term used in the early years of the State, less often heard today.

byurokratia. Literally, "bureaucracy"; more loosely, "red tape," overly complex procedures in government and public agencies; rigidity and inefficiency of officials. Example: "*Yesh harbei byurokratia sham.*" "There's a lot of bureaucracy there."

dugriyut. The quality of speaking franking and directly; characteristic of *sabras,* natives of Israel. Typical opener to frank statement: "*ani agid l'cha dugri*" . . . "I'll tell you frankly . . ." See Katriel (1986) and chapter 4.

Eretz Yisrael. Literally, "land of Israel," a phrase denoting the territory of Palestine. Used by nationalist-rightist groups to denote not only a geographical entity but a social-religious entity calling up primordial ties among Jews. See Kimmerling (1985) and chapter 4.

freier. (From the Yiddish). "A fool, a person easily duped or who doesn't know the score." According to Ben-Amotz and Ben-Yehuda, "A person likely to fall into a trap, an easy victim of a trick" (Ben-Amotz and Ben-Yehuda 1972: 191). Example: *Freier*

---

* This list includes a few terms which were not necessarily discussed in the text. Key to pronunciation:
  "a" as in "father"
  "e" as in "men"
  "i" as in "seen"
  "o" as in "comb"
  "ch" as in "Loch Lomond"

307

hu adam shekal l'sader oto. A *freier* is a man who is easily tricked."
See *sader,* below, and chapter 4.

gibush. Literally, "crystallization, consolidation." Used, for example,
in the phrase *gibush hakvutza,* "crystallization of the group." Refers
to creation and strengthening of group ties, in schools, the army,
the kibbutz, etc. See chapter 4 and Katriel and Nesher (1986).

haf'alat k'sharim ishi'im. Using personal connections, putting such
connections to work. See *k'sharim* below. Example: "*Ech hu kibel
et ha'avoda? Hu hif'il k'sharim ishi'im.*" "How did he get the job?
He used personal connections."

hamedina shebaderech. "The state on the way, the state being created." Term used in the Mandate period. Illegal behavior like
stealing arms from the British was justified by saying it was *l'ma'an
hamedina shebaderech*—for the sake of the state in the making.
See chapter 4 and Sprinzak (1986).

hanal mianash. Abbreviation for *ha'adam hanizkar lael hu mianshei
shlomenu*—"the above-mentioned person is one of ours." In the
formative years persons seeking protektzia would often appear
before an official with a note with nothing but this abbreviation
on it, signed by "Moshe" or "Chaimke." See chapter 4.

Kol Yisrael chaverim. An aphorism meaning "All Israel—all Jews—
are friends." More loosely, "All Jews (must) help one another."

Kol Yisrael arevim ze l'ze. Aphorism meaning "All Israel—all Jews—
are guarantors of one another."

K'sharim, k'sharim ishi'im. Connections, personal connections. People say, "*Yesh lo k'sharim tovim sham.*" "He has good connections
there."

la'asot skandal. "To make a scandal," to expose a person's misdoings
by telling others, getting the story into the media, etc.

l'harim kisei. Literally, "to lift a chair;" figuratively, to threaten with
physical violence, by throwing a chair or other means. See epigram
of this book.

l'harim yad. Literally, "to lift a hand or arm"; figuratively, to threaten.

l'harim telefon. Literally, "to lift the telephone"; Colloquially, to
enlist protektzia via the telephone. See epigram of this book.

l'histader. To manage, to know how to arrange affairs in a savvy way. To cope successfully, despite obstacles. See chapter 4 and Elon (1972).

litsor uvdot. Literally, "to create facts." To do things in a hurry, without waiting for permission, or for all relevant evidence to come in; to engage in pioneering activity in a pragmatic manner and against a background of obstacles. See chapter 4.

Medinat Yisrael. "The State of Israel." The term denoting the nation as a political entity; contrasts with *Eretz Yisrael* in connoting civil rather than primordial ties. See Kimmerling (1985) and chapter 4.

mishelanu. Literally, "from ours," more loosely, "one of ours," parallel to the Yiddish *fun unzereh,* "from ours." Used by political party members in speaking of whether persons are loyal to the party or not. See chapter 4 and Ben-Yehuda (1981).

mishpacha; mishpacha achat. "Family; one family." Used to speak of the Jews in Israel; all Jews are *mishpacha achat*—one family.

mishpachtiyut. Familism; an orientation which puts loyalty to the group and concern for its welfare over individual interests. See chapter 4.

pakid. Clerk, bureaucrat.

protektzia. Activation of personal connections; term brought to Palestine by Eastern European settlers. Includes bribery as well as personal favors, in Eastern Europe; in Israel, denotes only use of personal connections. See chapters 1 and 4.

sader; l'sader. Neutrally, to arrange, to order, make order; colloquially, to dupe someone, to put someone down, to "fix" him or her. Example given by Ben-Amotz and Ben-Yehuda 1972: *"shamata ech she'Leibovitz sider et Ben Gurion?"* "Did you hear how Leibovitz duped, 'fixed' Ben Gurion?"

sarsur. Neutrally, "intermediary, mediator;" secondarily, "pimp, procurer." Used by Grossman (1987) for Arabs in the West Bank who serve as go-betweens between the Israeli authorities and local residents. See chapter 9 and Grossman (1987, 1988).

shmor li v'eshmor l'cha. "You take care of, watch over me, and I will take care of, watch over you." Expression pertaining to reciprocity, mutual help among Jews, especially in opposition to hostile others.

Vitamin P. Vitamin "P"; protektzia. Popular nickname for protektzia. Example given by Ben-Amotz and Ben-Yehuda (1972): *"Smoch alav; hu yistader; lo chaser lo Vitamin P."* "Depend on him; he will manage; he doesn't lack for Vitamin P."

waasta. Arabic for use of personal connections, services of mediator.

waastonerim. Hebraized term for purveyors of waasta in the Arab community, especially in the West Bank. Used by Grossman (1987).

Notes

CHAPTER I

1. Institutions for the investigation of complaints have generally been created in socialist societies too, although their functions may be different. See, Gellhorn (1966a), the listings in International Ombudsman Institute (1980; 1983), and the discussion of complaints in chapter 2. Institutions for the airing of grievances also existed in regimes not based on rational-legal authority. Feudal emperors often had a day set aside to hear grievances of their subjects.

2. The word *success* should be interpreted as neutrally as possible. If an idea or practice is successfully adopted, this may not necessarily mean a better state of things than before, but merely that a plan to bring something about was fulfilled.

3. There is a growing tradition of experimental social-psychological research on the sense of injustice (e.g., Folger, 1984). A hypothesis deriving from this research is that those who perceive themselves to be in a situation of negative equity, vis-à-vis Israeli society, will choose illegitimate means to obtain what they want. The main thrust of findings in the present study point in quite another direction. For the theoretical formulation which guided the analysis, see chapter 3. For the results, see especially chapter 5. Hypotheses about use of protektzia deriving from equity theory have been tested in an M.A. thesis by Levenstein (1986).

4. See Anderson (1982).

5. See Weeks (1973); International Ombudsman Institute (1980; 1983).

6. For other discussions of the goals of ombudsmen, see Rowat (1968); Anderson (1969); Hill (1976: 12–13).

7. Huntington's criteria are complexity, coherence, adaptability and autonomy. See Huntington (1965; 1969).

8. Apparently, Anderson included Zambia in his listing of developing nations adopting the ombudsman at the national level, despite the fact that in this country the role is not strictly a classically independent one. See Anderson (1982). The International Ombudsman Institute has begun listing the legislative and executive ombudsmen separately in its annual survey of ombudsmen and other complaint-handling systems. See International Ombudsman Institute (1983).

9. See section IV.E below.

10. In addition to Almond and Verba (1965), see Verba and Nie (1972); Verba et al., (1978); Barnes, Kasse et al., (1978); Almond and Verba (1980).

11. Thus, Verba and Nic give as examples enlisting the aid of a Congressman to bring a son home from the Peace Corps, asking the state commissioner of insurance to help in the collection of an unpaid hospitalization claim, petitioning a state senator to intervene with the county social-service administration to reverse a decision, urging a local councilman to pressure for extension of a sidewalk, and asking a precinctman about a patronage job (Verba and Nie, 1972: 66). Strictly speaking, only the requests for help with the hospitalization and disability claims would fall under the rubric of the present study. In both, something has happened which the citizen perceives to be detrimental to his or her interests, leading the citizen to take action. The requests for help about bringing a son home or having a sidewalk put in are better called petitions—new influence attempts.

12. Examples are Rosengren and Lefton (1970); Katz and Danet (1973a, 1973b); Katz, et al. (1975); McKinlay (1975); Hasenfeld and English (1974); Danet (1981); Goodsell (1981).

13. See, for example, Katz and Danet (1973b, Part IV); Katz, et al. (1975); Hill (1976); Nader (1980); Goodsell (1981).

14. There is debate among students of dispute-processing as to how to define a dispute. Cf. also Lempert (1980–81); Mather and Yngevesson, (1980–81); Felstiner, Abel, and Sarat (1980–81).

15. For a representative sampling of the functionalist views of the 1960's, see papers in Heidenheimer (1970); for critiques incorporating post-functionalist views, see Ben- Dor (1974); Caiden and Caiden (1977); and Werner (1983a).

16. For more details on Sebba's research, see chapters 2 and 4. There is an obvious overlap between the subject matter of patronage and brokerage, and of corruption. Anthropologists try to take a neutral position, whereas political scientists writing in the post-functionalist spirit tend to see the

behavior in question as something that must be stamped out. To put it another way, anthropologists identify with the natives, political scientists with Western values.

17. The consociational variant of the universalistic model of society grants basic titles such as citizenship on a universalistic basis, but access to major centers of power and to many goods is mediated to a large degree by representatives of the major consociational elements. See Daalder (1974) and Liphart (1968), both cited in Eisenstadt and Roniger (1980); for further details on Israeli society and its organizational cutlure, see chapter 4.

18. Tel Aviv also has a complaint-handling office, but it does not fulfill all the criteria of a classic ombudsman.

19. I am indebted to Eisenstadt and Roniger (1980, 1984) for calling to my attention the aptness of the term *abdication* from the universalistic system. They write of clients' abdication of their potentially autonomous acces to major markets, to positions of control over use of resources or to the center and to the setting-up of goods and services except through the mediation of some patron (whether person or organization). See Eisenstadt and Roniger (1980: 59–60 and 1984).

20. There is more to the story of my efforts to establish cooperation with Dr. Nebenzahl. To my amazement, although I had written the only existing, full-fledged article on evaluation of the ombudsman, published in a highly respectable journal (see Danet, 1978), and was living right in Jerusalem, where the conference was to take place, I was not invited to participate in the panel on evaluation. In fact, Dr. Nebenzahl invited me to his office to ask if I would "help write letters" to get certain persons to attend the conference. Of course, people do and do not get invited to conferences for all sorts of reasons. Either or both of two factors may have been operating. First was the possibility that local talent is perceived as less interesting than imported. The second was sheer sexism. When I asked how I could possibly sign such letters, because I was not a member of Dr. Nebenzahl's staff, he said, "Oh, I'll sign them!" Ironically, one of the panelists was taken ill at the last minute and I was asked to substitute for him!

Dr. Nebenzahl had planned to invite me to participate in a smaller ombudsman seminar which was to follow the plenary conference. Behind the scenes, I learned that if the academics invited to participate in the panel could not come, I would be asked. To put the final touches to the story, one of the panelists used his time to summarize my article.

21. It may not be possible to test empirically whether complaint-handling agencies are cooling-out devices, because an individual's political beliefs may color interpretations of findings, or may lead to the rejection of such agencies out of hand. Persons in favor of radical social change may view the processing of little injustices as trivial, even if it sometimes leads to administrative reform.

22. Caplan's (1980) work on contacts between East Jerusalem Arabs and the Israeli authorities after the Six Day War can provide a model of how to study organization-client contacts without becoming embroiled in broader political issues. Although Caplan never hid the fact that he is a Jew, at the time of his research he had not yet settled in Israel, and was a member of the faculty of Harvard University. Things are rather more complicated for Jewish social scientists living in Israel.

23. As far as at least urban Israeli Arabs are concerned, the 1980 questionnaire could have been translated into Arabic, and Arabic-speaking interviewers used. As complicated as the political context is for Israeli Arabs, today. I believe this can no longer be used as a rationalization for avoiding the research.

24. The study of organizational culture has burgeoned in the last decade. One approach documents cross-cultural differences in organizational functioning without necessarily attempting to explain what it is in a particular society that accounts for the differences observed. Cf. Faucheau (1977); Davis (1971); Haire, Giselli and Porter (1963); Hofstede (1979; 1980). Another approach studies the emergence and nature of the culture that develops within organizations (e.g., Schein, 1983; Jones, 1983; Martin et al., 1983). The present study attempts to synthesize the two approaches. I am interested in the effects of the wider culture and social structure on emergent organizational culture. For a sampling of recent work on organizational culture, see the special issue of the *Administrative Science Quarterly* edited by Jelinek, Smircich, and Hirsch (1983). Unlike most studies of organizational culture, in which what goes on among workers is studied, this book focusses on clients. Studies reviewed in chapter 2, like those of Goodsell (1976) or Price (1975), are clear exceptions.

25. For an exploratory study on these issues, yielding interesting findings about protektzia networks in Israel, see Ha-Ilan (1986).

CHAPTER II

1. The formulation of the ideas in this chapter has benefited in countless ways from discussions with students in my 1984–1985 seminar on "The Study of Organizational Culture," and with my former teaching assistant, Neta Ha-Ilan. Reuven Kahane and Alex Weingrod both made valuable comments on this chapter. Ehud Harari and Eyal Ben Ari, experts on Japanese society, provided corrective feedback to the speculations on Japan in Section VIII.

2. The mapping sentence is not a theory, but an attempt to order the various facets of a domain, as Guttman (1957; 1970) called them. In this scheme, I identify 10 critical facets of non-U behavior. For further expla-

nation of the nature and uses of mapping sentences, see Guttman (1957; 1970); Shye (1986); and Levy (1976).

3. The scheme is designed to cover both instances of illegitimate exchange, as when an official accepts a bribe in exchange for a service to which the client has no right, and those in which there is no exchange because the violation is private. The code for the former example would be

$$a^1\ b^1\ c^1\ d^1\ e^1\ f^1\ g^2\ h^1\ i^2\ j^2.$$

The act of bribing the official by the client would be coded separately as another instance of rule-violation. Acts in which no exchange takes place and which require no cooperation on the part of another person would be coded as not relevant in facets E, F, and I. Embezzlement in a private-sector firm would be coded

$$a^1\ b^3\ c^1\ d^1\ e^3\ f^4\ g^3\ h^2\ i^5\ j^1.$$

Of course, offenses like embezzlement and tax evasion do sometimes involve the cooperation of one or more others.

4. More exactly, I focus on instances of rule-violation in which at least two persons are party to the violation. As explained in chapter 1, use of personal connections necessarily involves one or more third parties.

5. Strictly speaking, there is, of course, no private sector in the monolithic societies, because the production and distribution of all goods and services are the responsibility of the state. Still, as I argue below, the features relevant for analysis of the allocation of consumer goods, even in these societies, are partly different from those relevant for the analysis of services.

6. See Kiggundu, et al. (1983).

7. I am indebted to Reuven Kahane for this point.

8. Similarly, the meaning of fairness is quite different in the private and public sectors. Dealers can charge everyone the same price, be efficient in their procedures and pleasant in their manner, and still cheat their customers. Thus, fairness in the private sector (or at least with respect to the price of things that cost money) means fairness in the balance between rewards and costs, not fairness in the application of universalistic rules.

9. True, even in capitalist systems, quasi-monopolistic conditions emerge over time, as large corporations merge and control markets. Still, relative to socialist countries, market conditions are more prevalent.

10. There *are* pockets in the West where traditional bazaar or market patterns persist. My experiences in the Portobello Road antique market in London revealed many similarities with my experiences in the bazaar of the Old City of Jerusalem. Although London transactions are not accompanied by cups of Turkish coffee, they are more leisurely than department store transactions, with time for discussions on matters of common interest to collectors and dealers, and do allow for bargaining over prices.

11. See, e.g., Zuckerman (1977); Barnes and Sani (1974); versus Tarrow (1967) and Allum (1973).

12. I took these data from the Annual Report for 1973 of the Jerusalem Complaints Commissioner; he, in turn, had taken them from a previous report of the French Médiateur.

13. For figures on the proportion of complaints found justified in Israel, up through 1977, see Danet (1978: Table 3). Criteria for deciding whether a complaint is justified can never be fully objective, and no doubt vary not only from one society to another but from one ombudsman to another, and from one official to another even in the same office. Still, I believe that it is worthwhile to analyze such data. For further discussion of problems of interpreting such data, see Danet (1978).

14. Hill's (1976) book-length study of the New Zealand ombudsman contains information on problems complained about.

15. But recall the observation made in chapter 1 that some unknown proportion of complainants may be using complaint-handling devices as merely a means to try again, with no necessary sense of injustice involved. It is an empirical question just how many such users of complaint-handlers' services fall into this latter category.

16. There is a large literature on machine politics and party patronage. On the United States, see, for example, Merton (1957); Key (1964); Etzioni-Halevy (1979), chapter 3; on Britain, see, e.g., Gwyn (1962); Richards (1963); Clapham (1982); Doig (1984), and Etzioni-Halevy (1979) chapter 2.

17. Hirschmann (1970) has taken a different position from the traditional one that competition stimulates good service. He argued that where a choice is available to the customer, he or she will exit, going to another supplier, whereas in a monopolistic situation the customer will be strongly motivated to complain, thereby leading to improvement in quality. See Hirschmann (1970). Montias and Rose-Ackerman (1980) reached similar conclusions to those of Hirszowicz (1980) as to the ways in which over-bureaucratization and monopoly foster corruption.

18. A growing literature on the parallel economy in socialist countries has accumulated in the last decade. See, for example, Grossman (1977); Smith

(1976); Staats (1972); Katsenelenboigen (1977); Hirszowicz (1980); Wiles (1981); Schapiro and Godson (1982); Mars and Altman (1983).

19. See Nove (1977); Dyker (1982). In a BBC radio program on contemporary Russian literature on 22 May, 1983, Mary Seton-Watson discussed a short story which was called in translation "The Peddler," but more appropriately should probably have been called "The Pusher." Written by an author called Kashtana, the story appeared in *Novy Mir*, the chief official literary magazine in Russia. It told of the experiences of a factory pusher sent to mobilize chrome steel needed for his factory to meet its quota. He is given money "for the trip," and gets tips from other "peddlers" on how to get the supplies. He bribes a secretary and a hotel manageress with chocolates and face cream, and gains access to critical resources. Eventually, he is promoted to assistant head of the factory. Meanwhile, his boss is arrested for taking bribes. According to Ms. Seton-Watson, themes having to do with small-scale corruption, fixers, and bribery are more and more common in official Soviet literature. What is interesting is not only that the authors admit to the failure of socialism to produce persons who conform to official socialist morality, but that this admission is made in official publications.

20. Sebba debated the representativeness of his American and Russian interviewees. Because they had only been in Israel up to 1 year, and lived in Immigrant Absorption Centers, it is reasonable to argue that for the purposes of a pilot study, if not for a full-fledged one, these immigrants constituted a convenient base for cross-cultural research which would otherwise be impossible. Sebba also compared his results with answers of a sample of native Israelis.

21. The famous Chinese wall posters are an outlet for criticism, but apparently not for personal grievances. See Fraser (1982); Bonavia (1982). On letters to the editor in the People's Republic, see Chu and Chu (1981).

22. In the Ghanaian study, as in the Egyptian one, the higher the educational achievements of the officials and the higher their rank in the civil service, the more likely they were to express universalistic orientations. But in both cases, even among those of high rank and high education, the salience of particularistic pressures persisted (cf. Berger, 1957; Price, 1975). In a 1980 reassessment of Egyptian bureaucracy, Ayubi cited data showing that the educational attainments of top-level Egyptian civil servants are far higher on the average than those of comparable civil servants in the West, including the United States and the United Kingdom. Ayubi believes that Egyptian bureaucracy is less personalistic today than in the past, but provides no empirical evidence. See Ayubi (1980).

23. For more recent discussions of amoral familism in southern Italy, see Wichers (1964); Pizzorno (1966).

24. Note that these instances of exploitation of office to benefit family illustrate Andreski's (1970) distinction between *egoistic* and *solidaristic* graft. What is common in the West is private-regarding, egoistic violations of the U code; in the countries under discussion, these violations are strongly motivated by solidaristic considerations.

25. In both Spain and Italy the client approaching a gate-keeper to a resource often presents the calling card of the broker who sent him or her (Galt, 1974; Kenny, 1962).

26. See chapter 6 for my findings on the incidence of use of protektzia in Israel.

27. In an earlier study of the city of Detroit, in the United States, 41% had said that pull played an important part and another 28% said it played some part. See Janowitz et al. (1958: Table XI, 48). It is not clear from the way that Eldersveld et al. reported their findings whether the categories were exactly the same as in the Detroit study, and thus whether the Delhi and Detroit findings are strictly comparable. See Eldersveld et al. (1968: 28), Table 2.11. Crude as these results are, they have provided additional support for my contention that the United States functions in relatively universalistic fashion.

Galt (1974) provided a vivid example of how an Italian student at the University of Palermo, who had to live outside of Palermo and therefore rarely went to class, cultivated a personal relationship with a *bidello* (a minor university functionary) to make life easier. He gave the bidello gifts and tips, in exchange for which the bidello helped him to bypass long waiting lines and had the student's booklet signed to prove attendance.

28. Godparents are also sometimes brought in to serve as witnesses or best men at marriages (Davis, 1977).

29. I am indebted to Reuven Kahane for calling to my attention the notion of the delinquent community.

30. Matsushita, manufacturers of National products, are famous for their company song and code of values, which are recited together by all employees at the start of each working day. The code stresses the contribution of the company to wider social values, and not commitment to profit values.

31. In a personal communication Harari cautioned me that by some criteria, at least, resources are not plentiful in Japan. Still, the fact that it has one of the highest per capita incomes in the world persuades me that at least for the purposes of this exploratory analysis, scarcity is not present. A conversation with another Jerusalem colleague, Ben Ari, who lived for 2 years in Japan, strengthened my claim that bureaucracy is generally well-functioning.

32. Harari, a student of administration in Japan, could not think of a single empirical study of official-client encounters.

33. According to Nakane,

A common educational background comes next to institution or place of work in degree of function and is more effective than either family or local background. The "school clique" would come into function in the case of an interview, for example, where, other counts being equal, it proved difficult to choose between candidates . . . today . . . local background is by no means as vital as the "schoolclique", particularly at the level of the organization man (Nakane, 1973: 133).

As is quite well known, not only are Japanese not friendly with neighbors, but in anonymous situations they can be downright hostile and aggressive, as when they shove others out of the way to get a subway seat.

34. Although now 30 years old, this handbook was considered a valid enough source of evidence of life in contemporary Japan to be cited in a 1971 English-language publication by an author of Japanese origin himself. Ben Ari noted that the advice might be taken as strategy, rather than as a sign of how people actually feel in interaction with officials.

35. In some respects this discussion seems to imply that ordinary Japanese, even literate, fairly educated ones, might feel as at a disadvantage in bureaucratic settings in the manner described by the Greek peasants earlier. This may be overstating the case.

36. Harari and Ben Ari concurred that attitudes and behavior are changing and that urban-rural differences are considerable.

37. The concept of *on* means both a favor granted and the indebtedness that results from accepting it. See Lebra (1969; 1974).

CHAPTER III

1. Other groups may not have been exposed to the U code at all. Thus, clients lacking socialization to the U code may bring P expectations to encounters with officials who have come to identify with U values. Here the result will be not conflict within the individual, but interpersonal conflict between client and official.

2. A similar result emerged in the pilot study of appeals to four types of organizations. Variables like occupation predicted appeals to universalistic norms, but exposure to Israeli bureaucracy was correlated with appeals to the altruism of the official. See Katz and Danet (1966).

3. For a comprehensive review of theory and research on the relation between attitudes and behavior, see Fishbein and Ajzen (1975); Ajzen and Fishbein (1980). After a decade or so of discouragement in the search for

an adequate account of the discrepancy, there has been an upsurge of interest in the problem, with findings that begin to provide an explanation.

4. I am indebted to Stanley Cohen for calling Cressey's study to my attention. For more recent developments in control theories of deviance, and particularly in those varieties of them which emphasize the influence of situational factors, see, e.g., Downes and Rock (1982: chapter 9).

5. The direction of causality may also be the reverse, such that the belief that one cannot manage without it is a rationalization for behavior; see chapter 4.

6. Confirmation for this hypothesis was not found in the 1968 study. Although the numbers were in the expected direction, even among those reporting only positive experiences, admitted use of protektzia was very high. But as is indicated in the next section, there was no correlation between quality of personal experiences and the tendency to define oneself as needing protektzia.

7. There is, of course, a large literature in criminology on the effects of deterrence on behavior. This literature is concerned only with the effects of sanctions on acts which are illegal, whereas the concern in this book is mainly with acts which violate non-legal rules. On the deterrence issue in criminology, see, e.g., Zimring and Hawkins (1973).

8. Sociolinguists have spoken of norms of overt and covert prestige. Several studies have shown that officially denigrated speech forms sometimes enjoy covert prestige. Thus, Trudgill (1975) showed that the speech patterns of working class men in the British city of Norwich were better accounted for by a norm of covert prestige for lower-class speech than by the norm of overt prestige for upper class received pronunciation. The usefulness of this analogy to language is further demonstrated in Section VII below, where I introduce the concept of macro-level diculturalism.

9. Another aspect of the cost-benefit structure of the situation is the value of the desired resource: Other things equal, the greater the value of the resource, the more willing the client should be to use illegitimate means. Farrington (1979) cited three studies confirming this; e.g., the more valuable the prize at stake, the more children tended to cheat (cf. Dimitruk, 1971).

10. See the discussion of the concept of redress in chapter 1; see also Mayhew (1975).

11. A rare and colorful threat found in the content analysis of letters to Israeli customs officials (Danet, 1971) was, "Your decision could affect the plans of 20 families in Chicago to immigrate to Israel." In other words, "If you don't grant the request, we will tell them not to come, thereby depriving the state of valuable potential immigrants."

12. Actually, the line between inducements and activation of particularistic norms is very blurred. In any given instance, there may or may not be an established past relationship within which a normative obligation can be activated. To appeal to a politician may be to imply, "Do it for me and I will reward you with loyalty or my vote," or it may be an attempt to activate the norm, "You owe it to me because I voted for your party."

13. I assume that the term protektzia generally means the activation of literally personal connections, that is, persons with whom one is acquainted. Should the other types of patronage/brokerage investigated in the study also be labeled as protektzia? Would users think of them as protektzia? Perhaps I should have asked them. This is an empirical question, which should be kept separate from the analytical distinctions I am attempting to draw in this section. The empirical correlations between use of protektzia, as tapped by a direct, explicit question using this term, and use of the other four particularistic types (MK, Minister, political party, trade union), were quite low (see chapter VI).

14. This is a more refined distinction than Boissevain makes. He would call all four types organizational brokerage. See Boissevain (1974).

15. Although I believe low-level bribery to be relatively rare in Israel, according to Menachem Amir, a Hebrew University criminologist, there are certain "pockets" where it is widespread, e.g., the Registry of Motor Vehicles.

16. See especially Austin (1970).

17. A member of my seminar on "The Study of Organizational Culture" from Guatemala reported that such bribes are necessary there to get a driving license.

18. But as I have argued in other chapters, using pull is at the expense of others, strictly speaking. It could be argued that getting ahead of someone in the line when everyone has only brief business to arrange is not a serious deprivation. On the other hand, jumping the queue for a serious operation certainly may cause harm to others who are even more ill than the person who does it. But the point here is not whether the deprivation is or is not serious, but that this kind of reasoning can be used to resolve the dissonance between personal attitudes and behavior.

CHAPTER IV

1. Actually, although most of the Jewish population growth in Palestine starting around 1880 was through immigration, small numbers of Jews had continued to live there even during the 2000 years of dispersal.

2. However, in opposition to the value of respect for legitimate authority is a strong, countervailing trend of hostility to legitimate authority, to which

Nebenzahl alluded in the passage cited above. See the discussion of illegalism in Section V below.

3. For overviews of the history of immigration, see Eisenstadt (1954); Matras (1965), and Friedlander and Goldscheider (1979). A handy summary of immigration statistics is available in Avruch (1981), Appendix.

4. I take exception to Caiden's view of British public administration as condescending; perhaps it was condescending toward the "locals" in Palestine during the Mandate, but not necessarily so in its home territory today.

5. On institution-building during the period of the Yishuv, see Eisenstadt (1967).

6. More than 20 years have passed since Dror's observations. And Nebenzahl's words, cited at the beginning of this chapter, pertained to a period ending in 1973. Although there have been some changes, for instance, in professionalization of staff, by and large this characterization still fits.

7. These are traditional phrases from the period of the *galut,* or exile from the Promised Land.

8. See United Nations (1982), Tables 1-1 for Sweden and Israel.

9. This paragraph has benefited from discussion with Menachem and Delilah Amir.

10. Computed from Nachmias and Rosenbloom (1978), Table 3.2, 69. A hundred cases from their sample are unfortunately missing from the table. There is no explanation given as to why so many cases are missing.

11. The phrase *hanal mianash* is alive and well in 1987. A recent television program, called "Viewpoint," was devoted to a discussion of the politicization of public administration. In the background behind the moderator, as the logos for the program, was a poster with these very words. It is difficult to find references to the term in the social science literature. A recent reference to the phrase *anshei shlomenu* is in Sprinzak (1986): 156.

12. In Arabic *dugri* has both an original, literal meaning—"straight", as in "a straight road"—and a metaphorical one, as in "talking straight." The Hebrew usage is purely metaphorical. See Katriel (1986), chapter 2.

13. The term *sabra,* popularly used to denote Israelis, is also originally an Arabic word, pertaining to the fruit of a certain type of cactus which grows profusely in the area. Like the fruit, which has prickly thorns on the outside which must be carefully removed before enjoying the sweet fruit, Israelis are supposed to be prickly on the outside but sweet and with a heart of gold on the inside.

14. Since completion of this manuscript, Sprinzak has published an English-language article on illegalism; see Sprinzak (1988).

15. Attitudes toward law have a prominent place in the public agenda, as this manuscript is being completed. The prestigious daily newspaper *Ha'aretz*, read by intellectuals, recently took the unusual step of devoting the entire magazine section of its Friday edition to a series of articles on the topic. The issue was called "What's Happening to the Rule of Law?" and featured, among others, articles on the functioning of the current legal adviser (the man who replaced Zamir); on law-breakers as media heroes; on discrepancies between legal procedures inside Israel and the discriminatory ones operant in the occupied territories; on white-collar crime; on political ideology and attitudes toward law; and on the police as law-breakers. See *Ha'aretz*, March 6, 1987.

CHAPTER V

1. Because poorer people are somewhat less likely to own apartments, lower-class groups are slightly under-represented in the sample.

2. In 1974 three questions from the original 1968 study were asked again, in the context of the regular Continuing Survey of public opinion conducted by the Israel Institute of Applied Social Research (which also carried out the field work for both the 1968 and 1980, full-fledged studies). Although never written up in a separate report, the results for the three questions were cited by Maimon (1978). The figure of 14% approving the use of protektzia in the 1974 replication might be slightly higher than those for 1968 and 1980 because of sampling fluctuation. Although the 1968 sample included 1886 persons, and 1021 in the 1980 study, only 536 persons were interviewed in the 1974 replication.

3. Most Israelis live in relatively small apartments in condominium arrangements. Few own private homes, which are still considered a luxury. The range in number of persons per room, per family, is a good deal narrower than would be true for the affluent societies of the West. Consequently, housing density is a less effective measure of socio-economic status than in many other countries.

4. Two of his items were omitted and one new one was added. His item tapping perceptions of the complexity of government, and his question about the efficacy of complaining were omitted, and one added about local government. In the study, perceptions of the efficacy of complaining were kept separate.

5. The results for the public sector were very similar to those obtained for the year 1968. Because data on the private sector were collected for the first time in 1980, no comparison is available. The measure of private-sector contact was an index created from questions asking how recently respondents had had contact with nine types of places of business—grocery stores and

supermarkets, clothing and shoe stores, car agencies, and so forth, as well as with service-providers like plumbers and electricians.

6. In part, greater contact in the private sector probably reflects higher income—e.g., more money to spend.

7. In the 1968 study an indirect measure of need for protektzia was created by reworking answers to a question ostensibly only about actual use of it. In addition to three categories of use—(1) "many times;" (2) "a few times;" (3) "once or twice"—there were three options for those saying that they had not used it: (4) "No, because I didn't need it;" (5) "No, because I didn't want to use it;" and (6) "No, because I didn't have anyone to ask." Those choosing any category except the fourth were classified as having needed protektzia. In the 1980 study a direct question was asked about personal need for protektzia. In all presentations of findings in the following pages, wherever findings pertain to the 1980 study, they are based on the preferable direct measure. However, because this question was not asked in the 1968 study, all efforts to compare need for protektzia in 1968 and 1980 will necessarily be based on the indirect measure.

8. Because so many different variables were significantly associated with perceived need for protektzia, albeit at low levels, a step-wise regression analysis was carried out. The results narrowed the number of predictors down to four: age, frequency of negative experiences, length of residence, and frequency of contact generally; but the multiple correlation of these four variables with need was only 0.25. The single best predictor was age of interviewees.

9. See note 7.

10. I had expected the general level of subjective knowledgeability to have risen in the intervening 12 years. Given the increase in the number of channels available, the efforts of various institutions to publicize themselves, and the supposed growth of consumer consciousness, the index of feelings of subjective knowledgeability should have shown an increase.

11. Two sources of patterning in the belief in threats provided some support for the opposing hypothesis, that threats are the language of the weak. Women and those rating the quality of ethnic relations in Israeli society negatively both tended slightly more often to favor threats than did men, or those rating ethnic relations favorably. Yet, persons scoring high on the civic quiz favored them more than did those scoring poorly, counter to the idea that threats are used by the weak. On balance, then, these findings are consistent with the grand hypothesis—that illegitimate means are favored by the most, rather than by the least, integrated members of the society.

12. Unfortunately, I have no direct evidence as to the nature of the relationships called upon when protektzia is sought, as it was not investigated

in this study. On theoretical grounds, deriving mainly from analysis of the sources of solidarity among Jews in Israel (see chapter 4), I believe that spontaneous mobilization of networks tends to involve relatively symmetrical relationships, and that therefore the term protektzia is understood to pertain to such relationships. The empirical results of this study tended to confirm this interpretation. The data in Table V.9 show that, whatever the term protektzia calls up in people's minds, it must be quite different from what is called up by explicit reference to political figures, political parties, etc. For the latter are perceived to be far less effective, on the average, than unspecified protektzia.

Ha-Ilan (1986) investigated the mobilization of symmetrical versus asymmetrical ties in three areas: besides services to the public, the area studied in the present case, she also investigated ties mobilized in obtaining a job and in business deals between the public and private sectors. In the latter two areas, asymmetrical ties were more commonly mobilized than symmetrical ones, whereas in the former, symmetrical ones were the more common. Thus, her study provided some confirmation for the view expressed here.

CHAPTER VI

1. It is surprising that more people claimed access on the direct question than claimed need on the parallel direct question. Three hundred and nineteen persons had said that they had had no choice but to use protektzia (see chapter 5). One possible explanation is that the figure for access included people who used protektzia out of choice. I suspect that there is another explanation, namely, that people want to be perceived as having access because being able to use protektzia is a kind of status symbol.

2. See chapter 5, section IV.D and note 7.

3. Note that the data on access (indirect measure) and use are based on differing categorizations of the data from the original question on use of protektzia. This drop of 10% in use should not be taken as a sign that protektzia is gradually disappearing: On the contrary, the majority of findings of this study suggested quite the opposite, that it is at least as thoroughly entrenched as it was in 1968, and perhaps even more so.

4. For the debate on the ethnic gap see, e.g., Smooha (1978); Smooha and Peres (1980); Greenberg (1979); Bernstein and Antonovsky (1981); Fishelson et al., (1980); Shama and Idris (1977). As in all such debates, the controversy is complicated by differences as to what measures to use, which ones are most important, whether to emphasize absolute or relative gaps, and so on. Toward the end of this chapter I return to the question of the implications of the findings of this study on access to protektzia for Israel's ethnic gap.

5. Strictly speaking, at least according to the Weberian definition, power is the ability to influence another's behavior in spite of his or her opposition. Influence is the more general, more neutral term. As an umbrella term for a variety of types of influence attempts, protektzia probably includes some instances where voluntary compliance is involved, a few where there is latent coercion, and some where people exploit their rational-legal authority in organizations to give illegitimate orders to subordinates.

6. Smooha noted that the per capita expenditure of Middle Eastern Jews rose by 85%, or 7.1% annually between 1956–57 and 1968–69, whereas that of Europeans rose by 106% or 8.8% per year during the same period (Smooha, 1978: 155–156).

7. It would have been nice to show that matching Europeans and Middle Easterners for education washed away ethnic differences. The data in Table VI.5 do not show this to be so. Among those with at least some high school education, and both among immigrants and among second-generation persons, Europeans were a little more likely to report access. A complicating factor is the reluctance of some Europeans, mainly those of Western European or Anglo-Saxon origin, to bring themselves to say there was someone to whom they could turn. This measure of access to protektzia is thus not an entirely satisfactory indicator of perceived equality in Israeli society—it is flawed because, like the measure of perceived need for protektzia, it is influenced by the degree of past commitment to universalism in country of origin.

8. For explanations of log-linear procedures, see Knoke and Burke (1980) or Upton (1980). I am grateful to Zvi Richter, programmer for the sociology department, who spend a great deal of time preparing these analyses, as well as the parallel logit analysis of hybridization in use of complaint-channels, presented in chapter 8.

9. Knoke and Burke (1980: 31) suggested that p values falling within a range of about 0.10 to 0.35 are acceptable, commenting that higher probability levels may provide "too good" a fit—including unnecessary parameters.

10. These correlations between consistency and age and length of residence extend and confirm those between age, generation and length of residence, and general use of protektzia, displayed in Table V.2, but not discussed thus far in the text of this chapter.

11. As for length of residence, the data on reasons for use of protektzia did not fall into an orderly pattern. I had expected the tendency to cite time and trouble to rise neatly with seniority. True, natives were quite likely to cite this reason (this was already evident in the data for ethnic origin), but those in Israel since the late 1940's and early 1950's were about as likely to do so, whereas those old-timers who had been in Israel since before 1948 were extremely unlikely to do so. They were particularly high on the

tendency to say it was impossible to do without protektzia, a rare finding which goes against the main pattern of greater ease of coping for the haves.

CHAPTER VII

1. It is very difficult to interpret these rates of taking action. Several other researchers also investigated rates of complaining or taking action, but because different studies have used somewhat different measures, or investigated different time periods, comparison is generally not possible. A rare exception is the pair of studies by Miller and Sarat (1980–81) and Fitzgerald (1982), which enable comparison of the United States and Australia, primarily in the private sector. For a comparative study of rates of complaining in the public sector, see Friedmann's (1974) research on Canada and Britain. On the face of it opposing predictions can be developed for the response of Israelis to injustice, either as too passive—"sheep to the slaughter," an image evoked by the Holocaust—or as highly contentious individuals who relish an argument or a fight (see, e.g., Meyerhoff, 1978). One bit of evidence for the theory that Israelis are more passive than other nationals is the finding that, when asked to give reasons why they failed to seek redress of grievances, on the average, Israelis more often said "it wouldn't help" than did either Americans or Australians (cf. TARP, 1979, and Fitzgerald, 1982).

2. This is surprising. A secondary hypothesis of this study has been that citizens are stronger vis-a-vis organizations in the private than the public sector. I would have expected more use of third-party complaint-handlers in the private sector. This can be taken as evidence that the consumer movement has a long way to go in Israel. At the same time, data on the reasons for not complaining, referred to in note 1, are also pertinent to this issue and were in the direction of the hypothesis: People were a little more likely to say "it wouldn't help" in response to problems encountered in the public sector. Given that the difference wasn't very large, the safer generalization is that the consumer movement is indeed still quite weak in Israel.

3. The data for the private sector are much less interesting; three-quarters of all appeals were to universalistic-normative devices (returning to the seller, appealing to a higher official, appealing to a representative of the seller). A little over 1 fifth appealed to various devices implicitly or explicitly based on sanctions—small claims courts, a lawyer, negative publicity. Illegitimate threats again constituted a low 4% of all channel use in the private sector.

4. The number of categories in each variable depends on the number of channels from the original list of 12 now collapsed into the 6 motivational types. Thus, in the case of legitimate norms, the possible values are 0, 1, and 2, representing those having used neither the ombudsman nor the appeal to a supervisor, 1, for persons using one of the two channels, and the highest possible score of 2 for those having used both. Since four channels from

the original list are reclassified as channels based on legitimate sanctions, the resulting set of possible scores is from 0 to 4, and so on. Because protektzia and illegitimate threats are kept separate, these latter two variables are dichotomous—0 for non-use, and 1 for use.

5. The correlations between use of *protektzia* as a redress channel and use of organizational and political brokers may be slightly inflated because some people saying they had used *protektzia* in connection with a routine encounter may have thought of the same encounter when reporting that they had used either of these types of brokers. But the overlap is far from complete, because 214 persons said they had used protektzia in response to the general question, as opposed to only 130 on the question about protektzia as a redress channel; 46 persons had contacted a political VIP; 41 had contacted an MK; 19 approached a political party and 71 a union.

6. In a general sense, of course, to use any particularistic channel is to show some evidence of biculturalism, since the system is largely universalistic and citizens cannot avoid conforming with the official rules at least some of the time. But it is more interesting to look at explicit biculturalism.

7. Even the data on use of political VIPs at least partially followed the same pattern. While differences are very small, Western Europeans more often appeal to the Prime Minister or a Knesset member than the others. What is perhaps most surprising of all is that the Western European natives use threats more than the others (12%, compared to 2% to 5% among the other groups). Either this is yet another hint of the extent of their debureaucratization, or perhaps their threats are of a kind which is legitimate, after all. A client who explicitly threatens *la'asot skandal*—to make a scandal, not by overturning the furniture, for example, but by writing to the editor of a newspaper—is not engaging in illegitimate behavior. At the very least, these results conflict with other evidence that threats are the language of the weak, discussed earlier in this book. For the weakest group, the Middle Eastern immigrants, turned out to use illegitimate threats (if indeed they are illegitimate) less than half as often as the Western Europeans; moreover, Middle Eastern natives almost never use them at all.

8. The data on hybridization could be treated either as nominal data requiring cross-tabulation for analysis, or as a scale which lends itself to correlational analysis. Here, I have chosen to display cross-tabulations because it is the details about the hybrids which interest me and which would not be visible in Pearson correlations.

9. This indication of homogenization is consistent with that found for attitudes about the legitimacy of protektzia. In Chapter 5 I reported increased homogenization in the 1980 study on this latter variable. Another indication that haves are more likely to be hybrids than have nots is the finding that 41% of men were hybrids, compared to only 33% of women (not shown in Table VII.9).

10. Unfortunately, the sample did not include very many really new immigrants. To study the effects of past socialization in detail our research team would have to have worked with a very different sample, perhaps a stratified one, in which very new immigrants were compared with those in the country a few years and those who are old-timers. The feasibility of developing such a sample is limited these days, because immigration has dropped off, unless one chooses to work with particular ethnic groups, e.g., Ethiopian Jews or those coming from the Soviet Union. For a recent attempt to analyze difficulties of Ethiopians in dealing with the authorities, see Ben-Ezer (1985).

11. This problem of inferring change from the intensive investigation of different individuals in two different, not longitudinally designed studies was first encountered in the 1968 study. See the discussion of change in Danet and Hartman (1972a).

12. For details on the items which were included in this measure, see Appendix C, Section II.G.

13. All the findings reported so far deal with general tendencies, not with the history of action taken with respect to a particular problem. To complement these data on general redress behavior, we also collected information on channel use among those responding to a problem in their most recent encounter. There were 140 such persons, who had taken action of some kind in response to dissatisfaction with their most recent encounter in a public bureaucracy. Typologizing these persons according to the set of three basic types, we found that 76% had used U channels alone, 13% had used both U and P ones, and 11% had used only particularistic ones. The estimate of hybrids is far lower for a specific problem because so few individuals approach more than one channel on any one occasion.

14. See the log-linear analysis below; there, negative experience did turn out to be important, in interaction with need. That is, it seems that if negative experience leads people to see themselves as needing protektzia, they are likely to be hybrid complainants.

15. But the overlap is far from complete: Well over 300 persons saw themselves as needing *protektzia* and as having access, respectively, whereas only about 150 were hybrid complainants.

16. There were 65 hybrids who had also used protektzia routinely, whereas a much higher 237 persons had reported routine use of protektzia.

17. The total N for the data used in the logit analysis was 687, which is obviously higher than the 419 persons identified as users of at least one complaint channel. Originally, the logit analysis was to be carried out on the total sample, as was done for routine use of *protektzia* (see Chapter 6). In the first stages of the analysis, the data set was prepared incorporating

information on two variables which the analysis eventually excluded as not important, whether individuals were born in Israel or not, and whether they were Western European or not. Both because of missing information on these two variables, and that missing on others in the full set, over 300 persons were dropped. This was not considered serious, since the critical question was the identification of a reasonably large number of hybrids. Whereas the full total of hybrids was 153, 112 hybrids remained, in the logit analysis (this figure can be produced by totaling the last column in Table VII.12). This figure constitutes 73% of the full number of hybrids.

18. See note no. 11 above.

19. See Danet and Hartman (1972a).

Chapter VIII

1. With funding from the American National Science foundation, Elihu Katz assembled a team of four persons. Michael Gurevitch served as co-principal investigator and the two chief research assistants were Tsiyona Peled and myself.

2. It was already clear to Avruch (1981), who gently chastised us for clinging to the absorption-modernization paradigm (see Avruch, 1975, chap. 6). In the 1970's when he was gathering his material on American immigrants to Israel (some of which is cited in chapter 4), I rested from the study of bureaucracy and the public in Israel. There is, thus, a 12-year gap between the 1968 survey and the 1980 one.

3. Both Elihu Katz and I are native Americans. Michael Gurevitch, an Israeli who was brought to Israel as an infant, received his Ph.D. from M.I.T. Tsiyona Peled, a native-born Israeli, holds an M.A. from Boston University. Among my other collaborators, Hadassah Haas is the only one who is neither a native American nor a graduate of any American university. Harriet Hartman is another native American. The late Naomi Kies, still another American, who worked on the 1980 study, also received her Ph.D. from M.I.T.

4. Strictly speaking, it doesn't make sense to speak of a phenomenon being over-determined. Statistically, only 100% of the variance can ever be explained. What I mean is that any one or two of a larger number of factors may be sufficient to bring about the phenomenon, whereas all of them together virtually guarantee that the phenomenon will appear.

5. Berger (1957) and Price (1975) used hypothetical situations in which a respondent was asked to say whether he could expect particularistic treatment from a key person like a relative. See the discussion of expectations for particularistic treatment in chapter 3.

6. For an explanation of the distinction between biculturalism and diculturalism, see chapter 3, section VII.

CHAPTER IX

1. See chapter 1 for a discussion of the ambiguities of use of go-betweens like politicians, whether they just provide help, or whether they undermine universalistic arrangements.

2. This is consistent with other studies of rates of complaining. See the concluding discussion in chapter 7.

3. This discussion of protektzia as instrumental versus symbolic exchange has benefited from the work of Ha-Ilan (1986).

4. The word I have translated as *middleman/middlemen* is *sarsur*. Originally a high-register Hebrew term meaning "intermediary, mediator," it has also come to mean "pimp/procurer." Grossman may well have intended to exploit the double meaning of the term. *Middlemen* seems to be a fine compromise between the two in English because, at least in some contexts, it carries a slightly less noble or at least less neutral connotation than intermediary, something like the Yiddish *macher,* for "fixer," provider of services as go-between, and so forth. For social science discussions of waasta, see Farrag (1977) and Farsoun (1970). Since this manuscript was completed, Grossman's book has appeared in English; see Grossman (1988). In the English version of this passage, the word *sarsur* is translated as "agents." However, the opening paragraph of the chapter describes "the waastonaire (as) an intermediary—or, in other contexts, a pimp" (Grossman, 1988: 171).

References

Abegglen, James C. (1975). *Management and Worker: The Japanese Solution.* Tokyo: Kodansha.

Abel, Richard L., ed. (1982). *The Politics of Informal Justice: The American Experience.* New York: Academic. 2 vols.

Abel-Smith, Brian, Michael Zander and Rosalind Brooke (1973). *Legal Problems and the Citizen: A Study in Three London Boroughs.* London: Heinemann.

Abercrombie, N., and S. Hill (1976). "Paternalism and Patronage," *British Journal of Sociology, 27,* 413–429.

Ajzen, Icek, and Martin Fishbein (1980). *Understanding Attitudes and Predicting Behavior.* Englewood Cliffs, NJ: Prentice-Hall.

Allum, Peter Anthony (1973). *Politics and Society in Post-War Naples.* Cambridge: Cambridge University Press.

Almond, Gabriel, and Sidney Verba (1965). *The Civic Culture.* Boston: Little, Brown.

———, eds. (1980). *The Civic Culture Revisited.* Boston: Little, Brown.

Anderson, Stanley V. (1969). *Ombudsman Papers: American Experience and Proposals.* Berkeley: University of California, Institute of Governmental Studies.

——— (1982). "Ombud Research: A Bibliographical Essay," *Ombudsman Journal, 2,* 32–84.

Andreasen, Alan R. (1975). *The Disadvantaged Consumer.* New York: Free Press.

Andreski, Stanislav (1970). "Kleptocracy as a System of Government in Africa." In Arnold Heidenheimer, ed., *Political Corruption: Readings in Comparative Analysis.* New York: Holt, Rinehart and Winston. 346–357.

Argyle, Michael, Adrian Furnham, and J. Graham (1981). *Social Situations.* Cambridge: Cambridge University Press.

Austin, J.L. (1970). "A Plea for Excuses." In J.L. Austin, *Philosophical Papers.* Oxford: Oxford University Press. 175–204.

Avruch, Kevin (1981). *American Immigrants in Israel: Social Identities and Change.* Chicago: University of Chicago Press.

Ayubi, Nazih N.M. (1980). *Bureaucracy and Politics in Contemporary Egypt.* London: Ithaca.

Banfield, Edward (1958). *The Moral Basis of a Backward Society.* New York: Free Press.

Barkai, Chaim (1964). *The Public Sector, the Histradrut Sector, and the Private Sector in the Israeli Economy.* Jerusalem: Falk Institute: Sixth report (Hebrew).

Barlow, Robin, Harvey E. Brazer, and James N. Morgan (1966). *Economic Behavior of the Affluent.* Washington, DC: Brookings Institution.

Barnabas, A.P. (1969). *Citizens' Grievances and Administration.* New Delhi: Indian Institute of Public Administration.

Barnes, S., M. Kaase, *et al.* (1979). *Political Action: Mass Participation in Five Western Democracies.* Beverly Hills, CA: Sage.

———, and G. Sani (1974). "Mediterranean Political Culture and Italian Politics: An Interpretation," *British Journal of Political Science.*

Barnlund, Dean (1975). *Public and Private Self in Japan and the United States: Communicative Styles of Two Cultures.* Tokyo: Simul.

Bar-Yosef Weiss, Rivka (1968). "Desocialization and Re-socialization: The Adjustment Process of Immigrants," *The International Migration Review, 2,* 3, 27–42. Reprinted in In Ernest Krausz, ed., *Studies of Israeli Society.* New Brunswick, NJ: Transaction Books. vol. 1: *Migration Ethnicity and Community.* 19–37.

Bar-Yosef, Rivka and E.O. Schild (1966). "Pressures and Defenses in Bureaucratic Roles," *American Journal of Sociology, 75,* 665–673. Reprinted in Elihu Katz and Brenda Danet, eds., *Bureaucracy and the Public: a Reader in Official-Client Relations.* New York: Basic Books, 1973. 288–299.

Bawli, Dan (1982). *The Subterranean Economy.* New York: McGraw Hill.

Befu, Harumi (1974). "Gift-Giving in a Modernizing Japan." In Takie Sugiyama Lebra and William P. Lebra, eds., *Japanese Culture and Behavior: Selected Readings.* Honolulu: East-West Center, University of Hawaii. 208–221.

Ben-Amotz, Dahn, and Netiva Ben-Yehuda (1972). *The World Dictionary of Hebrew Slang.* Tel Aviv: Zmora, Betan (Hebrew).

Ben-Dor, Gabriel (1974). "Corruption, Institutionalization, and Political Development: The Revisionist Theses Revisited," *Comparative Political Studies, 7,* 63–83.

Ben-Ezer, Gadi (1985). "Cross-Cultural Misunderstandings: the Case of Ethiopian Immigrants," *Israel Social Science Research, 3,* 65–73.

Bensimon-Donath, Doris (1970). *Immigrants D'Afrique du Nord en Israel.* Paris: Anthropos.

Ben-Yehuda, Netiva (1981). *1948–Between Eras.* Jerusalem: Keter (Hebrew).

Berger, Morroe (1957). *Bureaucracy and Society in Modern Egypt.* Princeton: Princeton University Press.

Berger, Peter L., Brigitte Berger and Hansfried Kellner (1974). *The Homeless Mind: Modernization and Consciousness.* Harmondsworth: Penguin.

Bernstein, Basil (1971). *Class, Codes and Control.* London: Routledge & Kegan Paul.

Bernstein, Judith, and Aaron Antonovsky (1981). "The Integration of Ethnic Groups in Israel," *Jewish Journal of Sociology, 23,* 5–23.

Best, Arthur, and Alan R. Andreasen (1976). *Talking Back to Business: Voiced and Unvoiced Consumer Complaints.* Washington, DC: Center for the Study of Responsive Law.

—— (1977). "Consumer Response to Unsatisfactory Purchases: A Survey of Perceiving Defects, Voicing Complaints and Obtaining Redress," *Law and Society Review, 11,* 701–742.

Bhargava, Ganti Suryanarayana (1974). *India's Watergate: A Study of Political Corruption in India.* New Delhi: Heinemman.

Blau, Peter M. (1964). *Exchange and Power in Social Life.* New York: Wiley.

Blau, Peter M., and W. Richard Scott (1962). *Formal Organizations.* San Francisco: Chandler.

Blumenthal, Monica D., Robert L. Kahn, Frank M. Andrews, and Kendra B. Head (1972). *Justifying Violence: Attitudes of American Men.* Ann Arbor, MI: Institute for Social Research, University of Michigan.

Blum-Kulka, Shoshana, Brenda Danet, and Rimona Gherson (1985). "The Language of Requests in Israeli Society." In Joseph P. Forgas, ed., *Language in Social Situations*. New York: Springer-Verlag. 113–139.

Boissevain, Jeremy (1966). "Patronage in Sicily," *Man, 1,* 18–33.

———— (1974). *Friends of Friends: Networks, Manipulators and Coalitions.* Oxford: Basil Blackwell.

———— (1977). "When the Saints Go Marching Out: Reflections on the Decline of Patronage in Malta." In Ernest Gellner and John Waterbury, eds., *Patrons and Clients in Mediterranean Societies*. London: Duckworth. 81–96.

Bonavia, David (1982). *The Chinese: A Portrait*. Harmondsworth: Penguin.

Brown, Roger (1965). *Social Psychology*. New York: Free Press.

Buckle, Leonard G., and Suzann R. Thomas-Buckle (1982). "Doing unto Others: Dispute and Dispute Processing in an Urban American Neighborhood." In Roman Tomasic and Malcolm M. Feeley, eds., *Neighborhood Justice: Assessment of an Emerging Idea*. New York: Longman. 78–90.

Caiden, Gerald E. (1970). *Israel's Administrative Culture*. Berkeley: Institute of Governmental Studies, University of California.

———— (1980). *To Right Wrong: The Initial Ombudsman Experience in Israel.* Los Angeles and Tel Aviv: Ashdown.

————, ed. (1983). *International Handbook of the Ombudsman*. Westport, CT: Greenwood, 2 vols.

Caiden, Gerald E., and Naomi J. Caiden (1977). "Administrative Corruption," *Public Administration Review, 37,* 301–309.

Caiden, Gerald E., Niall MacDermott, and Ake Sandler (1983). "The Institution of the Ombudsman." In Gerald E. Caiden, ed., *International Handbook of the Ombudsman*. Westport, CT: Greenwood, vol. 1, chap. 1. 3–21.

Caplan, Gerald, with Ruth B. Caplan (1980). *Arab and Jew in Jerusalem: Explorations in Community Mental Health*. Cambridge, MA: Harvard University Press.

Caplovitz, David (1963). *The Poor Pay More: Consumer Practices of Low-Income Families*. New York: Free Press.

Cappelletti, Mauro, ed. (1981). *Access to Justice and the Welfare State*. Alphen aan den Rijn: Sijthoff.

Carmi, Yair (1968). "Favoritism in the Israeli Civil Service," *Public Administration in Israel and Abroad, 9,* 58–69.

Caudill, William (1961). "Around the Clock Patient Care in Japanese Psychiatric Hospitals—the Role of the Tsukisoi," *American Sociological Review, 26,* 643–655.

Central Bureau of Statistics (1974). *Statistical Abstract of Israel, 1973.* Jerusalem: Government Printing Office.

―――― (1981). *Statistical Abstract of Israel, 1980.* Jerusalem: Government Printing Office.

―――― (1982). *Statistical Abstract of Israel, 1981.* Jerusalem: Government Printing Office.

Chalidze, Valery (1974). *To Defend These Rights: Human Rights and the Soviet Union.* New York: Random House.

Chu, Godwin C., and Leonard L. Chu (1981). "Parties in Conflict: Letters to the Editor of the People's Daily," *Journal of Communication, 31,* 4, 74–91.

Clapham, Christopher, ed. (1982). *Private Patronage and Public Power: Political Clientelism in the Modern State.* London: Frances Pinter.

Coates, Dan, and Steven Penrod (1980–81). "Social Psychology and the Emergence of Disputes," *Law and Society Review, 15,* 3–4, special issue on "Dispute Processing and Civil Litigation." 654–680.

Cohen, Erik (1985). "Ethnicity and Legitimation in Contemporary Israel." In Ernest Krausz, ed., *Studies of Israeli Society,* vol. 3: *Politics and Society in Israel.* New Brunswick, NJ: Transaction Books. 320–333.

Connor, Walter D. (1979). *Socialism, Politics, and Equality: Hierarchy and Change in Eastern Europe and the USSR.* New York: Columbia University Press.

Craig, Ann L. and Wayne A. Cornelius (1980). "Political Culture in Mexico: Continuities and Revisionist Interpretations." In Gabriel A. Almond and Sidney Verba, eds., *The Civic Culture Revisited.* Boston: Little, Brown. 323–393.

Cressey, Donald (1953). *Other People's Money: A Study of the Social Psychology of Embezzlement.* Glencoe, IL: Free Press.

Crozier, Michael (1964). *The Bureaucratic Phenomenon.* Chicago: University of Chicago Press.

Curran, Barbara A. (1977). *The Legal Needs of the Public: The Final Report of a National Survey.* Chicago: American Bar Foundation.

Daalder, H. (1974). "The Consociational Democracy Theme," *World Politics, 26*, 604–621.

Danet, Brenda (1971). "The Language of Persuasion in Bureaucracy: 'Modern' and 'Traditional' Appeals to the Israel Customs Authorities," *American Sociological Review, 36*, 847–859.

―――― (1973). " 'Giving the Underdog a Break': Latent Particularism among Customs Officials." In Elihu Katz and Brenda Danet, eds., *Bureaucracy and the Public.* New York: Basic Books. 329–337.

―――― (1978). "Toward a Method to Evaluate the Ombudsman Role," *Administration and Society, 10*, 335–370.

―――― (1981). "Client-Organization Relationships." In Paul Nystrom and William H. Starbuck, eds., *Handbook of Organizational Design.* Oxford: Oxford University Press. vol. 2, 382–428.

―――― (1982). *Attitudes of the Israeli Public toward the Use of Protektzia.* Jerusalem: The Communications Institute, Hebrew University (Hebrew).

Danet, Brenda, and Michael Gurevitch (1972). "Presentation of Self in Appeals to Bureaucracy: An Empirical Study of Role Specificity," *American Journal of Sociology, 77*, 1165–1190.

Danet, Brenda, and Harriet Hartman (1972a). "On Protektzia: Orientations toward the Use of Personal Influence in Israeli Bureaucracy," *Journal of Comparative Administration, 3*, 405–434.

―――― (1972b). "Coping with Bureaucracy: the Israeli Case," *Social Forces, 51*, 7–22.

Danet, Brenda, and Tsiyona Peled (1973). "Jerusalem's Municipal Ombudsman," *City and Region, 2*, 68–80 (Hebrew).

Danet, Brenda, Mira Ben-Ari, and Pua Sczupak (1972). *The Telephone Services Authority: Attitudes of Staff toward Their Work, Communication with the Public.* Jerusalem: the Israel Institute of Applied Social Research, The Communications Institute, Hebrew University, and Management Sciences Branch, Ministry of Communications, State of Israel (Hebrew).

Danet, Brenda, Naomi Kies and Hadassah Haas (1981). *Uses and Effectiveness of Complaint-Handling Devices: An Interim Report.* Jerusalem: The Communications Institute, Hebrew University (Hebrew).

Davis, J. (1977). *People of the Mediterranean: an Essay in Comparative Social Anthropology.* London: Routledge & Kegan Paul.

Davis, Stanley (1971). *Comparative Management: Organizational and Cultural Perspectives.* Englewood Cliffs, N.J.: Prentice Hall.

Dhavan, Rajeev (1977). "Engrafting the Ombudsman idea on a Parliamentary Democracy—a Comment on the Lokpal Bill, 1977," *Journal of the Indian Law Institute, 19*, 257–282.

Dmitruk, Victor (1971). "Incentive Preference and Resistance to Temptation," *Child Development, 42*, 625–628.

Doig, Alan (1984). *Corruption and Misconduct in Contemporary British Politics.* Harmondsworth: Penguin.

Domhoff, G.W. (1970). *The Higher Circles.* New York: Vintage.

Dore, Ronald P. (1973). *British Factory, Japanese Factory.* Berkeley: University of California Press.

Downes, David, and Paul Rock (1982). *Understanding Deviance: A Guide to the Sociology of Crime and Rule-Breaking.* Oxford: Oxford University Press.

Dror, Yehezkel (1965). "Nine Main Characteristics of Governmental Administration in Israel." In The Viscount Samuel, ed., *Public Administration in Israel and Abroad, 1964,* vol. 5, Jerusalem: Israel Institute of Public Administration.

Duncanson, Dennis (1982). *Changing Qualities of Chinese Life.* London: Macmillan.

Dyker, David A. (1982). "Planning and the Workers." In Leonard Schapiro and Joseph Godson, eds., *The Soviet Worker.* London: Macmillan. 39–75.

Eisenstadt, S.N. (1954). *The Absorption of Immigrants.* London: Routledge, Kegan & Paul.

_____ (1959). "Bureaucracy, Bureaucratization and Debureaucratization," *Administrative Science Quarterly, 4*, 302–320.

_____ (1965). *Essays on Comparative Institutions.* New York: Wiley.

_____ (1967). *Israeli Society.* London: Weidenfeld & Nicholson.

_____ (1973). *Traditional Patrimonialism and Modern Neo-Patrimonialism.* London: Sage, Sage Research Papers.

_____ (1981). "Interactions between Organizations and Societal Stratification. In Paul Nystrom and William H. Starbuck, eds., *Handbook of Organizational Design.* Oxford: Oxford University Press. vol. 1, 309–322.

Eisenstadt, S.N., and Rene Lemarchand, eds. (1981). *Political Clientelism, Patronage and Development.* Beverly Hills, CA: Sage.

Eisenstadt, S.N., and Luis Roniger (1980). "Patron-Client Relations as a Model of Structuring Social Exchange," *Comparative Studies in Society and History, 22,* 42–77.

———— (1981). "The Study of Patron-Client Relations and Recent Developments in Sociological Theory." In S.N. Eisenstadt and Luis Roniger, *Patrons, Clients and Friends: Interpersonal Relations and the Structure of Trust in Society.* Cambridge: Cambridge University Press.

Eisinger, Peter K. (1972). "The Pattern of Citizen Contacts with Urban Officials," In Harlan Hahn, ed., *People and Politics in Urban Society,* Urban Affairs Annual Reviews, vol. 6. Beverly Hills, CA and London: Sage.

Ekeh, Peter P. (1974). *Social Exchange Theory: the Two Traditions.* London: Heinemann.

Elazar, Daniel (1985). "Israel's Compound Polity." In Ernest Krausz, ed. *Studies of Israeli Society.* New Brunswick, NJ: Transaction Books. vol. 3, *Politics and Society in Israel,* 43–80.

Eldersveld, Samuel J., and Bashiruddin Ahmed (1978). *Citizens and Politics: Mass Political Behavior in India.* Chicago: University of Chicago Press.

Eldersveld, Samuel J., V. Jagannadham, and A.P. Barnabas (1968). *The Citizen and the Administrator in a Developing Democracy: An Empirical Study in Delhi State.* New Delhi: Indian Institute of Public Administration.

Elizur, Yuval, and Eliahu Salpeter (1973). *Who Rules Israel?* New York: Harper and Row.

El-Makawi, Taher (1988). "*Waasta:* Orientations of the Arab Population in Israel and in the Occupied Territories toward the Use of Personal Connections in Bureaucratic Encounters." Jerusalem: Unpublished M.A. Thesis, Department of Communications, Hebrew University (Hebrew).

Elon, Amos (1972). *The Israelis: Founders and Sons.* London: Sphere.

Ervin-Tripp, Susan (1976). "Is Sybil There? The Structure of Some American English Directives," *Language in Society, 5,* 25–66.

Etzioni-Halevy, Eva (1975). "Some Patterns of Semi-Deviance on the Israeli Scene," *Social Problems, 22,* 356–367.

———— (1979). *Political Manipulation and Administrative Power: A Comparative Study.* London: Routledge & Kegan Paul.

Fallers, Lloyd A. (1956). *Bantu Bureaucracy.* Chicago: University of Chicago Press.

Farrag, Amina (1977). "The *Wastah* among Jordanian Villagers." In Ernest Gellner and John Waterbury, eds., *Patrons and Clients in Mediterranean Societies*. London: Duckworth. 225–238.

Farrington, David P. (1979). "Experiments on Deviance with Special Reference to Dishonesty," *Advances in Experimental Social Psychology*. New York: Academic Press. vol. 12, 208–253.

Farsoun, Samih K. (1970). "Family Structure and Society in Modern Lebanon." In Louise E. Sweet, ed., *Peoples and Cultures of the Middle East*. Garden City, NY: Natural History Press. 257–307.

Faucheau, C. (1977). "Strategy Formulation as a Cultural Process," *International Studies of Management and Organization, 7*, 127–138.

Felstiner, William L.F., Richard L. Abel, and Austin Sarat (1980–81). "The Emergence and Transformation of Disputes: Naming, Blaming, Claiming . . .", *Law and Society Review, 15*, 3–4, special issue on "Dispute Processing and Civil Litigation," 631–654.

Ferguson, Charles A. (1964). "Diglossia." In Dell Hymes, ed., *Language in Culture and Society*. New York: Harper and Row. 429–437.

Fishbein, Martin, and Icek Ajzen (1975). *Belief, Attitude, Intention and Behavior: An Introduction to Theory and Research*. Reading, MA: Addison-Wesley.

Fishman, Joshua A. (1967). "Bilingualism with and without Diglossia: Diglossia with and without Bilingualism," *Journal of Social Issues, 23*, 29–38.

Fishelson, Gideon, Yoram Weiss, and Mark Nili (1980). "Ethnic Origin and Income Differentials among Israeli Males, 1969–1976." In Asher Arian, ed., *Israel: a Developing Society*. Assen, the Netherlands: Van Gorcum. 253–276.

Fitzgerald, Jeffrey (1982). "Disputing and Non-Disputing in Legal and Nonlegal Contexts: An Analysis of Grievances, Claims, Disputes, Resort to the Law and Their Consequences in Two Cultures," paper presented at the Annual Meeting, Law and Society Association, Toronto, Canada, June 3–6, 1982.

Folger, Robert, ed. (1984). *The Sense of Injustice: Social Psychological Perspectives*. New York: Plenum.

Foster, George M. (1961). "The Dyadic Contract: A Model for the Social Structure of a Mexican Peasant Village," *American Anthropologist, 63*, 1173–1192.

―――― (1963). "The Dyadic Contract in Tzintzuntzan, II: Patron-Client Relationship," *American Anthropologist, 65*, 1280–1294.

Fraser, John (1982). *The Chinese: Portrait of a People.* Glasgow: Collins.

Friedlander, Dov, and Calvin Goldscheider (1979). *The Population of Israel.* London: Routledge & Kegan Paul.

Friedmann, Karl A. (1974). "Complaining: Comparative Aspects of Complaint Behavior and Attitudes toward Complaining in Canada and Britain." Administrative and Policy Studies Series, Sage Professional Paper, Series Number 03-019, vol. 2, 67 pp.

———— (1975). "Workload, Efficiency, Results," ms.

Furnham, Adrian and Michael Argyle, eds. (1981). *The Psychology of Social Situations.* Oxford: Pergamon.

Galanter, Marc (1981). "Justice in Many Rooms." In Mauro Cappelletti, ed., *Access to Justice and the Welfare State.* Alphen aan den Rijn: Sijthoff.

Galt, Anthony H. (1974). "Rethinking Patron-Client Relationships: the Real System and the Official System in Southern Italy," *Anthropological Quarterly, 47,* 182–202.

Geertz, Clifford (1973). "The Integrative Revolution." In Geertz, *The Interpretation of Cultures.* New York: Basic Books.

Gellhorn, Walter (1966a). *Ombudsmen and Others.* Cambridge, MA: Harvard University Press.

———— (1966b). *When Americans Complain.* Cambridge, MA: Harvard University Press.

Gellner, Ernest, and John Waterbury, eds. (1977). *Patrons and Clients in Mediterranean Societies.* London: Duckworth.

Globerson, Aryeh (1970). *The Administrative Elite in the Government Civil Service in Israel.* Tel Aviv: Hamidrasha Leminhal (Administrative College) (Hebrew).

Goffman, Erving, (1961). *Asylums.* Garden City, N.Y.: Anchor Books.

Goodsell, Charles T. (1976). "Cross-Cultural Comparison of Behavior of Postal Clerks toward Clients," *Administrative Science Quarterly, 21,* 140–150.

————, ed. (1981). *The Public Encounter: Delivering Human Services in the 1980s.* Bloomington, IN: University of Indiana Press.

Granovetter, Mark S. (1973). "The Strength of Weak Ties," *American Journal of Sociology, 78,* 1360–1380.

_____ (1974). *Getting a Job: A Study of Contacts and Careers*. Cambridge, MA: Harvard University Press.

Greenberg, Harold I. (1979). *Israel: Social Problems*. Tel Aviv: Dekel Academic Press.

Greenberg, Jerald (1984). "On the Apocryphal Nature of Inequity Distress." In Robert Folger, ed., *The Sense of Injustice: Social Psychological Perspectives*. New York: Plenum. 167–186.

Groves, Harold M. (1958). "Empirical Studies of Income Tax Compliance," *National Tax Journal, 11,* 291–.

Grossman, David (1987). *Yellow Wind.* Tel Aviv: Siman Kriah, Hakibbutz Hameuchad (Hebrew); (1988). Eng. transl., Haim Watzman, New York: Farrar, Straus and Giroux).

Grossman, Gregory (1977). "The 'Second Economy' of the USSR," *Problems of Communism, 26,* 5. 25–40.

Gurevitch, Michael (1961). *The Social Structure of Acquaintance Networks.* Unpublished Ph.D. dissertation, Cambridge, Mass.: M.I.T., Dept. of Political Science and Mass Communication.

Gurevitch, Michael, and Alex Weingrod (1978). "Who Knows Whom? Acquaintanceships and Contacts in the Israeli National Elite," *Human Relations, 31,* 195–214.

Guttman, Louis (1957). "Introduction to Facet Design and Analysis," *Proceedings of the International Congress of Psychology, Brussels.* Amsterdam: North-Holland.

_____ (1970). "Integration of Test Design and Analysis," *Proceedings of the 1969 Invitational Conference on Testing Problems.* Princeton: Educational Testing Service.

Guttsman, W.L. (1974). "Elite Recruitment and Political Leadership in Britain and Germany since 1950: a Comparative Study of MPs and Cabinets." In Ivor Crewe, ed., *Elites in Western Democracies.* London: Croom Helm. 89–125.

Gwyn, William B. (1962). *Democracy and the Cost of Politics in Britain.* London: Athlone.

Ha-Ilan, Neta (1986). "With a Little Help From My Friends: Social Aspects of the Use of *Protektzia.*" Unpublished M.A. thesis, Dept. of Sociology and Social Anthropology, Hebrew University (Hebrew).

Haire, Mason, Edwin E. Giselli and Lyman W. Porter (1963). "Cultural Patterns in the Role of the Manager," *Industrial Relations, 2,* 95–117.

Hammond Almanac (1983). Maplewood, N.J.: Hammond Almanac, Inc., vol. 14.

Handelman, Don (1976). "Bureaucratic Transactions: The Development of Official-Client Relationships in Israel." In Bruce Kapferer, ed., *Transaction and Meaning: Directions in the Anthropology of Exchange and Symbolic Behavior.* Philadelphia: Institute for the Study of Human Issues. 223–275.

Hannigan, John A. (1977). "The Newspaper Ombudsman and Consumer Complaints: An Empirical Assessment," *Law and Society Review, 11,* 679–699.

Hasenfeld, Yeheskel, and Richard A. English, eds. (1975). *Human Service Organizations: A Book of Readings.* Ann Arbor, MI: University of Michigan Press.

Hayashi, Chikio, S. Nishihara and T. Suzuki (1965). *Japanese National Character with Illustrations.* Tokyo: Shiseido (Japanese).

Heidenheimer, Arnold J., ed. (1970). *Political Corruption: Readings in Comparative Analysis.* New York: Holt, Rinehart and Winston.

Henslin, James M. (1970). "Guilt and Guilt Neutralization: Response and Adjustment to Suicide." In Jack D. Douglas, ed., *Deviance and Respectability: the Social Construction of Moral Meanings.* New York: Basic Books. 192–228.

Hill, Larry B. (1976). *The Model Ombudsman.* Princeton: Princeton University Press.

—— (1981). "Bureaucratic Monitoring Mechanisms." In Charles T. Goodsell, ed., *The Public Encounter.* Bloomington, IN: Indiana University Press. 160–186.

Hirschmann, Albert (1970). *Exist, Voice and Loyalty.* Cambridge, MA: Harvard University Press.

Hirszowicz, Maria (1980). *The Bureaucratic Leviathan: A Study in the Sociology of Communism.* Oxford: Martin Robertson.

Hofstede, Geert (1979). "Hierarchical Power Distance in Forty Countries." In Cornelis J. Lammers and David J. Hickson, eds., *Organizations Like and Unlike.* London: Routledge & Kegan Paul. 97–119.

—— (1980). *Culture's Consequences: International Differences in Work-Related Values.* Beverly Hills, CA: Sage.

Homans, George (1950). *Social Behavior: Its Elementary Forms.* New York: Harcourt Brace & World.

Hunter, Floyd (1959). *Top Leadership, USA.* Chapel Hill, NC: University of North Carolina Press.

Huntington, Samuel P. (1965). "Political Development and Political Decay," *World Politics, 17,* 386–430.

——— (1969). *Political Order in Changing Societies.* New Haven: Yale University Press.

Hurvitz, Leon (1981). *The State as Defendant: Governmental Accountability and the Redress of Individual Grievances.* London: Aldwych.

Ike, Nobutaka (1972). *Japanese Politics: Patron-Client Democracy.* New York: Knopf.

Inbar, Michael, and Chaim Adler (1977). *Ethnic Integration in Israel: a Case Study of Moroccan Brothers Who Settled in France and Israel.* New Brunswick, NJ: Transaction Books.

Inkeles, Alex (1969). "Making Men Modern: On the Causes and Consequences of Individual Change in Six Developing Countries," *American Journal of Sociology, 75,* 208–225.

——— (1972). "Participant Citizenship in Six Developing Countries." In John C. Pierce and Richard A. Pride, eds., *Cross-National Micro-Analysis: Procedures and Problems.* Beverly Hills, Calif.: Sage, Sage Readers in Cross-National Research, vol. 2.

Inkeles, Alex, and Kent Geiger (1952). "Critical Letters to the Soviet Press: Areas and Modes of Complaint," *American Sociological Review, 17,* 694–703.

Inkeles, Alex, and David H. Smith (1974). *Becoming Modern: Individual Change in Six Developing Countries.* Cambridge, MA: Harvard University Press.

International Ombudsman Institute (1980). *Ombudsman and Other Complaint-Handling Systems Survey,* vol. 9. Edmonton, Alberta: Law Center, International Ombudsman Institute, University of Alberta.

——— (1983). *Ombudsman and Other Complaint-Handling Systems Survey,* vol. 12. Edmonton, Alberta: Law Center, International Ombudsman Institute, University of Alberta.

Ishino, Iwao (1953). "The Oyabun-Kobun: A Japanese Ritual Kinship Institution," *American Anthropologist, 55,* 695–707.

Jain, S.N. (1983). "The Ombudsman Idea in India." In Gerald C. Caiden, ed., *International Handbook of the Ombudsman.* Westport, CT: Greenwood. vol. 1. 317–320.

Janowitz, Morris, Deil Wright and William Delany (1958). *Public Administration and the Public: Perspectives toward Government in a Metropolitan Community.* Ann Arbor, MI: Institute of Public Administration, University of Michigan.

Jelinek, Mariann, Linda Smircich, and Paul Hirsch, eds. (1983). "Organizational Culture." Special issue, *Administrative Science Quarterly, 28.*

Johnson, Chalmers (1982). *MITI and the Japanese Miracle.* Stanford: Stanford University Press.

Jones, Gareth R. (1983). "Transaction Cost, Property Rights and Organizational Culture: An Exchange Perspective," *Administrative Science Quarterly, 28,* 454–467.

Jubas, Harry (1974). "The Adjustment Process of Americans and Canadians in Israel and Their Integration into Israeli Society." Unpublished Ph.D. dissertation, Michigan State University.

Kahane, Reuven (1984a). "Hypotheses on Patronage and Social Change: A Comparative Perspective," *Ethnology, 23,* 13–24.

―――― (1984b). *Patterns of Corruption (and Deviation from Accepted Norms in Public Institutions in Israeli Society).* Jerusalem: Akademon (Hebrew).

Kaiser, Robert G. (1976). *Russia: The People and the Power.* Harmondsworth: Penguin.

Karikas, Angela (1980). "Solving Problems in Philadelphia: an Ethnography of a Congressional District Office." In Laura Nader, ed., *No Access to Law.* New York: Academic. 345–378.

Katriel, Tamar (1986). *Talking Straight: Dugri Speech in Israeli Sabra Culture.* Cambridge: Cambridge University Press.

Katriel, Tamar, and Perla Nesher (1986). "*Gibush:* The Rhetoric of Cohesion in Israeli School Culture," *Comparative Education Review, 30,* 2, 216–231.

Katsenelenboigen, Aron (1977). "Colored Markets in the Soviet Union," *Soviet Studies, 29,* 62–85.

Katz, Daniel, Barbara A. Gutek, Robert L. Kahn, and Eugenia Barton (1975). *Bureaucratic Encounters: a Pilot Study in the Evaluation of Government Services.* Ann Arbor, MI: Institute for Social Research, the University of Michigan.

Katz, David, and Aaron Antonovsky (1973). "Bureaucracy and Immigrant Adjustment," *International Migration Review, 7,* 247–256.

Katz, Elihu, and Brenda Danet (1966). "Petitions and Persuasive Appeals: A Study of Official-Client Relations," *American Sociological Review, 31,* 811–822. Reprinted in Elihu Katz and Brenda Danet, eds., *Bureaucracy and the Public.* New York: Basic Books, 1973. 174–190.

—— (1973a). *Bureaucracy and the Public: A Reader in Official-Client Relations.* New York: Basic Books.

—— (1973b). "Communication between Bureaucracy and the Public: A Review of the Literature." In Wilbur Schramm, Ithiel Pool, Nathan Maccoby, Edwin Parkes and Frederick Frey, eds., *Handbook of Communication.* Chicago: Rand McNally. 666–705.

Katz, Elihu, and S.N. Eisenstadt (1960). "Some Sociological Observations on the Response of Israeli Organizations to New Immigrants," *Administrative Science Quarterly, 3,* 113–133. Reprinted in Elihu Katz and Brenda Danet, eds., *Bureaucracy and the Public.* New York: Basic Books, 1973. 73–88.

Katz, Elihu, Michael Gurevitch, Brenda Danet, and Tsiyona Peled (1969). "Petitions and Prayers: a Content-Analysis of Persuasive Appeals," *Social Forces, 47,* 447–463.

Kawashima, Takeyoshi (1967). *Japanese Consciousness of Law.* Tokyo: Iwanami (Japanese).

Kenny, Michael (1962). *A Spanish Tapestry.* Bloomington, IN: University of Indiana Press.

—— (1977). "Patterns of Patronage in Spain." In Steffen W. Schmidt, Laura Guasti, Carl H. Lande and James C. Scott, eds., *Friends, Followers, and Factions.* Berkeley: University of California Press. 335–359.

Key, V.O., Jr. (1964). *Politics, Parties and Pressure Groups.* New York: Crowell. 5th ed.

Kiggundu, Moses J., Jan J. Jorgensen, and Taieb Hafsi (1983). "Administrative Theory and Practice in Developing Countries: A Synthesis," *Administrative Science Quarterly, 28,* 66–84.

Kimmerling, Baruch (1985). "Between the Primordial and the Civil Definitions of the Collective Identity: *Eretz Israel* or the State of Israel?" In Erik Cohen, Moshe Lissak, and Uri Almagor, eds., *Comparative Social Dynamics: Essays in Honor of S.N. Eisenstadt.* Boulder and London: Westview Press. 262–283.

—— (1988). "Boundaries and Frontiers of the Israeli System: Analytical Conclusions." In Baruch Kimmerling, ed., *The Israeli State and So-*

ciety; Boundaries and Frontiers. Albany, NY: State University of New York Press.

King, Donald W., and Kathleen A. McEvoy (1976). *A National Survey of the Complaint-Handling Procedures Used by Consumers.* Rockville, MD.: King Research.

Kish, Leslie (1965). *Survey Sampling.* New York: Wiley.

Knoke, David, and Peter J. Burke (1980). "Log-Linear Models." Sage University Paper, Quantitive Applications in the Social Sciences Series, no. 20.

Krendel, Ezra S. (1970). "A Case Study of Citizen Complaints as Social Indicators." *INEEET Transactions on Systems Science and Cybernetics.* Vol. SSC-6, 265–272.

Ladinsky, Jack, and Charles Susmilch (1981). "Conceptual and Operational Issues of Measuring Consumer Disputing Behavior," paper prepared for the Annual Meeting, Midwest Sociological Association, Minneapolis, Minnesota, April, 1981.

——— (1982). "Community Factors in the Brokerage of Consumer Product and Service Problems," paper presented at the Annual Meeting, Law and Society Association, Toronto, Canada, June 3–6, 1982.

Lammers, Cornelis J., and David J. Hickson, eds. (1979). *Organizations Like and Unlike: International and Inter-Institutional Studies in the Sociology of Organizations.* London: Routledge & Kegan Paul.

Lande, Carl H. (1977). "Introduction: The Dyadic Basis of Clientelism." In Steffen W. Schmidt, Laura Guasti, Carl H. Lande and James C. Scott, eds., *Friends, Followers and Factions.* Berkeley: University of California Press. xiii–xxxvii.

Law and Society Review (1974–1975). *Law and Society Review,* issue on "Litigation and Dispute Processing," *9,* 1,2.

——— (1977). *Law and Society Review, 11,* 4.

——— (1980–81). *Law and Society Review, 15,* 3–4, special issue on "Dispute Processing and Civil Litigation."

Lebra, Takie Sugiyama (1969). "Reciprocity and the Asymmetric Principle: An Analytical Reappraisal of the Japanese Concept of *On,*" *Psychologica, 12,* 129–138. Reprinted in Takie Sugiyama Lebra and William P. Lebra, eds., *Japanese Culture and Behavior: Selected Readings.* Honolulu: University of Hawaii. 192–207.

———(1976). *Japanese Patterns of Behavior.* Honolulu: University of Hawaii.

Lemarchand, Rene, and Keith Legge (1972). "Political Clientelism and Development: A Preliminary Analysis," *Comparative Politics, 4,* 149–178.

Lempert, Richard (1980–81). "Grievances and Legitimacy: the Beginnings and End of Dispute Settlement," *Law and Society Review, 15,* 3–4, special issue on "Dispute Processing and Civil Litigation," 707–716.

Lerner, Melvin J., and Sally C. Lerner, eds. (1981). *The Justice Motive in Social Behavior.* New York: Plenum.

Levenstein, Dov (1986). "*Protektzia* and Perceptions of Equity." Unpublished M.A. thesis, Dept. of Labor Relations, Tel Aviv University (Hebrew).

Levy, Shlomit (1976). "Use of the Mapping Sentence for Coordinating Theory and Research: a Cross-Cultural Example," *Quality and Quantity, 10,* 117–125.

Lévi-Strauss, Claude (1949). *Les Structures Elementaires de la Parente.* Paris: Presses Universitaires de France.

———— (1969). *The Elementary Structures of Kinship.* Boston: Beacon (translation of 1967 revised edition).

Liphart A. (1968). *The Politics of Accommodation: Pluralism and Democracy in the Netherlands.* Beverly Hills, CA: University Press.

Littlewood, Paul (1974). "Strings and Kingdoms: The Activities of a Political Mediator in Southern Italy," *Archives Europeennes de Sociologie, 15,* 33–51.

Lundvik, Ulf (1982). "A Brief Survey of the History of the Ombudsman," *Ombudsman Journal, 2,* 85–94.

Lustick, Ian (1980). *Arabs in the Jewish State: Israel's Control of a National Minority.* Austin and London: University of Texas Press.

Maimon, Zvi (1978). "Favoritism and Protektzia among Israeli Workers," *International Management Review, 19,* 85–97.

Mars, Gerald (1982). *Cheats at Work: An Anthropology of Workplace Crime.* London: Allen and Unwin.

Mars, Gerald, and Yochanan Altman (1983). "The Cultural Bases of Soviet Georgia's Second Economy," *Soviet Studies, 35,* 546–560.

Marsh, Robert M., and Hiroshi Mannari (1976). *Modernization and the Japanese Factory.* Princeton: Princeton University Press.

Martin, Joanne, Martha S. Feldman, Mary Jo Hatch, and Sim B. Sitkin, (1983). "The Uniqueness Paradox in Organizational Stories," *Administrative Science Quarterly, 28,* 438–453.

Marx, Emanuel (1972). "Some Social Contexts of Personal Violence." In Max Gluckman, ed., *The Allocation of Responsibility*. Manchester: Manchester University Press.

_____ (1973). "Coercive Violence in Official-Client Relationships," *Israel Studies in Criminology, 2,* 43–44.

_____ (1976). *The Social Context of Violent Behavior: A Social Anthropological Study in an Israeli Immigrant Town.* London: Routledge & Kegan Paul.

_____ (1980). "State and Citizen in Israel: An Essay in Macro-Anthropology," paper presented to the Burg Wartenstein Symposium no. 84, "The Exercise of Power in Complex Organizations," July 19–27, 1980.

Mason, Robert, and Lyle D. Calvin (1978). "A Study of Admitted Income Tax Evasion," *Law and Society Review, 13,* 73–90.

Mather, Lynn, and Barbara Yngevesson (1980–81). "Language, Audience, and the Transformation of Disputes," *Law and Society Review, 15,* 3–4, special issue on "Dispute Processing and Civil Litigation," 775–822.

Mathiason, John R., and John D. Powell (1972). "Participation and Efficacy: Aspects of Peasant Involvement in Political Mobilization," *Comparative Politics, 4,* 303–329.

Matras, Judah (1965). *Social Change in Israel.* Chicago: Aldine.

Matthews, Mervyn (1978). *Privilege in the Soviet Union: A Study of Elite Lifestyles under Communism.* London: Allen and Unwin.

Mattice, Michael C. (1980). "Media in the Middle: A Study of the Mass Media Complaint Managers." In Laura Nader, ed., *No Access to Law.* New York: Academic. 485–522.

Mayhew, Leon H. (1975). "Institutions of Representation: Civil Justice and the Public," *Law and Society Review, 9,* 401–430.

McKinlay, John (1975). "Clients and Organizations." In John McKinlay, ed., *Processing People: Cases in Organizational Behavior.* London: Holt, Rinehart and Winston. 339–378.

Medding, Peter Y. (1972). *Mapai in Israel.* Cambridge: Cambridge University Press.

Merton, Robert K. (1957). "Manifest and Latent Functions." In *Social Theory and Social Structure.* New York: Free Press. rev. ed., 195–206.

Meyerhoff, Barbara (1978). *Number Our Days.* New York: Simon and Schuster.

Milbraith, L., and G. Goel (1977). *Political Participation*. Chicago: Rand McNally.

Miller, Richard E., and Austin Sarat (1980–81). "Grievances, Claims and Disputes: Assessing the Adversary Culture," *Law and Society Review, 15,* 3–4, special issue on "Dispute Processing and Civil Litigation," 525–566.

Mills, C. Wright (1940). "Situated Actions and Vocabularies of Motive," *American Sociological Review, 5,* 904–913.

———— (1956). *The Power Elite*. New York: Oxford University Press.

Minami, Hiroshi (1953; 1971). *The Psychology of the Japanese People*. Tokyo: University of Tokyo Press.

Mintz, Sidney W., and Eric R. Wolf (1977). "An Analysis of Ritual Co-Parenthood (Compadrazgo)." In Steffen W. Schmidt, Laura Guasti, Carl H. Lande, and James C. Scott, eds., *Friends, Followers and Factions,* Berkeley: University of California Press. 1–14.

Montias, J.M., and Susan Rose-Ackerman (1980). "Corruption in a Soviet-Type Economy: Theoretical Considerations." Paper prepared for the Conference on "The Second Economy of the USSR," Kennan Institute for Advanced Russian Studies and National Council on Soviet and East European Research, January, 1980.

Nachmias, David, and David H. Rosenbloom (1978). *Bureaucratic Culture: Citizens and Administrators in Israel*. London: Croom Helm.

Nader, Laura, ed. (1969). *Law in Culture and Society*. Chicago: Aldine.

Nader, Laura ed. (1980). *No Access to Law: Alternatives to the American Judicial System*. New York: Academic.

Nader. Laura and Harry F. Todd, Jr., eds. (1978). *The Disputing Process: Law in Ten Societies*. New York: Columbia University Press.

Nakane, Chie (1973). *Japanese Society*. Harmondsworth: Penguin. 2nd ed.

Nebenzahl, I.E. (1974). "The Control of State Administration in Israel," *Public Administration in Israel and Abroad, 1973, 14,* 9–15.

Nelson, Barbara J. (1979). "Clients and Bureaucracies: Applicant Evaluations of Public Human Service and Benefit Programs." Paper presented at the Annual Meeting, American Political Science Association, Washington, D.C.

———— (1980). "Help-Seeking from Public Authorities: Who Arrives at the Agency Door," *Policy Sciences, 12,* 175–192.

———— (1981). "Client Evaluations of Social Programs." In Charles T. Good-sell,ed., *The Public Encounter,* Bloomington, IN: University of Indiana Press, 23–42.

Nove, Alec (1977). *The Soviet Economic System.* London: Allen and Unwin.

Nutini, Hugo, and Betty Bell (1980). *Ritual Kinship: the Structure and Historical Development of the Compadrazgo System in Rural Tlaxcala.* Princeton: Princeton University Press.

Ofer, Gur (1983). "Civil Public Expenditure in Israel," Discussion paper no. 12.83, Jerusalem: Falk Institute for Economic Research in Israel. 1–95 (Hebrew).

Ouchi, William (1981). *Theory Z.* Reading, MA: Addison-Wesley.

Palen, Frank S. (1979). "Media Ombudsmen: A Critical Review," *Law and Society Review, 13,* 3, 799–850.

Parsons, Talcott (1951). *The Social System.* New York: Free Press.

Pasquale, Richard T., and Anthony G. Athos (1982). *The Art of Japanese Management.* Harmondsworth: Penguin.

Peres, Yochanan (1977). *Ethnic Relations in Israel.* Tel Aviv: Tel Aviv University and Sifriat Hapoalim. 2nd ed. (Hebrew).

Peters, John G., and Susan Welch (1978). "Political Corruption in America: A Search for Definitions and a Theory, or If Political Corruption is in the Mainstream of American Politics, Why Is It Not in the Main-stream of American Politics Research?" *American Political Science Review, 72,* 974–984.

Pitts, Jesse R. (1963). "Continuity and Change in Bourgeois France." In Stanley Hoffman, Charles P. Kindleberger, Laurence Wylie, Jessee R. Pitts, Jean-Baptiste Burosell, Francois Goguel, eds., *In Search of France: The Economy, Society and Political System in the Twentieth Century.* New York: Harper Torchbooks. 235–304.

Pizzorno, Alessandro (1966). "Amoral Familism and Historical Marginality," *International Review of Community Development, 15–16,* 55–66.

Pool, Ithiel de Sola, and Manfred Kochen (1978). "Contacts and Influence," *Social Networks, 1,* 5–51.

Price, Robert M. (1975). *Society and Bureaucracy in Contemporary Ghana.* Berkeley: University of California Press.

Rajecki, D.W. (1982). *Attitudes: Themes and Advances.* Sunderland, MA: Sinauer.

Raphaeli, Nimrod (1970). "The Senior Civil Service in Israel: Some Characteristics," *Public Administration, 48,* 169–178.

Reischauer, Edwin O. (1981). *The Japanese.* Cambridge, MA: Harvard University Press.

Richards, Peter G. (1963). *Patronage in British Government.* London: Allen & Unwin.

Riggs, Fred (1964). *Administration in Developing Countries.* Boston: Houghton Mifflin.

———— (1973). *Prismatic Society Revisited.* Morristown, NJ: General Learning Press.

Roberts, Simon (1979). *Order and Dispute: an Introduction to Legal Anthropology.* Harmondsworth: Penguin.

Roos, Leslie L., Jr., and Noralou P. Roos (1971). *Managers of Modernization.* Cambridge, MA: Harvard University Press.

Roos, Leslie L., Jr., and Frederick A. Starke (1981). "Organizational Roles." In Paul Nystrom and William H. Starbuck, eds., *Handbook of Organization al Design.* Oxford: Oxford University Press. vol. 1, 290–308.

Rosengren, William R., and Mark Lefton, eds. (1970). *Organizations and Clients: Essays in the Sociology of Service.* Columbus, OH: Charles E. Merrill.

Ross, H. Laurence, and Neil O. Littlefield (1973). "Complaint as a Problem-Solving Mechanism," *Law and Society Review, 12,* 199–216.

Rotenberg, Mordecai (1983). *Dialogue with Deviance: the Hasidic Ethic and the Theory of Social Contraction.* Philadelphia: ISHI Institute for the Study of Human Issues.

Rowat, Donald, ed. (1968). *The Ombudsman: Citizen's Defender.* Toronto: University of Toronto Press. rev. ed.

Sampson, Steven L. (1983). "Bureaucracy and Corruption as Anthropological Problems: A Case Study from Romania," *Folk, 25,* 63–95.

———— (1984). "Rumors in Socialist Romania," *Survey,* 28.

———— (1985). "The Informal Sector in Eastern Europe." Paper presented at the Fourth International Conference on Bureaucracy, Vancouver, Canada, September, 1985.

Schapiro, Leonard, and Joseph Godson (1982). *The Soviet Worker: Illusions and Realities.* London: Macmillan.

Schein, E.H. (1983). "The Role of the Founder in Creating Organizational Culture," *Organizational Dynamics,* summer, 13–28.

Schmidt, Steffen W., Laura Guasti, Carl H. Lande, and James C. Scott, eds. (1977). *Friends, Followers and Factions: A Reader in Political Clientelism.* Berkeley: University of California Press.

Schmidt, Stuart M. (1977). "Client-Oriented Evaluation of Public-Agency Effectiveness," *Administration and Society, 8,* 403–422.

Schrag, Philip G. (1972). *Counsel for the Deceived: Case Studies in Consumer Fraud.* New York: Random House.

Schwartz, Richard D., and Sonya Orleans (1970). "On Legal Sanctions." In Richard D. Schwartz and Jerome H. Skolnick, eds., *Society and the Legal Order: Cases and Materials in the Sociology of Law.* New York: Basic Books. 533–546.

Scott, Ian (1982). "The Ombudsman in Fiji: Patterns of Mediation and Institutionalization," *Ombudsman Journal, 2,* 1–20.

——— (1983). "Ombudsmen in Underdeveloped Countries." In Gerald C. Caiden, ed., *International Handbook of the Ombudsman.* Westport, Conn.: Greenwood, vol. 2. 113–122.

Scott, James C. (1972). *Comparative Political Corruption.* Englewood-Cliffs, N.J.: Prentice-Hall.

Scott, Marvin B., and Stanford M. Lyman (1970a). "Accounts." In Stanford M. Lyman and Marvin B. Scott, *A Sociology of the Absurd.* New York: Meredith. 111–144.

——— (1970b). "Accounts, Deviance and Social Order." In Jack D. Douglas, ed., *Deviance and Respectability: the Social Construction of Moral Meanings.* New York: Basic Books. 89–119.

Sebba, Leslie (1983). "Attitudes of New Immigrants to White-Collar Crime: A Cross-Cultural Exploration," *Human Relations, 36,* 1091–1110.

Seeger, Murray (1982). "Eyewitness to Failure." In Leonard Schapiro and Joseph Godson, eds., *The Soviet Worker.* London: Macmillan. 76–105.

Selznick, Philip (1957). *Leadership in Administration.* New York: Harper.

Seton-Watson, Hugh (1967). *Eastern Europe Between the Wars: 1918–1941.* New York: Harper and Row. 3rd ed.

Shama, Avraham, and Mark Idris (1977). *Immigration without Integration: Third World Jews in Israel.* Cambridge, MA: Schenkman.

Shamgar-Handelman, Lea (1981). "Administering to War Widows in Israel: The Impact of Law and Bureaucracy on the Formation of a Category of Client," *Social Analysis, 9,* 24–47.

———— (1986). *Beyond the Glory of Heroism: Israeli War Widows.* Mount Holyoke, MA: Bergin and Garvey.

Shapiro, Yonatan (1977). *Democracy in Israel.* Ramat Gan: Massada.

Shils, Edward (1957). "Primordial, Personal, Sacred and Civil Ties," *British Journal of Sociology, 8,* 130–145.

Shokeid, Moshe (1980). "Reconciling with Bureaucracy; Middle Eastern Immigrants' *Moshav* in Transition," *Economic Development and Cultural Change, 29,* 1, 187–205.

Shye, Samuel, ed. (1986). *Theory Construction and Data Analysis in the Behavioral Sciences.* San Francisco: Jossey-Bass.

Silbey, Susan S. (1980–81). "Case Processing: Consumer Protection in an Attorney General's Office," *Law and Society Review, 15,* 3–4, special issue on "Dispute Processing and Civil Litigation," 823–848.

Small Claims Study Group (J. Weiss, Project Director) (1972). *Little Injustices: Small Claims Courts and the American Consumer.* Cambridge, MA: Quincy House, Harvard College. 2 vols.

Smart, Nick (1983). "Classes, Clients and Corruption in Sicily." In Michael Clarke, ed., *Corruption: Causes, Consequences, Control.* London: Frances Pinter. 127–145.

Smith, Hedrick (1976). *The Russians.* New York: Ballantine.

Smooha, Sammy (1978). *Israel: Pluralism and Conflict.* London: Routledge & Kegan Paul.

Smooha, Sammy, and Yochanan Peres (1980). "The Dynamics of Ethnic Inequalities: the Case of Israel." In Ernest Krausz, ed., *Studies of Israeli Society.* New Brunswick, New Jersey: Transaction Books. vol. 1: *Migration, Ethnicity and Community.* 165–181.

Spicer, M.W., and S.B. Lundstedt (1976). "Understanding Tax Evasion," *Public Finance, 31,* 295–305.

Sprinzak, Ehud (1981). "Illegalism in Israeli Political Culture." *A Study Day, 1980.* Jerusalem: Levi Eshkol Institute for Economic, Social and Political Research and Magnes Press. 8–33 (Hebrew).

———— (1984). *Illegalism in Israeli Political Culture.* Final Report Jerusalem: Jerusalem Institute for the Study of Israel (Hebrew).

———— (1986). *Every Man Whatsoever Is Right In His Own Eyes: Illegalism in Israeli Society.* Tel Aviv: Sifriat Poalim (Hebrew).

———— (1988). "Illegalism in Israeli Political Culture: Theoretical and Historical Footnotes to the Pollard Affair and the Shin Bet Cover-Up," *The Jerusalem Quarterly, 47,* 77–94.

356   PULLING STRINGS

Staats, Steven J. (1972). "Corruption in the Soviet System," *Problems of Communism, 21,* 40–47.

Steele, Eric H. (1975). "Fraud, Dispute and the Consumer: Responding to Consumer Complaints," *University of Pennsylvania Law Review, 123,* 1107–1186.

Strumpel, Burkhard (1969). "The Contribution of Survey Research to Public Finance." In Alan T. Peacock, ed., *Quantitative Analysis in Public Finance.* New York: Praeger.

Sykes, Gresham M., and David Matza (1957). "Techniques of Neutralization," *American Sociological Review, 22,* 667–669.

TARP, Inc. (1979). (Technical Assistance Research Programs, Inc.) *Consumer Complaint Handling in America: Final Report.* Washington, DC:

Tarrow, Sidney (1967). *Peasant Communism in Southern Italy.* New Haven: Yale University Press.

Teveth, Shabtai (1972). *Moshe Dayan: the Soldier, the Man, the Legend.* Jerusalem: Weidenfeld and Nicholson

Theodorson, George A., and Achilles G. Theodorson (1969). *A Modern Dictionary of Sociology.* New York: Crowell.

Tittle, Charles R., and Alan R. Rowe (1973). "Moral Appeal, Sanction Threat, and Deviance: An Experimental Test," *Social Problems, 20,* 488–498.

Travers, Jeffrey, and Stanley Milgram (1969). "An Experimental Study of the Small-World Problem," *Sociometry, 32,* 425–443.

Trudgill, Peter (1975). "Sex, Covert Prestige, and Linguistic Change in the Urban British English of Norwich." In Barrie Thorne and Nancy M. Henley, eds., *Language and Sex: Dominance and Difference.* Rowley, MA: Newbury House. 88–104.

United Nations (1982). *Yearbook of National Accounts Statistics 1980.* New York: United Nations. 2 vols.

Upton, G.S.G. (1980). *The Analysis of Cross-Tabulated Data.* New York: Wiley.

Uslaner, Eric M. (1985). "Casework and Institutional Design: Redeeming Promises in the Promised Land," *Legislative Studies Quarterly, 10,* 35–52.

Verba, Sidney, and Norman Nie (1972). *Participation in America: Political Democracy and Social Equality.* New York: Harper & Row.

Verba, Sidney, Norman H. Nie, and Jae-on Kim (1978). *Participation and Political Equality: A Seven-Nation Comparison.* Cambridge: Cambridge University Press.

Vogel, Ezra, ed. (1975). *Modern Japanese Organization and Decision Making.* Berkeley: University of California Press.

————— (1979). *Japan as Number One: Lessons for America.* Cambridge, MA: Harvard University Press.

Vogel, Joachim (1974). "Taxation and Public Opinion in Sweden: An Interpretation of Recent Survey Data," *National Tax Journal, 27,* 499–513.

Voss, Allen R. (1979). *Hearings Before the Subcommittee on Oversight of the Committee on Ways and Means, House of Representatives, on the Underground Economy, July 16, 1979.*

Walster, Elaine, E. Berscheid, and G.W. Walster (1978). Equity: Theory and Research. Boston: Allyn & Bacon.

Warland, Rex H., Robert O. Herrman, and Jane Willits (1975). "Dissatisfied Consumers: Who Gets Upset and Who Takes Action," *Journal of Consumer Affairs, 9,* 148–163.

Waterbury, John (1973). "Endemic and Planned Corruption in a Monarchical Regime," *World Politics, 21,* 533–555.

Weber, Max (1943). "Bureaucratization." In J.P. Mayer, ed., *Max Weber and German Politics.* London: Faber and Faber. Appendix I, 95–99.

Weeks, Kent W. (1973). *Ombudsmen Around the World: A Comparative Chart.* Berkeley: Institute of Governmental Studies.

Weiman, Gabriel (1982). "Dealing with Bureaucracy: the Effectiveness of Different Persuasive Appeals," *Social Psychology Quarterly, 45,* 136–144.

————— (1983). "The Not-So-Small-World: Ethnicity and Acquaintance Networks in Israel," *Social Networks, 5,* 289–302.

Weingrod, Alex, and Michael Gurevitch (1977). "Who Are the Israeli Elites?" *Jewish Journal of Sociology, 19–20,* 67–77.

Weller, Leonard (1974). *Sociology in Israel.* Westport, CT: Greenwood.

Werner, Simcha B. (1983a). "New Directions in the Study of Administrative Corruption," *Public Administration Review, 43,* 146–154.

————(1983b). "The Development of Political Corruption: A Case Study of Israel," *Political Studies, 31,* 620–639.

White, Caroline (1980). *Patrons and Partisans: A Study of Politics in Two Southern Italian Communities*. Cambridge: Cambridge University Press.

Wichers, A.J. (1964). "Amoral Familism Reconsidered," *Sociologia Ruralis*, 4, 167–181.

Wiles, Peter J.D. (1981). *Die Parallelwirtschaft*. Sonder veroffentliching des Bundesinstituts fur Ostwissenschaftliche und Internationale Studien. Cologne: Bois.

Wolf, Eric R. (1966). "Kinship, Friendship, and Patron-Client Relations." In Michael Banton, ed., *The Social Anthropology of Complex Societies*. London: Tavistock Publications. 1–22.

Wolfsfeld, Gadi (1988). *The Politics of Provocation: Participation and Protest in Israel*. Albany, NY: State University of New York Press, series on Studies of Israeli Society.

Zimring, Franklin E., and Gordon J. Hawkins (1973). *Deterrence*. Chicago: University of Chicago Press.

Zuckerman, Alan (1977). "Clientelist Politics in Italy." In Ernest Gellner and John Waterbury, eds., *Patrons and Clients*. London: Duckworth. 63–79.

Index

Note: Page numbers in *italics* denote figures; Page numbers followed by "t" denote tables.